The Theory of Splines and Their Applications

MATHEMATICS IN SCIENCE AND ENGINEERING

A SERIES OF MONOGRAPHS AND TEXTBOOKS

Edited by Richard Bellman
University of Southern California

1. Tracy Y. Thomas. Concepts from Tensor Analysis and Differential Geometry. Second Edition. 1965
2. Tracy Y. Thomas. Plastic Flow and Fracture in Solids. 1961
3. Rutherford Aris. The Optimal Design of Chemical Reactors: A Study in Dynamic Programming. 1961
4. Joseph LaSalle and Solomon Lefschetz. Stability by Liapunov's Direct Method with Applications. 1961
5. George Leitmann (ed.). Optimization Techniques: With Applications to Aerospace Systems. 1962
6. Richard Bellman and Kenneth L. Cooke. Differential-Difference Equations. 1963
7. Frank A. Haight. Mathematical Theories of Traffic Flow. 1963
8. F. V. Atkinson. Discrete and Continuous Boundary Problems. 1964
9. A. Jeffrey and T. Taniuti. Non-Linear Wave Propagation: With Applications to Physics and Magnetohydrodynamics. 1964
10. Julius T. Tou. Optimum Design of Digital Control Systems. 1963
11. Harley Flanders. Differential Forms: With Applications to the Physical Sciences. 1963
12. Sanford M. Roberts. Dynamic Programming in Chemical Engineering and Process Control. 1964
13. Solomon Lefschetz. Stability of Nonlinear Control Systems. 1965
14. Dimitris N. Chorafas. Systems and Simulation. 1965
15. A. A. Pervozvanskii. Random Processes in Nonlinear Control Systems. 1965
16. Marshall C. Pease, III. Methods of Matrix Algebra. 1965
17. V. E. Benes. Mathematical Theory of Connecting Networks and Telephone Traffic. 1965
18. William F. Ames. Nonlinear Partial Differential Equations in Engineering. 1965
19. J. Aczél. Lectures on Functional Equations and Their Applications. 1966
20. R. E. Murphy. Adaptive Processes in Economic Systems. 1965
21. S. E. Dreyfus. Dynamic Programming and the Calculus of Variations. 1965
22. A. A. Fel'dbaum. Optimal Control Systems. 1965

MATHEMATICS IN SCIENCE AND ENGINEERING

23. A. Halanay. Differential Equations: Stability, Oscillations, Time Lags. 1966
24. M. Namik Oğuztöreli. Time-Lag Control Systems. 1966
25. David Sworder. Optimal Adaptive Control Systems. 1966
26. Milton Ash. Optimal Shutdown Control of Nuclear Reactors. 1966
27. Dimitris N. Chorafas. Control System Functions and Programming Approaches. (In Two Volumes.) 1966
28. N. P. Erugin. Linear Systems of Ordinary Differential Equations. 1966
29. Solomon Marcus. Algebraic Linguistics; Analytical Models. 1967
30. A. M. Liapunov. Stability of Motion. 1966
31. George Leitmann (ed.). Topics in Optimization. 1967
32. Masanao Aoki. Optimization of Stochastic Systems. 1967
33. Harold J. Kushner. Stochastic Stability and Control. 1967
34. Minoru Urabe. Nonlinear Autonomous Oscillations. 1967
35. F. Calogero. Variable Phase Approach to Potential Scattering. 1967
36. A. Kaufmann. Graphs, Dynamic Programming, and Finite Games. 1967
37. A. Kaufmann and R. Cruon. Dynamic Programming: Sequential Scientific Management. 1967
38. J. H. Ahlberg, E. N. Nilson, and J. L. Walsh. The Theory of Splines and Their Applications. 1967

In preparation

Y. Sawaragi, Y. Sunahara, and T. Nakamizo. Statistical Decision Theory in Adaptive Control Systems

A. Kaufmann and R. Faure. Introduction to Operations Research

Richard Bellman. Introduction to the Mathematical Theory of Control Processes (In Three Volumes.)

E. Stanley Lee. Quasilinearization and Invariant Bedding

Willard Miller, Jr. Lie Theory and Special Functions

Paul B. Bailey, Lawrence F. Shampine, and Paul E. Waltman. Nonlinear Two Point Boundary Value Problems

This page intentionally left blank

The Theory of Splines and Their Applications

J. H. AHLBERG

UNITED AIRCRAFT RESEARCH LABORATORIES
EAST HARTFORD, CONNECTICUT

E. N. NILSON

PRATT & WHITNEY AIRCRAFT COMPANY
EAST HARTFORD, CONNECTICUT

J. L. WALSH

UNIVERSITY OF MARYLAND
COLLEGE PARK, MARYLAND

1967

ACADEMIC PRESS New York and London

ACADEMIC PRESS INC.
111 Fifth Avenue, New York, New York 10003

United Kingdom Edition published by
ACADEMIC PRESS INC. (LONDON) LTD.
Berkeley Square House, London W.1

Library of Congress Catalog Card Number: 66-30115

PRINTED IN THE UNITED STATES OF AMERICA

PREFACE

Spline functions constitute a relatively new subject in analysis. During the past decade both the theory of splines and experience with their use in numerical analysis have undergone a considerable degree of development. Discoveries of new and significant results are of frequent occurrence.

It is useful at this juncture, nevertheless, to make some serious effort to organize and present material already developed up to this time. Much of this has become standardized. On the other hand, there are several areas where the theory is not yet complete. This book contains much of the material published since 1956 together with a considerable amount of the authors' own research not previously presented; it also reflects a considerable amount of practical experience with splines on the part of the authors.

In the interests of holding the present volume to a reasonable size, certain areas related to splines have been omitted. Thus the work of Schoenberg and his associates on the use of splines in the smoothing of equidistant data has not been included, nor is there any treatment of the theory of splines of complex argument. We hope, nevertheless, that the material presented will provide the reader with the necessary background for both theoretical and applied work in what promises to be a very active and extensive area.

In Chapter I there is a brief description of what is meant by a spline; this is followed by a survey of the development of spline theory since 1946 when Schoenberg first introduced the concept of a mathematical spline. We develop in Chapters II and IV, respectively, the theory of cubic splines and polynomial splines of higher degree from an algebraic point of view; the methods employed depend heavily on the equations used to define the spline. In particular, these chapters contain much of the material basic for applications. In Chapters III and V we reconsider cubic and polynomial splines of higher degree from a different point of view which reveals more clearly their deeper structure. Although the resulting theorems are not so sharp as their counterparts in Chapters II and IV, they are more easily carried over to new settings. This is done in Chapters VI, VII, and VIII, in which we consider in turn generalized splines, doubly cubic splines, and two-dimensional generalized splines.

We wish to express our deep gratitude to all those who have contributed to making this book a reality. Specifically, we wish to thank the United Aircraft Research Laboratories, the Pratt & Whitney Division of the United Aircraft Corporation, Harvard University, and the University of Maryland, whose support has made possible much of our research in spline theory.

May, 1967

J. H. AHLBERG
E. N. NILSON
J. L. WALSH

CONTENTS

PREFACE . . . vii

Chapter I **Introduction**

1.1. What Is a Spline? . . . 1
1.2. Recent Developments in the Theory of Splines . . . 2

Chapter II **The Cubic Spline**

2.1. Introduction . . . 9
2.2. Existence, Uniqueness, and Best Approximation . . . 16
2.3. Convergence . . . 19
2.4. Equal Intervals . . . 34
2.5. Approximate Differentiation and Integration . . . 42
2.6. Curve Fitting . . . 50
2.7. Approximate Solution of Differential Equations . . . 52
2.8. Approximate Solution of Integral Equations . . . 57
2.9. Additional Existence and Convergence Theorems . . . 61

Chapter III **Intrinsic Properties of Cubic Splines**

3.1. The Minimum Norm Property . . . 75
3.2. The Best Approximation Property . . . 77
3.3. The Fundamental Identity . . . 78
3.4. The First Integral Relation . . . 79
3.5. Uniqueness . . . 82
3.6. Existence . . . 84
3.7. General Equations . . . 84
3.8. Convergence of Lower-Order Derivatives . . . 87
3.9. The Second Integral Relation . . . 89
3.10. Raising the Order of Convergence . . . 91
3.11. Convergence of Higher-Order Derivatives . . . 93
3.12. Limits on the Order of Convergence . . . 95
3.13. Hilbert Space Interpretation . . . 97
3.14. Convergence in Norm . . . 98
3.15. Canonical Mesh Bases and Their Properties . . . 101
3.16. Remainder Formulas . . . 103
3.17. Transformations Defined by a Mesh . . . 105
3.18. A Connection with Space Technology . . . 107

Chapter IV The Polynomial Spline

4.1. Definition and Working Equations 109
4.2. Equal Intervals 124
4.3. Existence 132
4.4. Convergence 135
4.5. Quintic Splines of Deficiency 2, 3 143
4.6. Convergence of Periodic Splines on Uniform Meshes 148

Chapter V Intrinsic Properties of Polynomial Splines of Odd Degree

5.1. Introduction 153
5.2. The Fundamental Identity 154
5.3. The First Integral Relation 155
5.4. The Minimum Norm Property 156
5.5. The Best Approximation Property 157
5.6. Uniqueness 159
5.7. Defining Equations 160
5.8. Existence 165
5.9. Convergence of Lower-Order Derivatives 166
5.10. The Second Integral Relation 168
5.11. Raising the Order of Convergence 170
5.12. Convergence of Higher-Order Derivatives 172
5.13. Limits on the Order of Convergence 174
5.14. Hilbert Space Interpretation 174
5.15. Convergence in Norm 176
5.16. Canonical Mesh Bases and Their Properties 179
5.17. Kernels and Integral Representations 182
5.18. Representation and Approximation of Linear Functionals . . . 185

Chapter VI Generalized Splines

6.1. Introduction 191
6.2. The Fundamental Identity 192
6.3. The First Integral Relation 193
6.4. The Minimum Norm Property 195
6.5. Uniqueness 196
6.6. Defining Equations 197
6.7. Existence 199
6.8. Best Approximation 200
6.9. Convergence of Lower-Order Derivatives 201
6.10. The Second Integral Relation 204
6.11. Raising the Order of Convergence 206
6.12. Convergence of Higher-Order Derivatives 208
6.13. Limits on the Order of Convergence 211
6.14. Hilbert Space Interpretation 213
6.15. Convergence in Norm 216
6.16. Canonical Mesh Bases 219

6.17. Kernels and Integral Representations . . . 220
6.18. Representation and Approximation of Linear Functionals . . . 221

Chapter VII **The Doubly Cubic Spline**

7.1. Introduction . . . 235
7.2. Partial Splines . . . 237
7.3. Relation of Partial Splines to Doubly Cubic Splines . . . 238
7.4. The Fundamental Identity . . . 240
7.5. The First Integral Relation . . . 242
7.6. The Minimum Norm Property . . . 242
7.7. Uniqueness and Existence . . . 243
7.8. Best Approximation . . . 244
7.9. Cardinal Splines . . . 245
7.10. Convergence Properties . . . 247
7.11. The Second Integral Relation . . . 248
7.12. The Direct Product of Hilbert Spaces . . . 249
7.13. The Method of Cardinal Splines . . . 251
7.14. Irregular Regions . . . 254
7.15. Surface Representation . . . 258
7.16. The Surfaces of Coons . . . 262

Chapter VIII **Generalized Splines in Two Dimensions**

8.1. Introduction . . . 265
8.2. Basic Definition . . . 266
8.3. The Fundamental Identity . . . 267
8.4. Types of Splines . . . 269
8.5. The First Integral Relation . . . 270
8.6. Uniqueness . . . 271
8.7. Existence . . . 272
8.8. Convergence . . . 274
8.9. Hilbert Space Theory . . . 275

Bibliography . . . 277

INDEX . . . 281

This page intentionally left blank

CHAPTER I

Introduction

1.1. What Is a Spline?

It seems appropriate to begin a book on spline theory by defining a spline in its simplest and most widely used form, and also to indicate the motivation leading to this definition. For many years, long, thin strips of wood or some other material have been used much like French curves by draftsmen to fair in a smooth curve between specified points. These strips or splines are anchored in place by attaching lead weights called "ducks" at points along the spline. By varying the points where the ducks are attached to the spline itself and the position of both the spline and the duck relative to the drafting surface, the spline can be made to pass through the specified points provided a sufficient number of ducks are used.

If we regard the draftsman's spline as a thin beam, then the Bernoulli-Euler law

$$M(x) = EI[1/R(x)]$$

is satisfied. Here $M(x)$ is the bending moment, E is Young's modulus, I is the geometric moment of inertia, and $R(x)$ is the radius of curvature of the elastica, i.e., the curve assumed by the deformed axis of the beam. For small deflections, $R(x)$ is replaced by $1/y''(x)$, where $y(x)$ denotes the elastica. Thus we have

$$y''(x) = (1/EI)M(x).$$

Since the ducks act effectively as simple supports, the variation of $M(x)$ between duck positions is linear.

The mathematical spline is the result of replacing the draftsman's spline by its elastica and then approximating the latter by a piecewise cubic (normally a different cubic between each pair of adjacent ducks) with certain discontinuities of derivatives permitted at the junction points (the ducks) where two cubics join.

In its simple form, the mathematical spline is continuous and has both a continuous first derivative and a continuous second derivative. Normally, however, there is a jump discontinuity in its third derivative at the junction points. This corresponds to the draftsman's spline having continuous curvature with jumps occurring in the rate of change of curvature at the ducks. For many important applications, this mathematical model of the draftsman's spline is highly realistic.

In practice, the draftsman does not place the ducks at the specified points through which his spline must pass. Moreover, there is not usually a one-to-one correspondence between the specified points and the ducks. On the other hand, when the mathematical analog is used, it is common practice to interpolate to the specified points at the junction points and to keep the number of specified points and junction points (including the endpoints) the same.

In the next section, we outline the recent history of the mathematical spline approximation. From this history, some of the properties of the mathematical spline become evident. Also, a considerable extension of the concept of a spline from that approximating the draftsman's tool is apparent.

1.2. Recent Developments in the Theory of Splines

The spline approximation in its present form first appeared in a paper by Schoenberg [1946].* As indicated in Section 1.1, there is a very close relationship between spline theory and beam theory. Sokolnikoff [1956, pp. 1–4] provides a brief but very readable account of the development of beam theory. From the latter, one might anticipate some of the recent developments in the theory of splines, particularly the *minimum curvature property*. As suggested in Schoenberg's paper [1946], approximations employed in actuarial work also frequently involve concepts that relate them closely to the spline.

After 1946, Schoenberg, together with some of his students, continued these investigations of splines and monosplines. In particular, Schoenberg and Whitney [1949; 1953] first obtained criteria for the existence of certain splines of interpolation. For the case of splines of even order with interpolation at the junction points, a simpler approach to the question of existence due to Ahlberg, Nilson, and Walsh [1964; 1965] is now possible; it makes use of a basic integral relation obtained for cubic

* Data in square brackets refer to items in the Bibliography.

splines of interpolation to a function $f(x)$ on a mesh Δ by Holladay [1957] which asserts

$$\int_a^b |f''(x)|^2\,dx = \int_a^b |S''_\Delta(f;x)|^2\,dx + \int_a^b |f''(x) - S''_\Delta(f;x)|^2\,dx.$$

Here $S_\Delta(f;x)$ denotes the spline of interpolation to $f(x)$ on Δ.

In this book, we refer to this integral relation as the *first integral relation.* The establishment of the first integral relation for certain cubic splines of interpolation was Holladay's proof of the following theorem.

Theorem (Holladay). *Let Δ: $a = x_0 < x_1 < \cdots < x_N = b$ and a set of real numbers $\{y_i\}$ $(i = 0, 1, \ldots, N)$ be given. Then of all functions $f(x)$ having a continuous second derivative on $[a, b]$ and such that $f(x_i) = y_i$ $(i = 0, 1, \ldots, N)$, the spline function $S_\Delta(f;x)$ with junction points at the x_i and with $S''_\Delta(f;a) = S''_\Delta(f;b) = 0$ minimizes the integral*

$$\int_a^b |f''(x)|^2\,dx. \tag{1.2.1}$$

Much of the present-day theory of splines began with this theorem and its proof. Since the integral (1.2.1) is often a good approximation to the integral of the square of the curvature for a curve $y = f(x)$, the content of Holladay's theorem is often called the *minimum curvature property*. Its close relation to the minimization of potential energy of a deflected beam is apparent.*

In this book, we consider a number of generalizations of the simple cubic spline. In these generalizations, there are analogs of Holladay's theorem; but, since there is no relation to curvature in these new settings, we use the name *minimum norm property* instead. This is meaningful, since in each case there is an associated Hilbert space, for now denoted by $\mathcal{H}$, in which (1.2.1) or its counterpart is the square of the norm of $f(x)$.

It was not until 1964 that the Hilbert space aspect of spline theory evolved. At that time, the authors (Ahlberg, Nilson, and Walsh [abs. 1964; 1964]) introduced some orthonormal bases for the space $\mathcal{H}$ which consisted entirely of splines or, somewhat more precisely, of equivalence classes of splines. In terms of any orthonormal basis for $\mathcal{H}$, a function $f(x)$ in $\mathcal{H}$ has, of course, for any positive integer N, a best approximation by linear combinations of the first N basis elements.

* The potential energy of a statically deflected beam is equal to the work done on the beam to produce the deflections; this in turn is proportional to the integral of the square of the curvature of the elastica of the beam (cf. Sokolnikoff [1956, p. 2]).

If $\|\cdot\|_{\mathscr{H}}$ denotes the norm of $\mathscr{H}$, $U_i(x)$ $(i = 1, 2, \ldots)$ denotes the basis elements, and

$$U(x) = \sum_{i=1}^{N} a_i U_i(x), \tag{1.2.2}$$

then $\|f - U\|_{\mathscr{H}}$ is minimized when a_i is the coefficient of $U_i(x)$ in the expansion of $f(x)$ in terms of the complete basis.

It is desirable to have another characterization of this best approximation, particularly if the alternative characterization facilitates its determination. Such a characterization is available. In 1962, the authors (Walsh, Ahlberg, and Nilson [1962]) obtained the result: *given a mesh* Δ: $a = x_0 < x_1 < \cdots < x_N = b$, *then of all simple periodic cubic splines on* Δ *the spline that interpolates to a periodic function* $f(x)$ *at the mesh points furnishes the best approximation in the preceding sense.* Since then, a number of extensions of this result have been obtained: Ahlberg, Nilson, and Walsh [abs. 1963; abs. 1964a,b; 1964; 1965], deBoor [1963], Schoenberg [1964c], Greville [1964a], and deBoor and Lynch [abs. 1964; 1966].

In Chapters III, V, and VI of this book, we develop the Hilbert space theory of splines for cubic splines, polynomial splines of odd degree, and generalized splines, respectively. We define $\mathscr{H}$ as a function space of classes of functions; we then show that $\mathscr{H}$ is a Hilbert space with respect to an appropriate choice of norm. The symbol $\mathscr{H}$, however, is replaced by other notation.

The convergence of the spline approximations $S_\Delta^{(\alpha)}(f; x)$ to the approximated functions $f^{(\alpha)}(x)$ as the mesh norm $\|\Delta\| = \max|x_{j+1} - x_j|$ approaches zero has also come under close scrutiny. The first results were obtained by the authors (Walsh, Ahlberg, and Nilson [1962]) for cubic splines and utilized the first integral relation. Under the assumption that $f(x)$ is in $C^2[a, b]$, it was shown for splines of interpolation to $f(x)$ at the mesh points that $S_\Delta^{(\alpha)}(f; x)$ converges uniformly to $f^{(\alpha)}(x)$ for $\alpha = 0, 1$. A more detailed analysis was made by Ahlberg and Nilson [abs. 1961; 1962; 1963]. In particular, it was shown that, if $f(x)$ is in $C^2[a, b]$, then $S_\Delta''(f; x)$ converges uniformly to $f''(x)$ provided the mesh spacing approaches uniformity as $\|\Delta\|$ approaches zero. This mesh restriction was later removed by Sharma and Meir [abs. 1964; 1966].

For $f(x)$ in $C^4[a, b]$, Birkhoff and deBoor [abs. 1964; 1964] have shown that

$$|f^{(\alpha)}(x) - S_\Delta^{(\alpha)}(f; x)| < K\|\Delta\|^{4-\alpha} \qquad (\alpha = 0, 1, \ldots, 4) \tag{1.2.3}$$

provided the ratio $R_\Delta \equiv \max_i \|\Delta\|/|x_i - x_{i-1}|$ is bounded. On the other hand, for weaker restrictions on $f(x)$ such as $f(x)$ is in $C[a, b]$ or

$f(x)$ is in $C^1[a, b]$, appropriate convergence properties have been obtained by Ahlberg, Nilson, and Walsh [abs. 1966]. In addition, the convergence of polynomial splines of odd degree has been investigated by Ahlberg, Nilson, and Walsh [abs. 1963; 1965], Schoenberg [1964], and Ziegler [abs. 1965]; the convergence of multidimensional splines by Ahlberg, Nilson, and Walsh [abs. 1964a; 1964; 1965a]; and the convergence of generalized splines by the same authors [abs. 1964b; 1964; 1965a].

Many of these convergence results depend on the fine structure of the linear system of equations defining the spline. In Chapters II and IV, we develop spline theory from this point of view. On the other hand, a number of convergence results can be established without appeal to the defining equations. In particular, for polynomial splines of degree $2n - 1$ this can be done with respect to the convergence of derivatives through order $n - 1$. Moreover, with the aid of the integral relation

$$\int_a^b \{f^{(n)}(x) - S_\Delta^{(n)}(f; x)\}^2 \, dx = \int_a^b \{f(x) - S_\Delta(f; x)\} f^{(2n)}(x) \, dx, \qquad (1.2.4)$$

which was established by Ahlberg, Nilson, and Walsh [1965a] under a variety of conditions, convergence of derivatives through order $2n - 2$ can be established. This was shown for generalized splines, polynomial splines of odd degree being a special case of the latter. We refer to the integral relation (1.2.4) as the *second integral relation*; on a suitable function space, it is a manifestation of the Riesz theorem concerning the representation of linear functionals. In Chapters III, V, and VI, this approach is developed. The basic result is

$$| f^{(\alpha)}(x) - S_\Delta^{(\alpha)}(f; x) | \leqslant K \| \Delta \|^{2n-\alpha-1} \qquad (\alpha = 0, 1, \ldots, 2n - 1) \qquad (1.2.5)$$

provided R_Δ is bounded. For cubic splines, this result is weaker than (1.2.3). Whether $2n - \alpha - 1$ can be replaced in general by $2n - \alpha$ is an open question.

The theory of splines has been extended in a number of directions. Of considerable importance is the extension to several dimensions. A start was made by Birkhoff and Garabedian [1960], but the first truly successful extension was made by deBoor [abs. 1961; 1962], who demonstrated (deBoor [1962]) both the existence and uniqueness of certain bicubic splines* of interpolation. Later Ahlberg, Nilson, and Walsh [abs. 1964a; 1965b] extended the first integral relation to splines in several dimensions. As a result, existence, uniqueness, the minimum

* We employ henceforth the terminology $f(t, s)$ *is a double cubic* rather than $f(t, s)$ *is a bicubic* to imply that $f(t, s)$ is a cubic in t for each s and a cubic in s for each t. A *doubly cubic spline* is a double cubic in each subrectangle defined by a two-dimensional mesh.

norm property, and the best approximation property were obtained for a variety of multidimensional splines. Questions of convergence were reduced to similar questions in one dimension, for which answers were known. In Chapters VII and VIII, we consider *multidimensional splines.*

Another direction of generalization has been the replacement of the operator D^{2n} associated with a polynomial spline of degree $2n - 1$ (here $D \equiv d/dx$) by the operator L^*L, where

$$L \equiv a_n(x)D^n + a_{n-1}(x)D^{n-1} + \cdots + a_0(x) \tag{1.2.6}$$

and L^* is the formal adjoint of L. In each mesh interval, a spline $S(x)$ now satisfies the equation $L^*LS = 0$ rather than the equation $D^{2n}S = 0$. Splines defined in this manner are called *generalized splines.* The first step in this direction was taken by Schoenberg [1964c], who considered "trigonometric splines." The complete generalization followed: Greville [1964]; Ahlberg, Nilson, and Walsh [abs. 1964b; 1964; 1965a]; deBoor and Lynch [abs. 1964]. A more abstract approach to spline theory has been made by Atteia [1965] and his colleagues at Grenoble.

The operator $L \equiv D(D - \sigma)$ has been considered by Schweikert [1966], who termed the resulting splines "splines in tension." When σ is properly chosen, these splines have some advantages over cubic splines, as well as some disadvantages; in particular, they tend to suppress the occurrence of inflexion points not indicated by the data but concentrate the curvature near the junction points. Generalized splines are the subject matter of Chapters VI and VIII.

The approximation of a linear functional $\mathscr{L}$ by a second linear functional $\hat{\mathscr{L}}$ such that the remainder $\mathscr{R} \equiv \mathscr{L} - \hat{\mathscr{L}}$ annihilates polynomials of degree $n - 1$ has been given considerable attention by Sard [1963]. Under reasonable restrictions,

$$\mathscr{R}f = \int_a^b \mathscr{K}(\mathscr{R}; t) f^{(n)}(t)\, dt; \tag{1.2.7}$$

the kernel $\mathscr{K}(\mathscr{R}; t)$ is called a *Peano kernel.* Sard [1963] has sought to determine $\hat{\mathscr{L}}$ such that

$$\int_a^b \mathscr{K}(\mathscr{R}; t)^2\, dt$$

is minimized, and for a variety of functionals $\mathscr{L}$ he has so determined $\hat{\mathscr{L}}$. In 1964, Schoenberg succeeded in showing that, for $\hat{\mathscr{L}}$ of the form

$$\hat{\mathscr{L}}f = a_0 f(x_0) + a_1 f(x_1) + \cdots + a_N f(x_N)$$

and with mild restrictions on $\mathscr{L}$, the optimum $\hat{\mathscr{L}}$ results when $\hat{\mathscr{L}}f = \mathscr{L}S_\Delta(f; x)$, where $S_\Delta(f; x)$ is the simple (see below) polynomial spline (of degree $2n - 1$) interpolating to $f(x)$ on Δ: $a = x_0 < x_1 < \cdots < x_N = b$. This result has been generalized (Ahlberg, Nilson, and Walsh [abs. 1965]; Ahlberg and Nilson [1966]) to $\hat{\mathscr{L}}$ of the form

$$\begin{aligned}\hat{\mathscr{L}}f = {} & a_{0,0}f(x_0) + \cdots + a_{N,0}f(x_N) \\ & + a_{0,1}f'(x_0) + \cdots + a_{N,1}f'(x_N) \\ & + \cdots \\ & + a_{0,p}f^{(p)}(x_0) + \cdots + a_{N,p}f^{(p)}(x_N),\end{aligned} \tag{1.2.8}$$

with $p \leqslant n - 2$ and certain $a_{i,j} = 0$ *ab initio*. For generalized splines, (1.2.7) becomes

$$\mathscr{R}f = \int_a^b \mathscr{K}(\mathscr{R}; t)Lf(t)\,dt,$$

and the kernel $\mathscr{K}(\mathscr{R}; t)$ depends on L (cf. also deBoor and Lynch [1966]). We consider these matters in Chapters III, V, VI, and VIII.

The generalization of Schoenberg's results for approximating functionals required the introduction of splines of a somewhat different character. The following terminology facilitates a partial indication of the nature of these differences.

A spline of order $2n$ is *simple* when there is at most a jump discontinuity in the $(2n - 1)$th derivative at a mesh point. In most instances, the splines under consideration are simple splines. When jumps in derivatives of order greater than $2n - k - 1$ are permitted at an interior mesh point x_i, the spline is said to be of *deficiency k at x_i*. If the spline is of deficiency k at all interior mesh points, it is said to be of *deficiency k*. We impose, however, the restriction $0 \leqslant k \leqslant n$. In this terminology, a solution of $L^*Lf = 0$ in $[a, b]$ has deficiency zero, and a simple spline has deficiency one.

The requirement that certain a_{ij} in (1.2.8) vanish *ab initio* often imposes even more complicated and irregular continuity requirements on the splines employed. Such splines are called *heterogenous splines* and are considered in detail in Chapters VI and VIII. They were introduced by Ahlberg, Nilson, and Walsh [abs. 1965] for studying the approximation of linear functionals.

The work of Golomb and Weinberger on "optimal" approximation of linear functionals (cf. Golomb and Weinberger [1959]) is very closely related to spline theory. In many instances the functions $\bar{u}(x)$ entering into their approximations are splines of interpolation. Nevertheless this is not pointed out in the above reference; the development proceeds along different lines and the functions $\bar{u}(x)$ appear only as solutions of a variational problem. Holladay's theorem which makes the direct connection to spline theory apparent is not mentioned. More recently, however, Secrest [1966] has recognized the relationship.

CHAPTER II

The Cubic Spline

2.1. Introduction

The natural starting point for a study of spline functions is the cubic spline. Its close relation with the draftsman's spline that results from the thin-beam approximation leads to many of its important properties and motivates much of its application to problems in numerical analysis.

The spline proves to be an effective tool in the elementary processes of interpolation and approximate integration. An outstanding characteristic, however, is its effectiveness in numerical differentiation. To a considerable extent, this is a consequence of the strong convergence properties that it possesses. On the other hand, the best approximation and minimum norm properties developed in Chapter III are also important contributors to this effectiveness.

In this introductory section, the basic working equations of the spline are given, together with the procedures necessary for the common applications of the spline. These are followed in Sections 2.2 and 2.3 by a presentation of the existence and convergence properties of greatest interest. In Sections 2.4 and 2.5, equal-interval splines are discussed and special formulas presented for numerical differentiation and integration for this case. In Section 2.6, the application to the solution of linear differential equations is introduced. The chapter is concluded with a derivation of convergence and existence properties that require more incisive methods of analysis.

In the mathematical spline, we consider an interval $a \leqslant x \leqslant b$, and subdivide it by a mesh of points corresponding to the locations of the ducks:

$$\Delta: \quad a = x_0 < x_1 < \cdots < x_N = b.$$

An associated set of ordinates is prescribed:

$$Y: \quad y_0, y_1, \ldots, y_N.$$

We seek a function $S_\Delta(Y; x)$, which we shall denote by $S_\Delta(x)$ or $S_{\Delta,Y}(x)$ when there is no ambiguity (and by $S_{\Delta,Y}$ when the argument x is suppressed) which is continuous together with its first and second derivatives on $[a, b]$, coincides with a cubic in each subinterval $x_{j-1} \leqslant x \leqslant x_j$ $(j = 1, 2, \ldots, N)$, and satisfies $S_\Delta(Y; x_j) = y_j$ $(j = 0, 1, \ldots, N)$. The function $S_\Delta(Y; x)$, or $S_\Delta(x)$, is said to be a *spline with respect to the mesh* Δ, *or a spline on* Δ, interpolating to the values y_j at the mesh locations. The spline is said to be *periodic of period* $(b - a)$ if the condition

$$S_\Delta^{(p)}(a+) = S_\Delta^{(p)}(b-) \qquad (p = 0, 1, 2)$$

is satisfied.

It is traditional to designate by M_j the "moment" $S''_\Delta(x_j)$ $(j = 0, 1, \ldots, N)$, even though this is not the true moment of the beam in the usual sense of the word. Thus we have on $[x_{j-1}, x_j]$ from the linearity of the second derivative the equation

$$S''_\Delta(x) = M_{j-1} \frac{x_j - x}{h_j} + M_j \frac{x - x_{j-1}}{h_j}, \tag{2.1.1}$$

where $h_j = x_j - x_{j-1}$. If we integrate twice and evaluate the constants of integration, we obtain the equations

$$S_\Delta(x) = M_{j-1} \frac{(x_j - x)^3}{6h_j} + M_j \frac{(x - x_{j-1})^3}{6h_j} + \left(y_{j-1} - \frac{M_{j-1} h_j^2}{6}\right) \frac{x_j - x}{h_j} + \left(y_j - \frac{M_j h_j^2}{6}\right) \frac{x - x_{j-1}}{h_j}, \tag{2.1.2}$$

$$S'_\Delta(x) = -M_{j-1} \frac{(x_j - x)^2}{2h_j} + M_j \frac{(x - x_{j-1})^2}{2h_j} + \frac{y_j - y_{j-1}}{h_j} - \frac{M_j - M_{j-1}}{6} h_j. \tag{2.1.3}$$

From (2.1.3) we have, for the one-sided limits of the derivative, the expressions

$$\begin{aligned} S'_\Delta(x_j-) &= \frac{h_j}{6} M_{j-1} + \frac{h_j}{3} M_j + \frac{y_j - y_{j-1}}{h_j}, \\ S'_\Delta(x_j+) &= -\frac{h_{j+1}}{3} M_j - \frac{h_{j+1}}{6} M_{j+1} + \frac{y_{j+1} - y_j}{h_{j+1}}. \end{aligned} \tag{2.1.4}$$

In virtue of (2.1.1) and (2.1.2), the functions $S''_\Delta(x)$ and $S_\Delta(x)$ are continuous on $[a, b]$. The continuity of $S'_\Delta(x)$ at x_j yields by means of (2.1.4) the condition

$$\frac{h_j}{6} M_{j-1} + \frac{h_j + h_{j+1}}{3} M_j + \frac{h_{j+1}}{6} M_{j+1} = \frac{y_{j+1} - y_j}{h_{j+1}} - \frac{y_j - y_{j-1}}{h_j}. \tag{2.1.5}$$

For the periodic spline, Eqs. (2.1.5) ($j = 1, 2, \ldots, N-1$) give $N-1$ simultaneous equations in the quantities $M_1, M_2, \ldots, M_N$. We require in this case that (2.1.5) be valid for $j = N$ as well. Here $y_N = y_0$, $M_N = M_0$, and we prescribe $y_{N+1} = y_1$, $M_{N+1} = M_1$, $h_{N+1} = h_1$.

For the nonperiodic spline, two additional conditions must be specified, the "end conditions," to determine the $N+1$ quantities $M_0, M_1, \ldots, M_N$. Specifying the slope of the spline at a and b gives the analog of the doubly cantilevered beam. For $S_\Delta'(a) = y_0'$ and $S_\Delta'(b) = y_N'$ we obtain from (2.1.4) the relations

$$2M_0 + M_1 = \frac{6}{h_1}\left(\frac{y_1 - y_0}{h_1} - y_0'\right), \quad M_{N-1} + 2M_N = \frac{6}{h_N}\left(y_N' - \frac{y_N - y_{N-1}}{h_N}\right).$$

Setting $M_0 = 0$ and $M_N = 0$ corresponds to placing simple supports at the ends. The condition

$$M_0 - \lambda M_1 = 0, \qquad 1 > \lambda > 0$$

is equivalent to placing a simple support at $x_{-1} = (x_0 - \lambda x_1)/(1 - \lambda)$ and requiring that the entire curve over $x_{-1} \leqslant x \leqslant x_1$ be the arc of a cubic. A common choice of λ is $\frac{1}{2}$.

We are generally concerned with end conditions, which, for convenience, we write in the form

$$2M_0 + \lambda_0 M_1 = d_0, \qquad \mu_N M_{N-1} + 2M_N = d_N. \tag{2.1.6}$$

We introduce the notation

$$\lambda_j = \frac{h_{j+1}}{h_j + h_{j+1}}, \qquad \mu_j = 1 - \lambda_j \qquad (j = 1, 2, \ldots, N-1).$$

The continuity requirement (2.1.5) then becomes

$$\mu_j M_{j-1} + 2M_j + \lambda_j M_{j+1} = 6\,\frac{[(y_{j+1} - y_j)/h_{j+1}] - [(y_j - y_{j-1})/h_j]}{h_j + h_{j+1}}. \tag{2.1.7}$$

For the nonperiodic spline, the defining equations (2.1.6) and (2.1.7) are now written as

$$\begin{bmatrix} 2 & \lambda_0 & 0 & \cdots & 0 & 0 & 0 \\ \mu_1 & 2 & \lambda_1 & \cdots & 0 & 0 & 0 \\ 0 & \mu_2 & 2 & \cdots & 0 & 0 & 0 \\ \vdots & \vdots & \vdots & & \vdots & \vdots & \vdots \\ 0 & 0 & 0 & \cdots & 2 & \lambda_{N-2} & 0 \\ 0 & 0 & 0 & \cdots & \mu_{N-1} & 2 & \lambda_{N-1} \\ 0 & 0 & 0 & \cdots & 0 & \mu_N & 2 \end{bmatrix} \begin{bmatrix} M_0 \\ M_1 \\ M_2 \\ \vdots \\ M_{N-2} \\ M_{N-1} \\ M_N \end{bmatrix} = \begin{bmatrix} d_0 \\ d_1 \\ d_2 \\ \vdots \\ d_{N-2} \\ d_{N-1} \\ d_N \end{bmatrix}, \tag{2.1.8}$$

where d_j ($j = 1, 2,..., N-1$) represents the right-hand member of (2.1.7). For the periodic spline, the defining equations are

$$\begin{bmatrix} 2 & \lambda_1 & 0 & \cdots & 0 & 0 & \mu_1 \\ \mu_2 & 2 & \lambda_2 & \cdots & 0 & 0 & 0 \\ 0 & \mu_3 & 2 & \cdots & 0 & 0 & 0 \\ \vdots & \vdots & \vdots & & \vdots & \vdots & \vdots \\ 0 & 0 & 0 & \cdots & 2 & \lambda_{N-2} & 0 \\ 0 & 0 & 0 & \cdots & \mu_{N-1} & 2 & \lambda_{N-1} \\ \lambda_N & 0 & 0 & \cdots & 0 & \mu_N & 2 \end{bmatrix} \begin{bmatrix} M_1 \\ M_2 \\ M_3 \\ \vdots \\ M_{N-2} \\ M_{N-1} \\ M_N \end{bmatrix} = \begin{bmatrix} d_1 \\ d_2 \\ d_3 \\ \vdots \\ d_{N-2} \\ d_{N-1} \\ d_N \end{bmatrix}, \tag{2.1.9}$$

with $M_0 = M_N$ and $\lambda_N = h_1/(h_N + h_1)$, $\mu_N = 1 - \lambda_N$.

For many applications, it is more convenient to work with the slopes $m_j = S'_\Delta(x_j)$ rather than with the moments M_j. Here we find that on $[x_{j-1}, x_j]$ we have the equations

$$S_\Delta(x) = m_{j-1}\frac{(x_j - x)^2(x - x_{j-1})}{h_j^2} - m_j\frac{(x - x_{j-1})^2(x_j - x)}{h_j^2} + y_{j-1}\frac{(x_j - x)^2[2(x - x_{j-1}) + h_j]}{h_j^3} + y_j\frac{(x - x_{j-1})^2[2(x_j - x) + h_j]}{h_j^3}, \tag{2.1.10}$$

$$S'_\Delta(x) = m_{j-1}\frac{(x_j - x)(2x_{j-1} + x_j - 3x)}{h_j^2} - m_j\frac{(x - x_{j-1})(2x_j + x_{j-1} - 3x)}{h_j^2} + \frac{y_j - y_{j-1}}{h_j^3}6(x_j - x)(x - x_{j-1}). \tag{2.1.11}$$

Moreover, the second derivative takes the form

$$S''_\Delta(x) = -2m_{j-1}\frac{2x_j + x_{j-1} - 3x}{h_j^2} - 2m_j\frac{2x_{j-1} + x_j - 3x}{h_j^2} + 6\frac{y_j - y_{j-1}}{h_j^3}(x_j + x_{j-1} - 2x), \tag{2.1.12}$$

so that the limiting values from the two sides of x_j are

$$\begin{aligned} S''_\Delta(x_j-) &= \frac{2m_{j-1}}{h_j} + \frac{4m_j}{h_j} - 6\frac{y_j - y_{j-1}}{h_j^2}, \\ S''_\Delta(x_j+) &= -\frac{4m_j}{h_{j+1}} - \frac{2m_{j+1}}{h_{j+1}} + 6\frac{y_{j+1} - y_j}{h_{j+1}^2}. \end{aligned} \tag{2.1.13}$$

The continuity condition is here imposed on $S''_\Delta(x)$ at x_j ($j = 1, 2,..., N-1$). There results the requirement

$$\frac{1}{h_j}m_{j-1} + 2\left(\frac{1}{h_j} + \frac{1}{h_{j+1}}\right)m_j + \frac{1}{h_{j+1}}m_{j+1} = 3\frac{y_j - y_{j-1}}{h_j^2} + 3\frac{y_{j+1} - y_j}{h_{j+1}^2}, \tag{2.1.14}$$

or, in more convenient form, the equation

$$\lambda_j m_{j-1} + 2m_j + \mu_j m_{j+1} = 3\lambda_j \frac{y_j - y_{j-1}}{h_j} + 3\mu_j \frac{y_{j+1} - y_j}{h_{j+1}}. \quad (2.1.15)$$

The equation system for the nonperiodic spline is, therefore,

$$\begin{bmatrix} 2 & \mu_0 & 0 & \cdots & 0 & 0 & 0 \\ \lambda_1 & 2 & \mu_1 & \cdots & 0 & 0 & 0 \\ 0 & \lambda_2 & 2 & \cdots & 0 & 0 & 0 \\ \vdots & \vdots & \vdots & & \vdots & \vdots & \vdots \\ 0 & 0 & 0 & \cdots & 2 & \mu_{N-2} & 0 \\ 0 & 0 & 0 & \cdots & \lambda_{N-1} & 2 & \mu_{N-1} \\ 0 & 0 & 0 & \cdots & 0 & \lambda_N & 2 \end{bmatrix} \begin{bmatrix} m_0 \\ m_1 \\ m_2 \\ \vdots \\ m_{N-2} \\ m_{N-1} \\ m_N \end{bmatrix} = \begin{bmatrix} c_0 \\ c_1 \\ c_2 \\ \vdots \\ c_{N-2} \\ c_{N-1} \\ c_N \end{bmatrix}, \quad (2.1.16)$$

where the general end conditions $2m_0 + \mu_0 m_1 = c_0$, $\lambda_N m_{N-1} + 2m_N = c_N$ are employed. The quantity c_j $(j = 1, 2, \ldots, N-1)$ represents the right-hand member of (2.1.15).

For the periodic case, the equations are

$$\begin{bmatrix} 2 & \mu_1 & 0 & \cdots & 0 & 0 & \lambda_1 \\ \lambda_2 & 2 & \mu_2 & \cdots & 0 & 0 & 0 \\ 0 & \lambda_3 & 2 & \cdots & 0 & 0 & 0 \\ \vdots & \vdots & \vdots & & \vdots & \vdots & \vdots \\ 0 & 0 & 0 & \cdots & 2 & \mu_{N-2} & 0 \\ 0 & 0 & 0 & \cdots & \lambda_{N-1} & 2 & \mu_{N-1} \\ \mu_N & 0 & 0 & \cdots & 0 & \lambda_N & 2 \end{bmatrix} \begin{bmatrix} m_1 \\ m_2 \\ m_3 \\ \vdots \\ m_{N-2} \\ m_{N-1} \\ m_N \end{bmatrix} = \begin{bmatrix} c_1 \\ c_2 \\ c_3 \\ \vdots \\ c_{N-2} \\ c_{N-1} \\ c_N \end{bmatrix}. \quad (2.1.17)$$

The end conditions are now classified in terms of the M_j as follows:

at $x = a$:

$$\text{(i)} \quad 2M_0 + M_1 = \frac{6}{h_1}\left(\frac{y_1 - y_0}{h_1} - y_0'\right),$$

$$\text{(ii)} \quad 2M_0 = 2y_0'',$$

$$\text{(iii)} \quad 2M_0 + \lambda_0 M_1 = d_0,$$

(2.1.18)

at $x = b$:

$$\text{(i)} \quad M_{N-1} + 2M_N = \frac{6}{h_N}\left(y_N' - \frac{y_N - y_{N-1}}{h_N}\right),$$

$$\text{(ii)} \quad 2M_N = 2y_N'',$$

$$\text{(iii)} \quad \mu_N M_{N-1} + 2M_N = d_N,$$

and, in terms of the m_j,

$$\text{at} \quad x = a:$$

$$
\begin{aligned}
&\text{(i)} && 2m_0 = 2y_0', \\
&\text{(ii)} && 2m_0 + m_1 = 3\frac{y_1 - y_0}{h_1} - \frac{h_1}{2} y_0'', \\
&\text{(iii)} && 2m_0 + \mu_0 m_1 = c_0, \\
& && \text{at} \quad x = b: \\
&\text{(i)} && 2m_N = 2y_N', \\
&\text{(ii)} && m_{N-1} + 2m_N = 3\frac{y_N - y_{N-1}}{h_N} + \frac{h_N}{2} y_N'', \\
&\text{(iii)} && \lambda_N m_{N-1} + 2m_N = c_N .
\end{aligned}
\tag{2.1.19}
$$

Here y_0'' and y_N'' are prescribed values of the spline second derivative at the ends of the interval. Moreover, these two sets are equivalent provided

$$\mu_0 = 4(1 - \lambda_0)/(4 - \lambda_0), \qquad \lambda_N = 4(1 - \mu_N)/(4 - \mu_N),$$

$$c_0 = -\frac{d_0 h_1}{4 - \lambda_0} + 6\frac{2 - \lambda_0}{4 - \lambda_0}\frac{y_1 - y_0}{h_1}, \quad c_N = \frac{d_N h_N}{4 - \mu_N} + 6\frac{2 - \mu_N}{4 - \mu_N}\frac{y_N - y_{N-1}}{h_N}.$$

It is readily verified that the right-hand members of (2.1.7) and (2.1.15) are three times the values of the second and first derivatives at x_j, respectively, of the parabola through (x_{j-1}, y_{j-1}), (x_j, y_j), and (x_{j+1}, y_{j+1}) having vertical axis. This fact has special significance relative to the problem of curve fitting with higher-order splines and is examined in detail in Chapter IV.

A very efficient algorithm is available for solving the system of equations (2.1.8) or (2.1.16). Given the equations

$$
\begin{aligned}
b_1 x_1 + c_1 x_2 &= d_1, \\
a_1 x_1 + b_2 x_2 + c_2 x_3 &= d_2, \\
a_3 x_2 + b_3 x_3 + c_3 x_4 &= d_3, \\
&\cdots \\
a_{n-1} x_{n-2} + b_{n-1} x_{n-1} + c_{n-1} x_n &= d_{n-1}, \\
a_n x_{n-1} + b_n x_n &= d_n,
\end{aligned}
$$

form $(k = 1, 2, \ldots, n)$

$$
\begin{aligned}
p_k &= a_k q_{k-1} + b_k && (q_0 = 0), \\
q_k &= -c_k / p_k, && \\
u_k &= (d_k - a_k u_{k-1}) / p_k && (u_0 = 0).
\end{aligned}
\tag{2.1.20}
$$

Successive elimination of x_1, x_2,..., x_{n-1} from 2nd, 3rd,..., nth equations yields the equivalent equation system

$$\begin{aligned} x_k &= q_k x_{k+1} + u_k \qquad (k = 1,..., n-1), \\ x_n &= u_n , \end{aligned} \tag{2.1.21}$$

whence x_n, x_{n-1},..., x_1 are successively evaluated.

For matrices with dominant main diagonal, with which we are primarily concerned, this procedure is stable in the sense that errors rapidly damp out ($0 < c_k/p_k < 1$). We note also that the quantities p_k and q_k in the application to the spline depend upon the mesh Δ but not upon the ordinates at the mesh locations. Thus, several spline constructions on the same mesh may be carried out with the computation of only one set of p_k's and q_k's.

An extension of this procedure is used for the periodic spline. For the equations

$$\begin{aligned} b_1x_1 + c_1x_2 + a_1x_n &= d_1 , \\ a_2x_1 + b_2x_2 + c_2x_3 &= d_2 , \\ &\cdots \\ a_{n-1}x_{n-2} + b_{n-1}x_{n-1} + c_{n-1}x_n &= d_{n-1} , \\ c_nx_1 + a_nx_{n-1} + b_nx_n &= d_n , \end{aligned}$$

we effectively solve for x_1,..., x_{n-1} in terms of x_n by means of the first $n - 1$ equations and then determine x_n from the last equation. In addition to the quantities p_k, q_k, u_k determined previously, we therefore calculate for $k = 1, 2,..., n$ the quantities

$$s_k = -a_k s_{k-1}/p_k \qquad (s_0 = 1) \tag{2.1.22}$$

so that Eqs (2.1.21) are replaced by the relations

$$x_k = q_k x_{k+1} + s_k x_n + u_k \qquad (k = 1,..., n-1).$$

If we write the equation

$$x_k = t_k x_n + v_k \qquad (k = 1, 2,..., n-1), \tag{2.1.23}$$

then we have

$$\begin{aligned} t_k &= q_k t_{k+1} + s_k \qquad (t_n = 1), \\ v_k &= q_k v_{k+1} + u_k \qquad (v_n = 0). \end{aligned}$$

We determine t_{k-1},..., t_1, v_{k-1},..., v_1 and evaluate x_n from the equation

$$c_n(t_1x_n + v_1) + a_n(t_{n-1}x_n + v_{n-1}) + b_nx_n = d_n .$$

We then determine x_{n-1},..., x_1 from (2.1.23).

We note that, when a_k, b_k, and c_k are all constant, the quantities p_k and q_k can be obtained from a solution of a second-order difference equation. Set $p_k = h_k/h_{k-1}$ with h_0 taken as 1. Then, with $a_k = a$, $b_k = b$, and $c_k = c$ for all k, we have from (2.1.20) the relations

$$p_k = aq_{k-1} + b, \qquad q_k = -c/p_k,$$

so that there results the difference equation

$$h_k - bh_{k-1} + ach_{k-2} = 0.$$

A similar property holds for the periodic spline.

2.2. Existence, Uniqueness, and Best Approximation

For most cases of interest, the proof of the existence of the spline function involves merely an application of Gershgorin's theorem (cf. Todd [1962, p. 227]), which states that the eigenvalues of the matrix $(a_{i,j})$ $(i, j = 1, 2, \ldots, n)$ lie in the union of the circles

$$| z - a_{ii} | = \sum_{j \neq i} | a_{i,j} | \qquad (1 \leqslant i \leqslant n)$$

in the complex plane. A matrix with dominant main diagonal $(| a_{ii} | > \sum_{j \neq i} | a_{i,j} |)$ is nonsingular. In (2.1.9) and (2.1.17), the sum $\sum_{j \neq 1} | a_{i,j} |$ is always equal to 1, with $a_{ii} = 2$. In (2.1.8) and (2.1.16), the condition for dominant main diagonal is that λ_0, μ_N, μ_0, λ_N be less than 2 in absolute value.

Thus it is seen that the periodic cubic spline with prescribed ordinates at mesh points always exists and is unique, the representation being given by (2.1.2) with the M_j uniquely determined by (2.1.9), and that the same is true in particular for nonperiodic splines having cantilevered ends (m_0 and m_N prescribed), having simple end support ($M_0 = 0$, $M_N = 0$), having prescribed end moments, or having simple supports at points beyond the mesh extremities (e.g., $M_0 = \lambda M_1$, $M_N = \mu M_{N-1}$, $0 < \lambda < 1$, $0 < \mu < 1$).

A general existence theorem covering a much wider class of nonperiodic cubic splines is given in Section 2.9. There it will be necessary to prove special properties of the coefficient matrix.

We remark that more than one spline may be associated with a set of values for the quantities M_j. Replacing y_j by $y_j + mx_j + C$ for fixed m and C does not affect the right-hand member of (2.1.7). Boundary conditions (2.1.18) possess the same property. Thus, $S_\Delta(Y; x) + mx + C =$

$S_\Delta(\tilde{Y}; x)$, where $\tilde{y}_j = y_j + mx_j + C$. For the periodic case, we may only say that $S_\Delta(Y; x) + C = S_\Delta(\tilde{Y}; x)$, with $\tilde{y}_j = y_j + C$. (The only periodic linear function is a constant.)

A related question concerns the arbitrariness of the quantities M_j or m_j. Is there always some spline associated with an arbitrarily prescribed set of values of M_j or m_j ? It is seen for periodic splines that adding the corresponding members of (2.1.5) ($j = 1, 2,..., N$) gives the necessary condition

$$\sum_{j=1}^{N} (h_j + h_{j+1})M_j = 0.$$

It may be seen, however, that any set of values of the M_j satisfying this relationship is an admissible set. If we designate the left-hand member of (2.1.5) by ϕ_j, then the preceding equation implies $\sum_{j=1}^{N} \phi_j = 0$. Set $(y_1 - y_N)/h_1 = c$. Then $(y_j - y_{j-1})/h_j = c + \phi_1 + \cdots + \phi_{j-1}$ ($j = 2,..., N$). The equation system requires $(y_1 - y_N)/h_1 = c + \phi_1 + \cdots + \phi_N$, but this is equal to c. We now have the relations

$$\begin{aligned}
y_1 &= y_N + h_1 c, \\
y_2 &= y_1 + h_2(c + \phi_1), \\
&\cdots \\
y_N &= y_{N-1} + h_N(c + \phi_1 + \cdots + \phi_{N-1}).
\end{aligned}$$

These equations have a one-parameter family of solutions (parameter y_N) iff we take $c = [\sum_{j=2}^{N} h_j(\phi_1 + \cdots + \phi_{j-1})]/(a - b)$, which is a known function of the given M_j's. It is readily seen for nonperiodic splines that there is no restriction upon the quantities M_j.

The corresponding problem for the slopes m_j is somewhat more complex. If we designate by $3\psi_j$ the left-hand member of (2.1.14) and set $(y_1 - y_N)/h_1^2 = c$, Eqs. (2.1.14) ($j = 1,..., N$) require that the following equations be satisfied:

$$\begin{aligned}
(y_2 - y_1)/h_2^2 &= \psi_1 - c, \\
(y_3 - y_2)/h_3^2 &= \psi_2 - \psi_1 + c, \\
&\cdots \\
(y_N - y_{N-1})/h_N^2 &= \psi_{N-1} - \psi_{N-2} + \cdots + (-1)^{N-2}\psi_1 + (-1)^{N-1}c, \\
(y_1 - y_N)/h_1^2 &= \psi_N - \psi_{N-1} + \cdots + (-1)^{N-1}\psi_1 + (-1)^N c.
\end{aligned}$$

These are consistent iff $\psi_N - \psi_{N-1} + \cdots + (-1)^{N-1} \psi_1 + (-1)^N c = c$. This is equivalent to the condition

$$\sum_{j=1}^{N} (-1)^j \left(\frac{1}{h_j} + \frac{1}{h_{j+1}}\right) m_j - \frac{m_1 + m_N}{h_1} [1 - (-1)^N] = c[1 - (-1)^N].$$

The resulting system of equations has a one-parameter family of solutions for $(y_1, \ldots, y_N)$ iff in addition

$$c[h_1^2 - h_2^2 + \cdots + (-1)^{N-1}h_N^2] = -[h_2^2\psi_1 + h_3^2(\psi_2 - \psi_1) + \cdots + h_N^2(\psi_{N-1} - \psi_{N-2} + \cdots + (-1)^{N-2}\psi_1)].$$

We restrict our attention here to the case in which the intervals are of equal length. If N is odd, these requirements are equivalent to $\psi_1 + \psi_2 + \cdots + \psi_N = 0$ and $c = \psi_1 + \psi_3 + \cdots + \psi_N$. If N is even, there exists a two-parameter family of solutions $y_{2j} = y_N + h^2(\psi_1 + \cdots + \psi_{2j-1})$, $y_{2j+1} = y_N + h^2c + h^2(\psi_2 + \cdots + \psi_{2j})$ (parameters y_N and c) iff $\psi_1 + \cdots + \psi_{2N-1} = \psi_2 + \cdots + \psi_{2N} = 0$, that is, iff

$$m_1 + m_3 + \cdots + m_{N-1} = m_2 + m_4 + \cdots + m_N = 0.$$

Equations (2.1.7) or, alternatively, (2.1.14), are given added significance if we consider the following extremal problem. Let $f''(x)$ be continuous. For a given mesh Δ, let $f_j = f(x_j)$ and let $S_\Delta(f; x)$ denote the periodic spline of interpolation to $f(x)$ or, alternatively, the non-periodic spline satisfying end conditions (2.1.18i). Thus, $S_\Delta(f; x_j) = f_j$.

Let $S_\Delta(x)$ be any cubic spline on Δ. Form the integral

$$E = \int_a^b [f''(x) - S_\Delta''(x)]^2\, dx.$$

The quantity E is, of course, a measure of the approximation of $S_\Delta''(x)$ to $f''(x)$ on $[a, b]$. Let M_j denote $S_\Delta''(x_j)$. Expanding the integral and integrating by parts gives E the form

$$E = \int_a^b [f''(x)]^2\, dx - \sum_{j=1}^N (f_j'M_j - f_{j-1}'M_{j-1}) + 2\sum_{j=1}^N (f_j - f_{j-1})\frac{M_j - M_{j-1}}{h_j} + \sum_{j=1}^N \frac{h_j}{3}(M_{j-1}^2 + M_{j-1}M_j + M_j^2), \tag{2.2.1}$$

where $f_0' = f_N'$, $f_0 = f_N$, $M_0 = M_N$ if $f(x)$ and $S_\Delta(x)$ have period $b - a$. The function E has a stationary point in the nonperiodic case when the conditions

$$\frac{\partial E}{\partial M_0} = \frac{h_1}{3}\left\{2M_0 + M_1 - \frac{6}{h_1}\left(\frac{f_1 - f_0}{h_1} - f_0'\right)\right\} = 0,$$

$$\frac{\partial E}{\partial M_j} = 2\left\{\frac{h_j}{6}M_{j-1} + \frac{h_j + h_{j+1}}{3}M_j + \frac{h_{j+1}}{2}M_{j+1} - 3\left(\frac{f_{j+1} - f_j}{h_{j+1}} - \frac{f_j - f_{j-1}}{h_j}\right)\right\} = 0 \quad (j = 1, 2, \ldots, N-1), \tag{2.2.2}$$

$$\frac{\partial E}{\partial M_N} = \frac{h_N}{3}\left\{M_{N-1} + 2M_N - \frac{6}{h_N}\left(f_N' - \frac{f_N - f_{N-1}}{h_N}\right)\right\} = 0$$

are satisfied. In the periodic case, a stationary point exists when the second relation is valid for $j = 1, 2,..., N$. These conditions are equivalent to (2.1.8) with boundary conditions (2.1.18i) or to (2.1.9). Consequently, the function E has a stationary point among the various choices of M_j iff $S_\Delta(x) \equiv S_\Delta(f; x)$.

We shall show that this stationary point is actually a minimum point. Denote by $(\bar{M}_0, \bar{M}_1,..., \bar{M}_N)$ and $(\bar{M}_1,..., \bar{M}_N)$ the solutions of these equation systems for the nonperiodic and periodic cases, respectively; that is, $\bar{M}_j = S''_\Delta(f; x_j)$. We rearrange the expression for E as follows: multiply the algebraic expressions in Eqs. (2.2.2), with $\bar{M}_j$ in place of M_j, by $-2M_0, -2M_1,..., -2M_N$, respectively, and add to the right-hand side of (2.2.1). We obtain expressions for E in the forms

$$E = \int_a^b [f''(x)]^2\,dx + \sum_{j=1}^N \frac{h_j}{3}[M_{j-1}^2 + M_{j-1}M_j + M_j^2 - 2M_{j-1}\bar{M}_{j-1} - M_{j-1}\bar{M}_j - M_j\bar{M}_{j-1} - 2M_j\bar{M}_j]$$

$$= \int_a^b [f''(x)]^2\,dx + \sum_{j=1}^N \frac{h_j}{3}[(M_{j-1} - \bar{M}_{j-1})^2 + (M_{j-1} - \bar{M}_{j-1})(M_j - \bar{M}_j) + (M_j - \bar{M}_j)^2] - \sum_{j=1}^N \frac{h_j}{3}[\bar{M}_{j-1}^2 + \bar{M}_{j-1}\bar{M}_j + \bar{M}_j^2]$$

$$= \int_a^b [f''(x)]^2\,dx + \int_a^b [S''_\Delta(x) - S''_\Delta(f; x)]^2\,dx - \int_a^b [S''_\Delta(f; x)]^2\,dx.$$

Observe that the first and third terms in the last member are independent of the choice of M_j. It is evident, therefore, that E is minimum for $S''_\Delta(x) = S''_\Delta(f; x)$. This is the *best approximation property* of the spline interpolation. In Chapter III, this and other related extremal properties are explored by more elegant and powerful means.

2.3. Convergence

The effectiveness of the spline in approximation can be explained to a considerable extent by its striking convergence properties. If $f^{(q)}(x)$ is continuous on $[a, b]$ $(q = 0, 1, 2, 3, \text{ or } 4)$, we find that $S_\Delta(f; x)$ converges to $f(x)$ on a sequence of meshes at least as rapidly as the approach to zero of the qth power of the mesh norm $\|\Delta\| = \max_j h_j$. (To compare with the degree of convergence of more general approximating sequences, see Davis [1963, Chapter XIII].) Similarly, $S_\Delta^{(p)}(f; x)$ converges to $f^{(p)}(x)$ $(0 \leqslant p \leqslant q)$ at least as rapidly as the $(q - p)$th power of the mesh norm. In some cases, it is required that the ratio of maximum interval length to minimum interval length in the respective meshes be bounded, but for many cases of interest it is required only that the limit of the mesh norm be zero. These rates, moreover, are optimal.

For purposes of demonstrating convergence, it is necessary to have at hand certain properties of the inverses of the coefficient matrices in (2.1.8), (2.1.9), or, alternatively, (2.1.16), (2.1.17). For the situations in which λ_0, μ_N or λ_N, μ_0 are less than 2 in magnitude, the convergence proofs are relatively simple. In this section, we restrict our attention to such situations, postponing to Section 2.9 the derivation of the more incisive properties of the inverse matrix essential to the general case.

If B is an $n \times n$ matrix and we take the norm on the space of n-tuples $x = (x_1, x_2, \ldots, x_n)$ to be the sup norm,

$$\| x \| = \max_{1 \leqslant i \leqslant n} | x_i |,$$

then the induced norm on the matrix B (cf. Taylor [1958, Chapter III]) is the row-max norm. To see this, express the linear transformation associated with B as

$$y_i = \sum_{j=1}^{n} b_{ij} x_j \qquad (1 \leqslant i \leqslant n).$$

Then we have

$$\| y \| = \max_i | y_i | \leqslant \| x \| \max_i \sum_{j=1}^{n} | b_{ij} |.$$

Thus the induced norm B satisfies

$$\| B \| = \sup_{x \neq 0} \frac{\| Bx \|}{\| x \|} \leqslant \max_i \sum_{j=1}^{n} | b_{ij} |.$$

Taking i^* to be the index of a row yielding a maximum value for $\sum_{j=1}^{n} | b_{ij} |$ and setting $x_j = 1$ if $b_{i^*j} \geqslant 0$, -1 if $b_{i^*j} < 0$, gives here the relation

$$\| y \| = \sum_{j=1}^{n} b_{i^*j} x_j = \sum_{j=1}^{n} | b_{i^*j} | = \| x \| \max_i \sum_{j=1}^{n} | b_{ij} |.$$

It follows that we have the equation

$$\| B \| = \max_i \sum_j | b_{ij} | .$$

Assume now that the main diagonal of B is dominant. For a given x, choose k so that $\| x \| = | x_k |$. Then

$$\| y \| = \| Bx \| = \max_i \left| \sum_{j=1}^{n} b_{ij} x_j \right|$$

$$\geqslant \left| \sum_{j=1}^{n} b_{kj} x_j \right|$$

$$\geqslant \left[| b_{kk} | - \sum_{j \neq k} | b_{kj} | \right] \| x \|$$

$$\geqslant \min_i \left[| b_{ii} | - \sum_{j \neq i} | b_{ij} | \right] \| x \|.$$

Since B^{-1} exists and $x = B^{-1}y$, we obtain the bound on $\| B^{-1} \|$:

$$\| B^{-1} \| = \sup_{y \neq 0} \frac{\| B^{-1} y \|}{\| y \|} \leqslant \left\{ \min_i \left[| b_{ii} | - \sum_{j \neq i} | b_{ij} | \right] \right\}^{-1}.$$

Denote by A and $\tilde{A}$ the coefficient matrices in (2.1.8) and (2.1.9), respectively. In (2.1.8), assume that λ_0 and μ_N are numerically less than 2. Then in the nonperiodic case we have the inequality

$$\| A^{-1} \| \leqslant \max[(2 - \lambda_0)^{-1}, (2 - \mu_N)^{-1}, 1]. \tag{2.3.1}$$

For the periodic spline, we have

$$\| \tilde{A}^{-1} \| \leqslant 1. \tag{2.3.2}$$

Let B and $\tilde{B}$ denote the coefficient matrices in (2.1.16) and (2.1.17), with $| \mu_0 | < 2$ and $| \lambda_N | < 2$ in (2.1.16). Then we obtain

$$\| B^{-1} \| \leqslant \max[(2 - \mu_0)^{-1}, (2 - \lambda_N)^{-1}, 1], \tag{2.3.3}$$

$$\| \tilde{B}^{-1} \| \leqslant 1. \tag{2.3.4}$$

Now take $\{\Delta_k\}$ to be a sequence of meshes on $[a, b]$:

$$\Delta_k: \quad a = x_{k,0} < x_{k,1} < \cdots < x_{k,N_k} = b. \tag{2.3.5}$$

Set

$$h_{k,j} = x_{k,j} - x_{k,j-1} \tag{2.3.6}$$

and define the norm of Δ_k to be

$$\| \Delta_k \| = \max_{1 \leqslant j \leqslant N_k} (h_{k,j}).$$

We shall be concerned with sequences $\{\Delta_k\}$ for which $\|\Delta_k\| \to 0$ as $k \to \infty$. Under certain circumstances, we shall also require the additional restriction on the meshes Δ_k that

$$R_{\Delta_k} \equiv \max_{1 \leqslant j \leqslant N_k} \frac{\|\Delta_k\|}{h_{k,j}} \leqslant \beta < \infty. \tag{2.3.7}$$

In particular, we require this restriction in the first convergence theorem:

Theorem 2.3.1. *Let $f(x)$ be continuous on $[a, b]$. Let $\{\Delta_k\}$ be a sequence of meshes on $[a, b]$ with $\lim_{k\to\infty} \|\Delta_k\| = 0$ and satisfying (2.3.7). If $S_{\Delta_k}(x)$ is the periodic spline of interpolation to $f(x)$ on Δ_k, or the nonperiodic spline of interpolation satisfying end conditions (2.1.18iii) with $\sup_k \max[|\lambda_{k,0}|, |\mu_{k,N_k}|] < 2$ and $\|\Delta_k\|^2(|d_{k,0}| + |d_{k,N_k}|) \to 0$ as $k \to \infty$, then we have uniformly with respect to x in $[a, b]$*

$$f(x) - S_{\Delta_k}(x) = o(\|1\|). \tag{2.3.8}$$

If, in addition, $f(x)$ satisfies a Hölder condition on $[a, b]$ of order $\alpha(0 < \alpha \leqslant 1)$, then

$$f(x) - S_{\Delta_k}(x) = O(\|\Delta_k\|^\alpha) \tag{2.3.9}$$

uniformly with respect to x in $[a, b]$, provided $\|\Delta_k\|^{2-\alpha}(|d_{k,0}| + |d_{k,N_k}|)$ is bounded in the nonperiodic case.

Proof. On $[x_{j-1}, x_j]$, we have from (2.1.2) the relation

$$S_\Delta(x) - f(x) = M_{j-1}\frac{(x_j - x)[(x_j - x)^2 - h_j^2]}{6h_j} + M_j\frac{(x - x_{j-1})[(x - x_{j-1})^2 - h_j^2]}{6h_j}$$
$$+ \left(\frac{f_j + f_{j-1}}{2} - f(x)\right) + (f_j - f_{j-1})\frac{x_j + x_{j-1} - 2x}{2h_j}, \tag{2.3.10}$$

where, for simplicity, we have dropped the mesh index k.

If $A_{i,j}^{-1}$ are the elements of the inverse of the coefficient matrix A in (2.1.8), then we find

$$M_j = 3\sum_{i=1}^{N-1} A_{j,i}^{-1}\frac{[(f_{i+1} - f_i)/h_{i+1}] - [(f_i - f_{i-1})/h_i]}{h_i + h_{i+1}} + A_{j,0}^{-1}d_0 + A_{j,N}^{-1}d_N.$$

Let $\mu(f; \delta)$ be the modulus of continuity of $f(x)$ on $[a, b]$. We note that the coefficients of M_{j-1} and M_j in (2.3.10) do not exceed $h_j^2/3^{5/2}$ in magnitude. Also by (2.3.7) follows the inequality

$$h_j^2\left|\frac{[(f_{i+1} - f_i)/h_{i+1}] - [(f_i - f_{i-1})/h_i]}{h_i + h_{i+1}}\right| \leqslant \tfrac{1}{2}\beta^2\mu(f; \|\Delta\|). \tag{2.3.11}$$

By (2.3.2), therefore, we have

$$h_j^2(|M_{j-1}| + |M_j|) \leqslant \|A^{-1}\|\{\tfrac{3}{2}\beta^2\mu(f; \|\Delta\|) + \|\Delta\|^2(|d_0| + |d_N|)\}. \quad (2.3.12)$$

In the periodic case, we have simply

$$h_j^2(|M_{j-1}| + |M_j|) = \|\tilde{A}^{-1}\|\tfrac{3}{2}\beta^2\mu(f; \|\Delta\|) \leqslant \tfrac{3}{2}\beta^2\mu(f; \|\Delta\|).$$

Thus we obtain from (2.3.10), in the nonperiodic case, the inequality

$$|S_\Delta(x) - f(x)| \leqslant [1/3^{5/2}]\|A^{-1}\|\{\tfrac{3}{2}\beta^2\mu(f; \|\Delta\|) + \|\Delta\|^2(|d_0| + |d_N|)\} + \mu(f; \|\Delta\|)(1 + \tfrac{1}{2}).$$

A corresponding inequality is evidently valid in the periodic case, and (2.3.8) follows.

If, furthermore, $f(x)$ satisfies a Hölder condition of order $\alpha(0 < \alpha \leqslant 1)$ on $[a, b]$, that is, if for some constant K

$$|f(x) - f(x')| \leqslant K|x - x'|^\alpha$$

for x and x' on $[a, b]$, then the right-hand member of (2.3.11) is replaced by the expression

$$\tfrac{1}{2}\beta^2 K\|\Delta\|^\alpha,$$

and the inequality

$$|S_\Delta(x) - f(x)| \leqslant [1/3^{5/2}]\|A^{-1}\| \cdot \|\Delta\|^\alpha\{\tfrac{3}{2}K(\beta^2 + 1) + \|\Delta\|^{2-\alpha}(|d_0| + |d_N|)\}$$

results. In the periodic case, we have

$$|S_\Delta(x) - f(x)| \leqslant [1/3^{5/2}]\|\tilde{A}^{-1}\| \cdot \|\Delta\|^\alpha \cdot \tfrac{3}{2}K(\beta^2 + 1).$$

This completes the proof of the theorem. It is evident that the corresponding result for end conditions (2.1.19iii) is valid. Here we make the restriction that $\sup_k\{\max[|\mu_{k,0}|, |\lambda_{k,N_k}|]\} < 2$; furthermore, we require that $\|\Delta_k\|(|c_{k,0}| + |c_{k,N_k}|) \to 0$ as $k \to \infty$ for (2.3.8) and that $\|\Delta_k\|^{1-\alpha}(|c_{k,0}| + |c_{k,N_k}|)$ be bounded with respect to k for (2.3.9).

It is worth noting at this point a connection with certain properties of polynomials investigated by Fejér. Fejér [1930] showed, for a polynomial $g(x)$ of degree $2n - 1$ which satisfies at the Tchebycheff abscissas $\xi_k^{(n)}$ $(k = 1, 2, \ldots, n)$ on $[-1, 1]$ the inequalities $|g(\xi_k^{(n)})| \leqslant A$ and $|g'(\xi_k^{(n)})| \leqslant B$, that on $[-1, 1]$, $|g(x)| \leqslant A + \lambda_n B$, where λ_n is independent of the polynomial g and $\lambda_n \to 0$ as $n \to \infty$. He had previously demonstrated [1916] that if a polynomial $X_n(x)$ of degree $2n - 1$ interpolates to a function $f(x)$ of $C[-1, 1]$ at these Tchebycheff abscissas with $X_n'(\xi_k^{(n)}) = 0$, then $X_n(x)$ converges uniformly to $f(x)$ on $[-1, 1]$.

Consider here the representation (2.1.10) for a spline $S_\Delta(x)$ which is valid even if $S_\Delta(x)$ is not in $C^2[a, b]$. We note that, if we set $\sigma = (x - x_{j-1})/h_j$ on $[x_{j-1}, x_j]$, we have

$$S_\Delta(x) = m_{j-1}h_j(1-\sigma)^2\sigma - m_jh_j\sigma^2(1-\sigma) + y_{j-1}(1-\sigma)^2(2\sigma+1) + y_j\sigma^2[2(1-\sigma)+1].$$

Hence, if $|y_k| \leqslant A$ and $|m_k| \leqslant B$ for $k = 0, 1,..., N$, then on $[x_{j-1}, x_j]$

$$S_\Delta(x) \leqslant A + (h_j/4)B.$$

Thus we obtain the following lemma.

Lemma 2.3.1. *If a cubic spline $S_\Delta(x)$ on an arbitrary mesh Δ on $[a, b]$ satisfies the inequalities*

$$|S_\Delta(x_k)| \leqslant A, \qquad |S'_\Delta(x_k)| \leqslant B,$$

then we have on $[a, b]$

$$|S_\Delta(x)| \leqslant A + (\|\Delta\|/4)B.$$

It is important to remark that in this lemma $S_\Delta(x)$ is a piecewise cubic with continuous first derivatives. No assumptions have been made on $S''_\Delta(x)$. Using terminology that will be developed more completely in subsequent chapters, we speak of such splines as being of *deficiency* 2, splines with continuous second derivatives generally as being of *deficiency* 1. A spline that is a single cubic arc we designate as being of *deficiency* 0.

We note next that if we employ splines of deficiency 2 which interpolate to a continuous function $f(x)$ at points of a mesh Δ on $[a, b]$ and at these points have derivative 0, we obtain the analog of Fejér's result of 1916:

Lemma 2.3.2. *Let $\{\Delta_k\}$ be a sequence of meshes on $[a, b]$ with $\|\Delta_k\| \to 0$ as $k \to \infty$. Let $f(x)$ be of class $C[a, b]$. Let $\hat{S}_{\Delta_k}(x)$ be the spline of deficiency 2 interpolating to $f(x)$ at the points of Δ_k and there having derivative 0. Then the sequence $\{\hat{S}_{\Delta_k}(x)\}$ converges uniformly to $f(x)$ on $[a, b]$. In fact,*

$$|f(x) - \hat{S}_{\Delta_k}(x)| \leqslant 2\mu(f; \|\Delta\|/2).$$

Proof. The existence of such splines is evident: at the extremities of each interval of Δ_k, we have prescribed the value of a cubic and its first derivative. Next, the spline $\hat{S}_{\Delta_k}(x)$ is monotone on each interval of Δ_k. Thus on $[x_{k,j-1}, x_{k,j}]$ we have

$$|f(x) - \hat{S}_{\Delta_k}(x)| \leqslant |f(x) - f(x_{k,j-1})| + |\hat{S}_{\Delta_k}(x_{k,j-1}) - \hat{S}_{\Delta_k}(x)|$$
$$\leqslant 2\mu(f; h_{k,j}/2).$$

The following lemma involves somewhat more relaxed requirements on the spline involved. Its proof is evident.

Lemma 2.3.3. *Let $\{\Delta_k\}$ be a sequence of meshes on $[a, b]$, with $\| \Delta_k \| \to 0$ as $k \to \infty$. Let $\hat{S}_{\Delta_k}(x)$ and $\hat{T}_{\Delta_k}(x)$ be two splines on Δ_k which coincide at the mesh locations. If $\max_j | \hat{S}'_{\Delta_k}(x_{k,j})| \| \Delta_k \| \to 0$ and $\max_j | \hat{T}'_k(x_{k,j})| \| \Delta_k \| \to 0$ as $k \to \infty$, then on $[a, b]$*

$$\hat{S}_{\Delta_k}(x) - \hat{T}_{\Delta_k}(x) = o(1)$$

uniformly with respect to x in $[a, b]$.

Let us now return to Theorem 2.3.1. With no additional mesh restriction, we have the splines $\hat{S}_{\Delta_k}(x)$ of deficiency 2 of Lemma 2.3.2 converging uniformly to $f(x)$ on $[a, b]$. With the additional mesh restriction (2.3.7), we find for the splines $S_{\Delta_k}(x)$ of the theorem, using the boundedness with respect to k of $\| A^{-1} \|$ and $\| \tilde{A}^{-1} \|$ in (2.1.16) and (2.1.17), that

$$\max_j | S'_k(x_{k,j}) | \| \Delta_k \| \to 0.$$

Thus, by Lemma 2.3.3, $[S_{\Delta_k}(x) - \hat{S}_{\Delta_k}(x)] \to 0$, and by Lemma 2.3.2, $S_{\Delta_k}(x) \to f(x)$, both uniformly with respect to x in $[a, b]$. This alternative proof of Theorem 2.3.1 indicates somewhat more clearly the role of the mesh restriction (2.3.7).

If we assume that $f'(x)$ is continuous on $[a, b]$, then the spline and its derivative converge. Furthermore we no longer require the condition (2.3.7) on the sequence of meshes to be satisfied.

Theorem 2.3.2. *Let $\{\Delta_k\}$ be a sequence of meshes on $[a, b]$ with $\lim_{k\to\infty} \| \Delta_k \| = 0$. Let $f(x)$ be of class $C'[a, b]$. Let the splines of interpolation $S_{\Delta_k}(x)$ satisfy end condition (2.1.19i) or be periodic if $f(x)$ is periodic. Then we have, uniformly with respect to x in $[a, b]$,*

$$[f^{(p)}(x) - S^{(p)}_{\Delta_k}(x)] = o(\| \Delta_k \|^{1-p}) \qquad (p = 0, 1). \tag{2.3.13}$$

If $f'(x)$ satisfies a Hölder condition on $[a, b]$ of order $\alpha(0 < \alpha \leqslant 1)$, then (uniformly with respect to x in $[a, b]$)

$$[f^{(p)}(x) - S_{\Delta_k}^{(p)}(x)] = O(\| \Delta_k \|^{1+\alpha-p}) \qquad (p = 0, 1). \tag{2.3.14}$$

Proof. Let $m_k = (m_{k,0}, m_{k,1}, ..., m_{k,N_k})^{\mathrm{T}}$, $c_k = (c_{k,0}, c_{k,1}, ..., c_{k,N_k})^{\mathrm{T}}$, $f_k = (f_{k,0}, f_{k,1}, ..., f_{k,N_k})^{\mathrm{T}}$ in the nonperiodic case, with corresponding expressions for the periodic case. For a given Δ_k, let B_k denote the coefficient matrix in (2.1.17), or (2.1.16) with end condition (i) and the first and last equations written as $3m_{k,0} = 3f'(a) \equiv c_{k,0}$, $3m_{k,N_k} = 3f'(b) \equiv c_{k,N_k}$. Then

$$B_k(m_k - c_k/3) = (I_k - B_k/3)c_k,$$

where I_k is the $(N_k + 1) \times (N_k + 1)$ or $N_k \times N_k$ unit matrix. The right-hand member is, accordingly, in the nonperiodic and periodic cases,

$$\frac{1}{3}\begin{bmatrix} c_{k,0} - c_{k,1} \\ \lambda_1(c_{k,1} - c_{k,0}) - \mu_1(c_{k,2} - c_{k,1}) \\ \lambda_2(c_{k,2} - c_{k,1}) - \mu_2(c_{k,3} - c_{k,2}) \\ \vdots \\ c_{k,N_k} - c_{k,N_k-1} \end{bmatrix}, \qquad \frac{1}{3}\begin{bmatrix} \lambda_1(c_{k,1} - c_{k,N_k}) - \mu_1(c_{k,2} - c_{k,1}) \\ \lambda_2(c_{k,2} - c_{k,1}) - \mu_2(c_{k,3} - c_{k,2}) \\ \lambda_3(c_{k,3} - c_{k,2}) - \mu_3(c_{k,4} - c_{k,3}) \\ \vdots \\ \lambda_{N_k}(c_{k,N_k} - c_{k,N_k-1}) - \mu_{N_k}(c_{k,1} - c_{k,N_k}) \end{bmatrix}.$$

The norm of neither of these vectors exceeds $\mu(f'; 3\|\Delta_k\|) \leqslant 3\mu(f'; \|\Delta_k\|)$, and so $\| m_k - c_k \| \leqslant \| B_k^{-1} \| \cdot 3\mu(f'; \| \Delta_k \|) \leqslant 3\mu(f'; \| \Delta_k \|)$. Now $c_{k,j} = f'(\xi_{k,j})$ at some location $\xi_{k,j}$ in $[x_{k,j-1}, x_{k,j}]$ in the periodic case, and the same is true for $1 \leqslant j \leqslant N_k - 1$ in the nonperiodic situation. Of course, $c_{k,0} = 3f'(a)$, and $c_{k,N_k} = 3f'(b)$ in the latter instance. Thus, we obtain $\| m_k - f_k' \| \leqslant 4\mu(f'; \| \Delta_k \|)$.

As a result, we find for x on $[x_{k,j-1}, x_{k,j}]$ that we have from (2.1.11) (dropping the mesh index k)

$$\begin{aligned} &\left| S_\Delta'(x) - \frac{f_j - f_{j-1}}{h_j} \right| \\ &= \Bigg| \left[\frac{3}{h_j^2}\left(x - \frac{x_{j-1} + x_j}{2}\right)^2 - \frac{1}{4}\right] \\ &\quad \cdot \left[(m_{j-1} - f_{j-1}') + (m_j - f_j') + \left(f_{j-1}' + f_j' - 2\frac{f_j - f_{j-1}}{h_j}\right)\right] \\ &\quad + \frac{1}{h_j}\left(x - \frac{x_j + x_{j-1}}{2}\right)[(m_j - f_j') - (m_{j-1} - f_{j-1}') + (f_j' - f_{j-1}')] \Bigg| \\ &\leqslant 5\mu(f'; \| \Delta \|) + \tfrac{9}{2}\mu(f'; \| \Delta \|). \end{aligned}$$

Thus, since $|f'(x) - (f_j - f_{j-1})/h_j| \leqslant \mu(f'; h_j)$, we obtain the inequality

$$|f'(x) - S'(x)| \leqslant \tfrac{21}{2}\mu(f'; \|\Delta\|).$$

If $|f'(x) - f'(x')| \leqslant K|x - x'|^\alpha$ on $[a, b]$, then we see immediately that

$$|f'(x) - S_\Delta'(x)| \leqslant \tfrac{21}{2}K\|\Delta\|^\alpha.$$

Because of the interpolation property, we have on $[x_{j-1}, x_j]$ the relation

$$|f(x) - S_\Delta(x)| = \left|\int_{x_{j-1}}^{x} [f'(x) - S_\Delta'(x)]\, dx\right|$$

$$\leqslant \tfrac{21}{2}\mu(f'; \|\Delta\|) \cdot \|\Delta\|.$$

Equations (2.3.13) and (2.3.14) now follow. The case of the general end condition (2.1.19iii) will be considered in Section 2.9.

Essentially the same method of proof applies to the situation in which $f''(x)$ is continuous on $[a, b]$. The following theorem extends somewhat the results of Sharma and Meir [abs. 1964; 1966] by admitting more general conditions on $f(x)$.

Theorem 2.3.3. *Let $f(x)$ be of class $C^2[a, b]$. Let $\{\Delta_k\}$ be a sequence of meshes on $[a, b]$ with $\lim_{k\to\infty} \|\Delta_k\| = 0$. If the splines of interpolation $S_{\Delta_k}(x)$ to $f(x)$ on Δ_k satisfy end conditions (2.1.18i) or (2.1.18ii), or if $S_{\Delta_k}(x)$ and $f(x)$ are periodic, then we have*

$$[f^{(p)}(x) - S_{\Delta_k}^{(p)}(x)] = o(\|\Delta_k\|^{2-p}) \qquad (p = 0, 1, 2), \tag{2.3.15}$$

uniformly with respect to x in $[a, b]$. If $f''(x)$ satisfies a Hölder condition on $[a, b]$ of order α $(0 < \alpha \leqslant 1)$, then

$$[f^{(p)}(x) - S_{\Delta_k}^{(p)}(x)] = O(\|\Delta_k\|^{2+\alpha-p}) \qquad (p = 0, 1, 2) \tag{2.3.16}$$

uniformly with respect to x in $[a, b]$.

Proof. We set $M_k = (M_{k,0}, M_{k,1}, \ldots, M_{k,N_k})^T$, $d_k = (d_{k,0}, d_{k,1}, \ldots, d_{k,N_k})^T$ in the nonperiodic case and $(M_{k,1}, \ldots, M_{k\,N_k})^T$, $(d_{k,1}, \ldots, d_{k,N_k})^T$ in the periodic case. Let A_k denote the coefficient matrix in (2.1.8) or (2.1.9) associated with the mesh Δ_k. Then (2.1.8) for end condition (i) and (2.1.9) can be written in the form

$$A_k(M_k - d_k/3) = (I_k - A_k/3)d_k, \tag{2.3.17}$$

where I_k is a unit matrix. The right-hand member, in these two cases, takes the forms (dropping the mesh index k)

$$\frac{1}{3}\begin{bmatrix} d_0 - d_1 \\ \mu_1(d_1 - d_0) - \lambda_1(d_2 - d_1) \\ \mu_2(d_2 - d_1) - \lambda_2(d_3 - d_2) \\ \vdots \\ d_{N_k} - d_{N_k-1} \end{bmatrix}, \qquad \frac{1}{3}\begin{bmatrix} \mu_1(d_1 - d_{N_k}) - \lambda_1(d_2 - d_1) \\ \mu_2(d_2 - d_1) - \lambda_2(d_3 - d_2) \\ \mu_3(d_3 - d_2) - \lambda_3(d_4 - d_3) \\ \vdots \\ \mu_{N_k}(d_{N_k} - d_{N_k-1}) - \lambda_{N_k}(d_1 - d_{N_k}) \end{bmatrix}.$$

We note that $d_j/6$ is the divided difference (Hildebrand [1956, p. 38]) $f[x_{j-1}, x_j, x_{j+1}]$ in the periodic case, and when $j \neq 0$ or N is the non-periodic case,

$$\frac{d_j}{6} = \frac{[(f_{j+1} - f_j)/h_{j+1}] - [(f_j - f_{j-1})/h_j]}{h_j + h_{j+1}} = f[x_{j-1}, x_j, x_{j+1}].$$

This is equal to $\frac{1}{2}f''(\xi_j)$ at some location ξ_j in the interval $x_{j-1} < x < x_{j+1}$. It is also true by the Taylor theorem that quantity $d_0/6$,

$$\frac{d_0}{6} = \frac{[(f_1 - f_0)/h_1] - f_0'}{h_1},$$

is equal to $\frac{1}{2}f''(\xi_0)$ at some location in the first interval, and a similar assertion can be made for d_N.

It follows, therefore, that $\|(I_k - A_k/3)\, d_k\| \leqslant \mu(f''; 3\|\Delta_k\|) \leqslant 3\mu(f''; \|\Delta_k\|)$, and we obtain from (2.3.17) the inequality

$$\begin{aligned} \| M_k - d_k/3 \| &\leqslant \| A_k^{-1} \| \cdot \| (I_k - A_k/3)d_k \| \\ &\leqslant 3\mu(f''; \|\Delta_k\|), \end{aligned}$$

since $\| A_k^{-1} \| \leqslant 1$.

It is clear that $\|f_k'' - d_k/3\| \leqslant \mu(f''; \|\Delta_k\|)$, and it follows that $\| M_k - f_k'' \| \leqslant 4\mu(f''; \|\Delta_k\|)$. From the piecewise linearity of $S_{\Delta_k}''(x)$, we obtain the inequality

$$| f''(x) - S_{\Delta_k}''(x) | \leqslant 5\mu(f''; \|\Delta_k\|).$$

If $f''(x)$ satisfies a Hölder condition of order α on $[a, b]$, then we find for some K independent of k and x

$$| f''(x) - S_{\Delta_k}''(x) | \leqslant 5K\|\Delta_k\|^{\alpha}.$$

In consequence of the interpolation property of $S_{\Delta_k}(x)$, an application of Rolle's theorem yields the fact that in every interval $[x_{k,j-1}, x_{k,j}]$ there exists a point $\xi_{k,j}$ for which $f'(\xi_{k,j}) = S'_{\Delta_k}(\xi_{k,j})$. Thus on this interval we find that

$$|f'(x) - S'_{\Delta_k}(x)| = \left| \int_{\xi_{k,j}}^{x} [f''(x) - S''_{\Delta_k}(x)] \right| dx \leqslant 5 \| \Delta_k \| \mu(f''; \| \Delta_k \|),$$

and a second integration yields the property

$$|f(x) - S_{\Delta_k}(x)| \leqslant \tfrac{5}{2} \| \Delta_k \|^2 \mu(f''; \| \Delta_k \|).$$

Relations (2.3.16) and (2.3.17) are an immediate consequence. The nonperiodic case involving end condition (2.1.18ii) is included by writing the first and last of Eqs. (2.1.8) as $3M_{k,0} = 3f''(a) \equiv d_{k,0}$ and $3M_{k,N_k} = 3f''(b) \equiv d_{k,N_k}$. We still have $\| A_k^{-1} \| \leqslant 1$.

The convergence properties become even more striking as we increase the smoothness of $f(x)$. Birkhoff and deBoor [1964] showed that, for the nonperiodic splines of interpolation satisfying end condition (i), if $f'''(x)$ is absolutely continuous in $[a, b]$, then $S'''_{\Delta_k}(x)$ converges uniformly to $f'''(x)$ provided the mesh condition (2.3.7) is satisfied. Moreover, if $f^{iv}(x)$ is continuous, then $f^{(p)}(x) - S^{(p)}_{\Delta_k}(x)$ is of order $O(\| \Delta_k \|^{4-p})$ $(p = 0, 1, \ldots, 4)$ uniformly with respect to x in $[a, b]$. We present here a somewhat simpler proof of slightly stronger forms of these theorems.

Theorem 2.3.4. *Let $f(x)$ be of class $C^3[a, b]$. Let $\{\Delta_k\}$ be a sequence of meshes on $[a, b]$ with $\lim_{k\to\infty} \| \Delta_k \| = 0$ and satisfying (2.3.7). Then for the splines of interpolation $S_{\Delta_k}(x)$ satisfying end condition (2.1.18) (i) or (ii), or periodic if $f(x)$ is periodic, we have, uniformly with respect to x in $[a, b]$,*

$$[f^{(p)}(x) - S^{(p)}_{\Delta_k}(x)] = o(\| \Delta_k \|^{3-p}) \qquad (p = 0, 1, 2, 3) \tag{2.3.18}$$

If $f'''(x)$ satisfies a Hölder condition on $[a, b]$ of order α $(0 < \alpha \leqslant 1)$, then

$$[f^{(p)}(x) - S^{(p)}_{\Delta_k}(x)] = O(\| \Delta_k \|^{3+\alpha-p}) \qquad (p = 0, 1, 2, 3) \tag{2.3.19}$$

uniformly with respect to x in $[a, b]$.

Proof. Consider, first, Eqs. (2.1.8) with $\lambda_0 = \mu_N = 1$. Set

$$\sigma_j = (M_j - M_{j-1})/h_j,$$

the third derivative of the spline in $[x_{j-1}, x_j]$. In (2.1.8), subtract from each equation but the first its predecessor, obtaining

$$\begin{aligned} (1+\lambda_1)h_1\sigma_1 + \lambda_1 h_2\sigma_2 &= d_1 - d_0, \\ \mu_1 h_1\sigma_1 + (1+\mu_1+\lambda_2)h_2\sigma_2 + \lambda_2 h_3\sigma_3 &= d_2 - d_1, \\ \mu_2 h_2\sigma_2 + (1+\mu_2+\lambda_3)h_3\sigma_3 + \lambda_3 h_4\sigma_4 &= d_3 - d_2, \\ \cdots & \qquad\qquad (2.3.20) \\ \mu_{N-2}h_{N-2}\sigma_{N-2} + (1+\mu_{N-2}+\lambda_{N-1})h_{N-1}\sigma_{N-1} + \lambda_{N-1}h_N\sigma_N &= d_{N-1} - d_{N-2}, \\ \mu_{N-1}h_{N-1}\sigma_{N-1} + (1+\mu_{N-1})h_N\sigma_N &= d_N - d_{N-1}. \end{aligned}$$

Divide through by $(h_1 + h_2)$, $(h_1 + h_2 + h_3)$, $(h_2 + h_3 + h_4)$,..., $(h_{N-2} + h_{N-1} + h_N)$, $(h_{N-1} + h_N)$. The right-hand members become the column vector $r = (r_1, r_2, ..., r_N)^T$, where

$$r_1 = 6\,\frac{[f_0, f_1, f_2] - \{([f_0, f_1] - f_0')/h_1\}}{h_1 + h_2},$$

$$r_N = 6\,\frac{\{(f_N' - [f_{N-1}, f_N])/h_N\} - [f_{N-2}, f_{N-1}, f_N]}{h_{N-1} + h_N},$$

$$r_j = 6[f_{j-2}, f_{j-1}, f_j, f_{j+1}] \qquad (j = 2, ..., N-1).$$

Here $[f_j, f_{j+1}, ..., f_{j+k}] = f[x_j, x_{j+1}, ..., x_{j+k}]$ denotes the kth divided difference of $f(x)$ on the points x_j, $x_{j+1}, ..., x_{j+k}$. Note that the following relations are valid:

$$\frac{1 - \mu_{j-1}\lambda_j}{h_{j-1} + h_j + h_{j+1}} = \frac{\mu_{j-1}\mu_j}{h_{j-1}} = \frac{\lambda_{j-1}\mu_j}{h_j} = \frac{\lambda_{j-1}\lambda_j}{h_{j+1}}, \qquad \frac{h_j}{h_{j+1}} = \frac{\mu_j}{\lambda_j}.$$

Thus we obtain from (2.3.20) the set of equations

$$\begin{aligned} (1+\lambda_1)\mu_1\sigma_1 + \lambda_1^2\sigma_2 &= r_1, \\ \frac{\mu_1^2\mu_2}{1-\mu_1\lambda_2}\sigma_1 + \frac{(1+\mu_1+\lambda_2)\lambda_1\mu_2}{1-\mu_1\lambda_2}\sigma_2 + \frac{\lambda_1\lambda_2^2}{1-\mu_1\lambda_2}\sigma_3 &= r_2, \\ \cdots & \qquad\qquad (2.3.21) \\ \frac{\mu_{N-2}^2\mu_{N-1}}{1-\mu_{N-2}\lambda_{N-1}}\sigma_{N-2} & \\ + \frac{(1+\mu_{N-2}+\lambda_{N-1})\lambda_{N-2}\mu_{N-1}}{1-\mu_{N-2}\lambda_{N-1}}\sigma_{N-1} + \frac{\lambda_{N-2}\lambda_{N-1}^2}{1-\mu_{N-2}\lambda_{N-1}}\sigma_N &= r_{N-1}, \\ \mu_{N-1}^2\sigma_{N-1} + (1+\mu_{N-1})\lambda_{N-1}\sigma_N &= r_N. \end{aligned}$$

Although the coefficient matrix here collapses for $\lambda_1 = \cdots = \lambda_{N-1} = \frac{1}{2}$ to a dominant-diagonal matrix, the main diagonal is not generally dominant. The coefficient matrix C, however, can be represented by a matrix possessing this property multiplied by two diagonal matrices:

$$C = EDF,$$

where

$$E = \begin{bmatrix} \mu_1 & & & & & & 0 \\ & \dfrac{\mu_1\mu_2}{1 - \mu_1\lambda_2} & & & & & \\ & & \dfrac{\mu_1\mu_2\mu_3}{(1 - \mu_2\lambda_3)\lambda_1} & & & & \\ & & & \cdots & & & \\ & & & & \dfrac{\mu_1\mu_2 \cdots \mu_{N-2}}{(1 - \mu_{N-3}\lambda_{N-2})\lambda_1 \cdots \lambda_{N-4}} & & \\ & & & & & \dfrac{\mu_1\mu_2 \cdots \mu_{N-1}}{(1 - \mu_{N-2}\lambda_{N-1})\lambda_1 \cdots \lambda_{N-3}} & \\ 0 & & & & & & \dfrac{\mu_1\mu_2 \cdots \mu_{N-1}}{\lambda_1 \cdots \lambda_{N-2}} \end{bmatrix}, \quad F = \begin{bmatrix} 1 & & & & & 0 \\ & \dfrac{\lambda_1}{\mu_1} & & & & \\ & & \dfrac{\lambda_1\lambda_2}{\mu_1\mu_2} & & & \\ & & & \cdots & & \\ & & & & \dfrac{\lambda_1 \cdots \lambda_{N-2}}{\mu_1 \cdots \mu_{N-2}} & \\ 0 & & & & & \dfrac{\lambda_1 \cdots \lambda_{N-1}}{\mu_1 \cdots \mu_{N-1}} \end{bmatrix},$$

$$D = \begin{bmatrix} 1 + \lambda_1 & \lambda_1 & 0 & 0 & \cdots & 0 \\ \mu_1 & 1 + \mu_1 + \lambda_2 & \lambda_2 & 0 & \cdots & 0 \\ 0 & \mu_2 & 1 + \mu_2 + \lambda_3 & \lambda_3 & \cdots & 0 \\ & & \cdots & & & \\ 0 & \cdots & 0 & \mu_{N-2} & 1 + \mu_{N-2} + \lambda_{N-1} & \lambda_{N-1} \\ 0 & \cdots & 0 & 0 & \mu_{N-1} & 1 + \mu_{N-1} \end{bmatrix}.$$

It is clear that $\| D^{-1} \| \leqslant 1$.

If now, for all i, j, the intervals of the mesh satisfy the restriction

$$h_i/h_j \leqslant \beta < \infty,$$

then we have the inequality

$$\frac{1}{\beta} \leqslant \frac{\lambda_i}{\mu_i} \frac{\lambda_{i+1}}{\mu_{i+1}} \cdots \frac{\lambda_{i+p-1}}{\mu_{i+p-1}} = \frac{h_{i+p}}{h_i} \leqslant \beta.$$

Furthermore, we see that

$$\frac{1}{1 + 2\beta} \leqslant \frac{\mu_j\mu_{j+1}}{1 - \mu_j\lambda_{j+1}} = \frac{1}{1 + h_{j+1}/h_j + h_{j+2}/h_j} \leqslant 1,$$

$$\frac{1}{1 + \beta} \leqslant \mu_j \leqslant \frac{\beta}{1 + \beta} \leqslant 1 \qquad (1 \leqslant j \leqslant N - 1).$$

Thus it follows that

$$\| C^{-1} \| \leqslant (1 + 2\beta)\beta^2.$$

Let $\sigma = (\sigma_1, \ldots, \sigma_N)^{\mathrm{T}}$, and from $C\sigma = r$ obtain the equation

$$C(\sigma - r) = (I - C)r =$$

$$\begin{bmatrix} 1 - \mu_1(1+\lambda_1) & -\lambda_1^2 & 0 & \cdots & 0 & 0 \\ \dfrac{-\mu_1^2\mu_2}{(1-\mu_1\lambda_2)} & 1\dfrac{(1+\mu_1+\lambda_2)\lambda_1\mu_2}{1-\mu_1\lambda_2} & \dfrac{-\lambda_1\lambda_2^2}{1-\mu_1\lambda_2} & \cdots & 0 & 0 \\ & & \cdots & & & \\ 0 & 0 & 0 & \cdots & -\mu_{N-1}^2 & 1-\lambda_{N-1}(1+\mu_{N-1}) \end{bmatrix} r.$$

The sum of elements in each row is zero. Thus the last member is the vector

$$\begin{bmatrix} -\lambda_1^2(r_2 - r_1) \\ -\dfrac{\lambda_1\lambda_2^2}{1-\mu_1\lambda_2}(r_3 - r_2) + \dfrac{\mu_1^2\mu_2}{1-\mu_1\lambda_2}(r_2 - r_1) \\ \cdots \\ -\dfrac{\lambda_{N-2}\lambda_{N-1}^2}{1-\mu_{N-2}\lambda_{N-1}}(r_N - r_{N-1}) + \dfrac{\mu_{N-2}^2\mu_{N-1}}{1-\mu_{N-2}\lambda_{N-1}}(r_{N-1} - r_{N-2}) \\ \mu_{N-1}^2(r_N - r_{N-1}) \end{bmatrix}.$$

If $f'''(x)$ is continuous on $[a, b]$, then $| r_{j+1} - r_j |$ can be made arbitrarily small. Since $(1 - \mu_j\lambda_{j+1})^{-1} \leqslant 1 + 3\beta$, the step function $S_\Delta'''(x)$ can be made uniformly close to $f'''(x)$ by taking $\| \Delta \|$ sufficiently small. In fact, $| r_{j+1} - r_j | \leqslant \mu(f'''; 4\| \Delta \|) \leqslant 4\mu(f'''; \| \Delta \|)$, and

$$\| \sigma - r \| \leqslant K_2\mu(f''', \| \Delta \|),$$

where $K_2 = (1 + 2\beta)\beta^2 \cdot 2(1 + 3\beta) \cdot 4$. Since on $[x_{j-1}, x_j]$ we have $| f'''(x) - r_j | \leqslant \mu(f''', 3\| \Delta \|)$, it follows that

$$| S_\Delta'''(x) - f'''(x) | \leqslant (3 + K_2)\mu(f''', \| \Delta \|). \tag{2.3.22}$$

If $f'''(x)$ satisfies a Hölder condition of order α, $0 < \alpha \leqslant 1$, on $[a, b]$, then

$$| S_\Delta'''(x) - f'''(x) | = O(\| \Delta \|^\alpha)$$

uniformly with respect to x on $[a, b]$. In particular, if $f^{iv}(x)$ is continuous on $[a, b]$, then

$$| S_\Delta'''(x) - f'''(x) | \leqslant (3 + K_2) \max_{a \leqslant x \leqslant b} | f^{iv}(x) | \cdot \| \Delta \|.$$

Only minor modifications are required for end condition (ii). The first and last equations of (2.1.8) are written as $3M_0 = d_0 = 3f''(a)$ and $3M_N = d_N = 3f''(b)$. The quantities $2 + \lambda_1$ and $2 + \mu_{N-1}$ replace

$1 + \lambda_1$ and $1 + \mu_{N-1}$ in the first and last lines of (2.3.20), (2.3.21), and the matrix D.

The periodic case requires a slight change in the handling of the coefficient matrices. In this case $C = EDF$, where

$$E = \begin{bmatrix} \dfrac{\mu_1\lambda_N}{1-\mu_N\lambda_1} & & & & & 0 \\ & \dfrac{\mu_1\mu_2}{1-\mu_1\lambda_2} & & & & \\ & & \dfrac{\mu_1\mu_2\mu_3}{(1-\mu_2\lambda_3)\lambda_1} & & & \\ & & & \cdot & & \\ & & & & \cdot & \\ 0 & & & & & \dfrac{\mu_1\mu_2\cdots\mu_N}{(1-\mu_{N-1}\lambda_N)\,\lambda_1\cdots\lambda_{N-2}} \end{bmatrix}, \qquad F = \begin{bmatrix} 1 & & & & & 0 \\ & \dfrac{\lambda_1}{\mu_1} & & & & \\ & & \dfrac{\lambda_1\lambda_2}{\mu_1\mu_2} & & & \\ & & & \cdot & & \\ & & & & \cdot & \\ 0 & & & & & \dfrac{\lambda_1\lambda_2\cdots\lambda_{N-1}}{\mu_1\mu_2\cdots\mu_{N-1}} \end{bmatrix},$$

$$D = \begin{bmatrix} 1+\mu_N+\lambda_1 & \lambda_1 & 0 & \cdots & 0 & 0 & \mu_N \\ \mu_1 & 1+\mu_1+\lambda_2 & \lambda_2 & \cdots & 0 & 0 & 0 \\ 0 & \mu_2 & 1+\mu_2+\lambda_3 & \cdots & 0 & 0 & 0 \\ \vdots & \vdots & \vdots & & \vdots & \vdots & \vdots \\ 0 & 0 & 0 & \cdots & \mu_{N-2} & 1+\mu_{N-2}+\lambda_{N-1} & \lambda_{N-1} \\ \lambda_N & 0 & 0 & \cdots & 0 & \mu_{N-1} & 1+\mu_{N-1}+\lambda_N \end{bmatrix}$$

In this, we have used the fact that, in the periodic case, $\lambda_1\lambda_2\cdots\lambda_N = \mu_1\mu_2\cdots\mu_N$. The bound on $\| C^{-1} \|$ is as before, and we obtain again (2.3.22).

The third derivative, $S_\Delta'''(x)$, however, has jump discontinuities at mesh points so that simple integration cannot be employed to obtain inequalities on the second derivatives. To study the second derivative, then, we note the relation for second divided differences:

$$\frac{\dfrac{f_{j+1}-f_j}{h_{j+1}} - \dfrac{f_j - f_{j-1}}{h_j}}{h_j + h_{j+1}} = \frac{f_j''}{2} + \frac{\dfrac{1}{h_{j+1}}\displaystyle\int_{x_j}^{x_{j+1}} (x_{j+1}-t)^2 f'''(t)\,dt - \dfrac{1}{h_j}\displaystyle\int_{x_{j-1}}^{x_j} (x_{j-1}-t)^2 f'''(t)\,dt}{2(h_j+h_{j+1})}.$$

Using (2.1.5) and the interpolation property of $S_\Delta(x)$, we obtain

$$f_j'' - M_j = \frac{\dfrac{1}{h_{j+1}}\displaystyle\int_{x_j}^{x_{j+1}} (x_{j+1}-t)^2[f'''(t)-\sigma_{j+1}]\,dt - \dfrac{1}{h_j}\displaystyle\int_{x_{j-1}}^{x_j} (x_{j-1}-t)^2(f'''(t)-\sigma_j)\,dt}{h_j+h_{j+1}}.$$

On $[x_{j-1}, x_j]$, we evidently have

$$f''(x) - S''_\Delta(x) = f''_j - M_j + \int_{x_j}^{x} [f'''(t) - \sigma_{j+1}]\, dt,$$

and we obtain from this relation the inequality

$$|f''(x) - S''_\Delta(x)| \leqslant \max_j \left(\frac{2}{3} \frac{h_j^2 + h_{j+1}^2}{h_j + h_{j+1}} + h_j\right) \max_{[x_{j-1}, x_j]} |f'''(x) - S'''_\Delta(x)|$$
$$\leqslant \tfrac{5}{3} \| \Delta \| (3 + K_2)\mu(f'''; \| \Delta \|),$$

where we have made use of (2.3.22). The corresponding properties for $S'_\Delta(x) - f'(x)$ and $S_\Delta(x) - f(x)$ now follow by integration and the application of Rolle's theorem as before.

Two further properties serve to complete this initial presentation of spline convergence properties. We only mention these here and postpone their proofs to Sections 2.9 and 3.12.

If $f^{iv}(x)$ is continuous on $[a, b]$ and if $\{\Delta_k\}$ has the properties $\| \Delta_k \| \to 0$ as $k \to \infty$, $\| \Delta_k \| / \min_j h_{k,j} \leqslant \beta < \infty$, and $\max_j | \lambda_{k,j} - \frac{1}{2} | \to 0$, then

$$\lim_{k\to\infty} \max_j \left| \frac{S'''_{\Delta_k}(x_{k,j}+) - S'''_{\Delta_k}(x_{k,j}-)}{\| \Delta_k \|} - \frac{f^{iv}(x_{k,j})}{2} \right| = 0.$$

Thus the jumps in the spline third derivative are tied directly to the fourth derivative of the approximated function.

Finally, the uniform rate of convergence of $S^{(p)}_{\Delta_k}(x) - f^{(p)}(x)$ to zero was shown to be $o(\| \Delta_k \|^{\gamma-p})$ when $f(x)$ is of class $C^\gamma[a, b]$ ($\gamma = 0, 1, 2, 3, 4$; $0 \leqslant p \leqslant \gamma$) and to be $O(\| \Delta_k \|^{4-p})$ when $f(x)$ is of class $C^4[a, b]$ ($0 \leqslant p \leqslant 3$). In Section 3.12 it will be shown that it may be no higher than $O(\| \Delta_k \|^{4-p})$, unless $f(x)$ is itself a cubic polynomial.

2.4. Equal Intervals

In the case in which the intervals of the mesh Δ on $[a, b]$ are of equal length, the inverses of the coefficient matrices (2.1.8) and (2.1.9) or (2.1.16) and (2.1.17) take on relatively simple forms. These permit the immediate application of the spline to standard problems of numerical analysis.

Introduce the $n \times n$ determinant

$$D_n(\lambda) = \begin{vmatrix} 2 & \lambda & & & \\ 1-\lambda & 2 & \lambda & & \\ & \cdots & & & \\ & & 1-\lambda & 2 & \lambda \\ & & & 1-\lambda & 2 \end{vmatrix}. \tag{2.4.1}$$

This determinant, where $D_{-1}(\lambda) = 0$, $D_0(\lambda) = 1$, and $D_1(\lambda) = 2$, satisfies the difference equation

$$D_n(\lambda) - 2D_{n-1}(\lambda) + \lambda(1 - \lambda)D_{n-2}(\lambda) = 0,$$

so that

$$D_n(\lambda) = \frac{[1 + (1 - \lambda + \lambda^2)^{1/2}]^{n+1} - [1 - (1 - \lambda + \lambda^2)^{1/2}]^{n+1}}{2(1 - \lambda + \lambda^2)^{1/2}}. \tag{2.4.2}$$

We set $D_n = D_n(\frac{1}{2})$, $D_0 = 1$, $D_{-1} = 0$. Then we have

$$D_n = \frac{(1 + 3^{1/2}/2)^{n+1} - (1 - 3^{1/2}/2)^{n+1}}{3^{1/2}}. \tag{2.4.3}$$

Define the $n \times n$ determinant

$$Q_n(\alpha) = \begin{vmatrix} 2 & \alpha & & & \\ \frac{1}{2} & 2 & \frac{1}{2} & & \\ & \frac{1}{2} & 2 & \frac{1}{2} & \\ & & \cdots & & \\ & & & \frac{1}{2} & 2 \end{vmatrix}.$$

Here $Q_1(\alpha) = 2$. We define $Q_0(\alpha) = 1$. For $n \geqslant 1$,

$$Q_n(\alpha) = 2D_{n-1} - (\alpha/2)D_{n-2}, \tag{2.4.4}$$

and $Q_n(\alpha)$ satisfies the same difference equation as D_n. The coefficient determinant $|A|$ in (2.1.8) satisfies the equations

$$\begin{aligned} |A| &= 2Q_N(\mu_N) - \lambda_0 Q_{N-1}(\mu_N)/2 \\ &= 2Q_N(\lambda_0) - \mu_N Q_{N-1}(\lambda_0)/2. \end{aligned} \tag{2.4.5}$$

We obtain the elements of the inverse A^{-1} of the coefficient matrix in (2.1.8) in the case of equal intervals from the cofactors of the transpose matrix:

$$\left.\begin{aligned} A^{-1}_{i,j} &= \frac{(-1)^{i+j}Q_i(\lambda_0)Q_{N-j}(\mu_N)}{2^{j-i}\,|A|} && (0 < i \leqslant j \leqslant N), \\ A^{-1}_{i,j} &= \frac{(-1)^{i+j}Q_j(\lambda_0)Q_{N-i}(\mu_N)}{2^{i-j}\,|A|} && (0 \leqslant j \leqslant i < N), \\ A^{-1}_{0,j} &= \frac{(-1)^{j}\lambda_0 Q_{N-j}(\mu_N)}{2^{j-1}\,|A|} && (0 < j \leqslant N), \\ A^{-1}_{N,j} &= \frac{(-1)^{N+j}\mu_N Q_j(\lambda_0)}{2^{N-j-1}\,|A|} && (0 \leqslant j < N). \end{aligned}\right\} \tag{2.4.6}$$

The inverse matrix $\tilde{A}^{-1}$ for the periodic spline becomes particularly interesting if the intervals of Δ are of equal length. The matrix is now a circulant matrix (cf. Muir [1960]). Each row may be obtained by advancing each element of the preceding row to the next following position. Properties of such matrices play an important role in the development of polynomial splines and are examined in some detail in Chapter IV.

For the determinant $|\tilde{A}|$ of coefficients in the periodic case (2.2.6) with equal intervals, we obtain the relation

$$|\tilde{A}| = 2D_{N-1} - D_{N-2}/2 + (-2)^{1-N}. \tag{2.4.7}$$

Let $d_0^{(N)}, d_1^{(N)}, \ldots, d_{N-1}^{(N)}$ be the elements of the first row of $\tilde{A}^{-1}$, and adopt the convention $d_{N+j}^{(N)} = d_j^{(N)} = d_{-j}^{(N)}$. Then we have

$$\tilde{A}_{i,j}^{-1} = d_{j-i}^{(N)}. \tag{2.4.8}$$

The quantities $d_k^{(N)}$ are again found directly from the cofactors of the coefficient matrix, which is symmetric:

$$d_k^{(N)} = [(-2)^{-N+k} D_{k-1} + (-2)^{-k} D_{N-k-1}]/|A| \qquad (0 \leqslant k \leqslant N-1). \tag{2.4.9}$$

For Eqs. (2.1.16), the determinant $|B|$ of the matrix satisfies the equations

$$\begin{aligned} |B| &= 2Q_N(\mu_0) - \lambda_N Q_{N-1}(\mu_0)/2 \\ &= 2Q_N(\lambda_N) - \mu_0 Q_{N-1}(\lambda_N)/2, \end{aligned} \tag{2.4.10}$$

whereas for (2.1.17) we have $\tilde{B} = \tilde{A}$ and hence $|\tilde{B}| = |\tilde{A}|$.

In the nonperiodic case, the moment

$$M_i = \sum_{j=0}^{N} A_{i,j}^{-1} d_j$$

is seen to be given by

$$M_i = A_{i,0}^{-1} d_0 + \frac{3}{h^2}\Big\{A_{i,1}^{-1} f_0 + (A_{i,2}^{-1} - 2A_{i,1}^{-1}) f_1 + \sum_{j=2}^{N-2} (A_{i,j-1}^{-1} - 2A_{i,j}^{-1} + A_{i,j+1}^{-1}) f_j$$
$$+ (A_{i,N-2}^{-1} - 2A_{i,N-1}^{-1}) f_{N-1} + A_{i,N-1}^{-1} f_N\Big\} + A_{i,N-1}^{-1} d_N,$$

if we require the spline to assume the value f_j at $x_j = a + jh$. For $j \neq i$, we have the relations

$$A_{i,j-1}^{-1} - 2A_{i,j}^{-1} + A_{i,j+1}^{-1} = -6A_{i,j}^{-1} \qquad (1 < j < N-1),$$
$$A_{i,0}^{-1} - 2A_{i,1}^{-1} + A_{i,2}^{-1} = -6A_{i,1}^{-1} + (1 - 2\lambda_0) A_{i,0}^{-1} \; (i \neq 1),$$
$$A_{i,N-2}^{-1} - 2A_{i,N-1}^{-1} + A_{i,N}^{-1} = -6A_{i,N-1}^{-1} + (1 - 2\mu_N) A_{i,N}^{-1} \; (i \neq N-1),$$

whereas

$$A^{-1}_{i,i-1} - 2A^{-1}_{i,i} + A^{-1}_{i,i+1} = 2 - 6A^{-1}_{i,i} \qquad (1 < i < N-1),$$

$$A^{-1}_{1,0} - 2A^{-1}_{1,1} + A^{-1}_{1,2} = 2 - 6A^{-1}_{1,1} + A^{-1}_{1,0}(1 - 2\lambda_0),$$

$$A^{-1}_{N-1,N-2} - 2A^{-1}_{N-1,N-1} + A^{-1}_{N-1,N} = 2 - 6A^{-1}_{N-1,N-1} + A^{-1}_{N-1,0}(1 - 2\mu_N).$$

Thus we obtain the representation for the moments,

$$M_i = A^{-1}_{i,0}\left[d_0 + \frac{6}{h^2}(f_0 - \lambda_0 f_1)\right] - \frac{18}{h^2}\sum_{j=0}^{N} A^{-1}_{i,j}f_j$$

$$+ \frac{6}{h^2}f_i + A^{-1}_{i,N}\left[d_N + \frac{6}{h^2}(f_N - \mu_N f_{N-1})\right]. \qquad (2.4.11)$$

In the periodic case, we obtain

$$M_i = \frac{18}{h^2}\sum_{j=1}^{N} \tilde{A}^{-1}_{i,j}f_j + \frac{6}{h^2}f_i. \qquad (2.4.12)$$

The quantities $A^{-1}_{i,j}$ and $\tilde{A}^{-1}_{i,j}$ decay rapidly as j departs from i. Thus it is necessary in the evaluation of the quantities M_j to employ only a few terms centered at x_j. In addition, the limiting values of the coefficients in (2.4.11) and (2.4.12) as $N \to \infty$ may frequently be used, affording considerable simplification in applications of the spline.

Set

$$r = 1 + 3^{1/2}/2, \qquad s = 1 - 3^{1/2}/2, \qquad \sigma = -1/(2r) = -2s = -(s/r)^{1/2};$$

then we find directly that

$$D_n = \frac{r^{n+1} - s^{n+1}}{r - s}, \qquad \frac{D_{n-1}}{r^n} = \frac{1 - \sigma^{2n}}{2 + \sigma}.$$

Using the fact that $2 + \sigma = -(2 + 1/\sigma) = 3^{1/2}$, we obtain the relation

$$\tilde{A}^{-1}_{i,j} = d^{(N)}_{|j-i|} = \frac{\sigma^{N-|j-i|} + \sigma^{|j-i|}}{(2+\sigma)(1-\sigma^N)}. \qquad (2.4.13)$$

For the nonperiodic spline, those situations in which $\lambda_0 = \mu_N = \alpha$ are of particular interest. With $\alpha = 1$ is associated the end condition (2.1.18i); with $\alpha = 0$, (2.1.18ii); $\alpha = -2$ gives a parabolic runout. This last case is related to the condition $M_0 = M_1$, $M_{N-1} = M_N$, which has special significance when neither the end slopes nor end moments are known. The existence and convergence properties of such splines will be covered in Section 2.9.

It is easily seen that, for $n \geqslant 1$,

$$\frac{Q_n(\alpha)}{r^n} = \frac{2(1-\sigma^{2n}) + \alpha\sigma(1-\sigma^{2n-2})}{2+\sigma},$$
$$\frac{|A|}{r^N} = \frac{(2+\alpha\sigma)^2 - \sigma^{2N}(2+\alpha\sigma^{-1})^2}{2+\sigma}. \tag{2.4.14}$$

Thus for $0 < i \leqslant j \leqslant N$ and for $i = j = 0$,

$$A_{i,j}^{-1} = \frac{\sigma^{j-i}[Q_i(\alpha)/r^i]\cdot[Q_{N-j}(\alpha)/r^{N-j}]}{|A|/r^N},$$

so that

$$A_{i,j}^{-1} = \frac{\sigma^{j-i}[2+\alpha\sigma-\sigma^{2i-1}(2\sigma+\alpha)][2+\alpha\sigma-\sigma^{2N-2j-1}(2\sigma+\alpha)]}{(2+\sigma)[(2+\alpha\sigma)^2-\sigma^{2N-2}(2\sigma+\alpha)^2]} \quad (0 < i \leqslant j < N), \tag{2.4.15a}$$

and

$$A_{i,N}^{-1} = \frac{\sigma^{N-i}[2+\alpha\sigma-\sigma^{2i-1}(2\sigma+\alpha)]}{(2+\alpha\sigma)^2-\sigma^{2N-2}(2\sigma+\alpha)^2} \quad (0 < i \leqslant N). \tag{2.4.15b}$$

For $0 < j \leqslant N$,

$$A_{0,j}^{-1} = \frac{\sigma^j\cdot 2\alpha Q_{N-j}(\alpha)/r^{N-j}}{|A|/r^N},$$

so that

$$A_{0,j}^{-1} = \frac{\sigma^j\cdot 2\alpha[2+\alpha\sigma-\sigma^{2N-2j-1}(2\sigma+\alpha)]}{(2+\alpha\sigma)^2-\sigma^{2N-2}(2\sigma+\alpha)^2} \quad (0 < j < N), \tag{2.4.15c}$$

and

$$A_{0,N}^{-1} = \frac{\sigma^N 2\alpha(2+\sigma)}{(2+\alpha\sigma)^2-\sigma^{2N-2}(2\sigma+\alpha)^2}. \tag{2.4.15d}$$

To complete the evaluation of $A_{i,j}^{-1}$, we remark that in consequence of (2.4.6) we have $A_{i,j}^{-1} = A_{j,i}^{-1}$ $(0 < i < N, 0 < j < N)$, whereas $A_{i,j}^{-1} = A_{N-i,N-j}^{-1}$ for unrestricted i and j.

For the three cases referred to in the foregoing:

End Condition (i) $(\alpha = 1)$

$$A_{i,j}^{-1} = \frac{\sigma^{j-1}(1+\sigma^{2i})(1+\sigma^{2N-2j})}{(2+\sigma)(1-\sigma^{2N})} \quad (0 < i \leqslant j < N),$$

$$A_{i,N}^{-1} = \frac{\sigma^{N-i}(1+\sigma^{2i})}{(2+\sigma)(1-\sigma^{2N})} \quad (0 < i \leqslant N),$$

$$A_{0,j}^{-1} = \frac{2\sigma^j(1+\sigma^{2N-2j})}{(2+\sigma)(1-\sigma^{2N})} \quad (0 < j < N),$$

$$A_{0,N}^{-1} = \frac{2\sigma^N}{(2+\sigma)(1-\sigma^{2N})}.$$

End Condition (ii) ($\alpha = 0$)

$$A_{i,j}^{-1} = \frac{\sigma^{j-i}(1-\sigma^{2i})(1-\sigma^{2N-2j})}{(2+\sigma)(1-\sigma^{2N})} \qquad (0 < i \leqslant j < N),$$

$$A_{i,N}^{-1} = \frac{\sigma^{N-i}(1-\sigma^{2i})}{2(1-\sigma^{2N})} \qquad (0 < i \leqslant N),$$

$$A_{0,j}^{-1} = 0 \qquad (0 < j \leqslant N).$$

Parabolic Runout ($\alpha = -2$)

$$A_{i,j}^{-1} = \frac{\sigma^{j-i}(1+\sigma^{2i-1})(1+\sigma^{2N-2j-1})}{(2+\sigma)(1-\sigma^{2N-2})} \qquad (0 < i \leqslant j < N),$$

$$A_{i,N}^{-1} = \frac{\sigma^{N-i}(1+\sigma^{2i-1})}{2(1-\sigma)(1-\sigma^{2N-2})} \qquad (0 < i \leqslant N),$$

$$A_{0,j}^{-1} = \frac{-2\sigma^{j}(1+\sigma^{2N-2j-1})}{(1-\sigma)(1-\sigma^{2N-2})} \qquad (0 < j < N),$$

$$A_{0,N}^{-1} = -\frac{\sigma^{N}(2+\sigma)}{(1-\sigma)^2(1-\sigma^{2N-2})}.$$

The elements $B_{i,j}^{-1}$ for equal spacing are obtained from expressions (2.4.6) by replacing λ_0, μ_N by μ_0, λ_N. Of course, $\tilde{B}_{i,j}^{-1} = \tilde{A}_{i,j}^{-1}$. In order to obtain the expression m_i corresponding to (2.4.11), we write

$$\begin{aligned} m_i &= \sum_{j=0}^{N} B_{i,j}^{-1} c_j \\ &= B_{i,0}^{-1} c_0 + \sum_{j=1}^{N-1} B_{i,j}^{-1} \frac{3}{2h}(f_{j+1} - f_{j-1}) + B_{i,N}^{-1} c_N \\ &= B_{i,0}^{-1}(c_0 - f_1) - B_{i,1}^{-1} f_0 + \sum_{j=1}^{N-1} (B_{i,j-1}^{-1} - B_{i,j+1}^{-1}) f_j + B_{i,N-1}^{-1} f_N \\ &\quad + B_{i,N}^{-1}(f_{N-1} + c_N). \end{aligned} \tag{2.4.16}$$

It is seen from the discussion following (2.1.19) that for the determination of the $B_{i,j}^{-1}$ from (2.4.15a–d) the values of α in the three cases are 0, 1, 2, respectively. The first two are therefore available from the foregoing, whereas the case $\alpha = 2$ gives a parabolic runout:

Parabolic Runout ($\alpha = 2$)

$$B_{i,j}^{-1} = \frac{\sigma^{j-i}(1-\sigma^{2i-1})(1-\sigma^{2N-2j-1})}{(2+\sigma)(1-\sigma^{2N-2})} \qquad (0 < i \leqslant j < N),$$

$$B_{i,N}^{-1} = \frac{\sigma^{N-i}(1-\sigma^{2i-1})}{2(1+\sigma)(1-\sigma^{2N-2})} \qquad (0 < i \leqslant N),$$

$$B_{0,j}^{-1} = \frac{2\sigma^{j}(1-\sigma^{2N-2j-1})}{(1+\sigma)(1-\sigma^{2N-2})} \qquad (0 < j < N),$$

$$B_{0,N}^{-1} = \frac{(2+\sigma)\sigma^N}{(1+\sigma)^2(1-\sigma^{2N-2})}.$$

In the periodic situation, (2.4.16) is replaced by

$$\begin{aligned} m_i &= \frac{3}{2h}\sum_{j=1}^{N}(\tilde{B}_{i,j-1}^{-1} - \tilde{B}_{i,j+1}^{-1})f_j \\ &= \frac{3}{h}\sum_{j=1}^{[(N-1)/2]}\frac{\sigma^{N-j}-\sigma^j}{1-\sigma^N}(f_{i+j}-f_{i-j}), \end{aligned} \qquad (2.4.17)$$

where the brackets denote "integral part of."

The limiting values of $\tilde{A}_{i,j}^{-1}$ as $N \to \infty$ play a useful role. We have

$$d_{j-1}^{(\infty)} = \lim_{N\to\infty} d_{j-i}^{(N)} = \lim_{N\to\infty} \tilde{A}_{i,j}^{-1} = \frac{\sigma^{|j-i|}}{2+\sigma}.$$

The error in approximating $\tilde{A}_{i,j}^{-1}$ by $d_{j-i}^{(\infty)}$ is given by

$$\tilde{A}_{i,j}^{-1} - d_{j-i}^{(\infty)} = \frac{\sigma^{N-|j-i|}+\sigma^{N+|j-i|}}{(2+\sigma)(1-\sigma^N)}.$$

Even in the nonperiodic case, this is a useful approximation except near the ends of the interval, inasmuch as $\sigma \doteq -0.268$. The values of $d_k^{(\infty)}$ for $k \leqslant 7$ are

$k =$	0	1	2	3	4	5	6	7
$d_k^{(\infty)} =$	0.57735	−0.15470	0.04145	−0.01111	0.00298	−0.00080	0.00021	−0.00006

Table 2.4.1 presents the quantities $d_k^{(N)}$ that serve as the elements of $\tilde{A}^{-1}$: $\tilde{A}_{i,j}^{-1} = d_{j-i}^{(N)}$.

TABLE 2.4.1

VALUES OF $d_k^{(N)}$, $N = 2,\ldots, 17$

k	$N = 2$	$N = 3$	$N = 4$	$N = 5$	$N = 6$	$N = 7$	$N = 8$	$N = 9$
0	0.66667	0.55556	0.58333	0.57576	0.57778	0.57724	0.57738	0.57734
1	−0.33333	−0.11111	−0.16667	−0.15152	−0.15556	−0.15447	−0.15476	−0.15468
2	—	—	0.08333	0.03030	0.04444	0.04065	0.04167	0.04139
3	—	—	—	—	−0.02222	−0.00813	−0.01190	−0.01089
4	—	—	—	—	—	—	0.00595	0.00218

k	$N = 10$	$N = 11$	$N = 12$	$N = 13$	$N = 14$	$N = 15$	$N = 16$	$N = 17$
0	0.57735	0.57735	0.57735	0.57735	0.57735	0.57735	0.57735	0.57735
1	−0.15470	−0.15470	−0.15470	−0.15470	−0.15470	−0.15470	−0.15470	−0.15470
2	0.04147	0.04145	0.04145	0.04145	0.04145	0.04145	0.04145	0.04145
3	−0.01116	−0.01109	−0.01111	−0.01111	−0.01111	−0.01111	−0.01111	−0.01111
4	0.00319	0.00292	0.00299	0.00297	0.00298	0.00298	0.00298	0.00298
5	−0.00159	−0.00058	−0.00085	−0.00078	−0.00080	−0.00080	−0.00080	−0.00080
6	—	—	0.00043	0.00016	0.00023	0.00021	0.00021	0.00021
7	—	—	—	—	−0.00011	−0.00004	−0.00006	−0.00006
8	—	—	—	—	—	—	0.00003	0.00001

The corresponding elements of the inverse matrix for the nonperiodic spline for the cases considered in Table 2.4.1 may be determined from the following identities, which are readily verified. For $\alpha = 1$,

$$A^{-1}_{i,j} = d^{(2N)}_{j-i} + d^{(2N)}_{j+i} \quad (0 < i \leqslant j < N), \qquad A^{-1}_{0,j} = 2d^{(2N)}_{j} \quad (0 < j < N),$$

$$A^{-1}_{i,N} = \tfrac{1}{2}[d^{(2N)}_{N-i} + d^{(2N)}_{N+i}] \quad (0 < i \leqslant N), \qquad A^{-1}_{0,N} = d^{(2N)}_{N}.$$

For $\alpha = 0$,

$$A^{-1}_{i,j} = d^{(2N)}_{j-i} - d^{(2N)}_{j+i} \qquad (0 < i \leqslant j < N), \qquad A^{-1}_{0,j} = 0 \qquad (0 < j \leqslant N),$$

$$A^{-1}_{i,N} = \frac{(2+\sigma)^2}{2}\,[d^{(2N)}_0 d^{(2N)}_{N+i} - d^{(2N)}_N d^{(2N)}_i] \qquad (0 < i \leqslant N).$$

For $\alpha = -2$,

$$A^{-1}_{i,j} = d^{(2N-2)}_{j-i} + d^{(2N-2)}_{j+i-1} \quad (0 < i \leqslant j < N), \qquad A^{-1}_{0,j} = d^{(2N-2)}_{j} + d^{(2N-2)}_{j-1} \quad (0 < j < N),$$

$$A^{-1}_{i,N} = -\tfrac{1}{4}[d^{(2N-2)}_{N-i} + d^{(2N-2)}_{N+i-1}] \ (0 < i \leqslant N), \qquad A^{-1}_{0,N} = -\tfrac{1}{4}[d^{(2N-2)}_{N} + d^{(2N-2)}_{N-1}].$$

In order to obtain $B_{i,j}^{-1}$ for $\alpha = 2$, we have

$$B_{i,j}^{-1} = d_{j-i}^{(2N-2)} - d_{j+i-1}^{(2N-2)} \quad (0 < i \leqslant j < N), \quad B_{0,j}^{-1} = d_j^{(2N-2)} - d_{j-1}^{(2N-2)} \quad (0 < j < N),$$

$$B_{i,N}^{-1} = \tfrac{1}{4}[d_{N-i}^{(2N-2)} - d_{N+i-1}^{(2N-2)}] \quad (0 < i \leqslant N), \qquad B_{0,N}^{-1} = \tfrac{1}{4}[d_N^{(2N-2)} - d_{N-1}^{(2N-2)}].$$

2.5. Approximate Differentiation and Integration

Among the most important applications of the spline to numerical analysis and the areas where its versatility and flexibility are particularly evident are numerical differentiation and integration. From Theorem 2.3.4, it is evident that in approximate integration a fourth-order process results even for unequal intervals. For approximate differentiation, the error is $O(h^3)$, but there is more to add to this picture. The resulting derivatives at mesh points are "smooth", a property attributable partly to the best approximation characteristic exhibited in Section 2.2 and partly to the minimum curvature property developed in Chapter III.

We have for the periodic spline, from Eqs. (2.1.15), the relations

$$m_i = 3 \sum_{j=1}^{N} \tilde{B}_{i,j}^{-1} \left[\lambda_j \frac{f_j - f_{j-1}}{h_j} + \mu_j \frac{f_{j+1} - f_j}{h_{j+1}}\right], \tag{2.5.1}$$

and, for the nonperiodic spline, the relations

$$m_i = B_{i,0}^{-1} c_0 + 3 \sum_{j=1}^{N-1} B_{i,j}^{-1} \left[\lambda_j \frac{f_j - f_{j-1}}{h_j} + \mu_j \frac{f_{j+1} - f_j}{h_{j+1}}\right] + B_{i,N}^{-1} c_N . \tag{2.5.2}$$

For equal intervals, we have the formulas (2.4.15) and (2.4.16). In the case of unequal intervals, however, it is rarely worthwhile to compute the quantities $B_{i,j}^{-1}$. The algorithm at the end of Section 2.1 should be used to determine the slopes m_j directly or to determine the moments M_j whence the slopes may be found by (2.1.4):

$$\begin{aligned} m_i &= \frac{h_i}{6} M_{i-1} + \frac{h_i}{3} M_i + \frac{f_i - f_{i-1}}{h_i} \qquad (0 < i \leqslant N), \\ m_i &= -\frac{h_{i+1}}{3} M_i - \frac{h_{i+1}}{6} M_{i+1} + \frac{f_{i+1} - f_1}{h_{i+1}} \qquad (0 \leqslant i < N). \end{aligned} \tag{2.5.3}$$

A slight rearrangement of (2.5.2) and (2.5.3), however, yields an important property of the slopes m_i. We have from (2.5.1) the equation

$$m_i = 3 \sum_{j=1}^{N} \frac{f_i - f_{j-1}}{h_j} [\lambda_j \tilde{B}_{i,j}^{-1} + \mu_{j-1} \tilde{B}_{i,j-1}^{-1}], \tag{2.5.4}$$

and from (2.5.2) we obtain the equation

$$m_i = B_{i,0}^{-1} c_0 + 3\lambda_1 B_{i,1}^{-1} \frac{f_1 - f_0}{h_1} + 3 \sum_{j=1}^{N-1} \frac{f_j - f_{j-1}}{h_j} [\lambda_j B_{i,j}^{-1} + \mu_{j-1} B_{i,j-1}^{-1}]$$

$$+ 3\mu_{N-1} B_{i,N-1}^{-1} \frac{f_N - f_{N-1}}{h_N} + B_{i,N}^{-1} c_N . \tag{2.5.5}$$

EXAMPLE 2.5.1

DETERMINATION OF SLOPES AND SECOND DERIVATIVES FOR A NOZZLE CONTOUR (END SLOPES PRESCRIBED)

x	y	y'	M	y'' (spline-on-spline) ($\lambda_0 = \mu_N = 1$)
0	5.160	−0.04400	−0.00490	−0.00145
1	5.110	−0.04450	0.00380	−0.00255
2	5.070	−0.04780	−0.01031	−0.00266
3	5.020	−0.04924	0.00743	−0.00087
4	4.972	−0.04923	−0.00741	0.00186
5	4.921	−0.05083	0.00420	−0.01135
6	4.860	−0.08343	−0.06941	−0.05907
7	4.738	−0.16442	−0.09257	−0.09313
8	4.528	−0.25486	−0.08830	−0.08270
9	4.228	−0.36231	−0.09423	−0.12118
10	3.829	−0.45763	−0.12878	−0.04087
11	3.373	−0.38834	0.26736	0.15803
12	3.094	−0.19400	0.12135	0.19970
13	2.985	0.00043	0.26724	0.20913
14	3.100	0.21077	0.15369	0.17807
15	3.375	0.32662	0.07801	0.05750
16	3.720	0.34276	−0.04571	0.01209
17	4.050	0.32733	0.01483	−0.00700
18	4.380	0.32793	−0.01362	−0.00440
19	4.700	0.31094	−0.02037	−0.01245
20	5.000	0.28830	−0.02492	−0.01635
21	5.280	0.27586	0.00004	−0.01530
22	5.550	0.25826	−0.03524	−0.01258
23	5.580	0.25110	0.02093	−0.00867
24	6.050	0.23733	−0.04848	−0.01557
25	6.275	0.22458	0.02299	−0.00891
26	6.500	0.21433	−0.04349	−0.01754
27	6.700	0.19308	0.00099	−0.01646
28	6.890	0.18334	−0.02046	−0.00577
29	7.070	0.18354	0.02085	−0.00331
30	7.250	0.16250	−0.06292	−0.00960

It is possible to show for equal intervals that the summation

$$3 \sum_{j=1}^{N} B_{i,j}^{-1} \frac{f_j - f_{j-1}}{h} = 3 \sum_{j=1}^{N} \frac{\sigma^{N-|j-i|} + \sigma^{|j-i|}}{(2+\sigma)(1-\sigma^N)} \frac{f_j - f_{j-1}}{h}$$

is a *smoothing* of the quantities $(f_j - f_{j-1})/h_j$ in the sense of Schoenberg [1946], and the calculation of m_i involves an additional averaging of such sums. Related conclusions can be drawn for (2.5.5).

It should be noted again here, however, that the right-hand member of (2.1.15) is the slope at x_j of the parabola through the points (x_{j-1}, y_{j-1}), (x_j, y_j), and (x_{j+1}, y_{j+1}), and that in consequence these slopes of parabolas represent a smoothing of the quantities m_j.

The fact that m_i represents a smoothing of the quantities $(f_j - f_{j-1})/h$ is in marked contrast to the behavior of the M_j's. It may be seen from (2.1.7) that the second divided differences $f[x_{j-1}, x_j, x_{j+1}]$ themselves represent a smoothing of the quantities M_j.

It is important to take these characteristics into account in applications of the spline to problems in which smooth second derivatives are required. One such class of problems involves the determination of flow patterns of a compressible gas by the "streamline" procedure. Here it is necessary to obtain streamline curvatures that are smooth as well as accurate, for the stability of the numerical procedure is usually involved. The spline has proved to be an effective tool in determining second derivatives by the following device: first determine streamline slopes by the usual method; then spline-fit the slopes themselves and use the resulting derivatives as the second derivatives required. Example 2.5.1 employs a typical streamline for a convergent-divergent nozzle to illustrate the effect of this device. Here M_j represents the usual spline second derivative; y_j'' represents the spline-on-spline second derivative. In both cases, end conditions $M_0 = M_1$, $M_{N-1} = M_N$ have been used.

The integral of the spline over $\{a, b\}$ results directly from (2.1.2). We obtain the relation

$$\int_{x_{j-1}}^{x_j} S_\Delta(x)\, dx = \frac{f_{j-1} + f_j}{2} h_j - \frac{M_{j-1} + M_j}{24} h_j^3. \tag{2.5.6}$$

Thus we are led to the formula

$$\int_a^b S_\Delta(x)\, dx = \sum_{j=1}^{N} \frac{f_{j-1} + f_j}{2} h_j - \sum_{j=1}^{N} \frac{M_{j-1} + M_j}{24} h_j^3. \tag{2.5.7}$$

For the case of unequal intervals it is preferable, as indicated in the case of numerical differentiation, to evaluate the moments M_j by the spline algorithm in Section 2.1 and in this way evaluate the integral on the left.

When the intervals $[x_{j-1}, x_j]$ are of equal length, Eq. (2.5.7) becomes

$$\int_a^b S_\Delta(x)\,dx = h\sum_{j=1}^{N}\frac{f_{j-1}+f_j}{2} - \frac{h^3}{12}\sum_{j=1}^{N}\frac{M_{j-1}+M_j}{2}.$$

For the periodic spline, this is simply the trapezoidal rule, since $M_1 + M_2 + \cdots + M_N = 0$.

If we sum the left-hand members of (2.1.5), we obtain for the nonperiodic spline the equation

$$\frac{h_1}{6}M_0 + \left(\frac{h_1}{3}+\frac{h_2}{2}\right)M_1 + \frac{1}{2}\sum_{j=2}^{N-2}(h_j + h_{j+1})M_j + \left(\frac{h_{N-1}}{2}+\frac{h_N}{3}\right)M_{N-1}$$

$$+\frac{h_N}{6}M_N = \frac{f_N - f_{N-1}}{h_N} - \frac{f_1 - f_0}{h_1}. \qquad (2.5.8)$$

Thus, for equal intervals, (2.5.7) becomes

$$\int_a^b S_\Delta(x)\,dx = h\left(\tfrac{5}{12}f_0 + \tfrac{13}{12}f_1 + f_2 + \cdots + f_{N-2} + \tfrac{13}{12}f_{N-1} + \tfrac{5}{12}f_N\right)$$
$$-(h^3/72)(2M_0 + M_1 + M_{N-1} + 2M_N). \qquad (2.5.9)$$

For the end conditions in which $\lambda_0 = \mu_N = \alpha$, which are those of principal concern to us, we have $A_{i,j}^{-1} = A_{N-i,N-j}^{-1}$. Set

$$E_j \equiv E_j(\alpha) = 2A_{0,j}^{-1} + A_{1,j}^{-1} + A_{N-1,j}^{-1} + 2A_{N,j}^{-1}.$$

Then (2.4.11) gives the equation

$$(2M_0 + M_1 + M_{N-1} + 2M_N) = E_0[d_0 + d_N + (6/h^2)(f_0 + f_N - \alpha f_1 - \alpha f_{N-1})]$$
$$+ (6/h^2)(2f_0 + f_1 + f_{N-1} + 2f_N) - (18/h^2)\sum_{j=0}^{N} E_j f_j.$$

By (2.4.6), we obtain the relation

$$E_0 = [2Q_N(\alpha) - \tfrac{1}{2}Q_{N-1}(\alpha) + (-2)^{1-N}Q_1(\alpha) + (-2)^{2-N}\alpha]/|A|,$$

which, by (2.4.14), is shown to yield

$$E_0 = \frac{[(2+\alpha\sigma) - \sigma^N(2+\alpha\sigma^{-1})](1-\sigma^N)(2+\sigma)}{(2+\alpha\sigma)^2 - \sigma^{2N}(2+\alpha\sigma^{-1})^2} = \frac{(1-\sigma^N)(2+\sigma)}{2+\alpha\sigma+\sigma^N(2+\alpha\sigma^{-1})}.$$

Similarly, we find for $0 < j < N$ that

$$E_j = -4(1-\alpha)\frac{\sigma^{N-j}+\sigma^j}{2+\alpha\sigma+\sigma^N(2+\alpha\sigma^{-1})}. \qquad (2.5.10)$$

We note further that $E_0 = 1 - E_1/4$. Thus, (2.5.9) becomes

$$\int_a^b S_\Delta(x)\,dx = -(h^3/72)\,E_0(d_0 + d_N) + (\tfrac{1}{4} + \tfrac{1}{6}E_0)h(f_0 + f_N)$$
$$+ \{2 - [1 - (\alpha/12)]E_0\}h(f_1 + f_{N-1}) + h\sum_{j=2}^{N-2}(1 + \tfrac{1}{4}E_j)f_j\,. \tag{2.5.11}$$

A rapid procedure for calculating the numerical values of these coefficients for arbitrary α is afforded by the following algorithm. Set $G_n = (-2)^n D_n$ so that

$$G_{n+2} + 4G_{n+1} + G_n = 0.$$

Also set

$$F_{2n} = \frac{2G_{n-2} + G_{n-3}}{3G_{n-1} + G_{n-2}}, \qquad F_{2n+1} = \frac{5G_{n-2} + G_{n-3}}{5G_{n-1} + G_{n-2}}\,.$$

It may be verified directly that

$$F_{2n} = \frac{\sigma + \sigma^{2n-1}}{1 + \sigma^{2n}}, \qquad F_{2n+1} = \frac{\sigma + \sigma^{2n}}{1 + \sigma^{2n+1}},$$

and that, for $0 \leqslant j \leqslant N$,

$$\frac{\sigma^j + \sigma^{N-j}}{1 + \sigma^N} = G_{j-1}F_N - G_{j-2}\,.$$

Thus,

$$E_0(\alpha) = \frac{2 + F_N}{2 + \alpha F_N}, \qquad E_j(\alpha) = -4(1 - \alpha)\frac{G_{j-1}F_N - G_{j-2}}{2 + F_N}\,.$$

We include a table of these quantities for small n, Table 2.5.1.

Coefficients for the case $d_0 = d_N = 0$, $\alpha = 0$ are given in Table 2.5.2 and those for $d_0 = d_N = 0$, $\alpha = -2$ in Table 2.5.3. The elements in the first of these tables were given previously by Holladay [1957] and are presented here again for convenience. Numerators of coefficients are displayed in the body of each table; denominators are indicated at the left of each row.

Curiously enough, this gives the trapezoidal rule, Simpson's rule, and the three-eighth's rule for one, two, and three intervals. In Chapters V and VI there is a detailed examination of the fundamental relationship between splines and approximate integration formulas, as well as the approximation of continuous linear functionals in general.

TABLE 2.5.1

n	G_n	$2G_n + G_{n-1}$	$5G_n + G_{n-1}$	F_n
−3	4	—	—	—
−2	−1	2	−1	—
−1	0	−1	−1	—
0	1	2	5	−2
1	−4	−7	−19	1
2	15	26	71	$-\frac{1}{2}$
3	−56	−97	−265	$-\frac{1}{5}$
4	209	362	989	$-\frac{2}{7}$
5	−780	−1,351	−3,691	$-\frac{5}{19}$
6	2,911	5,042	13,775	$-\frac{7}{26}$
7	−10,864	−18,817	−51,409	$-\frac{19}{71}$
8	40,545	70,226	191,861	$-\frac{26}{97}$
9	−151,316	−262,087	−716,035	$-\frac{71}{265}$
10	564,719	978,122	2,672,279	$-\frac{97}{362}$

TABLE 2.5.2

$\frac{1}{2}$	1	1								
$\frac{1}{8}$	3	10	3							
$\frac{1}{10}$	4	11	11	4						
$\frac{1}{28}$	11	32	26	32	11					
$\frac{1}{38}$	15	43	37	37	43	15				
$\frac{1}{104}$	41	118	100	106	100	118	41			
$\frac{1}{142}$	56	161	137	143	143	137	161	56		
$\frac{1}{388}$	153	440	374	392	386	392	374	440	153	
$\frac{1}{530}$	209	601	511	535	529	529	535	511	601	209

TABLE 2.5.3

$\frac{1}{2}$	1	1								
$\frac{1}{3}$	1	4	1							
$\frac{1}{8}$	3	9	9	3						
$\frac{1}{36}$	13	44	30	44	13					
$\frac{1}{96}$	35	115	90	90	115	35				
$\frac{1}{44}$	16	53	40	46	40	53	16			
$\frac{1}{360}$	131	433	330	366	366	330	433	131		
$\frac{1}{492}$	179	592	450	504	486	504	450	592	179	
$\frac{1}{448}$	163	539	410	458	446	446	458	410	539	163

In Example 2.5.2, we indicate the application of the spline approximation to the evaluation of first and second derivatives of the function sin x on the interval $[0, 2\pi]$. Interval lengths of 20° and 10° are used. Second derivatives using the M_j and also spline-on-spline second derivatives are indicated. The use of a variety of end conditions permits the estimation of the extent of the effect of end conditions. We consider four cases: (a) $M_0 = M_N = 0$; (b) $M_0 = M_1$, $M_{N-1} = M_N$; (c) y'_0 and y'_N prescribed at their correct values; and (d) spline periodic. Because of symmetry, only half of the entries are exhibited.

The spline-on-spline calculation for y'' is exhibited for cases b and d in which the same type spline is employed as in the basic fit. The improvement in y'' so calculated is evident by comparison with the sin x entries. The quality of the periodic y' and periodic spline-on-spline y'' for both 10° and 20° intervals is noteworthy.*

EXAMPLE 2.5.2

FITTING OF SIN x, 10° INTERVALS, CASES a, b

		$M_0 = M_N = 0$		$M_0 = M_1$, $M_{N-1} = M_N$		Case b
$18x/\pi$	sin x	y'	y''	y'	y''	y'' (spline-on-spline)
0	0.00000	1.00005	−0.00000	1.00700	−0.13797	−0.09541
1	0.17365	0.98478	−0.17494	0.98292	−0.13797	−0.18053
2	0.34202	0.93966	−0.34212	0.94015	−0.35203	−0.33132
3	0.50000	0.86606	−0.50119	0.86593	−0.49854	−0.50507
4	0.64279	0.76603	−0.64516	0.76606	−0.64587	−0.64101
5	0.76604	0.64279	−0.76706	0.64278	−0.76687	−0.76661
6	0.86603	0.49999	−0.86924	0.49999	−0.86929	−0.86588
7	0.93969	0.34201	−0.94107	0.34201	−0.94106	−0.93968
8	0.98481	0.17366	−0.98814	0.17366	−0.98814	−0.98471
9	1.00000	0.00000	−1.00184	0.00000	−1.00184	−1.00018
10	0.98481	−0.17367	−0.98825	−0.17367	−0.98825	−0.98467
11	0.93969	−0.34199	−0.94061	−0.34199	−0.94061	−0.93954
12	0.86603	−0.50000	−0.86997	−0.50000	−0.86997	−0.86628
13	0.76604	−0.64281	−0.76654	−0.64281	−0.76654	−0.76594
14	0.64279	−0.76603	−0.64551	−0.76603	−0.64551	−0.64272
15	0.50000	−0.86602	−0.50030	−0.86602	−0.50030	−0.49993
16	0.34202	−0.93966	−0.34348	−0.93966	−0.34348	−0.34202
17	0.17365	−0.98482	−0.17408	−0.98482	−0.17408	−0.17396
18	0.00000	−1.00003	−0.00023	−1.00003	−0.00023	+0.00018

* The excellent quality of the periodic spline-on-spline second derivative was obtained using 6 decimal places in the data and the approximation, valid for large N,

$$y''_i = \Sigma_j (9/4h^2)[d_j^{\infty}(i + 2/3^{1/2})/3^{1/2}][f_{i+j+2} - 2f_{i+j} + f_{i+j-2}].$$

10° Intervals, Cases c, d

	$y'_0 = y'_N = 1$		Periodic		Periodic
$18x/\pi$	y'	y''	y'	y''	y'' (spline-on-spline)
0	1.00000	−0.00093	1.00005	0.00000	−0.00000
1	0.98479	−0.17519	0.98478	−0.17494	−0.17375
2	0.93965	−0.34205	0.93965	−0.34212	−0.34196
3	0.86606	−0.50121	0.86606	−0.50019	−0.50002
4	0.76603	−0.64516	0.76603	−0.64516	−0.64280
5	0.64279	−0.76706	0.64279	−0.76706	−0.76600
6	0.49999	−0.86924	0.49999	−0.86924	−0.86594
7	0.34201	−0.94107	0.34201	−0.94107	−0.93970
8	0.17366	−0.98814	0.17366	−0.98814	−0.98479
9	0.00000	−1.00184	0.00000	−1.00184	−0.99996
10	−0.17367	−0.98825	−0.17367	−0.98825	−0.98479
11	−0.34199	0.94061	−0.34199	−0.94061	−0.93970
12	−0.50000	−0.86997	−0.50000	−0.86997	−0.86594
13	−0.64281	−0.76654	−0.64281	−0.76654	−0.76600
14	−0.76603	−0.64551	−0.76603	−0.64551	−0.64280
15	−0.86602	−0.50030	−0.86602	−0.50030	−0.50002
16	−0.93966	−0.34348	−0.93966	−0.34348	−0.34196
17	−0.98482	−0.17408	−0.98482	−0.17408	−0.17375
18	−1.00003	−0.00023	−1.00003	−0.00023	−0.00000

20° Intervals, Cases a, b

		$M_0 = M_N = 0$		$M_0 = M_1$ $M_{N-1} = M_N$		Case b
$18x/\pi$	sin x	y'	y''	y'	y''	y''(spline-on-spline)
0	0.00000	0.99989	−0.0	1.02734	−0.27235	−0.19056
2	0.34202	0.93962	−0.34533	0.93227	−0.27235	−0.35391
4	0.64279	0.76600	−0.64950	0.76797	−0.66905	−0.62260
6	0.86603	0.49995	−0.87481	0.49942	−0.86957	−0.87575
8	0.98481	0.17363	−0.99489	0.17377	−0.99629	−0.98078
10	0.98481	−0.17362	−0.99472	−0.17366	−0.99435	−0.98612
12	0.86603	−0.49996	−0.87505	−0.49995	−0.87515	−0.86531
14	0.64279	−0.76599	−0.64916	−0.76599	−0.64917	−0.64285
16	0.34202	−0.93962	0.34569	−0.93962	−0.34569	−0.34200
18	0.00000	−0.99992	0.00022	−0.99992	+0.00022	−0.00011

20° Intervals, Cases c, d

	$y'_0 = y'_N = 1$		Periodic		Periodic
$18x/\pi$	y'	y''	y'	y''	y'' (spline-on-spline)
0	1.00000	−0.00105	0.99989	0.00000	0.00000
2	0.93959	−0.34504	0.93962	0.34533	−0.34198
4	0.76600	−0.64957	0.76600	0.64950	−0.64279
6	0.49995	−0.87479	0.49995	0.87481	−0.86589
8	0.17363	−0.99489	0.17363	−0.99489	−0.98469
10	−0.17362	−0.99472	−0.17362	−0.99472	−0.98469
12	−0.49996	−0.87505	−0.49996	−0.87505	−0.86589
14	−0.76599	−0.64916	−0.76599	−0.64916	−0.64279
16	−0.93962	−0.34569	−0.93962	−0.34569	−0.34198
18	−0.99992	−0.00022	−0.99992	−0.00022	0.00000

2.6. Curve Fitting

The specific objective of much of the development of one-dimensional splines is, of course, the fitting of a curve. Nevertheless, curve-fitting remains an art, and it is necessary to point out some of the techniques and artifices employed on splines used in the practice of this art.

It is generally desirable to employ more or less uniform distributions of mesh points when this is practical. When a long and short interval are in juxtaposition, oscillations frequently result which are not attributable directly to the data.

The effect of the end condition chosen for a given arc, when this choice is within one's discretion, dampens rapidly as one moves in from the extremities of the arc. The necessity to determine more or less accurately the slope at the end of the arc, however, is a problem one frequently meets in curve fitting. The choice of end condition does have some effect upon the value of this slope. If flex points appear to be appropriate at the extremities, use $M_0 = M_N = 0$. In the absence of other motivation, our own choice is $M_0 = M_1$, $M_{N-1} = M_N$. The resulting fit, however, may exhibit a strong behavior on the part of the quantities M_j near the extremities with which this particular end condition appears to conflict. Frequently, in this situation, the more general end conditions $M_0 = \lambda_0 M_1$, $M_N = \mu_N M_{N-1}$ may be employed with λ_0 and μ_N adjusted so as to be consistent with that behavior.

A related problem concerns the fitting of an arc near an end of which the slope and curvature are both numerically decreasing, e.g., $y = x^{1/2}$, $0 \leqslant x \leqslant 10$, near the end $x = 10$. This behavior does not represent a natural runout for a cubic, and the fit will not be good if the mesh distance increases materially as we approach this end. Likewise, a good fit by a spline at the $x = 0$ end of this arc is prevented by the existence of a vertical tangent there.

Some of the difficulties arising in the curve-fitting may be eliminated by a suitable change of coordinates. Many problems are intrinsic, however, and a technique of application of the spline is required which circumvents the difficulties presented. A highly effective procedure is the use of a parametric representation. Suppose $P_j\,(x_j\,,\, y_j)\,(j=0, 1,..., N)$ represent $N + 1$ points appearing on an arc C in the order given. If s_j is the cumulative chordal distance,

$$s_j = \sum_{i=1}^{j} \overline{P_{i-1}P_i}\,,$$

we spline-fit x versus s and y versus s. If desired, we can then approximate numerically the lengths of the segments of the resulting curve $x = x(s)$, $y = y(s)$ and construct a new fit of x and y against the *cumulative arc length*, although this step usually results in no perceptible change in the curve itself.

A rather striking example is the fitting of x and y against cumulative chord length for the unit circle using periodic splines. Using eight points (45° apart) gives a maximum error of 0.00112 in the radius. For 12 points (30° apart), the maximum error in the radius is 0.000165. As a matter of interest, even for 4 points the error is less than 1 %. We remark that with this device we have effectively accomplished an intrinsic parametric spline representation.

The advantages in such a representation are many. The geometric configuration of the arc is of much less concern than for the conventional spline. Fitting a simple closed curve by a periodic spline in polar coordinates r and θ with respect to some pole inside the curve may be effective if no half-line from the pole intersects the curve more than once or is tangent to the curve. The arc-length representation presents no such limitation. We may fit curves as well in three dimensions, forming splines for x, y, and z in terms of chord length or arc length.

Care must be taken, of course, that the curves being fitted actually possess the continuity conditions required. Using a single spline curve to fit an arc consisting of a piece of a circle and a tangent line at its extremity results in oscillations near the junctions due to the curvature discontinuity. Slope and curvature discontinuities (in two dimensions) when the fit is y versus x should be handled by terminating the splines at these locations or by appropriate spacing of points near the point of curvature discontinuity. The latter itself should not be a mesh point. In the use of a parametric fit employing cumulative chord length, the situation is far less critical. Appropriate spacing suffices even though the curvature discontinuity location is taken as a mesh point.

2.7. Approximate Solution of Differential Equations

The spline may frequently be used to advantage in the solution of initial- and boundary-value problems in ordinary differential equations. The method to be described is of general application, but we restrict our discussion here to a two-point boundary-value problem for a second-order equation. Consider the problem

$$\begin{aligned} Ly &= y'' + p(x)y' + q(x)y = r(x) \qquad (a \leqslant x \leqslant b), \\ a_1y(a) &+ a_2y'(a) = a_0\,, \qquad b_1y(b) + b_2y'(b) = b_0\,. \end{aligned} \tag{2.7.1}$$

Let us introduce here the *cardinal splines* associated with boundary condition (2.1.18i). The *cardinal splines* are a set of $N + 3$ independent splines forming a basis for all cubic splines on the mesh Δ: $a = x_0 < x_1 < \cdots < x_N = b$. We define these in the following way: $A_{\Delta,k}(x)$ $(k = 0, 1,..., N)$ and $B_{\Delta,k}(x)$ $(k = 0, N)$ are cubic splines on Δ with

$$\begin{aligned} &A_{\Delta,k}(x_j) = \delta_{k,j}\,(j = 0, 1,..., N), \quad A'_{\Delta,k}(x_i) = 0\,(i = 0 \text{ and } N), \quad k = 0, 1,..., N, \\ &B_{\Delta,k}(x_j) = 0\,(j = 0, 1,..., N), \quad B'_{\Delta,k}(x_i) = \delta_{k,i}\,(i = 0 \text{ and } N), k = 0 \text{ and } N. \end{aligned} \tag{2.7.2}$$

Here $\delta_{k,j}$ is the Kronecker delta.

We may express the spline satisfying end condition (2.1.18i) and interpolating on Δ to the solution of the differential equation in the form

$$S_\Delta(y; x) = \sum_{j=0}^{N} A_{\Delta,j}(x)y(x_j) + y'(a)B_{\Delta,0}(x) + y'(b)B_{\Delta,N}(x). \tag{2.7.3}$$

Set $E_\Delta(y; x)$ equal to the difference between $y(x)$ and $S_\Delta(y; x)$:

$$E_\Delta(y; x) = y(x) - S_\Delta(y; x). \tag{2.7.4}$$

If there exists a solution $y(x)$ of (2.7.1) which is of class $C^2[a, b]$ and is unique, then $E_\Delta^{(\alpha)}(y; x) = o\,(\|\Delta\|^{2-\alpha})$ $(\alpha = 0, 1, 2)$ uniformly with respect to x in $[a, b]$. If $f(x)$ possesses a higher order of regularity, then the approach of $E_\Delta^{(\alpha)}$ to zero is correspondingly higher in accordance with the results of Section 2.3.

Using (2.7.4), we form the difference

$$\begin{aligned} LS_\Delta(y; x) - r(x) &= S''_\Delta(y; x) + p(x)S_\Delta'(y; x) + q(x)S_\Delta(y; x) - r(x) \\ &= G_\Delta(y; x), \end{aligned}$$

where $G_\Delta(y; x) = -E''_\Delta(y; x) - p(x)E_\Delta'(y; x) - q(x)E_\Delta(y; x)$. We have $G_\Delta(y; x) = o(\| 1 \|)$. Substituting from (2.7.3) into (2.7.1) now gives the equation

$$\sum_{j=0}^{N} y(x_j)LA_{\Delta,j}(x) + y'(a)LB_{\Delta,0}(x) + y'(b)LB_{\Delta,N}(x) - r(x) = G_\Delta(y; x). \tag{2.7.5}$$

Thus the ordinates $y_j = y(x_j)$ $(j = 0, 1, \ldots, N)$ and the slopes $y_0' = y'(a)$, $y_N' = y'(b)$ satisfy the equations

$$\left.\begin{aligned} &\sum_{j=0}^{N} y_j LA_{\Delta,j}(x_i) + y_0' LB_{\Delta,0}(x_i) + y_N' LB_{\Delta,N}(x_i) = r(x_i) + G_\Delta(y; x_i) \\ &\qquad\qquad\qquad\qquad (i = 0, 1, 2, \ldots, N), \\ &a_1 y_0 + a_2 y_0' = a_0, \qquad b_1 y_N + b_2 y_N' = b_0 . \end{aligned}\right\} \tag{2.7.6}$$

We introduce the notation

$$\begin{aligned} Y_\Delta &= (y_0', y_0, y_1, \ldots, y_N, y_N')^{\mathrm{T}}, \\ G_\Delta &= (0, G_\Delta(y; x_0), \ldots, G_\Delta(y; x_N), 0)^{\mathrm{T}}, \\ R_\Delta &= (a_0, r(x_0), \ldots, r(x_N), b_0)^{\mathrm{T}}, \end{aligned}$$

and let H_Δ represent the matrix

$$H_\Delta = \begin{bmatrix} a_2 & a_1 & 0 & \cdots & 0 & 0 \\ LB_{\Delta,0}(x_0) & LA_{\Delta,0}(x_0) & LA_{\Delta,1}(x_0) & \cdots & LA_{\Delta,N}(x_0) & LB_{\Delta,N}(x_0) \\ \vdots & \vdots & \vdots & & \vdots & \vdots \\ LB_{\Delta,0}(x_N) & LA_{\Delta,0}(x_N) & LA_{\Delta,1}(x_N) & \cdots & LA_{\Delta,N}(x_N) & LB_{\Delta,N}(x_N) \\ 0 & 0 & 0 & \cdots & b_1 & b_2 \end{bmatrix}.$$

Then we have

$$H_\Delta Y_\Delta = R_\Delta + G_\Delta .$$

The quantities $G_\Delta(y; x_i)$ are, of course, unknown. The method consists of replacing these by zero and then determining from $H_\Delta Y_\Delta^* = R_\Delta$ the approximation Y_Δ^* of Y_Δ. If we have the property that H_Δ^{-1} exists and that $\| H_\Delta^{-1} G_\Delta \| \to 0$ as $\| \Delta \| \to 0$, then the solutions of the modified equation

$$H_\Delta Y_\Delta^* = R_\Delta \tag{2.7.7}$$

define splines that converge uniformly to $y(x)$ on $[a, b]$. In particular, this conclusion follows if the norms $\| H_\Delta^{-1} \|$ are uniformly bounded.

For purposes of illustration, we now consider the problem

$$\begin{aligned} y'' - \alpha^2 y = 0, \qquad 0 \leqslant x \leqslant 1, \\ y(0) = y(1) = 1. \end{aligned} \tag{2.7.8}$$

Here H_Δ is the matrix

$$\begin{bmatrix} 0 & 1 & 0 & & 0 & 0 \\ B''_{\Delta,0}(x_0) & A''_{\Delta,0}(x_0)-\alpha^2 & A''_{\Delta,1}(x_0) & \cdots & A''_{\Delta,N}(x_0) & B''_{\Delta,N}(x_0) \\ B''_{\Delta,0}(x_1) & A''_{\Delta,0}(x_1) & A''_{\Delta,1}(x_1)-\alpha^2 & \cdots & A''_{\Delta,N}(x_1) & B''_{\Delta,N}(x_1) \\ \vdots & \vdots & \vdots & & \vdots & \vdots \\ B''_{\Delta,0}(x_N) & A''_{\Delta,0}(x_N) & A''_{\Delta,1}(x_N) & \cdots & A''_{\Delta,N}(x_N)-\alpha^2 & B''_{\Delta,N}(x_N) \\ 0 & 0 & 0 & & 1 & 0 \end{bmatrix}.$$

Premultiply the members of Eq. (2.7.7) in this case by the $(N+3)\times(N+3)$ matrix

$$\begin{bmatrix} 1 & 0 & \cdots & 0 & 0 \\ 0 & & & & 0 \\ \vdots & & \left[\;A\;\right] & & \vdots \\ 0 & & & & 0 \\ 0 & 0 & \cdots & 0 & 1 \end{bmatrix}, \tag{2.7.9}$$

where A is the coefficient matrix in (2.1.8) with $\lambda_0 = \mu_N = 1$. The resulting equation is

$$\begin{bmatrix} 0 & 1 & 0 & 0 & \cdots & 0 & 0 & 0 \\ -\dfrac{6}{h_1} & -\dfrac{6}{h_1^2}-2\alpha^2 & \dfrac{6}{h_1^2}-\lambda_0\alpha^2 & 0 & \cdots & 0 & 0 & 0 \\ 0 & \dfrac{6}{h_1(h_1+h_2)}-\mu_1\alpha^2 & -\dfrac{6}{h_1h_2}-2\alpha^2 & \dfrac{6}{h_2(h_1+h_2)}-\lambda_1\alpha^2 & \cdots & 0 & 0 & 0 \\ 0 & 0 & \dfrac{6}{h_2(h_2+h_3)}-\mu_2\alpha^2 & -\dfrac{6}{h_2h_3}-2\alpha^2 & \cdots & 0 & 0 & 0 \\ 0 & 0 & 0 & \dfrac{6}{h_3(h_3+h_4)}-\mu_3\alpha^2 & \cdots & 0 & 0 & 0 \\ \vdots & \vdots & & & & \vdots & \vdots & \vdots \\ 0 & 0 & \cdots & & & \dfrac{6}{h_N^2}-\mu_N\alpha^2 & -\dfrac{6}{h_N^2}-2\alpha^2 & \dfrac{6}{h_N} \\ 0 & 0 & \cdots & & & 0 & 1 & 0 \end{bmatrix} \cdot \begin{bmatrix} y_0' \\ y_0 \\ y_1 \\ y_2 \\ y_3 \\ \vdots \\ y_N \\ y_N' \end{bmatrix} = \begin{bmatrix} 1 \\ 0 \\ 0 \\ 0 \\ 0 \\ \vdots \\ 0 \\ 1 \end{bmatrix}$$

In these equations, replace $-y_0' + (y_1 - y_0)h_1$ by u_0, $y_N' - (y_N - y_{N-1})/h_N$ by u_N. Interchange the first and second equations of the resulting set, and the last and next to last. The modified equations are

$$\begin{bmatrix} \frac{6}{h_1} & -2\alpha^2 & -\lambda_0\alpha^2 & 0 & \cdots & 0 & 0 \\ 0 & 1 & 0 & 0 & \cdots & 0 & 0 \\ 0 & \frac{6}{h_1(h_1+h_2)} - \mu_1\alpha^2 & -\frac{6}{h_1h_2} - 2\alpha^2 & \frac{6}{h_2(h_1+h_2)} - \lambda_1\alpha^2 & \cdots & 0 & 0 \\ \vdots & \vdots & & & & \vdots & \vdots \\ 0 & 0 & \cdots & 0 & 0 & 1 & 0 \\ 0 & 0 & \cdots & 0 & -\mu_N\alpha^2 & -2\alpha^2 & \frac{6}{h_N} \end{bmatrix} \begin{bmatrix} u_0 \\ y_0 \\ y_1 \\ \vdots \\ y_N \\ u_N \end{bmatrix} = \begin{bmatrix} 0 \\ 1 \\ 0 \\ \vdots \\ 1 \\ 0 \end{bmatrix}.$$

Here the coefficient matrix is clearly diagonal dominant if $\| \Delta \|$ is sufficiently small, and the norm of the inverse matrix is uniformly bounded.

In this process, the error vector G_Δ is multiplied by the matrix (2.7.9), which has a bounded norm, and by the inverse of the coefficient matrix in (2.7.10), which likewise has a bounded norm. Thus, convergence of the splines to $y(x)$ follows; indeed,

$$\| [y'(x_0) - y_0'^*, y(x_0) - y_0^*, \ldots, y(x_N) - y_N^*, y'(x_N) - y_N'^*] \| \to 0$$

as $\| \Delta \| \to 0$.

Table 2.7.1 gives, to five decimal places, the exact solution of the problem $y'' - 100y = 0$, $0 \leqslant x \leqslant 1$, $y(0) = y(1) = 1$, together with the spline approximations employing 10 and 20 intervals. The exact solution is $y = [\cosh 10(x - 0.5)]/\cosh 5$. Because of the symmetry, only the first half of the interval [0, 1] is covered.

TABLE 2.7.1

x	Exact y	$y(N = 10)$	$y(N = 20)$	Exact y'	$y'(N = 10)$	$y'(N = 20)$
0.00	1.00000	1.00000	1.00000	−9.9991	−10.1152	−10.1028
0.05	0.60657	—	0.60333	—	—	—
0.10	0.36799	0.35107	0.36406	—	—	—
0.15	0.22332	—	0.21975	—	—	—
0.20	0.13566	0.12343	0.13277	—	—	—
0.25	0.08263	—	0.08042	—	—	—
0.30	0.05070	0.04390	0.04906	—	—	—
0.35	0.03170	—	0.03049	—	—	—
0.40	0.02079	0.01075	0.01987	—	—	—
0.45	0.01520	—	0.01444	—	—	—
0.50	0.01348	0.01065	0.01277	—	—	—

One should note also at this point that, once the spline solution has been completed, the information required for spline interpolation between mesh points is available. This is particularly significant when, as part of a longer calculation, the solution of the boundary-value problem is required at various locations in the interval $[a, b]$. An important instance also is the use of an automatic plotter that frequently requires interpolation at a great many intermediate points.

Nonlinear differential equations are effectively handled by the method of splines when used in conjunction with the quasilinearization techniques introduced by Bellman and Kalaba [1965]. Here the problem

$$y'' = f(x, y, y'), \qquad a \leqslant x \leqslant b;$$
$$A[y(a), y'(a)] = 0, \quad B[y(b), y'(b)] = 0$$

is solved by the iterative procedure

$$y''_{n+1} = f_y(x, y_n, y'_n)(y_{n+1} - y_n) + f_{y'}(x, y_n, y'_n)(y'_{n+1} - y'_n),$$

with the linearized boundary conditions

$$A_y[y_n(0), y'_n(0)][y_{n+1}(0) - y_n(0)] + A_{y'}[y_n(0), y'_n(0)][y'_{n+1}(0) - y'_n(0)] = 0,$$
$$B_y[y_n(0), y'_n(0)][y_{n+1}(0) - y_n(0)] + B_{y'}[y_n(0), y'_n(0)][y'_{n+1}(0) - y'_n(0)] = 0.$$

For the case of equal intervals, the moments for the cardinal splines introduced previously may be obtained directly from the results of Section 2.4. We have end condition (2.1.18i), so that $\lambda_0 = \mu_N = 1$ in the coefficient matrix A of (2.1.8). Thus,

$$\begin{bmatrix}
B''_{\Delta,0}(x_0) & A''_{\Delta,0}(x_0) & A''_{\Delta,1}(x_0) & \cdots & A''_{\Delta,N}(x_0) & B''_{\Delta,N}(x_0) \\
B''_{\Delta,0}(x_1) & A''_{\Delta,0}(x_1) & A''_{\Delta,1}(x_1) & \cdots & A''_{\Delta,N}(x_1) & B''_{\Delta,N}(x_1) \\
B''_{\Delta,0}(x_2) & A''_{\Delta,0}(x_2) & A''_{\Delta,1}(x_2) & \cdots & A''_{\Delta,N}(x_2) & B''_{\Delta,N}(x_2) \\
\vdots & \vdots & \vdots & & \vdots & \vdots \\
B''_{\Delta,0}(x_{N-2}) & A''_{\Delta,0}(x_{N-2}) & A''_{\Delta,1}(x_{N-2}) & \cdots & A''_{\Delta,N}(x_{N-2}) & B''_{\Delta,N}(x_{N-2}) \\
B''_{\Delta,0}(x_{N-1}) & A''_{\Delta,0}(x_{N-1}) & A''_{\Delta,1}(x_{N-1}) & \cdots & A''_{\Delta,N}(x_{N-1}) & B''_{\Delta,N}(x_{N-1}) \\
B''_{\Delta,0}(x_N) & A''_{\Delta,0}(x_N) & A''_{\Delta,1}(x_N) & \cdots & A''_{\Delta,N}(x_N) & B''_{\Delta,N}(x_N)
\end{bmatrix}$$

$$= A^{-1} \begin{bmatrix}
-6/h & -6/h & 6/h & 0 & 0 & \cdots & & 0 & 0 \\
0 & 3/h^2 & -6/h^2 & 3/h^2 & 0 & \cdots & & 0 & 0 \\
0 & 0 & 3/h^2 & -6/h^2 & 3/h^2 & \cdots & & 0 & 0 \\
0 & 0 & 0 & 3/h^2 & -6/h^2 & \cdots & & 0 & 0 \\
\vdots & \vdots & & & & & & \vdots & \vdots \\
0 & 0 & & \cdots & -6/h^2 & 3/h^2 & 0 & 0 & 0 \\
0 & 0 & & \cdots & 3/h^2 & -6/h^2 & 3/h^2 & 0 & 0 \\
0 & 0 & & \cdots & 0 & 3/h^2 & -6/h^2 & 3/h^2 & 0 \\
0 & 0 & & \cdots & 0 & 0 & 6/h & -6/h & 6/h
\end{bmatrix}.$$

The elements of the inverse matrix A^{-1} are given in Section 2.4. We have, in fact,

$$A_{i,j}^{-1} = \frac{(\sigma^{-i} + \sigma^{i})(\sigma^{j-N} + \sigma^{N-j})}{(2+\sigma)(\sigma^{-N} - \sigma^{N})} \qquad (0 < i \leqslant j < N),$$

$$A_{i,N}^{-1} = \frac{(\sigma^{-i} + \sigma^{i})}{(2+\sigma)(\sigma^{-N} - \sigma^{N})} \qquad (0 < i \leqslant N),$$

$$A_{0,j}^{-1} = \frac{2(\sigma^{N-j} + \sigma^{j-N})}{(2+\sigma)(\sigma^{-N} - \sigma^{N})} \qquad (0 < j < N),$$

$$A_{0,0}^{-1} = \frac{2}{(2+\sigma)(\sigma^{-N} - \sigma^{N})} \cdot$$

with $A_{i,j}^{-1} = A_{j,i}^{-1}$ $(0 < i < N, 0 < j < N)$ and $A_{i,j}^{-1} = A_{N-j,N-i}^{-1}$ for all i and j. These quantities can be evaluated using the methods set forth in Section 2.4 or directly computed from the property that $\sigma^k + \sigma^{-k}$ and $\sigma^{-k} - \sigma^k$ are solutions of the difference equation $u_{n+2} + 4u_{n+1} + u_n = 0$.

2.8. Approximate Solution of Integral Equations

Consider the linear integral equation

$$y(x) = f(x) + \lambda \int_a^b k(x, t) y(t)\, dt, \tag{2.8.1}$$

where $f(x)$ and $k(x, t)$ are continuous, $a \leqslant x \leqslant b$, $a \leqslant t \leqslant b$. Introduce the $N + 1$ cardinal splines defined by the end conditions $M_0 = M_1$, $M_{N-1} = M_N$, here designated $A_{\Delta,j}(x)$, $j = 0, 1,\ldots, N$. Thus,

$$A''_{\Delta,j}(x_0) = A''_{\Delta,j}(x_1), \qquad A''_{\Delta,j}(x_{N-1}) = A''_{\Delta,j}(x_N),$$

$$A_{\Delta,j}(x_i) = \delta_{i,j} \qquad (i, j = 0, 1,\ldots, N).$$

The spline of interpolation of this type is

$$S_\Delta(x) = \sum_{j=0}^{N} y_j A_{\Delta,j}(x),$$

where $y_j = y(x_j)$. If $E_\Delta(x) = y(x) - S_\Delta(x)$, then

$$S_\Delta(x) = f(x) + \lambda \int_a^b k(x, t) S_\Delta(t)\, dt + G_\Delta(x),$$

$$G_\Delta(x) = \lambda \int_a^b k(x, t) E_\Delta(t)\, dt - E_\Delta(x).$$

Here $E_\Delta(x) = o(\| \Delta \|^\alpha)$ if $f(x)$ and $k(x, t)$ are of class $C^\alpha[a, b]$ ($\alpha = 0, 1, 2, 3$).

We proceed much as in the case of the linear differential equation in the preceding section. We determine $y_0, y_1, \ldots, y_N$ by replacing $G_\Delta(x_j)$ by 0 for $j = 0, 1, \ldots, N$. Thus,

$$\sum_{i=0}^{N} y_i A_{\Delta,i}(x_j) = f(x_j) + \lambda \int_a^b k(x_j, t) \sum_{i=0}^{N} y_i A_{\Delta,i}(t)\, dt \qquad (j = 0, 1, \ldots, N).$$

The integrals

$$I_{j,i} = \lambda \int_a^b k(x_j, t) A_{\Delta,i}(t)\, dt$$

are evaluated in closed form if this can be done conveniently [note that $A_{\Delta,i}(t)$ is piecewise cubic] or approximated numerically. If the latter course of action is followed, we note that, inasmuch as the cardinal splines $A_{\Delta,i}(t)$ have already been determined, little additional work is required to spline-fit each $k(x_j, t)$ for this integral approximation.

It is required then to solve the system of equations

$$\begin{bmatrix} I_{0,0} - 1 & I_{0,1} & I_{0,2} & \cdots & I_{0,N} \\ I_{1,0} & I_{1,1} - 1 & I_{1,2} & \cdots & I_{1,N} \\ I_{2,0} & I_{2,1} & I_{2,2} - 1 & \cdots & I_{2,N} \\ & & & & \\ I_{N,0} & I_{N,1} & I_{N,2} & \cdots & I_{N,N} - 1 \end{bmatrix} \cdot \begin{bmatrix} y_0 \\ y_1 \\ y_2 \\ \\ y_N \end{bmatrix} = \begin{bmatrix} -f_0 \\ -f_1 \\ -f_2 \\ \\ -f_N \end{bmatrix}.$$

The convergence of the splines so obtained as $\| \Delta \| \to 0$, in the case in which 1 is not a characteristic value of the homogeneous integral equation, rests on the corresponding proof for the case in which trapezoidal integration is used (cf. Goursat-Bergmann [1964, p. 46 ff]).

From an algebraic point of view, it is usually simpler to employ the spline in its standard form (2.1.2) in making this application to integral equations. As an example, we consider the integral equation associated with the two-point boundary-value problem (2.7.8):

$$y(x) = 1 + \int_0^1 k(x, t) y(t)\, dt, \qquad (2.8.2)$$

where

$$\begin{aligned} k(x, t) &= \alpha^2(x - 1)t \qquad (0 \leqslant t \leqslant x), \\ &= \alpha^2 x(t - 1) \qquad (x \leqslant t \leqslant 1). \end{aligned}$$

We replace $y(x)$ by the spline $S_\Delta(x)$ determined by

$$y_i = 1 + \alpha^2(x_i - 1) \int_0^{x_i} tS_\Delta(t)\, dt + \alpha^2 x_i \int_{x_i}^1 (t - 1)S_\Delta(t)\, dt$$

for $i = 0, 1, \ldots, N$.

We have, of course, $y_0 = y_N = 1$, and we use this fact to reduce the number of equations by 2. For $0 < i < N$ we obtain

$$\begin{aligned} y_i = 1 &+ \alpha^2(x_i - 1) \sum_{j=1}^{i} \Big\{ M_{j-1} \int_{x_{j-1}}^{x_i} \frac{(x_j - t)^3 t\, dt}{6h_j} + M_j \int_{x_{j-1}}^{x_j} \frac{(t - x_{j-1})^3 t\, dt}{6h_j} \\ &+ \left(y_{j-1} - M_{j-1}\frac{h_j^2}{6}\right) \int_{x_{j-1}}^{x_j} \frac{t(x_j - t)}{h_j}\, dt + \left(y_j - M_j \frac{h_j^2}{6}\right) \int_{x_{j-1}}^{x_j} \frac{t(t - x_{j-1})}{h_j}\, dt \Big\} \\ &+ \alpha^2 x_i \sum_{j=i+1}^{N} \Big\{ M_{j-1} \int_{x_{j-1}}^{x_j} (t - 1)\frac{(x_j - t)^3}{6h_j}\, dt + M_j \int_{x_{j-1}}^{x_j} (t - 1)\frac{(t - x_{j-1})^3}{6h_j}\, dt \\ &+ \left(y_{j-1} - M_{j-1}\frac{h_j^2}{6}\right) \int_{x_{j-1}}^{x_j} \frac{(t - 1)(x_j - t)}{h_j}\, dt \\ &+ \left(y_j - M_{j-1}\frac{h_j^2}{6}\right) \int_{x_{j-1}}^{x_j} \frac{(t - 1)(t - x_{j-1})}{h_j}\, dt \Big\}. \end{aligned}$$

The integrals are evaluated, and we obtain directly for equal intervals ($h_j = h$, $j = 1, \ldots, N$; $Nh = 1$)

$$\begin{aligned} y_i = 1 &- \alpha^2(N - i) \Big\{ h^5 \Big[-\frac{1}{12}\sum_{j=1}^{i-1} jM_j - \frac{1}{24} iM_i - \frac{7}{360}(M_0 - M_i) \Big] \\ &+ h^3 \Big[\sum_{j=1}^{i-1} jy_j + \frac{1}{2} iy_i + \frac{1}{6}(y_0 - y_i) \Big] \Big\} \\ &- \alpha^2 i \Big\{ h^5 \Big[-\frac{1}{12} \sum_{j=i+1}^{N-1} (N - j)M_j - \frac{1}{24}(N - i)M_i - \frac{7}{360}(M_N - M_i) \Big] \\ &+ h^3 \Big[\sum_{j=i+1}^{N-1} (N - j)y_j + \frac{N - i}{2} y_i + \frac{1}{6}(y_N - y_i) \Big] \Big\}. \end{aligned}$$

By multiplying respective members of the 2nd, 3rd,..., ith equations of (2.1.8) by $1, 2, \ldots, (i - 1)$ and adding, we obtain

$$\sum_{j=1}^{i-1} jM_j = \frac{1}{3}\left[-\frac{1}{2} M_0 + \frac{1}{2} iM_{i-1} - \frac{1}{2}(i-1)M_i \right] + \frac{1}{h^2}[y_0 - iy_{i-1} + (i - 1)y_i],$$

and, similarly,

$$\sum_{i=i+1}^{N-1} (N-j)M_j = \frac{1}{3}\left[-\frac{1}{2}M_N + \frac{1}{2}(N-i)M_{i+1} - \frac{1}{2}(N-i-1)M_i\right]$$
$$+ \frac{1}{h^2}[y_N - (N-i)y_{i+1} + (N-i-1)y_i].$$

With an application of (2.1.5), the term in M_{i-1}, M_i, M_{i+1}, namely

$$\frac{(N-i)i}{72} M_{i-1} + \left(\frac{(N-i)i}{18} - \frac{N}{180}\right) M_i + \frac{(N-i)i}{72} M_{i+1},$$

becomes

$$-\frac{N}{180} M_i + \frac{(N-i)i}{12} \frac{y_{i+1} - 2y_i + y_{i-1}}{h^2}.$$

We note that $M_0 = \alpha^2 y_0 = \alpha^2$, $M_1 = \alpha^2 y_N = \alpha^2$, so that we are involved with end condition (2.1.18ii).

The quantity M_i is expressed in terms of $y_1, ..., y_{N-1}$ by means of (2.4.11) using the quantities $A_{i,j}^{-1}$ for end conditions (ii) (Section 2.4):

$$M_i = A_{i,0}^{-1}\left(\alpha^2 + \frac{6}{h^2}\right) - \frac{18}{h^2}\sum_{j=0}^{N} A_{i,j}^{-1} y_j + \frac{6}{h^2} y_i + A_{i,N}^{-1}\left(\alpha^2 + \frac{6}{h^2}\right).$$

There results the following equation system for the quantities $y_1, ..., y_{N-1}$ when N is even: for $i = 1, 2, ..., N/2$,

$$y_i = 1 + \frac{\alpha^4 h^4}{180}\left(1 - \frac{\theta_i}{2}\right) + \frac{\alpha^2 h^2}{30}\left(\theta_i - \frac{5}{2}\right) + \frac{\alpha^2 h^2}{20} y_i$$
$$+ \frac{\alpha^2 h^2}{10}\left\{\sum_{j=1}^{i} (\phi_j \theta_i - 10j) y_j + \sum_{j=i+1}^{N/2-1} (\phi_i \theta_j - 10i) y_j + \frac{1}{2}(\phi_i \theta_{N/2} - 10i) y_{N/2}\right\},$$

where

$$\theta_i = \frac{\sigma^{N/2-i} + \sigma^{i-N/2}}{\sigma^{N/2} + \sigma^{-N/2}}, \qquad \phi_i = \frac{\sigma^{-i} - \sigma^i}{2 + \sigma}.$$

The comparison with the exact solution (see Section 2.7) is given in Table 2.8.1 for the case in which $N = 20$.

In the present instance, it is evident from (2.8.2) that $y''(x) - \alpha^2 y(x) = 0$. In the general case, the end condition for the spline is determined by differentiation in the integral equation to obtain a restriction on M_0 and M_N.

TABLE 2.8.1

x	Exact y	Spline integral equation method
0.00	1.00000	1.00000
0.05	0.60657	0.60656
0.10	0.36799	0.36802
0.15	0.22332	0.22334
0.20	0.13566	0.13568
0.25	0.08263	0.08264
0.30	0.05070	0.05070
0.35	0.03170	0.03170
0.40	0.02079	0.02080
0.45	0.01520	0.01520
0.50	0.01348	0.01348

The present example includes a considerable part of the structure employed in the general case in which the kernel $k(x, t)$ is itself spline-fitted at each level x_i in order to approximate the integrals involved.

2.9. Additional Existence and Convergence Theorems

The existence of the spline of interpolation was demonstrated in Section 2.2 under the assumption that $|\lambda_0| < 2$ and $|\mu_N| < 2$ in (2.1.8) or under comparable restrictions in (2.1.16). In order to extend these existence results, it is necessary to examine in some detail properties of the coefficient matrix in (2.1.8) or (2.1.16). We complete here the proof of the general existence theorem.

Theorem 2.9.1. *The periodic spline $S_\Delta(x)$ on the mesh Δ: $a = x_0 < x_1 < \cdots < x_N = b$ with prescribed ordinates $y_0, y_1, \ldots, y_N = y_0$ always exists. The nonperiodic spline with end conditions (2.1.18iii) [or (2.1.1.19iii)] exists provided $\lambda_0 < 4$ and $\mu_N < 4$ (or $\mu_0 < 4$ and $\lambda_N < 4$).*

It remains to complete the proof for the nonperiodic situation in which we require only that λ_0 and μ_N be less than 4. (The condition $\mu_0 < 4$, $\lambda_N < 4$ is equivalent to this one.) For $k > j$, we define

$$D(\lambda_j, \ldots, \lambda_k) = \begin{vmatrix} 2 & \lambda_j & & & \\ 1-\lambda_{j+1} & 2 & \lambda_{j+1} & & \\ & & \cdots & & \\ & & 1-\lambda_{k-1} & 2 & \lambda_{k-1} \\ & & & 1-\lambda_k & 2 \end{vmatrix}, \tag{2.9.1}$$

together with the conventions $D(\lambda_j, ..., \lambda_k) = 2, 1, 0$ for $k = j$, $k = j - 1$, $k = j - 2$, respectively. For $k \geqslant j + 1$, we use the Laplace expansion for determinants and obtain the relation

$$D(\lambda_j, ..., \lambda_k) = D(\lambda_j, \lambda_{j+1})D(\lambda_{j+2}, ..., \lambda_k) - 2\lambda_{j+1}(1 - \lambda_{j+2})D(\lambda_{j+3}, ..., \lambda_k). \tag{2.9.2}$$

Thus, for $k \geqslant j + 1$, we have in the notation of continued fractions

$$\frac{D(\lambda_{j+2}, ..., \lambda_k)}{D(\lambda_j, ..., \lambda_k)} = \left\{ D(\lambda_j, \lambda_{j+1}) - \frac{2\lambda_{j+1}(1 - \lambda_{j+2})D(\lambda_{j+3}, ..., \lambda_k)}{D(\lambda_{j+2}, ..., \lambda_k)} \right\}^{-1}$$

$$= \frac{1}{D(\lambda_j, \lambda_{j+1})} \, \frac{2\lambda_{j+1}(1 - \lambda_{j+2})}{2-} \, \frac{\lambda_{j+2}(1 - \lambda_{j+3})}{2-} \cdots \frac{\lambda_{k-1}(1 - \lambda_k)}{2}. \tag{2.9.3}$$

The relationship between tridiagonal matrices (continuant matrices) and continued fractions which is entering here is indicated by Aitken [1958, p. 126].

The left-hand member of (2.9.3) is a linear fractional function of each of its arguments on the hypercube $0 \leqslant \lambda_i \leqslant 1$ $(j \leqslant i \leqslant k)$. Its denominator is different from zero on this hypercube by Gershgorin's theorem. When $\lambda_j = \cdots = \lambda_k = 0$, we have $D(\lambda_j, ..., \lambda_k) = 2^{k-j+1}$ $(k \geqslant j - 1)$. Thus, $D(\lambda_j, ..., \lambda_k)$ is positive on the hypercube. It takes on its maximum and minimum values for the hypercube at points where each λ_i is 0 or 1.

When $\lambda_{j+1} = 0$, the left-hand member in (2.9.3) is equal to $1/(4 - \lambda_j)$. When $\lambda_{j+1} = 1$, it is $\frac{1}{3}$ or $\frac{1}{4}$ according as λ_{j+2} is 0 or 1. Hence, if $0 \leqslant \lambda_i \leqslant 1$ $(j \leqslant i \leqslant k)$, we obtain the inequality

$$\frac{1}{4} \leqslant \frac{D(\lambda_{j+2}, ..., \lambda_k)}{D(\lambda_j, ..., \lambda_k)} \leqslant \frac{1}{3}. \tag{2.9.4}$$

If we note that

$$3 \leqslant D(\lambda_j, \lambda_{j+1}) \leqslant 4,$$

$$6 \leqslant D(\lambda_j, \lambda_{j+1}, \lambda_{j+2}) \leqslant 8,$$

we obtain by induction the following lemma.

Lemma 2.9.1. *If* $0 \leqslant \lambda_i \leqslant 1$ $(j \leqslant i \leqslant k)$ *and* $k > j$, *then*

$$\begin{Bmatrix} 3^{(k-j+1)/2}, & k - j \text{ odd} \\ 2 \cdot 3^{(k-j)/2}, & k - j \text{ even} \end{Bmatrix} \leqslant D(\lambda_j, ..., \lambda_k) \leqslant 2^{k-j+1}. \tag{2.9.5}$$

Consider now the coefficient determinant in (2.1.8), $D = D(\lambda_0, ..., \lambda_N)$, expanded first using minors of the first row and then using minors of the last row:

$$D = 4D(\lambda_1, ..., \lambda_{N-1}) - 2\lambda_0(1 - \lambda_1)D(\lambda_2, ..., \lambda_{N-1}) - 2\mu_N\lambda_{N-1}D(\lambda_1, ..., \lambda_{N-2}) + \lambda_0(1 - \lambda_1)\lambda_{N-1}\mu_N D(\lambda_2, ..., \lambda_{N-2}) . \qquad (2.9.6)$$

We find

$$\begin{aligned} D &= (4 - \lambda_0)(4 - \lambda_N)D(\lambda_2, ..., \lambda_{N-2}) && \text{for } \lambda_1 = 0 \text{ and } \lambda_{N-1} = 1, \\ &= 2(4 - \lambda_0)D(\lambda_2, ..., \lambda_{N-2}, 0) && \text{for } \lambda_1 = 0 \text{ and } \lambda_{N-1} = 0, \\ &= 2(4 - \lambda_N)D(1, \lambda_2, ..., \lambda_{N-2}) && \text{for } \lambda_1 = 1 \text{ and } \lambda_{N-1} = 1, \\ &= 4D(1, \lambda_2, ..., \lambda_{N-2}, 0) && \text{for } \lambda_1 = 1 \text{ and } \lambda_{N-1} = 0. \end{aligned}$$

From (2.9.5), it now follows for $\lambda_0 < 4$ and $\mu_N < 4$ that the coefficient determinant D in (2.1.8) satisfies

$$D \geqslant [\min(3, 4 - \lambda_0)] \cdot [\min(3, 4 - \mu_N)] \cdot \begin{Bmatrix} 3^{(N-3)/2}, & N \text{ odd} \\ 2 \cdot 3^{(N-4)/2}, & N \text{ even} \end{Bmatrix} > 0. \qquad (2.9.7)$$

The proof of the theorem is now complete.

We turn to the extension of Theorems 2.3.2 and 2.3.3 to cover more general end conditions. For this purpose, it is desirable to use properties of the elements of the inverse matrix which are of considerable interest for their own sake. These properties generally relate to the rate of decay of the magnitudes of the elements of the inverse matrix as we move away from the principal diagonal.

The elements of the inverse A^{-1} of the coefficient matrix in (2.1.8) are obtained directly from the cofactors of A. Thus,

$$A_{i,j}^{-1} = (-1)^{i+j}D(\lambda_0, ..., \lambda_{i-1})\lambda_i\lambda_{i+1} \cdots \lambda_{j-1}D(\lambda_{j+1}, ..., \lambda_N)/D \qquad (0 \leqslant i \leqslant j \leqslant N),$$

$$(2.9.8)$$

$$A_{i,j}^{-1} = (-1)^{i+j}D(\lambda_0, ..., \lambda_{j-1})(1-\lambda_{j+1}) \cdots (1-\lambda_i)D(\lambda_{i+1}, ..., \lambda_N)/D \quad (0 \leqslant j \leqslant i \leqslant N),$$

where λ_N means $1 - \mu_N$, and again D denotes the coefficient determinant.

We require two lemmas on the properties of these elements. If we expand $D(\lambda_j, ..., \lambda_k)$ for $j < k$ in minors of the first row, we obtain

$$D(\lambda_j, ..., \lambda_k) = 2D(\lambda_{j+1}, ..., \lambda_k) - (1 - \lambda_j)\lambda_{j+1}D(\lambda_{j+2}, ..., \lambda_k),$$

so that

$$\frac{D(\lambda_{j+1},\ldots,\lambda_k)}{D(\lambda_j,\ldots,\lambda_k)} = \left\{2 - \frac{\lambda_j(1-\lambda_{j+1})D(\lambda_{j+2},\ldots,\lambda_k)}{D(\lambda_{j+1},\ldots,\lambda_k)}\right\}^{-1}$$
$$= \frac{1}{2}\,\frac{\lambda_j(1-\lambda_{j+1})}{2-}\,\frac{\lambda_{j+1}(1-\lambda_{j+2})}{2-}\cdots\frac{\lambda_{k-1}(1-\lambda_k)}{2}$$

provided $D(\lambda_j,\ldots,\lambda_k) \neq 0$. This ratio is equal to $\frac{1}{2}$ when $\lambda_{j+1} = 1$ and to $2/(4-\lambda_j)$ when $\lambda_{j+1} = 0$. The ratio is a bilinear function of each of its arguments. The denominator is positive if $0 \leqslant \lambda_i \leqslant 1$ for $j < i < k$ and if, in addition, $\lambda_j < 4$ and $\mu_k < 4$. Under these conditions, we may conclude that

$$\min\left[\frac{1}{2}, \frac{2}{4-\lambda_j}\right] \leqslant \frac{D(\lambda_{j+1},\ldots,\lambda_k)}{D(\lambda_j,\ldots,\lambda_k)} \leqslant \max\left[\frac{1}{2}, \frac{2}{4-\lambda_j}\right]. \tag{2.9.9}$$

If we expand $D(\lambda_j,\ldots,\lambda_k)$ in minors of the last row, we obtain, for $0 \leqslant \lambda_i \leqslant 1$ $(j < i < k)$ and $\lambda_j < 4$, $\mu_k < 4$, the inequality

$$\min\left[\frac{1}{2}, \frac{2}{4-\mu_k}\right] \leqslant \frac{D(\lambda_j,\ldots,\lambda_{k-1})}{D(\lambda_j,\ldots,\lambda_k)} \leqslant \max\left[\frac{1}{2}, \frac{2}{4-\mu_k}\right]. \tag{2.9.10}$$

If we examine the proof of (2.9.4) we see immediately when $0 \leqslant \lambda_i \leqslant 1$ $(j < i < k)$ and $\lambda_j < 4$, $\mu_k < 4$ that we have

$$\min\left[\frac{1}{4}, \frac{1}{4-\lambda_j}\right] \leqslant \frac{D(\lambda_{j+2},\ldots,\lambda_k)}{D(\lambda_j,\ldots,\lambda_k)} \leqslant \max\left[\frac{1}{3}, \frac{1}{4-\lambda_j}\right]. \tag{2.9.11}$$

A similar derivation yields, under the same conditions, the inequality

$$\min\left[\frac{1}{4}, \frac{1}{4-\mu_k}\right] \leqslant \frac{D(\lambda_j,\ldots,\lambda_{k-2})}{D(\lambda_j,\ldots,\lambda_k)} \leqslant \max\left[\frac{1}{3}, \frac{1}{4-\mu_k}\right]. \tag{2.9.12}$$

The first of the lemmas required is as follows.

Lemma 2.9.2. *For $\lambda_0 < 4$, $0 \leqslant \lambda_i \leqslant 1$ $(0 < i < N)$, $\mu_N < 4$, and any integer p, $0 < p < N$, we have*

$$2^{-p}\min\left[1, \frac{4}{4-\lambda_0}\right] \leqslant \frac{D(\lambda_p,\ldots,\lambda_N)}{D(\lambda_0,\ldots,\lambda_N)}$$
$$\leqslant \begin{cases} \max\left[\frac{1}{2}, \frac{2}{4-\lambda_0}\right]\cdot 3^{-(p-1)/2}, & p \text{ odd} \\ \max\left[1, \frac{3}{4-\lambda_0}\right]\cdot 3^{-p/2}, & p \text{ even} \end{cases}, \tag{2.9.13}$$

$$2^{-(N-p)} \min\left[1, \frac{4}{4-\mu_N}\right] \leqslant \frac{D(\lambda_0, ..., \lambda_p)}{D(\lambda_0, ..., \lambda_N)}$$

$$\leqslant \begin{Bmatrix} \max\left[\frac{1}{2}, \frac{2}{4-\mu_N}\right] \cdot 3^{-(N-p-1)/2}, & N-p \text{ odd} \\ \max\left[1, \frac{3}{4-\mu_N}\right] \cdot 3^{-(N-p)/2}, & N-p \text{ even} \end{Bmatrix} \tag{2.9.14}$$

where $\mu_N = 1 - \lambda_N$.

Proof. For p odd,

$$\frac{D(\lambda_p, ..., \lambda_N)}{D(\lambda_0, ..., \lambda_N)} = \frac{D(\lambda_1, ..., \lambda_N)}{D(\lambda_0, ..., \lambda_N)} \cdot \prod_{j=1}^{(p-1)/2} \frac{D(\lambda_{2j+1}, ..., \lambda_N)}{D(\lambda_{2j-1}, ..., \lambda_N)}.$$

By (2.9.9) and (2.9.11), this ratio lies between the two quantities

$$\min\left[\frac{1}{2}, \frac{2}{4-\lambda_0}\right] \cdot \left(\frac{1}{4}\right)^{(p-1)/2}, \qquad \max\left[\frac{1}{2}, \frac{2}{4-\lambda_0}\right] \cdot \left(\frac{1}{3}\right)^{(p-1)/2}.$$

For p even,

$$\frac{D(\lambda_p, ..., \lambda_N)}{D(\lambda_0, ..., \lambda_N)} = \prod_{j=1}^{p/2} \frac{D(\lambda_{2j}, ..., \lambda_N)}{D(\lambda_{2j-2}, ..., \lambda_N)},$$

which, by (2.9.11), lies between the quantities

$$\min\left[\frac{1}{4}, \frac{1}{4-\lambda_0}\right] \cdot \left(\frac{1}{4}\right)^{(p/2)-1}, \qquad \max\left[\frac{1}{3}, \frac{1}{4-\lambda_0}\right] \cdot \left(\frac{1}{3}\right)^{(p/2)-1}.$$

This completes the demonstration of (2.9.13). Inequality (2.9.14) is similarly obtained using (2.9.10) and (2.9.12).

It should be noted that inequalities (2.9.13) and (2.9.14) are sharp. For suitable values of the quantities λ_i, the equality actually obtains.

Lemma 2.9.3. *For* $\lambda_0 < 4$, $0 \leqslant \lambda_i \leqslant 1$ $(0 < i < N)$, $\mu_N < 4$, *and* $0 < p < q < N$, *we have*

$$2^{-(q-p-1)} \leqslant \frac{D(\lambda_0, ..., \lambda_p) D(\lambda_q, ..., \lambda_N)}{D(\lambda_0, ..., \lambda_N)} \leqslant \begin{Bmatrix} 4 \cdot 3^{-(q-p+1)/2}, & q-p \text{ odd} \\ 2 \cdot 3^{-(q-p)/2}, & q-p \text{ even} \end{Bmatrix}. \tag{2.9.15}$$

Proof. We employ the Laplace expansion

$$\begin{aligned} D(\lambda_0, ..., \lambda_N) &= D(\lambda_0, ..., \lambda_p) D(\lambda_{p+1}, ..., \lambda_N) \\ &\quad - D(\lambda_0, ..., \lambda_{p-1}) \lambda_p (1 - \lambda_{p+1}) D(\lambda_{p+2}, ..., \lambda_N), \end{aligned} \tag{2.9.16}$$

which may be written as

$$D(\lambda_0, \ldots, \lambda_p)D(\lambda_{p+1}, \ldots, \lambda_{q-1})D(\lambda_q, \ldots, \lambda_N)$$
$$- D(\lambda_0, \ldots, \lambda_p)D(\lambda_{p+1}, \ldots \lambda_{q-2})\lambda_{q-1}(1 - \lambda_q)D(\lambda_{q+1}, \ldots, \lambda_N)$$
$$- D(\lambda_0, \ldots, \lambda_{p-1})\lambda_p(1 - \lambda_{p+1})D(\lambda_{p+2}, \ldots, \lambda_{q-1})D(\lambda_q, \ldots, \lambda_N)$$
$$+ D(\lambda_0, \ldots, \lambda_{p-1})\lambda_p(1 - \lambda_{p+1})D(\lambda_{p+2}, \ldots, \lambda_{q-2})\lambda_{q-1}(1 - \lambda p)D(\lambda_{p+1}, \ldots, \lambda_N), \tag{2.9.17}$$

if $0 \leqslant p \leqslant q - 2$ and $q \leqslant N$, since we define $D(\lambda_i, \ldots, \lambda_j) = 0$ if $j = i - 2$. We obtain for the second member of (2.9.15), when $0 < p < q - 2$ and $q < N$, the value

$$\{D(\lambda_{p+1}, \ldots, \lambda_{q-1})\}^{-1} \qquad \text{for } \lambda_p = 0 \text{ and } \lambda_q = 1,$$
$$\{D(\lambda_{p+1}, \ldots, \lambda_{q-1}) - \tfrac{1}{2}\lambda_{q-1}D(\lambda_{p+1}, \ldots, \lambda_{q-2})\}^{-1} \qquad \text{for } \lambda_p = 0 \text{ and } \lambda_q = 0,$$
$$\{D(\lambda_{p+1}, \ldots, \lambda_{q-1}) - \tfrac{1}{2}(1 - \lambda_{p+1})D(\lambda_{p+2}, \ldots, \lambda_{q-1})\}^{-1} \qquad \text{for } \lambda_p = 1 \text{ and } \lambda_q = 1,$$
$$\{D(\lambda_{p+1}, \ldots, \lambda_{q-1}) - \tfrac{1}{2}\lambda_{q-1}D(\lambda_{p+1}, \ldots, \lambda_{q-2})$$
$$-\tfrac{1}{2}(1 - \lambda_{p+1})D(\lambda_{p+2}, \ldots, \lambda_{q-1}) + \tfrac{1}{4}\lambda_{q-1}(1 - \lambda_{p+1})D(\lambda_{p+2}, \ldots, \lambda_{q-2})\}^{-1}$$
$$\text{for } \lambda_p = 1 \text{ and } \lambda_q = 0.$$

We have used here the properties $D(0, \lambda_{j+1}, \ldots, \lambda_k) = 2D(\lambda_{j+1}, \ldots, \lambda_k)$, $D(\lambda_j, \ldots, \lambda_{k-1}, 1) = 2D(\lambda_j, \ldots, \lambda_{k-1})$. A routine examination of the cases $\lambda_{p+1} = 0$ or 1, $\lambda_{q-1} = 0$ or 1, and the application of (2.9.9) and (2.9.10) yields

$$\{D(\lambda_{p+1}, \ldots, \lambda_{q-1})\}^{-1} \leqslant \frac{D(\lambda_0, \ldots, \lambda_p)D(\lambda_q, \ldots, \lambda_N)}{D(\lambda_0, \ldots, \lambda_N)} \leqslant \frac{4}{9}\{D(\lambda_{p+2}, \ldots, \lambda_{q-2})\}^{-1}.$$

Use of Lemma 2.9.1 gives (2.9.15).

We turn now to the extensions of Theorems 2.3.2 and 2.3.3 to more general end conditions.

Theorem 2.9.2. *Let $f(x)$ be of class $C^1[a, b]$. Let $\{\Delta_k\}$ be a sequence of meshes on $[a, b]$ with $\lim_{k\to\infty} \|\Delta_k\| = 0$. Let $S_{\Delta_k}(x)$ be a spline of interpolation to $f(x)$ on Δ_k satisfying end conditions (2.1.19iii) with $\inf_k(4 - \mu_{k,0}) > 0$, $\inf_k(4 - \lambda_{k,N_k}) > 0$, and $\mu_{k,0}$ and λ_{k,N_k} bounded as $k \to \infty$.*

(a) *If*

$$\epsilon_k' = c_{k,0} - (2 + \mu_{k,0})f'(a) \to 0 \qquad \textit{and} \qquad \epsilon_k'' = c_{k,N_k} - (2 + \lambda_{k,N_k})f'(b) \to 0$$

as $k \to \infty$, then $S'_{\Delta_k}(x)$ converges uniformly to $f'(x)$ on $[a, b]$, and

$$[S^{(p)}_{\Delta_k}(x) - f^{(p)}(x)] = o(\| \Delta_k \|^{1-p}) \qquad (p = 0, 1) \tag{2.9.18}$$

uniformly with respect to x in $[a, b]$.

(b) *If $c_{k,0}$ and c_{k,N_k} are bounded as $k \to \infty$, then (2.9.18) is valid on any closed subinterval of $a < x < b$, and $\{S_{\Delta_k}(x)\} \to f(x)$ uniformly on $[a, b]$.*

Proof (a). We introduce the $(N_k + 1) \times (N_k + 1)$ matrix G_k,

$$G_k = \begin{bmatrix} \frac{1}{3} & (1-\mu_{k,0})/9 & 0 & & \cdots & & 0 \\ 0 & \frac{1}{3} & 0 & & \cdots & & 0 \\ 0 & 0 & \frac{1}{3} & & \cdots & & 0 \\ & & & \ddots & & & \\ 0 & \cdots & & & \frac{1}{3} & 0 & 0 \\ 0 & \cdots & & & 0 & \frac{1}{3} & 0 \\ 0 & \cdots & & & 0 & (1-\lambda_{k,N_k})/9 & \frac{1}{3} \end{bmatrix}$$

and rewrite (2.1.16) in the form

$$B_k m_k - B_k G_k c_k = (I_k - B_k G_k) c_k , \tag{2.9.19}$$

where I_k is the unit matrix of order $N_k + 1$, and B_k is the coefficient matrix in (2.1.16) associated with Δ_k. The right-hand member of (2.9.19) is equal to the vector

$$\begin{bmatrix} \frac{1}{3}\left(c_{k,0} - \frac{2+\mu_{k,0}}{3} c_{k,1}\right) \\ -\frac{\lambda_{k,1}}{3}\left(c_{k,0} - \frac{2+\mu_{k,0}}{3} c_{k,1}\right) + \frac{\mu_{k,1}}{3}(c_{k,1} - c_{k,2}) \\ -\frac{\lambda_{k,2}}{3}(c_{k,1} - c_{k,2}) + \frac{\mu_{k,2}}{3}(c_{k,2} - c_{k,3}) \\ \vdots \\ -\frac{\lambda_{k,N_k-1}}{3}(c_{k,N_k-2} - c_{k,N_k-1}) - \frac{\mu_{k,N_k-1}}{3}\left(c_{k,N_k} - \frac{2+\lambda_{k,N_k}}{3} c_{k,N_k-1}\right) \\ \frac{1}{3}\left(c_{k,N_k} - \frac{2+\lambda_{k,N_k}}{3} c_{k,N_k-1}\right) \end{bmatrix} \tag{2.9.20}$$

Now $c_{k,i}/3$ $(0 < i < N)$ is equal to $f'(\xi)$ at some ξ in $x_{i-1} < x < x_{i+1}$. Thus, the norm of the vector (2.9.20) does not exceed the larger of the two quantities

$$\frac{1}{3}\,|\,\epsilon_k'\,| + \frac{2+\mu_{k,0}}{3}\, 2\mu(f'; \| \Delta_k \|) + 3\mu(f'; \| \Delta_k \|),$$

$$\frac{1}{3}\,|\,\epsilon_k''\,| + \frac{2+\lambda_{k,N_k}}{3}\, 2\mu(f'; \| \Delta_k \|) + 3\mu(f'; \| \Delta_k \|).$$

From (2.9.8) and Lemma 2.9.3, we see that $\| B_k^{-1} \|$ is bounded with respect to k. Thus, it follows from (2.9.19) that, as $k \to \infty$,

$$\| m_k - G_k c_k \| \to 0.$$

Also, $\| G_k c_k - [f'(x_{k,0}), f'(x_{k,1}), \dots, f'(x_{k,N_k})] \| \to 0$, since

$$\frac{1}{3} c_{k,0} + \frac{1 - \mu_{k,0}}{9} c_{k,1} - f'(a) = \frac{1}{3} \epsilon_k' + \frac{1 - \mu_{k,0}}{3} \left[\frac{c_{k,1}}{3} - f'(a) \right],$$

$$\frac{1}{3} c_{k,N_k} + \frac{1 - \lambda_{k,N_k}}{9} c_{k,N_k-1} - f'(b) = \frac{1}{3} \epsilon_k'' + \frac{1 - \lambda_{k,N_k}}{3} \left[\frac{c_{k,N_k-1}}{3} - f'(b) \right].$$

The remainder of the proof now follows precisely the pattern of proof of Theorem 2.3.2.

Proof (b). Suppose now that the quantities $c_{k,0}$ and c_{k,N_k} are assumed merely to be bounded as $k \to \infty$ and that $\mu_{k,0}$ and λ_{k,N_k} satisfy this condition also. For an interval $[a', b']$ with $a < a' < b' < b$, there are at least $n_k' = 1 + [(a' - a)/\| \Delta_k \|]$ mesh points in Δ_k at or to the left of a', and $n_k'' = 1 + [(b - b')/\| \Delta_k \|]$ at or to the right of b'. In forming the sums representing the components of $m_k - G_k c_k$ from (2.9.19) associated with mesh locations within $[a', b']$, it is seen that the first, second, next-to-last, and last components of (2.9.20) are multiplied, respectively, by quantities not exceeding

$$(1 - \lambda_{k,1}) \cdots (1 - \lambda_{k,n_k'}) \max \left\{ 1, \frac{4}{4 - \mu_{k,0}} \right\} \cdot 3^{-(n_k'+1)/2},$$

$$2(1 - \lambda_{k,2}) \cdots (1 - \lambda_{k,n_k'}) \max \left\{ 1, \frac{4}{4 - \mu_{k,0}} \right\} \cdot 3^{-n_k'/2},$$

$$2\lambda_{k,N_k-n_k''} \cdots \lambda_{k,N_k-2} \max \left\{ 1, \frac{4}{4 - \lambda_{k,N_k}} \right\} \cdot 3^{-n_k''/2},$$

$$\lambda_{k,N_k-n_k''} \cdots \lambda_{k,N_k-1} \max \left\{ 1, \frac{4}{4 - \lambda_{k,N_k}} \right\} \cdot 3^{-(n_k''+1)/2}.$$

[See (2.9.8) and Lemma 2.9.2.] Inasmuch as n_k' and n_k'' increase indefinitely as $k \to \infty$, we obtain

$$\lim_{k \to \infty} \{ \max_{a' \leq x_{k,j} \leq b'} | m_{k,j} - f'(x_{k,j}) | \} = 0.$$

The uniform convergence of $\{S_{\Delta_k}(x)\}$ and $\{S_{\Delta_k}'(x)\}$ to $f(x)$ and $f'(x)$ on $[a', b']$ now follows in the standard way.

In order to demonstrate uniform convergence of $\{S_{\Delta_k}(x)\}$ to $f(x)$ on $[a, b]$, we remark that the method of proof for (a) suffices to show that the quantities $m_{k,j}$ are bounded with respect to k under the conditions of (b). The uniform convergence of $\{S_{\Delta_k}(x)\}$ to $f(x)$ on $[a, b]$ is now a direct consequence of (2.1.10). We note that the term containing $y_{k,j-1}$ and $y_{k,j}$ is a cubic with extrema at $x_{k,j-1}$ and $x_{k,j}$ and hence monotone between.

The validity of the following corollaries is also evident.

Corollary 2.9.2.1. *Under the conditions of Theorem 2.9.2, if $f'(x)$ satisfies a Hölder condition on $[a, b]$ of order α $(0 < \alpha \leqslant 1)$, and if $\epsilon_k' = O(\| \Delta_k \|^\alpha)$, $\epsilon_k'' = O(\| \Delta_k \|^\alpha)$, then the right-hand member of (2.9.18) is replaced by $O(\| \Delta_k \|^{1+\alpha-p})$ $(p = 0, 1)$.*

Corollary 2.9.2.2. *If $f'(x)$ is continuous on $[a', b']$, $a < a' < b' < b$, and exists and is bounded for all x in $[a, b]$, then $\{S'_{\Delta_k}(x)\} \to f'(x)$ uniformly on $[a', b']$, and $\{S_{\Delta_k}(x)\} \to f(x)$ uniformly on $[a, b]$.*

The proof of the next theorem follows very closely the pattern of proof employed for Theorem 2.9.2 and will not be repeated.

Theorem 2.9.3. *Let $f(x)$ be of class $C^2[a, b]$. Let $\{\Delta_k\}$ be a sequence of meshes on $[a, b]$ with $\lim_{k\to\infty} \| \Delta_k \| = 0$. Let $S_{\Delta_k}(x)$ be a spline of interpolation to $f(x)$ on Δ_k satisfying end conditions (2.1.18iii) with $\inf_k(4 - \lambda_{k,0}) > 0$, $\inf_k(4 - \mu_{k,N_k}) > 0$, and $\lambda_{k,0}$ and μ_{k,N_k} bounded as $k \to \infty$.*

(a) *If*

$$\epsilon_k' = d_{k,0} - (2 + \lambda_{k,0})f''(a) \to 0 \qquad \text{and} \qquad \epsilon_k'' = d_{k,N_k} - (2 + \mu_{k,N_k})f''(b) \to 0$$

as $k \to \infty$, then $S''_{\Delta_k}(x)$ converges uniformly to $f''(x)$ on $[a, b]$, and we have

$$| S^{(p)}_{\Delta_k}(x) - f^{(p)}(x) | = o(\| \Delta_k \|^{2-p}) \qquad (p = 0, 1, 2) \tag{2.9.21}$$

uniformly with respect to x in $[a, b]$.

(b) *If $d_{k,0}$ and d_{k,N_k} are bounded as $k \to \infty$, then (2.9.21) is valid on any closed subinterval of $a < x < b$. Moreover, $\{S'_{\Delta_k}(x)\}$ and $\{S_{\Delta_k}(x)\}$ converge uniformly to $f'(x)$ and $f(x)$ on $[a, b]$.*

The analogs of the two corollaries carry over as well.

Corollary 2.9.3.1. *Under the conditions of Theorem 2.9.3, if $f''(x)$ satisfies a Hölder condition on $[a, b]$ of order α $(0 < \alpha \leqslant 1$, and if $\epsilon_k' = O(\| \Delta_k \|^\alpha)$*

and $\epsilon_k'' = O(\| \Delta_k \|^\alpha)$, *then the right-hand member of (2.9.21) is replaced by* $O(\| \Delta_k \|^{2+\alpha-p})$ $(p = 0, 1, 2)$.

Corollary 2.9.3.2. *If* $f''(x)$ *is continuous on* $[a', b']$ $(a < a' < b' < b)$ *and exists and is bounded for all* x *in* $[a, b]$, *then* $\{S''_{\Delta_k}(x)\} \to f''(x)$ *uniformly on* $[a', b']$, *and* $\{S^{(p)}_{\Delta_k}(x)\} \to f^{(p)}(x)$ *uniformly on* $[a, b]$ *for* $p = 0, 1$.

Other convergence results related to these can clearly be obtained. Existence of $f''(x)$ can be replaced by uniform boundedness of difference quotents. It is possible to obtain convergence at a single point when $f''(x)$ is known to exist at that point (Ahlberg and Nilson [1963]).

We turn now to a consideration of third and fourth derivatives.

Theorem 2.9.4. *Let* $f(x)$ *be of class* $C^3[a, b]$. *Let* $\{\Delta_k\}$ *be a sequence of meshes on* $[a, b]$ *with*

$$\lim_{k\to\infty} \| \Delta_k \| = 0 \qquad \text{and} \qquad \sup_k [\| \Delta_k \| / \min_j (x_{k,j} - x_{k,j-1})] = \beta < \infty.$$

Let the splines of interpolation $\{S_{\Delta_k}(x)\}$ *to* $f(x)$ *on* Δ_k *satisfy end condition (2.1.18iii) with* $\inf_k(4 - \lambda_{k,0}) > 0$, $\inf_k(4 - \mu_{k,N_k}) > 0$, *and* $\lambda_{k,0}$ *and* μ_{k,N_k} *bounded as* $k \to \infty$. *If*

$$\epsilon_k' = \frac{(2 + \lambda_{k,0})d_{k,1} - 3d_{k,0}}{h_{k,1} + h_{k,2}} - [(4 - \lambda_{k,0})\mu_{k,1} + (2 + \lambda_{k,0})\lambda_{k,1}]f'''(a),$$

$$\epsilon_k'' = \frac{3d_{k,N_k} - (2 + \mu_{k,N_k})d_{k,N_k-1}}{h_{k,N-1} + h_{k,N}} - [(4 - \mu_{k,N_k})\lambda_{k,N_k-1} + (2 + \mu_{k,N_k})\lambda_{k,N_k-1}]f'''(b),$$

both approach 0 *as* $k \to \infty$, *then on* $[a, b]$ *we have*

$$[S^{(p)}_{\Delta_k}(x) - f^{(p)}(x)] = o(\| \Delta_k \|^{3-p}) \qquad (p = 0, 1, 2, 3).$$

If $f'''(x)$ *satisfies a Hölder condition of order* α $(0 < \alpha \leqslant 1)$ *and if* ϵ_k' *and* ϵ_k'' *are both* $O(\| \Delta_k \|^\alpha)$, *then on* $[a, b]$

$$[S^{(p)}_{\Delta_k}(x) - f^{(p)}(x)] = O(\| \Delta_k \|^{3+\alpha-p}) \qquad (p = 0, 1, 2, 3).$$

Proof. The first and last of Eqs. (2.3.21) are here replaced by the general forms (dropping mesh index k):

$$[6 - (2 + \lambda_0)\mu_1]\mu_1\sigma_1 + (2 + \lambda_0)\lambda_1{}^2\sigma_2 = \frac{(2 + \lambda_0)d_1 - 3d_0}{h_1 + h_2},$$

$$(2 + \mu_N)\mu_{N-1}^2\sigma_{N-1} + [6 - (2 + \mu_N)\lambda_{N-1}]\lambda_{N-1}\sigma_N = \frac{3d_N - (2 + \mu_N)d_{N-1}}{h_{N-1} + h_N}.$$

If the resulting coefficient matrix is decomposed as was the matrix C of (2.3.21), we obtain again $E \cdot D \cdot F$, where D is now

$$\begin{bmatrix} 6-(2+\lambda_0)\mu_1 & (2+\lambda_0)\lambda_1 & 0 & \cdots & 0 & 0 \\ \mu_1 & 1+\mu_1+\lambda_2 & \lambda_2 & \cdots & 0 & 0 \\ \vdots & \vdots & & & \vdots & \vdots \\ 0 & 0 & \cdots & \mu_{N-2} & 1+\mu_{N-2}+\lambda_{N-1} & \lambda_{N-1} \\ 0 & 0 & \cdots & 0 & (2+\mu_N)\mu_{N-1} & 6-(2+\mu_N)\lambda_{N-1} \end{bmatrix}.$$

This matrix has dominant main diagonal and a uniformly bounded inverse if $\inf_k(4-\lambda_{k,0}) > 0$ and $\inf_k(4-\mu_{k,N_k}) > 0$. Thus, $\| C^{-1} \|$ is uniformly bounded.

We form the $N_k \times N_k$ matrix

$$H = \begin{bmatrix} 1 & 1-[(4-\lambda_0)\mu_1+(2+\lambda_0)\lambda_1] & 0 & \cdots & & 0 & 0 \\ 0 & 1 & 0 & \cdots & & 0 & 0 \\ 0 & 0 & 1 & \cdots & & 0 & 0 \\ \vdots & \vdots & & & & \vdots & \vdots \\ 0 & 0 & & \cdots & 0 & 1 & 0 \\ 0 & 0 & & \cdots & 0 & 1-[(4-\mu_N)\lambda_{N-1}+(2+\mu_N)\mu_{N-1}] & 1 \end{bmatrix}.$$

Then, if r represents the vector

$$\begin{bmatrix} \dfrac{(2+\lambda_0)d_1 - 3d_0}{h_1+h_2} \\ \dfrac{d_2-d_1}{h_1+h_2+h_3} \\ \vdots \\ \dfrac{d_{N-1}-d_{N-2}}{h_{N-2}+h_{N-1}+h_N} \\ \dfrac{3d_N-(2+\mu_N)d_{N-1}}{h_{N-1}+h_N} \end{bmatrix},$$

we have

$$C(\sigma - Hr) = (I - CH)r,$$

and the right-hand vector is

$$\begin{bmatrix} [1-6\mu_1+(2+\lambda_0)\mu_1{}^2]\{r_1-[(4-\lambda_0)\mu_1+(2+\lambda_0)\lambda_1]r_2\} \\ -\dfrac{\mu_1{}^2\mu_2}{1-\mu_1\lambda_2}\{r_1-[(4-\lambda_0)\mu_1+(2+\lambda_0)\lambda_1]r_2\} - \dfrac{\lambda_1\lambda_2{}^2}{1-\mu_1\lambda_2}(r_3-r_2) \\ \dfrac{\mu_2{}^2\mu_3}{1-\mu_2\lambda_3}(r_3-r_2) - \dfrac{\lambda_2\lambda_3{}^2}{1-\mu_2\lambda_3}(r_4-r_3) \\ \vdots \\ \dfrac{\mu_{N-2}^2\mu_{N-1}}{1-\mu_{N-2}\lambda_{N-1}}(r_{N-1}-r_{N-2}) + \dfrac{\lambda_{N-2}\lambda_{N-1}^2}{1-\mu_{N-2}\lambda_{N-1}}\{r_N-[(4-\mu_N)\lambda_{N-1}+(2+\mu_N)\mu_{N-1}]r_{N-1}\} \\ [1-6\lambda_{N-2}+(2+\mu_N)\lambda_{N-1}^2]\{r_N-[(4-\mu_N)\lambda_{N-1}+(2+\mu_N)\mu_{N-1}]r_{N-1}\} \end{bmatrix}.$$

The rate at which $\|(I - CH)\, r\|$ approaches zero is now evident, and the conclusions of the theorem follow from the boundedness of $\| C^{-1} \|$.

Our final result concerns a rather curious property of convergence to the $f^{iv}(x)$. For the sake of simplicity, we restrict our attention to the periodic cubic spline, although the argument can be carried through for nonperiodic splines as well.

We consider the jump in the spline third derivatives at x_j and set

$$\delta_j = \frac{\sigma_{j+1} - \sigma_j}{h_j + h_{j+1}}.$$

From the set of equations for the quantities σ_j,

$$\begin{bmatrix} \frac{(1+\mu_N+\lambda_1)\lambda_N\mu_1}{1-\mu_N\lambda_1} & \frac{\lambda_N\lambda_1^2}{1-\mu_N\lambda_1} & 0 & \cdots & \frac{\mu_N^2\mu_1}{1-\mu_N\lambda_1} \\ \frac{\mu_1^2\mu_2}{1-\mu_1\lambda_2} & \frac{(1+\mu_1+\lambda_2)\lambda_1\mu_2}{1-\mu_1\lambda_2} & \frac{\lambda_1\lambda_2^2}{1-\mu_1\lambda_2} & \cdots & 0 \\ \vdots & & & & \vdots \\ \frac{\lambda_{N-1}\lambda_N^2}{1-\mu_{N-1}\lambda_N} & \cdots & 0 & \frac{\mu_{N-1}^2\mu_N}{1-\mu_{N-1}\lambda_N} & \frac{(1+\mu_{N-1}+\lambda_N)\lambda_{N-1}\mu_N}{1-\mu_{N-1}\lambda_N} \end{bmatrix} \cdot \begin{bmatrix} \sigma_1 \\ \sigma_2 \\ \vdots \\ \sigma_N \end{bmatrix} = \begin{bmatrix} r_1 \\ r_2 \\ \vdots \\ r_N \end{bmatrix},$$

we obtain, by subtracting corresponding members of the jth from the $(j+1)$th equation and dividing the result by $h_{j-1} + h_j + h_{j+1} + h_{j+2}$, the equation

$$D\delta = g, \tag{2.9.22}$$

where $g_k/6$ is the fourth divided difference $f[x_{j-2}, x_{j-1}x_j, x_{j+1}, x_{j+2}]$,

$$D = \begin{bmatrix} \frac{\lambda_N\lambda_1\mu_1\mu_2(\theta_1+\theta_2)}{\lambda_N\lambda_1+\mu_1\mu_2} & \frac{\lambda_N\lambda_1^2\lambda_2^2\theta_2}{\lambda_N\lambda_1+\mu_1\mu_2} & 0 & \cdots & \frac{\mu_N^2\mu_1^2\mu_2\theta_1}{\lambda_N\lambda_1+\mu_1\mu_2} \\ \frac{\mu_1^2\mu_2^2\mu_3\theta_2}{\lambda_1\lambda_2+\mu_2\mu_3} & \frac{\lambda_1\lambda_2\mu_2\mu_3(\theta_2+\theta_3)}{\lambda_1\lambda_2+\mu_2\mu_3} & \frac{\lambda_1\lambda_2^2\lambda_3^2\theta_3}{\lambda_1\lambda_2+\mu_2\mu_3} & \cdots & 0 \\ \vdots & & & & \vdots \\ \frac{\lambda_{N-1}\lambda_N^2\lambda_1^2\theta_1}{\lambda_{N-1}\lambda_N+\mu_N\mu_1} & \cdots & 0 & \frac{\mu_{N-1}^2\mu_N^2\mu_1\theta_N}{\lambda_{N-1}\lambda_N+\mu_N\mu_1} & \frac{\lambda_{N-1}\lambda_N\mu_N\mu_1(\theta_N+\theta_1)}{\lambda_{N-1}\lambda_N+\mu_N\mu_1} \end{bmatrix},$$

and $\theta_j = (1 - \mu_{j-1}\lambda_j)^{-1}$. We multiply the rows of D by

$$(\lambda_N\lambda_1 + \mu_1\mu_2)/(\mu_1{}^2\mu_2),\ (\lambda_1\lambda_2 + \mu_2\mu_3)\lambda_N^2\lambda_1/[(\mu_1\mu_2)^2\mu_3],\ \ldots,$$
$$(\lambda_{N-2}\lambda_{N-1} + \mu_{N-1}\mu_N)(\lambda_N\lambda_1 \cdots \lambda_{N-3})^2\lambda_{N-2}/[(\mu_1 \cdots \mu_{N-1})^2\mu_N]$$
$$= (\lambda_{N-2}\lambda_{N-1} + \mu_{N-1}\mu_N)\mu_N/(\lambda_{N-1}^2\lambda_{N-2}),\ (\lambda_{N-1}\lambda_N + \mu_N\mu_1)/(\lambda_{N-1}\mu_1),$$

and the columns by

$$\mu_1/(\lambda_N^2\lambda_1),\ \mu_1{}^2\mu_2/[(\lambda_N\lambda_1)^2\lambda_2],\ldots,\ (\mu_1 \cdots \mu_{N-2})^2\mu_{N-1}/[(\lambda_N\lambda_1 \cdots \lambda_{N-2}^2)\lambda_{N-1}]$$
$$= \lambda_{N-1}/(\mu_{N-1}\mu_N^2),\ 1/(\lambda_N\mu_N).$$

We obtain as a result the matrix

$$\begin{bmatrix} \theta_1 + \theta_2 & \lambda_2\theta_2 & 0 & \cdots & 0 & \mu_N\theta_1 \\ \mu_1\theta_2 & \theta_2 + \theta_3 & \lambda_3\theta_3 & \cdots & 0 & 0 \\ \vdots & \vdots & & & \vdots & \vdots \\ 0 & 0 & \cdots & \mu_{N-2}\theta_{N-1} & \theta_{N-1} + \theta_N & \lambda_N\theta_N \\ \lambda_1\theta_1 & 0 & \cdots & 0 & \mu_{N-1}\theta_N & \theta_N + \theta_1 \end{bmatrix}.$$

If we assume for the meshes Δ under consideration that $\| \Delta \| / \min_j | h_j | \leqslant \beta < \infty$, we find again that $\| D^{-1} \|$ is bounded with respect to k. The sum of the elements in the jth row of D is

$$G_j = \frac{\mu_{j-1}^2\mu_j{}^2\mu_{j+1}\theta_j + \lambda_{j-1}\lambda_j\mu_j\mu_{j+1}(\theta_j + \theta_{j+1}) + \lambda_{j-1}\lambda_j{}^2\lambda_{j+1}^2\theta_{j+1}}{\lambda_{j-1}\lambda_j + \mu_j\mu_{j+1}}$$
$$= \frac{(\mu_{j-1}^2\mu_j/\lambda_{j-1}\lambda_j)\theta_j + \theta_j + \theta_{j+1} + (\lambda_j\lambda_{j+1}^2/\mu_j\mu_{j+1})\theta_{j+1}}{(1/\mu_j\mu_{j+1}) + (1/\lambda_{j-1}\lambda_j)}.$$

If the meshes Δ become asymptotically uniform as $k \to \infty$, that is, if

$$\max_j | \lambda_j - \tfrac{1}{2} | \to 0,$$

then $\max_j | G_j - \frac{1}{2} | \to 0$. In general, let G be the diagonal matrix with G_j the diagonal element in the jth row. Then for $G^{-1}D - I$, the sum of elements in each row is zero.

Write Eq. (2.9.22) as

$$D\delta - G^{-1}Dg = (I - G^{-1}D)g.$$

Let $f^{iv}(x)$ be continuous on $[a, b]$. The quantities $4g_j$ differ from $f^{iv}(x_j)$ by an amount $O(\| \Delta \|)$. Thus, $\|(I - G^{-1}D)g \| \to 0$ as $\| \Delta \| \to 0$. Since $\| D^{-1} \|$ is uniformly bounded, it is evident that $\| \delta - D^{-1}G^{-1}Dg \| \to 0$.

If the meshes become asymptotically uniform as $\| \Delta \| \to 0$, then $\| \delta - 2g \| \to 0$. Thus we have proved the following.

Theorem 2.9.5. *Let $f^{iv}(x)$ be continuous on $[a, b]$. Let $\{\Delta_k\}$ be a sequence of meshes on $[a, b]$ with $\lim_{k\to\infty} \| \Delta_k \| = 0$ and $\sup_k \| \Delta_k \| / [\min_j | h_{k,j} |] = \beta < \infty$. If, in addition, the meshes become asymptotically uniform as $k \to \infty$, we have*

$$\lim_{k\to\infty} \left[\max \left| \frac{S'''_{\Delta k}(x_{k,j}+) - S'''_{\Delta k}(x_{k,j}-)}{\| \Delta_k \|} - \frac{f^{iv}(x_{k,j})}{2} \right| \right] = 0.$$

CHAPTER III

Intrinsic Properties of Cubic Splines

3.1. The Minimum Norm Property

The treatment of cubic splines in Chapter II does not reveal the intrinsic structure of spline functions. Historically, too, this structure was well hidden; more than a decade elapsed after the introduction of the spline by Schoenberg [1946] before the first of the intrinsic properties was uncovered. This property, which we refer to as the *minimum norm property*, was obtained by Holladay [1957]. Before proceeding with the statement and proof of Holladay's theorem, we require some notation and terminology.

By $\mathscr{K}^n(a, b)$, we mean the class of all functions $f(x)$ defined on $[a, b]$ which possess an absolutely continuous $(n - 1)$th derivative on $[a, b]$ and whose nth derivative is in $L^2(a, b)$. We denote by $\mathscr{K}_P^n(a, b)$ the subclass of functions in $\mathscr{K}^n(a, b)$ which, together with their first $n - 1$ derivatives, have continuous periodic extensions to $(-\infty, \infty)$ of period $b - a$.

A function $f(x)$ is of type I′ if it has a first derivative that vanishes at $x = a$ and $x = b$. Two functions are in the same type I equivalence class if their difference is of type I′. A spline function $S(x)$ can be represented in many ways in terms of a finite number of parameters. If two of these parameters are $S'(a)$ and $S'(b)$, we say the representation is of type I and that $S(x)$ is of type I when it is represented in this manner. In a similar fashion, we say a function $f(x)$ is of type II′ if it has a second derivative that vanishes at $x = a$ and $x = b$. Two functions are in the same type II equivalence class if their difference is of type II′. A type II representation of a spline $S(x)$ is a representation into which $S''(a)$ and $S''(b)$ enter explicitly. We say that $S(x)$ is of type II when it is represented in this manner. The purpose of these definitions of "type" is to facilitate the discussion of cubic splines; they are modified later when splines other than cubic splines are considered.

The minimum norm property is expressed in Theorem 3.1.1, which follows, in a form slightly stronger than originally stated. The proof, however, is that of Holladay.

Theorem 3.1.1. *Let* Δ: $a = x_0 < x_1 < \cdots < x_N = b$ *and* $Y = \{y_i \mid i = 0, 1, \ldots, N\}$ *be given. Then of all functions* $f(x)$ *in* $\mathscr{K}^2(a, b)$ *such that* $f(x_i) = y_i$, *the type II′ cubic spline* $S_\Delta(Y; x)$ *minimizes*

$$\int_a^b |f''(x)|^2\, dx.$$

Moreover, $S_\Delta(Y; x)$ *is the unique admissible function that minimizes this integral.*

Proof. If $f(x)$ belongs to $\mathscr{K}^2(a, b)$, and if $f(x_i) = y_i$, then

$$\int_a^b |f''(x) - S''_\Delta(Y; x)|^2\, dx$$
$$= \int_a^b |f''(x)|^2\, dx - 2\int_a^b f''(x) \cdot S''_\Delta(Y; x)\, dx + \int_a^b |S''_\Delta(Y; x)|^2\, dx$$
$$= \int_a^b |f''(x)|^2\, dx - 2\int_a^b \{f''(x) - S''_\Delta(Y; x)\} \cdot S''_\Delta(Y; x)\, dx - \int_a^b |S''_\Delta(Y; x)|^2\, dx.$$

We have, however,

$$\int_a^b \{f''(x) - S''_\Delta(Y; x)\} \cdot S''_\Delta(Y; x)\, dx$$
$$= \sum_{i=1}^N \int_{x_{i-1}}^{x_i} \{f''(x) - S''_\Delta(Y; x)\} \cdot S''_\Delta(Y; x)\, dx,$$

and

$$\int_{x_{i-1}}^{x_i} \{f''(x) - S''_\Delta(Y; x)\} \cdot S''_\Delta(Y; x)\, dx$$
$$= \{f'(x) - S'_\Delta(Y; x)\} \cdot S''_\Delta(Y; x) \Big|_{x_{i-1}}^{x_i} - \int_{x_{i-1}}^{x_i} \{f'(x) - S'_\Delta(y; x)\} \cdot S'''_\Delta(Y; x)\, dx$$
$$= \{f'(x) - S'_\Delta(Y; x)\} \cdot S''_\Delta(Y; x) \Big|_{x_{i-1}}^{x_i} - \{f(x) - S_\Delta(Y; x)\} \cdot S'''_\Delta(Y; x) \Big|_{x_{i-1}}^{x_i}$$
$$= \{f'(x) - S'_\Delta(Y; x)\} \cdot S''_\Delta(Y; x) \Big|_{x_{i-1}}^{x_i},$$

since $S'''_\Delta(Y; x)$ is constant on each mesh interval $[x_{i-1}, x_i]$ and $f(x_i) = S_\Delta(Y; x_i) = y_i$ $(i = 0, 1, \ldots, N)$. In virtue of the continuity of $\{f'(x) - S'_\Delta(Y; x)\} \cdot S''_\Delta(Y; x)$ on $[a, b]$, it follows that

$$\int_a^b \{f''(x) - S''_\Delta(Y; x)\} \cdot S''_\Delta(Y; x)\, dx$$
$$= \sum_{i=1}^N \{f'(x) - S'_\Delta(Y; x)\} \cdot S''_\Delta(Y; x) \Big|_{x_{i-1}}^{x_i}$$
$$= \{f'(x) - S'_\Delta(Y; x)\} \cdot S''_\Delta(Y; x) \Big|_a^b = 0.$$

The last equality is true in view of the hypothesis that $S_\Delta(Y; x)$ is a type II′ spline. It now follows that

$$\int_a^b |f''(x)|^2\,dx - \int_a^b |S_\Delta''(Y; x)|^2\,dx = \int_a^b |f''(x) - S_\Delta''(Y; x)|^2\,dx. \qquad (3.1.1)$$

The right hand member is positive unless $S_\Delta''(Y; x) = f''(x)$ a.e., i.e., unless $S_\Delta(Y; x) \equiv f(x) + Ax + B$, which reduces to $f(x)$ since $S_\Delta(Y; x_i) = f(x_i)$ $(i = 0, N)$. This proves the theorem. Equation (3.1.1) is called the *first integral relation.*

The content of Holladay's theorem was anticipated to a degree by researchers in the theory of elastic beams dating back to the Bernoullis and Euler, (Sokolnikoff [1956, p. 1]), but the abstract formulation, the simplicity of Holladay's proof, and the integral relation (3.1.1) that this method of proof establishes represent a major contribution. Holladay, however, did not pursue the subject further and did not explore the far-reaching consequences of the first integral relation.

3.2. The Best Approximation Property

Let us introduce the pseudo-norm

$$\|f\| = \left\{\int_a^b f''(x)^2\,dx\right\}^{1/2} \qquad (3.2.1)$$

into $\mathscr{K}^2(a, b)$ and, for fixed $f(x)$ in $\mathscr{K}^2(a, b)$, consider $\|f - S_\Delta\|$, where $S_\Delta(x)$ is a cubic spline of prescribed type with respect to a fixed mesh Δ: $a = x_0 < x_1 < \cdots < x_N = b$. The question arises, "Does the spline $S_\Delta(f; x)$ of interpolation to $f(x)$ on Δ minimize $\|f - S_\Delta\|$?" We have given an affirmative answer to this question for several important situations in Section 2.3; we formulate this result for the periodic case.

Theorem 3.2.1. *Let Δ: $a = x_0 < x_1 < \cdots < x_N = b$ and $f(x)$ in $\mathscr{K}_P^2(a, b)$ be given. Then of all periodic cubic splines $S_\Delta(x)$, $S_\Delta(f; x)$ minimizes $\|f - S_\Delta\|$. If $\bar{S}_\Delta(x)$ also minimizes $\|f - S_\Delta\|$, then $\bar{S}_\Delta(x) = S_\Delta(f; x) + const.$*

The proof of Theorem 3.2.1 contained in Section 2.3 is classical in nature and requires the determination of stationary points. In Section 3.4, we generalize Holladay's argument and obtain an elegant proof that avoids determining stationary points and extends beyond the periodic case not only to type I splines and type II splines, but to situations where the splines involved are not simple. Although we are not yet in position to define a simple spline in complete generality, we say a cubic spline *is simple* if it is in $C^2[a, b]$.

The property expressed in Theorem 3.2.1 is called the *best approximation property* (Walsh *et al.* [1962]). Like the minimum norm property and a number of other important intrinsic properties that we subsequently develop, it can be obtained as a simple consequence of the first integral relation. This integral relation itself (as is apparent from Holladay's proof of the minimum norm property) is a consequence of a very general identity involving spline functions, and results when certain restrictions are imposed upon the splines involved. The identity plays a fundamental role in spline theory and allows it to proceed smoothly in situations where methods such as the standard minimization argument employed in the proof of Theorem 3.2.1 become very cumbersome. However, when direct methods, such as those employed in Chapter II, are applicable, they generally yield sharper results. This is particularly true with respect to rates of convergence. We now obtain the indicated identity explicitly and use it as a cornerstone for a theory of splines.

3.3. The Fundamental Identity

We can obtain the identity just mentioned and at the same time make more transparent the conditions under which the first integral relation is valid, if we again transform (as in Holladay's argument) the integral

$$\int_a^b \{D^2f(x) - D^2S_\Delta(x)\}\, D^2S_\Delta(x)\, dx$$

by integrating by parts twice. The operator notation $D^2f(x)$ rather than $f''(x)$ will make the generalizations in Chapter VI more natural. The result of this double integration by parts for each interval $x_{i-1} \leqslant x \leqslant x_i$ of the mesh Δ: $a = x_0 < x_1 < \cdots < x_N = b$ is

$$\begin{aligned}
\int_{x_{i-1}}^{x_i} & \{D^2f(x) - D^2S_\Delta(x)\}\, D^2S_\Delta(x)\, dx \\
&= \{Df(x) - DS_\Delta(x)\}\, D^2S_\Delta(x)\, \Big|_{x_{i-1}}^{x_i} \\
&\qquad - \{f(x) - S_\Delta(x)\}\, D^3S_\Delta(x)\, \Big|_{x_{i-1}}^{x_i} + \int_{x_{i-1}}^{x_i} \{f(x) - S_\Delta(x)\}\, D^4S_\Delta(x)\, dx \\
&= \{Df(x) - DS_\Delta(x)\}\, D^2S_\Delta(x)\, \Big|_{x_{i-1}}^{x_i} - \{f(x) - S_\Delta(x)\}\, D^3S_\Delta(x)\, \Big|_{x_{i-1}}^{x_i}
\end{aligned}$$

since $D^4S_\Delta(x)$ is identically zero on each open mesh interval $x_{i-1} < x < x_i$. Consequently,

$$\int_a^b \{D^2f(x) - D^2S_\Delta(x)\} D^2S_\Delta(x)\, dx = \{Df(x) - DS_\Delta(x)\} D^2S_\Delta(x) \Big|_a^b$$

$$- \sum_{i=1}^{N} \{f(x) - S_\Delta(x)\} D^3S_\Delta(x) \Big|_{x_{i-1}}^{x_i} \quad (3.3.1)$$

in view of the continuity of $\{Df(x) - DS_\Delta(x)\} D^2S_\Delta(x)$ on $[a, b]$. Generally, however, $D^3S_\Delta(x)$ is not continuous at the mesh points of Δ; this is the reason for the presence of the summation

$$\sum_{i=1}^{N} \{f(x) - S_\Delta(x)\} D^3S_\Delta(x) \Big|_{x_{i-1}}^{x_i}.$$

Substituting (3.3.1) in the identity

$$\| f - g \|^2 = \| f \|^2 - 2 \int_a^b \{D^2f(x) - D^2g(x)\} D^2g(x)\, dx - \| g \|^2 \quad (3.3.2)$$

with $g(x) = S_\Delta(x)$ gives the *fundamental identity*

$$\| f - S_\Delta \|^2 = \| f \|^2 - 2[\{Df(x) - DS_\Delta(x)\} D^2S_\Delta(x) \Big|_a^b$$

$$- \sum_{i=1}^{N} \{f(x) - S_\Delta(x)\} D^3S_\Delta(x) \Big|_{x_{i-1}}^{x_i}] - \| S_\Delta \|^2 \quad (3.3.3)$$

which is valid for any $f(x)$ in $\mathscr{K}^2(a, b)$ and any simple spline $S_\Delta(x)$ on an arbitrary mesh Δ: $a = x_0 < x_1 < \cdots < x_N = b$.

3.4. The First Integral Relation

When $S_\Delta(x) = S_\Delta(f; x) + \text{const}$, the summation

$$\sum_{i=1}^{N} \{f(x) - S_\Delta(x)\} D^3S_\Delta(x) \Big|_{x_{i-1}}^{x_i}$$

in the fundamental identity vanishes. If in addition $f(x)$ and $S_\Delta(x)$ are in $\mathscr{K}_P^2(a, b)$, or $f(x) - S_\Delta(x)$ is of type I′, or $S_\Delta(x)$ is of type II′, then the fundamental identity reduces to the first integral relation. These conditions are clearly only sufficient and not necessary, since, in particular, end conditions of mixed type may be imposed. We can even relax the continuity requirement on $S''_\Delta(x)$ and still obtain the first integral relation by requiring $S_\Delta'(x)$ to interpolate to $f'(x)$ at the mesh points of Δ; even this does not exhaust the possibilities. The following theorem is, in view of these remarks, a direct consequence of the fundamental identity.

Theorem 3.4.1. *If $f(x)$ is in $\mathscr{K}^2(a, b)$ and $S_\Delta(f; x)$ is a spline of interpolation to $f(x)$ on a mesh Δ: $a = x_0 < x_1 < \cdots < x_N = b$ and any of the conditions,* (a) *$f(x)$ and $S_\Delta(f; x)$ are periodic,* (b) *$f(x) - S_\Delta(f; x)$ is of type I',* (c) *$S_\Delta(f; x)$ is of type II', is satisfied, then*

$$\|f\|^2 = \|S_{\Delta,f}\|^2 + \|f - S_{\Delta,f}\|^2.$$

In the light of Theorem 3.4.1, let us re-examine Theorems 3.1.1 and 3.2.1. Since in Theorem 3.1.1 we have $S_\Delta(Y; x) \equiv S_\Delta(f; x)$ for any $f(x)$ in $\mathscr{K}^2(a, b)$ such that $f(x_i) = y_i$ $(i = 0, 1, \ldots, N)$ when $S_\Delta(Y; x)$ and $S_\Delta(f; x)$ are both of type II', Theorem 3.4.1 implies

$$\|f\|^2 - \|S_{\Delta,Y}\|^2 = \|f - S_{\Delta,Y}\|^2 \geqslant 0.$$

Consequently, we have

$$\int_a^b |S''_\Delta(Y; x)|^2 \, dx \leqslant \int_a^b |f''(x)|^2 \, dx$$

for any $f(x)$ in $\mathscr{K}^2(a, b)$ such that $f(x_i) = y_i$ $(i = 0, 1, \ldots, N)$, with equality if and only if $S''_\Delta(f; x) = f''(x)$ a.e. Thus, the minimum norm property is a direct consequence of the first integral relation. As we have already seen Holladay's argument constitutes a proof of this relation.

If $y_0 = y_N$ and both $f(x)$ and $S_\Delta(x)$ are restricted to $\mathscr{K}^2_P(a, b)$, then Theorem 3.4.1 implies the following.

Theorem 3.4.2. *Let Δ: $a = x_0 < x_1 < \cdots < x_N = b$ and $Y \equiv \{y_i \mid i = 0, 1, \ldots, N; y_0 = y_N\}$ be given. Then of all functions $f(x)$ in $\mathscr{K}^2_P(a, b)$ such that $f(x_i) = y_i$ $(i = 0, 1, \ldots, N)$, the periodic spline $S_\Delta(Y; x)$ minimizes*

$$\int_a^b |f''(x)|^2 \, dx$$

and is the unique admissible function that minimizes the integral.

It should be observed that, if $y_0 = y_N$, if $S_\Delta(Y; x)_P$ is the periodic spline of interpolation to Y, and if $S_\Delta(Y; x)$ is the corresponding type II' spline of interpolation, then

$$\int_a^b |S''_\Delta(Y; x)|^2 \, dx \leqslant \int_a^b |S''_\Delta(Y; x)_P|^2 \, dx,$$

where we have equality only when

$$S_\Delta(Y; x)_P \equiv S_\Delta(Y; x) + Ax + B \equiv S_\Delta(Y; x),$$

since $S_\Delta(Y; x)_P$ and $S_\Delta(Y; x)$ interpolate to the same values at $x = a$ and $x = b$. In this sense, Theorem 3.1.1 is stronger than Theorem 3.4.2.

We can formulate yet another analog of Theorem 3.1.1.

Theorem 3.4.3. *Let Δ: $a = x_0 < x_1 < \cdots < x_N = b$ and $Y = \{y'_0, y'_N, y_i \mid i = 0, 1,..., N\}$ be given. Then of all functions $f(x)$ in $\mathcal{K}^2(a, b)$ such that $f(x_i) = y_i$ $(i = 0, 1,..., N)$ and $f'(x_i) = y'_i$ $(i = 0, N)$, the type I spline $S_\Delta(Y; x)$ minimizes*

$$\int_a^b |f''(x)|^2 \, dx. \tag{3.4.1}$$

Moreover, $S_\Delta(Y; x)$ is the unique admissible function that minimizes this integral.

Proof. All but the uniqueness follows directly from Theorem 3.4.1. To see the uniqueness, observe that, if $g(x)$ also satisfies the condition of Theorem 3.4.3 and minimizes (3.4.1), then Theorem 3.4.1 implies that

$$\| g - S_{\Delta,Y} \|^2 = \| g \|^2 - \| S_{\Delta,Y} \|^2 = 0$$

or $g(x) \equiv S_\Delta(Y; x) + Ax + B = S_\Delta(Y; x)$, since $g^{(\alpha)}(a) = S_\Delta^{(\alpha)}(Y; a)$ for $\alpha = 0, 1$. If the requirement that $S'_\Delta(Y; x_i) = y'_i$ $(i = 0, 1)$ is omitted, the type II′ spline of interpolation to Y on Δ minimizes (3.4.1).

A spline function $S_\Delta(x)$ on Δ of a given type depends in a linear fashion on its values at the mesh points of Δ and on the values of its derivatives at $x = a$ and $x = b$. This is evident from (2.1.2), (2.1.8), and (2.1.9). Consequently, we have, under a variety of conditions,

$$S_\Delta(f + g; x) = S_\Delta(f; x) + S_\Delta(g; x), \tag{3.4.2}$$

although the decomposition is not unique. Some useful sets of end conditions which serve to make the decomposition (3.4.2) both valid and unique are as follows:

(a) $S_\Delta(f; x) - f(x)$, $S_\Delta(g; x) - g(x)$, and $S_\Delta(f + g; x) - f(x) - g(x)$ are all of type I′.

(b) $S_\Delta(f; x)$, $S_\Delta(g; x)$, and $S_\Delta(f + g; x)$ are all of type II′.

(c) $S_\Delta(f; x)$, $S_\Delta(g; x)$, and $S_\Delta(f + g; x)$ are all periodic.

In particular, we have

$$S_\Delta(f - S_\Delta; x) = S_\Delta(f; x) - S_\Delta(x) \tag{3.4.3}$$

for a number of end conditions on $S_\Delta(f - S_\Delta; x)$ and $S_\Delta(f; x)$. We can choose $S_\Delta(f - S_\Delta; x)$ to be periodic, of type II′, or such that $S_\Delta(f - S_\Delta; x) - f(x) + S_\Delta(x)$ is of type I′, and not only have (3.4.3) valid but also have the fundamental identity in each case reduce to

$$\|f - S_\Delta\|^2 - \|S_{\Delta,f-S_\Delta}\|^2 = \|f - S_\Delta - S_{\Delta,f-S_\Delta}\|^2 = \|f - S_\Delta - S_{\Delta,f} + S_\Delta\|^2$$
$$= \|f - S_{\Delta,f}\|^2,$$

which implies that $\|f - S_\Delta\| \geqslant \|f - S_{\Delta,f}\|$. When $S_\Delta(f - S_\Delta; x)$ is of type II′, we can modify condition (b) for the decomposition (3.4.2) and only require that $S_\Delta(f; x) - S_\Delta(x)$ be of type II′. This establishes Theorem 3.4.4, which is a generalization of Theorem 3.2.1. Observe that the strongest result is obtained when $f(x) - S_\Delta(f; x)$ is of type I′, since in this case no restriction is placed on $S_\Delta(x)$.

Theorem 3.4.4. *Let Δ: $a = x_0 < x_1 < \cdots < x_N = b$ and $f(x)$ in $\mathscr{K}^2(a, b)$ be given. If $S_\Delta(x)$ and $S_\Delta(f; x)$ are splines on Δ such that one of the conditions,* (a) *$f(x)$, $S_\Delta(x)$, and $S_\Delta(f; x)$ are in $\mathscr{K}_p^2(a, b)$,* (b) *$S_\Delta(x) - S_\Delta(f; x)$ is of type II′,* (c) *$f(x) - S_\Delta(f; x)$ is of type I′, is satisfied, then*

$$\|f - S_\Delta\| \geqslant \|f - S_{\Delta,f}\|.$$

If we have equality, then $S_\Delta(x) \equiv S_\Delta(f; x) + Ax + B$ except in the periodic case, where $A = 0$.

The decomposition (3.4.2) results from the possibility of finding a set of parameters upon which a spline $S_\Delta(x)$ depends linearly and which, together with continuity requirements, serves to define $S_\Delta(x)$. We refer to these parameters as *defining values*.

3.5. Uniqueness

In the present chapter, we have been relying hitherto on the results of Chapter II for the uniqueness and existence of the various splines under discussion. The assertions of all our theorems are correct and do not depend for their correctness on either existence or uniqueness, although, if we did not have at least existence, the theorems would be vacuous. A number of existence and uniqueness theorems of

Chapter II were obtained with relative ease due to the dominance of the main diagonal in the matrices involved. Indeed some of the important boundedness properties needed for convergence theorems of Chapter II were also obtained from this dominance. The investigation of splines of higher odd degree contained in Chapter IV is severely hampered by the absence of this diagonal dominance, and only limited existence and uniqueness theorems are obtained. In Chapter V, these difficulties are circumvented through an application of the first integral relation (in more general form).

In order to see this very useful application of the first integral relation, we proceed to establish the basic uniqueness and existence theorems for cubic splines by this method of argument.

Theorem 3.5.1. *Let Δ: $a = x_0 < x_1 < \cdots < x_N = b$ and $f(x)$ be given. If any of the conditions,* (a) *$f(x)$ and $S_\Delta(f; x)$ are periodic,* (b) *$f(x) - S_\Delta(f; x)$ is of type I′,* (c) *$f(x) - S_\Delta(f; x)$ is of type II′, is satisfied, then $S_\Delta(f; x)$ is unique.*

Proof. Suppose that $S_\Delta(f; x)$ and $\bar{S}_\Delta(f; x)$ are two splines of interpolation to $f(x)$ on Δ, both of which satisfy the same one of the conditions a, b, or c. In each of these cases, $S_\Delta(f; x) - \bar{S}_\Delta(f; x)$ is a spline of interpolation to the zero function $Z(x)$ such that the first integral relation holds, in virtue of Theorem 3.4.1. Thus,

$$\| Z - S_{\Delta,f} + \bar{S}_{\Delta,f} \|^2 = \| Z \|^2 - \| S_{\Delta,f} - \bar{S}_{\Delta,f} \|^2,$$

$$\| S_{\Delta,f} - \bar{S}_{\Delta,f} \|^2 = - \| S_{\Delta,f} - \bar{S}_{\Delta,f} \|^2.$$

It follows that

$$S_\Delta(f; x) \equiv \bar{S}_\Delta(f; x) + Ax + B.$$

Since both $S_\Delta(f; x)$ and $\bar{S}_\Delta(f; x)$ are splines of interpolation to $f(x)$ on Δ, $A = B = 0$.

In the proof of Theorem 3.5.1, the function $f(x)$ served only to determine an interpolation vector Y to which $S_\Delta(f; x)$ and $\bar{S}_\Delta(f, x)$ interpolate on Δ. The first integral relation was not applied to $f(x)$ but to $Z(x)$; consequently, the differentiability or even continuity of $f(x)$ is immaterial, and $f(x)$ may be regarded as an arbitrary function on $[a, b]$.

REMARK 3.5.1. The uniqueness asserted in Theorems 3.1.1, 3.4.2, and 3.4.3 implies the uniqueness of the splines there considered. Condition c, however, requires the slightly more elaborate argument given here.

3.6. Existence

We are now in a position to give an alternative proof of the existence of type I, type II, and periodic splines of interpolation which carries over to more general situations.

Theorem 3.6.1. *Let Δ: $a = x_0 < x_1 < \cdots < x_N = b$ and $f(x)$ be given. Then there exist type I and type II splines $S_\Delta(f; x)$ of interpolation to $f(x)$ on Δ in each type I and type II equivalence class. If $f(a) = f(b)$, there exists a periodic spline of interpolation to $f(x)$ on Δ.*

Proof. Since we consider only the values of $f(x)$ at mesh points, we can modify $f(x)$ so that its values on Δ are unchanged but the modified function $\tilde{f}(x)$ is in any specified type I or type II equivalence class. From Theorem 3.5.1, we can conclude that, if $S_\Delta(\tilde{f}; x)$ exists, it is unique. The splines in question will exist if the matrices in (2.1.8) and (2.1.9) are nonsingular. Both of these equations are of the form

$$A \cdot M = Y \tag{3.6.1}$$

where A is a matrix and both M and Y are vectors. The components of M are the values of $S''_\Delta(f; x)$ at the mesh points of Δ. If (3.6.1) had two distinct solutions M, we would have two distinct splines of interpolation to $f(x)$ on Δ—both periodic, both in the same type I equivalence class, or both in the same type II equivalence class. This, however, would contradict Theorem 3.5.1; consequently, (3.6.1) has a unique solution M. Since a unique solution of (3.6.1) for one Y implies the uniqueness of the solution for any Y, A^{-1} exists, and this proves the theorem.

Although Theorem 3.6.1 establishes the existence of A^{-1}, the method of proof does not place a bound on $\| A^{-1} \|$. In this sense, Theorem 3.6.1 is inferior to the existence theorems of Chapter II. Its superiority lies in its generality. Moreover, the first integral relation together with the second integral relation, which will be introduced in Section 3.9, to a very large degree compensates for the lack of the bound on $\| A^{-1} \|$.

3.7. General Equations

The matrix equations (2.1.8) and (2.1.9) obtained in Chapter II were derived from the hypothesis that $S''_\Delta(x)$ is continuous and piecewise linear. In Chapter IV, similar equations are obtained for higher-order splines of odd degree; but only under restrictions such as uniform spacing do these equations assume a simple form. There is, however, in all cases a system of approximately N equations in the same number of unknowns, where N is the number of mesh intervals. The representation of higher-order splines of odd degree in terms of these quantities is considerably more complex than in the case of cubic splines (cf. Section 4.1). The analogous procedure for generalized splines, which are investigated in Chapter VI, is unclear, since the linearity assumption is not valid. Consequently, each case requires special analysis.

Even in the case of generalized splines, it is possible to write down in a straightforward manner a system of $2nN$ equations in $2nN$ unknowns where again N is the number of mesh intervals and n is the order of the pertinent differential operator. Moreover, in each mesh interval the spline is easily represented in terms of these quantities. The matrices that arise have the property that only a limited number of subarrays contain nonzero entries. This allows the use of special inversion procedures on a computer which greatly reduce the storage required for performing the inversion. The matrices have the disadvantage, however, that, as the length of the mesh intervals approaches zero, the matrices approach a singular matrix. Moreover, when a special representation is possible, the system of equations is usually significantly smaller in size.

In order to derive these equations, let us alter our point of view and regard the construction of the cubic spline of interpolation as the problem of piecing together N solutions of the differential equation

$$D^4 f = 0, \tag{3.7.1}$$

each solution valid in a different open mesh interval of the mesh Δ: $a = x_0 < x_1 < \cdots < x_N = b$, such that the resultant spline $S_\Delta(f; x)$ interpolates to a prescribed function $f(x)$ on Δ, satisfies a definite set of end conditions, and is in $\mathscr{K}^3(a, b)$.

Any solution of (3.7.1) is a linear combination of four linearly independent solutions $u_i(x)$ $(i = 1, 2, 3, 4)$ that can be chosen such that $u_i^{(j)}(0) = \delta_{i-1,j}$ $(j = 0, 1, 2, 3)$. Specifically, we have $u_i(x) = x^{i-1}/(i-1)!$. It follows that, in any mesh interval $x_{i-1} \leqslant x \leqslant x_i$,

$$S_\Delta(f; x) = \sum_{j=1}^{4} c_{ij} u_j(x - x_{i-1}). \tag{3.7.2}$$

Since $S_\Delta(f; x_i) = f(x_i) = y_i$, we have $c_{i1} = y_{i-1}$ $(i = 1, 2, 3, \ldots, N)$. For $S_\Delta(f; x)$ to be in $\mathscr{K}^3(a, b)$, it is necessary that

$$\sum_{j=1}^{4} c_{ij} u_j^{(k)}(x_i - x_{i-1}) = \sum_{j=1}^{4} c_{i+1,j} u_j^{(k)}(0) = c_{i+1,k+1}$$
$$(k = 0, 1, 2;\ i = 1, 2, \ldots, N-1). \tag{3.7.3}$$

If $S_\Delta(f; x)$ is of type I, we have

$$c_{11} = y_0, \qquad c_{12} = y_0', \tag{3.7.4}$$
$$\sum_{j=1}^{4} c_{Nj} u_j(x_N - x_{N-1}) = y_N, \qquad \sum_{j=1}^{4} c_{Nj} u_j'(x_N - x_{N-1}) = y_N',$$

and, if $S_\Delta(f; x)$ is of type II,

$$c_{11} = y_0, \qquad c_{13} = y_0'',$$
$$\sum_{j=1}^{4} c_{Nj} u_j(x_N - x_{N-1}) = y_N, \qquad \sum_{j=1}^{4} c_{Nj} u_j''(x_N - x_{N-1}) = y_N''. \tag{3.7.5}$$

In the periodic case, these equations are replaced by

$$c_{11} = y_0 = y_N, \sum_{j=1}^{4} c_{Nj} u_j^{(k)}(x_N - x_{N-1}) = c_{1,k+1} \qquad (k = 0, 1, 2). \tag{3.7.6}$$

Let us set

$$A_i = \begin{bmatrix} 0 & 0 & 0 & 0 \\ u_1(x_i - x_{i-1}) & u_2(x_i - x_{i-1}) & u_3(x_i - x_{i-1}) & u_4(x_i - x_{i-1}) \\ u_1'(x_i - x_{i-1}) & u_2'(x_i - x_{i-1}) & u_3'(x_i - x_{i-1}) & u_4'(x_i - x_{i-1}) \\ u_1''(x_i - x_{i-1}) & u_2''(x_i - x_{i-1}) & u_3''(x_i - x_{i-1}) & u_4''(x_i - x_{i-1}) \end{bmatrix} \tag{3.7.7.1}$$
$$(i = 1, 2, \ldots, N),$$

$$B = \begin{bmatrix} 1 & 0 & 0 & 0 \\ -1 & 0 & 0 & 0 \\ 0 & -1 & 0 & 0 \\ 0 & 0 & -1 & 0 \end{bmatrix}, \tag{3.7.7.2}$$

$$C_0^{\mathrm{I}} = \begin{bmatrix} 1 & 0 & 0 & 0 \\ 0 & 1 & 0 & 0 \end{bmatrix}, \tag{3.7.7.3}$$

$$C_0^{\mathrm{II}} = \begin{bmatrix} 1 & 0 & 0 & 0 \\ 0 & 0 & 1 & 0 \end{bmatrix}, \tag{3.7.7.4}$$

$$C_N^{\mathrm{I}} = \begin{bmatrix} u_1(x_N - x_{N-1}) & u_2(x_N - x_{N-1}) & u_3(x_N - x_{N-1}) & u_4(x_N - x_{N-1}) \\ u_1'(x_N - x_{N-1}) & u_2'(x_N - x_{N-1}) & u_3'(x_N - x_{N-1}) & u_4'(x_N - x_{N-1}) \end{bmatrix}, \tag{3.7.7.5}$$

$$C_N^{\mathrm{II}} = \begin{bmatrix} u_1(x_N - x_{N-1}) & u_2(x_N - x_{N-1}) & u_3(x_N - x_{N-1}) & u_4(x_N - x_{N-1}) \\ u_1''(x_N - x_{N-1}) & u_2''(x_N - x_{N-1}) & u_3''(x_N - x_{N-1}) & u_4''(x_N - x_{N-1}) \end{bmatrix}, \tag{3.7.7.6}$$

$$C = (c_{11}, c_{12}, c_{13}, c_{14}, c_{21}, \cdots \quad \cdots, c_{N4})^{\mathrm{T}}, \tag{3.7.7.7}$$

$$Y = (y_0, \alpha y_0' + \beta y_0'', y_1, 0, 0, 0, y_2, 0, \cdots \quad \cdots, y_{N-1}, 0, 0, 0, y_N, \alpha y_N' + \beta y_N'')^{\mathrm{T}}. \tag{3.7.7.8}$$

Then

$$AC = Y \tag{3.7.7.9}$$

where, for type I splines,

$$A = \begin{bmatrix} C_0^{\mathrm{I}} & 0 & 0 & \cdots & 0 & 0 \\ A_1 & B & 0 & \cdots & 0 & 0 \\ 0 & A_2 & B & \cdots & 0 & 0 \\ & & \cdots & & & \\ 0 & 0 & 0 & \cdots & A_{N-1} & B \\ 0 & 0 & 0 & \cdots & 0 & C_N^{\mathrm{I}} \end{bmatrix} \qquad (\alpha = 1, \quad \beta = 0), \tag{3.7.7.10}$$

and, for type II splines,

$$A = \begin{bmatrix} C_0^{\mathrm{II}} & 0 & 0 & \cdots & 0 & 0 \\ A_1 & B & 0 & \cdots & 0 & 0 \\ 0 & A_2 & B & \cdots & 0 & 0 \\ & & \cdots & & & \\ 0 & 0 & 0 & \cdots & A_{N-1} & B \\ 0 & 0 & 0 & \cdots & 0 & C_N^{\mathrm{II}} \end{bmatrix} \qquad (\alpha = 0, \quad \beta = 1), \tag{3.7.7.11}$$

and, for periodic splines,

$$A = \begin{bmatrix} A_1 & B & 0 & \cdots & 0 & 0 \\ 0 & A_2 & B & \cdots & 0 & 0 \\ & & \cdots & & & \\ 0 & 0 & 0 & \cdots & A_{N-1} & B \\ B & 0 & 0 & \cdots & 0 & A_N \end{bmatrix} \tag{3.7.7.12}$$

with (3.7.7.8) replaced by

$$Y = (y_1, 0, 0, 0, y_2, 0, \ldots, y_N, 0, 0, 0)^{\mathrm{T}}. \tag{3.7.7.13}$$

In each case, the matrix A is nonsingular, since the representation (3.7.2) uniquely determines the coefficients c_{ij}. Thus, as in the proof of Theorem 3.6.1, two solutions of Eqs. (3.7.7) would give rise to two distinct splines of interpolation; this would contradict Theorem 3.5.1. Since we have $c_{i1} = y_{i-1}$ ($i = 1, 2, \ldots, N$), the size of the system of equations easily can be reduced from $4nN$ equations to $3nN$ equations.

3.8. Convergence of Lower-Order Derivatives

We now investigate the convergence of a sequence of splines of interpolation $\{S_{\Delta_N, f}\}$ ($N = 1, 2, \ldots$) defined on a sequence of meshes

$\{\Delta_N : a = x_0^N < x_1^N < \cdots < x_{m_N}^N = b\}$ such that $\| \Delta_N \| \to 0$ as $N \to \infty$. As in the convergence proofs of Chapter II, it is not required that $\Delta_{N_1} \subseteq \Delta_{N_2}$ for $N_1 \leqslant N_2$. One important notion in the discussions that follow is that, since $S_{\Delta_N}(f; x)$ interpolates to $f(x)$ on Δ_N, we know from Rolle's theorem that in every mesh interval $x_{i-1}^N < x < x_i^N$ $(i = 1, 2, \ldots, m_N)$ there exists an x_{iN} such that

$$f'(x_{iN}) = S'_{\Delta N}(f; x_{iN}). \tag{3.8.1}$$

Later we need the analogous result that in each interval $x_{i-2}^N < x < x_i^N$ $(i = 2, 3, \ldots, m_N)$ there exists an $\bar{x}_{iN}$ such that

$$f''(\bar{x}_{iN}) = S''_{\Delta N}(f; \bar{x}_{iN}). \tag{3.8.2}$$

Theorem 3.8.1. *Let*

$$\{\Delta_N : a = x_0^N < x_1^N < \cdots < x_{mN}^N = b\} \ (N = 1, 2, \ldots)$$

and $f(x)$ in $\mathscr{K}^2(a, b)$ be given with $\| \Delta_N \| \to 0$ as $N \to \infty$. Let $\{S_{\Delta_N, f}\}$ $(N = 1, 2, \ldots)$ be the corresponding sequence of splines of interpolation determined by one of the following conditions: (a) *$f(x)$ is in $\mathscr{K}_P^2(a, b)$, and $S_{\Delta_N}(f; x)$ is periodic $(N = 1, 2, \ldots)$,* (b) *$f(x) - S_{\Delta_N}(f; x)$ is of type I′ $(N = 1, 2, \ldots)$,* (c) *$S_{\Delta_N}(f; x)$ is of type II′ $(N = 1, 2, \ldots)$. Then we have*

$$\lim_{N \to \infty} | f^{(\alpha)}(x) - S_{\Delta N}^{(\alpha)}(f; x) | = 0 \qquad (\alpha = 0, 1) \tag{3.8.3}$$

uniformly for x in $[a, b]$.

Proof. Let x_{iN} in $[x_{i-1}^N, x_i^N]$ be such that $f'(x_{iN}) = S'_{\Delta_N}(f; x_{iN})$. Then

$$| f'(x) - S'_{\Delta_N}(f; x) | = \left| \int_{x_{iN}}^{x} \{f''(x) - S''_{\Delta_N}(f; x)\} \, dx \right|$$
$$\leqslant \left\{ \int_{x_{iN}}^{x} | f''(x) - S''_{\Delta_N}(f; x) |^2 \, | dx | \right\}^{1/2} | x - x_{iN} |^{1/2}$$

by Schwarz's inequality applied to $f''(x) - S''_{\Delta_N}(f; x)$ and 1. Consequently,

$$| f'(x) - S'_{\Delta N}(f; x) | \leqslant \| f - S_{\Delta N, f} \| \cdot | x - x_{iN} |^{1/2} \leqslant K \, | x - x_{iN} |^{1/2}, \tag{3.8.4}$$

where $K = 2\| f \|$, by Minkowski's inequality and the minimum norm property. If $\Delta_1 \subseteq \Delta_N$ $(N = 1, 2, \ldots)$, we may take $K = \| f - S_{\Delta_1, f} \|$, since in this case $S_{\Delta_1}(f; x)$ is a spline on Δ_N, and the best approximation property applies. Since there is an x_{iN} in every mesh interval, we can find one such that $|x - x_{iN}| \leqslant \|\Delta_N\|$, which implies that $S'_{\Delta_N}(f; x) \to f'(x)$ as $N \to \infty$ uniformly for x in $[a, b]$. Similarly for x_{i-1}^N such that $x_{i-1}^N \leqslant x \leqslant x_i^N$,

$$|f(x) - S_{\Delta_N}(f; x)| \leqslant \int_{\bar{x}}^{x} |f'(x) - S'_{\Delta_N}(f; x)| \, |dx| \leqslant \tfrac{1}{2}K \|\Delta_N\|^{3/2},$$

where $\bar{x}$ is equal to x_{i-1}^N or x_i^N, depending on which is closer to x. This proves the theorem.

Corollary 3.8.1.1. *If $\Delta_1 \subseteq \Delta_N$ $(N = 1, 2, \ldots)$, $\|\Delta_N\| \to 0$ as $N \to \infty$, and $S_{\Delta_N}(f; x)$ $(N = 1, 2, \ldots)$ is in a prescribed type II equivalence class, then*

$$\lim_{N\to\infty} S_{\Delta_N}^{(\alpha)}(f; x) = f^{(\alpha)}(x) \qquad (\alpha = 0, 1)$$

uniformly for x in $[a, b]$.

Proof. We may take K as $\|f - S_{\Delta_1, f}\|$ in virtue of the best approximation property.

Corollary 3.8.1.2. *Let $f(x)$, $\{\Delta_N\}$ $(N = 1, 2, \ldots)$, and $\{S_{\Delta_N}(f; x)\}$ $(N = 1, 2, \ldots)$ satisfy the conditions of Theorem 3.8.1 or Corollary 3.8.1.1. Then*

$$f^{(\alpha)}(x) = S_{\Delta_N}^{(\alpha)}(f; x) + O(\|\Delta_N\|^{(3-2\alpha)/2}) \qquad (\alpha = 0, 1) \qquad (3.8.5)$$

uniformly for x in $[a, b]$.

3.9. The Second Integral Relation

Let us examine in more detail the pseudo-norm

$$\|f\|^2 = \int_a^b |f''(x)|^2 \, dx \equiv \int_a^b |D^2 f(x)|^2 \, dx. \qquad (3.9.1)$$

If $f(x)$ is in $\mathscr{K}^4(a, b)$, then

$$\|f - S_\Delta\|^2 = \int_a^b \{D^2 f(x) - D^2 S_\Delta(x)\}^2 \, dx$$

$$= \sum_{j=1}^{N} \int_{x_{j-1}}^{x_j} \{D^2 f(x) - D^2 S_\Delta(x)\}^2 \, dx \qquad (3.9.2)$$

for any spline $S_\Delta(x)$ defined on a mesh Δ: $a = x_0 < x_1 < \cdots < x_N = b$. Moreover,

$$\int_{x_{j-1}}^{x_j} \{D^2f(x) - D^2S_\Delta(x)\}^2\, dx = \{Df(x) - DS_\Delta(x)\}\{D^2f(x) - D^2S_\Delta(x)\} \Big|_{x_{j-1}}^{x_j}$$
$$- \{f(x) - S_\Delta(x)\}\{D^3f(x) - D^3S_\Delta(x)\} \Big|_{x_{j-1}}^{x_j}$$
$$+ \int_{x_{j-1}}^{x_j} \{f(x) - S_\Delta(x)\}\{D^4f(x) - D^4S_\Delta(x)\}\, dx. \tag{3.9.3}$$

Substitution of (3.9.3) in (3.9.2) together with the continuity of $\{Df(x) - DS_\Delta(x)\}\{D^2f(x) - D^2S_\Delta(x)\}$ on $[a, b]$ and the equation

$$\int_a^b \{f(x) - S_\Delta(x)\}\, D^4S_\Delta(x)\, dx = 0$$

shows that

$$\|f - S_\Delta\|^2 = \{Df(x) - DS_\Delta(x)\}\{D^2f(x) - D^2S_\Delta(x)\} \Big|_a^b$$
$$- \sum_{j=1}^{N} \{f(x) - S_\Delta(x)\}\{D^3f(x) - D^3S_\Delta(x)\} \Big|_{x_{j-1}}^{x_j}$$
$$+ \int_a^b \{f(x) - S_\Delta(x)\}\, D^4f(x)\, dx. \tag{3.9.4}$$

The identity (3.9.4) is important in spline theory and is valid for any simple spline $S_\Delta(x)$ on any mesh Δ: $a = x_0 < x_1 < \cdots < x_N = b$ and any function $f(x)$ in $\mathscr{K}^4(a, b)$. Under a number of conditions on $S_\Delta(x)$, this identity reduces to

$$\|f - S_\Delta\|^2 \equiv \int_a^b \{D^2f(x) - D^2S_\Delta(x)\}^2\, dx = \int_a^b \{f(x) - S_\Delta(x)\}\, D^4f(x)\, dx, \tag{3.9.5}$$

which we refer to as the *second integral relation*. In particular, the following theorem is immediate from (3.9.4).

Theorem 3.9.1. *Let* Δ: $a = x_0 < x_1 < \cdots < x_N = b$ *and* $f(x)$ *in* $\mathscr{K}^4(a, b)$ *be given. If* $S_\Delta(f; x)$ *is the spline of interpolation to* $f(x)$ *on* Δ *satisfying one of the conditions* (a) $f(x) - S_\Delta(f; x)$ *is of type* I'; (b) $f(x) - S_\Delta(f; x)$ *is of type* II'; (c) $S_\Delta(f; x)$ *is periodic and* $f(x)$ *belongs to* $\mathscr{K}_P^4(a, b)$; *then*

$$\|f - S_{\Delta,f}\|^2 \equiv \int_a^b \{D^2f(x) - D^2S_\Delta(f; x)\}^2\, dx = \int_a^b \{f(x) - S_\Delta(f; x)\}\, D^4f(x)\, dx. \tag{3.9.6}$$

REMARK 3.9.1. If $f(x)$ is in $\mathscr{K}^2(a\ b)$, the statement "$f(x) - S_\Delta(f; x)$ is of type II" is not well defined, since $f''(x)$ may not exist at $x = a$ or $x = b$. In the present case, $f''(x)$ is in $\mathscr{K}^4(a, b)$, and so the statement is meaningful.

3.10. Raising the Order of Convergence

Let $f(x)$, $\{\Delta_N\}$ $(N = 1, 2, \ldots)$, and $\{S_{\Delta_N, f}\}$ $(N = 1, 2, \ldots)$ satisfy the conditions of Theorem 3.9.1. By the argument in Section 3.8, we have

$$|f^{(\alpha)}(x) - S^{(\alpha)}_{\Delta_N}(f; x)| \leqslant \|f - S_{\Delta_N, f}\| \cdot \|\Delta_N\|^{(3-2\alpha)/2} \qquad (\alpha = 0, 1), \quad (3.10.1)$$

and, since the second integral relation is valid, (3.10.1) becomes

$$\begin{aligned} &|f^{(\alpha)}(x) - S^{(\alpha)}_{\Delta_N}(f; x)| \\ &\leqslant \left\{\int_a^b |f(x) - S_{\Delta_N}(f; x)| \cdot |D^4 f(x)|\, dx\right\}^{1/2} \cdot \|\Delta_N\|^{(3-2\alpha)/2} \\ &\leqslant \left\{\int_a^b |D^4 f(x)|\, dx\right\}^{1/2} \cdot \{\sup_{x \in [a, b]} |f(x) - S_{\Delta_N}(f; x)|\}^{1/2} \cdot \|\Delta_N\|^{(3-2\alpha)/2} \qquad (\alpha = 0, 1). \end{aligned} \quad (3.10.2)$$

Setting $\alpha = 0$ and substituting the resulting inequality in the right-hand member of (3.10.2), we obtain

$$|f^{(\alpha)}(x) - S^{(\alpha)}_{\Delta_N}(f; x)| \leqslant \left\{\int_a^b |D^4 f(x)|\, dx\right\}^{J_1} \cdot \{\sup_{x \in [a, b]} |f(x) - S_{\Delta_N}(f; x)|\}^{J_2} \cdot \|\Delta_N\|^{J_3}, \quad (3.10.3.1)$$

where

$$J_1 = \tfrac{1}{2} + \tfrac{1}{4}, \qquad J_2 = \tfrac{1}{4}, \qquad J_3 = \{3(1 + \tfrac{1}{2}) - 2\alpha\}/2. \qquad (3.10.3.2)$$

Again setting $\alpha = 0$ in (3.10.3.1), substituting in the right-hand member of (3.10.2), and repeating this process, we obtain (3.10.3.1), but with

$$\left.\begin{aligned} J_1 &= \tfrac{1}{2} + \tfrac{1}{4} + \cdots + (\tfrac{1}{2})^{2^k} \\ J_2 &= (\tfrac{1}{2})^{2^k} \\ J_3 &= \{3(1 + \tfrac{1}{2} + \cdots + (\tfrac{1}{2})^{2^k - 1}) - 2\alpha\}/2 \end{aligned}\right\} \qquad (3.10.4)$$

at the end of k steps. But, since this is true for any positive integer k, it follows that

$$|f^{(\alpha)}(x) - S^{(\alpha)}_{\Delta_N}(f; x)| \leqslant \int_a^b |D^4 f(x)|\, dx \cdot \|\Delta_N\|^{3-\alpha} \qquad (\alpha = 0, 1). \qquad (3.10.5)$$

This result can be obtained in a more direct manner, for by (3.10.2) we have

$$\sup_{x\in[a,b]} | f(x) - S_{\Delta_N}(f; x) |$$
$$\leqslant \left\{\int_a^b | D^4f(x) | \, dx\right\}^{1/2} \cdot \{\sup_{x\in[a,b]} | f(x) - S_\Delta(f; x) |\}^{1/2} \cdot \| \Delta_N \|^{3/2}.$$

If

$$\sup_{x\in[a,b]} | f(x) - S_{\Delta_N}(f; x) | = 0,$$

there is nothing to prove; otherwise,

$$\sup_{x\in[a,b]} | f(x) - S_{\Delta_N}(f; x) |^{1/2} \leqslant \left\{\int_a^b | D^4f(x) | \, dx\right\}^{1/2} \cdot \| \Delta_N \|^{3/2}, \qquad (3.10.6)$$

which establishes (3.10.5) for $\alpha = 0$. Substituting (3.10.6) in (3.10.2) gives the general case.

We have established by this argument the following theorem.

Theorem 3.10.1. *Let*

$$\{\Delta_N : a = x_0^N < x_1^N < \cdots < x_{m_N}^N = b\} \; (N = 1, 2, \ldots)$$

and $f(x)$ *in* $\mathscr{K}^4(a, b)$ *be given with* $\| \Delta_N \| \to 0$ *as* $N \to \infty$. *If* $S_{\Delta_N}(f; x)$ *is a spline of interpolation to* $f(x)$ *on* Δ_N *and one of the conditions,* (a) $f(x) - S_{\Delta_N}(f; x)$ *is of type I'* $(N = 1, 2, \ldots)$, (b) $f(x) - S_{\Delta_N}(f; x)$ *is of type II'* $(N = 1, 2, \ldots)$, (c) $f(x)$ *is in* $\mathscr{K}_P^4(a, b)$ *and* $S_{\Delta_N}(f; x)$ *is periodic* $(N = 1, 2, \ldots)$, *is satisfied, then*

$$\sup_{x\in[a,b]} | f^{(\alpha)}(x) - S_{\Delta_N}^{(\alpha)}(f; x) | \leqslant \int_a^b | D^4f(x) | \, dx \cdot \| \Delta_N \|^{3-\alpha} \qquad (\alpha = 0, 1).$$

REMARK 3.10.1. If we replace (3.10.1) by the tighter inequality

$$| f^{(\alpha)}(x) - S_{\Delta_N}^{(\alpha)}(f; x) | \leqslant (\tfrac{1}{2})^{1-\alpha} \| f - S_{\Delta_N;f} \|$$
$$\cdot \| \Delta_N \|^{(3-2\alpha)/2} \qquad (\alpha = 0, 1), \qquad (3.10.7)$$

which was established in Section 3.8, then we obtain

$$\sup_{x\in[a,b]} | f^{(\alpha)}(x) - S_{\Delta_N}^{(\alpha)}(f; x) | \leqslant (\tfrac{1}{4})^{1-\alpha} \cdot \int_a^b | D^4f(x) | \, dx \cdot \| \Delta_N \|^{3-\alpha} \qquad (\alpha = 0, 1). \qquad (3.10.8)$$

3.11. Convergence of Higher-Order Derivatives

Let $f(x)$ in $\mathscr{K}^4(a, b)$, Δ: $a = x_0 < x_1 < \cdots < x_N = b$, and $S_\Delta(f; x)$ be given. Then, by (3.7.2) for $x_{i-1} \leqslant x \leqslant x_i$ $(i = 1, 2,\ldots, N)$,

$$S_\Delta(f; x) = \sum_{j=1}^{4} c_{ij} u_j(x - x_{i-1}). \tag{3.11.1}$$

Let $\delta_g^\alpha[c, d]$ denote the αth equally spaced difference quotient of an arbitrary function $g(x)$ on an arbitrary interval $[c, d]$, and interpret $\delta_g^0[c, d]$ as $g(c)$. Then there exists an $x_{i\alpha}$ in $[x_{i-1}, x_i]$ such that

$$\delta_{S_{\Delta,f}}^\alpha[x_{i-1}, x_i] = S_\Delta^{(\alpha)}(f; x_{i\alpha}) \qquad (\alpha = 0, 1, 2, 3).$$

It follows that

$$\delta_{S_{\Delta,f}}^\alpha[x_{i-1}, x_i] = \sum_{j=1}^{4} c_{ij} u_j^{(\alpha)}(x_{i\alpha} - x_{i-1}) \qquad (\alpha = 0, 1, 2, 3), \tag{3.11.2}$$

and when $\| \Delta \| \to 0$ these equations approach*

$$\delta_{S_{\Delta,f}}^\alpha[x_{i-1}, x_i] = c_{i,\alpha+1} \qquad (\alpha = 0, 1, 2, 3). \tag{3.11.3}$$

Consequently, for $\| \Delta \|$ sufficiently small, the system of equations (3.11.2) is solvable, and each c_{ij} is a linear combination of the four quantities $\delta_{S_{\Delta,f}}^\alpha[x_{i-1}, x_i]$ $(\alpha = 0, 1, 2, 3)$. We can, in addition, employ Theorem 3.10.1 to obtain the relations

$$| \delta_{S_{\Delta,f}}^0[x_{i-1}, x_i] - \delta_f^0[x_{i-1}, x_i] | = 0, \tag{3.11.4.1}$$

$$\begin{aligned} | \delta_{S_{\Delta,f}}^1[x_{i-1}, x_i] - \delta_f^1[x_{i-1}, x_i] | &= \left| \frac{\{S_\Delta(f; x_i) - f(x_i)\} - \{S_\Delta(f; x_{i-1}) - f(x_{i-1})\}}{h_i} \right| \\ &\leqslant 2 \int_a^b | D^4 f(x) | \, dx \cdot \frac{\| \Delta \|^3}{h_i}, \end{aligned} \tag{3.11.4.2}$$

* Observe that the functions $u_j^{(\alpha)}(x)$ $(j = 1, 2, 3, 4;\ \alpha = 0, 1, 2, 3)$ are continuous on $[0, b - a]$ and, hence, uniformly continuous and bounded on $[0, b - a]$. As $\| \Delta \| \to 0$, these functions remain fixed and only the points at which they are evaluated vary.

$$\begin{aligned}
&| \delta^2_{S_{\Delta},f}[x_{i-1}, x_i] - \delta^2_f[x_{i-1}, x_i] | \\
&\quad = | \{S_\Delta(f; x_i) - f(x_i)\} - 2\{S_\Delta(f; x_i - \tfrac{1}{2}h_i) - f(x_i - \tfrac{1}{2}h_i)\} \\
&\qquad + \{S_\Delta(f; x_{i-1}) - f(x_{i-1})\} | / (h_i^2/4) \\
&\quad \leqslant 4^2 \cdot \int_a^b | D^4 f(x) | \, dx \cdot \| \Delta \|^3 / h_i^2,
\end{aligned} \tag{3.11.4.3}$$

$$\begin{aligned}
&| \delta^3_{S_{\Delta},f}[x_{i-1}, x_i] - \delta^3_f[x_{i-1}, x_i] | \\
&\quad = | \{S_\Delta(f; x_i) - f(x_i)\} - 3\{S_\Delta(f; x_i - \tfrac{1}{3}h_i) - f(x_i - \tfrac{1}{3}h_i)\} \\
&\qquad + 3\{S_\Delta(f; x_i - \tfrac{2}{3}h_i) - f(x_i - \tfrac{2}{3}h_i)\} - \{S_\Delta(f; x_{i-1}) - f(x_{i-1})\} | \, (h_i^3/27) \\
&\quad \leqslant 3^3 \cdot 2^3 \cdot \int_a^b | D^4 f(x) | \, dx \cdot \| \Delta \|^3 / h_i^3,
\end{aligned} \tag{3.11.4.4}$$

where $h_i = x_i - x_{i-1}$. If $R_\Delta \equiv \max_i \{\| \Delta \| / h_i\}$, we have the general inequality

$$\begin{aligned}
&| \delta^\alpha_{S_{\Delta},f}[x_{i-1}, x_i] - \delta^\alpha_f[x_{i-1}, x_i] | \\
&\quad \leqslant (2\alpha R_\Delta)^\alpha \cdot \int_a^b | D^4 f(x) | \, dx \cdot \| \Delta \|^{3-\alpha} \qquad (\alpha = 0, 1, 2, 3).
\end{aligned} \tag{3.11.5}$$

We observe that an extra factor of $\frac{1}{4}$ can be obtained in the right-hand member of (3.11.5) in view of Remark 3.10.1.

Theorem 3.11.1. *Let a sequence of meshes*

$$\{\Delta_N : a = x_0^N < x_1^N < \cdots < x_{m_N}^N = b\} \; (N = 1, 2, \ldots)$$

with $\| \Delta_N \| \to 0$ *as* $N \to \infty$ *and* $f(x)$ *in* $\mathscr{K}^4(a, b)$ *be given. Let* $R_{\Delta_N} = \max_{i=1,\cdots,m_N} \| \Delta_N \| / (x_i^N - x_{i-1}^N)$ *be bounded with respect to* N, *and let* $\{S_{\Delta_N}(f; x)\}$ $(N = 1, 2, \ldots)$ *be a sequence of splines of interpolation to* $f(x)$ *satisfying one of the conditions,* (a) $f(x) - S_{\Delta_N}(f; x)$ *is of type* I' $(N = 1, 2, \ldots)$, (b) $f(x) - S_{\Delta_N}(f; x)$ *is of type* II' $(N = 1, 2, \ldots)$ *and* $\Delta_1 \subseteq \Delta_N$, (c) $f(x)$ *is in* $\mathscr{K}_P^4(a, b)$, *and each* $S_{\Delta_N}(f; x)$ *is periodic; then*

$$f^{(\alpha)}(x) = S^{(\alpha)}_{\Delta_N}(f; x) + O(\| \Delta_N \|^{3-\alpha}) \qquad (\alpha = 0, 1, 2, 3). \tag{3.11.6}$$

uniformly for x *in* $[a, b]$.

Proof. For some $x_{i\alpha}^N$ in $[x_{i-1}^N, x_i^N]$, we know

$$\delta^\alpha_f[x_{i-1}, x_i] = f^{(\alpha)}(x_{i\alpha}^N) \qquad (\alpha = 0, 1, 2, 3). \tag{3.11.7}$$

Consequently, (3.11.4) implies

$$|\delta^{\alpha}_{S_{\Delta_N},f}[x_{i-1}, x_i]| \leqslant |\delta^{\alpha}_{S_{\Delta_N},f}[x_{i-1}, x_i] - \delta^{\alpha}_{f}[x_{i-1}, x_i]| + |\delta^{\alpha}_{f}[x_{i-1}, x_i]|$$

$$\leqslant (2\alpha \sup_N R_{\Delta_N})^{\alpha} \cdot \int_a^b |D^4 f(x)|\, dx \cdot \|\Delta_N\|^{3-\alpha} + \sup_{x\in[a,b]} |f^{(\alpha)}(x)|$$

$$(\alpha = 0, 1, 2, 3),$$

which, by the hypotheses of our theorem, is bounded as $N \to \infty$. Since the matrix in Eqs. (3.11.2) approaches the identity matrix as $N \to \infty$ uniformly both with respect to the number and location of the mesh intervals $[x_{i-1}, x_i]$, it follows that all the coefficients determining the splines $S_{\Delta_N}(f; x)$ $(N = 1, 2,...)$ are uniformly bounded with respect to N. Therefore, $|S^{(\alpha)}_{\Delta_N}(f; x)|$ is uniformly bounded for $\alpha < 4$ and all N; thus, there exists a real number B such that $|S^{(3)}_{\Delta_N}(f; x)| \leqslant B$ for every N. Since in each mesh interval $[x^N_{i-2}, x^N_i]$ $(i = 2, 3,..., m_N)$ there is an x_{iN} for which $S''_{\Delta_N}(f; x_{iN}) = f''(x_{iN})$,

$$|f''(x) - S''_{\Delta_N}(f; x)| \leqslant \int_{x_{iN}}^{x} |f^{(3)}(x) - S^{(3)}_{\Delta_N}(f; x)|\,|dx|$$

$$\leqslant 2\{\sup_{x\in[a,b]} |f^{(3)}(x)| + B\} \cdot \|\Delta_N\|.$$

More generally, we have

$$|f^{(\alpha)}(x) - S^{(\alpha)}_{\Delta_N}(f; x)| \leqslant 2\{\sup_{x\in[a,b]} |f^{(3)}(x)| + B\} \cdot \|\Delta_N\|^{3-\alpha} \qquad (\alpha = 0, 1, 2).$$

In addition,

$$|f^{(3)}(x) - S^{(3)}_{\Delta_N}(f; x)| \leqslant \{\sup_{x\in[a,b]} |f^{(3)}(x)| + B\} \cdot \|\Delta_N\|^0,$$

which concludes the proof.

REMARK 3.11.1. Observe that, for $\alpha = 0$ and $\alpha = 1$, Theorem 3.10.1 gives more precise bounds on the rate of convergence. Perhaps even more important, no restriction is placed upon the meshes involved; in Theorem 3.11.1, R_{Δ_N} must be bounded as a function of N.

3.12. Limits on the Order of Convergence

In Sections 3.10 and 3.11, we established that

$$f^{(\alpha)}(x) = S^{(\alpha)}_{\Delta_N}(f; x) + O(\|\Delta_N\|^{3-\alpha}) \qquad (\alpha = 0, 1, 2, 3), \qquad (3.12.1)$$

and in Chapter II we established, by more special methods, that

$$f^{(\alpha)}(x) = S_{\Delta_N}^{(\alpha)}(f; x) + O(\| \Delta_N \|^{4-\alpha}) \qquad (\alpha = 0, 1, 2, 3, 4), \quad (3.12.2)$$

although the mesh restrictions and constants involved are not the same in both cases. In particular, the constant in (3.12.1) is proportional to $V_a{}^b[f^{(3)}]$, whereas the constant in (3.12.2) is {when $f(x)$ is in $C^4[a, b]$} proportional to $\| f^{(4)} \|_\infty$; here we have used the standard notations

$$V_a{}^b[f] = \int_a^b | f'(x) | \, dx$$

and

$$\| f \|_\infty = \sup_{x \in [a, b]} | f(x) |.$$

Remark 3.11.1 is indicative of the differences in the mesh restrictions that are required. We have the following theorem, which limits the rate of convergence.

Theorem 3.12.1. *Let* $\{\Delta_N\}$ *be a sequence of meshes with* $\| \Delta_N \| \to 0$ *as* $N \to \infty$ *and* $R \equiv \sup_N R_{\Delta_N} < \infty$. *Let* $f(x)$ *be in* $C^4[a, b]$ *and* $\mu > 0$. *If*

$$f(x) = S_{\Delta_N}(f; x) + O(\| \Delta_N \|^{4+\mu}) \qquad (3.12.3)$$

uniformly for x *in* $[a, b]$, *then*

$$D^4 f(x) \equiv 0.$$

Proof. Just as in Section 3.11, we can show

$$| \delta_{S_{\Delta_N}}^4 [x_{i-1}^N, x_i^N] - \delta_f^4 [x_{i-1}^N, x_i^N] | \leqslant 8^4 \cdot R^4 \cdot V_a{}^b[f^{(3)}] \cdot \| \Delta_N \|^\mu .$$

Thus, for any $\epsilon > 0$ and N sufficiently large, $| \delta_f^4 [x_{i-1}^N, x_i^N] | < \epsilon$, since $\delta_{S_{\Delta_N}}^4 [x_{i-1}^N, x_i^N] = 0$ for all N. In addition, we know that, for some x_{iN} in $[x_{i-1}^N, x_i^N]$, $\delta_f^4 [x_{i-1}^N, x_i^N] = f^{(4)}(x_{iN})$. Since $f^{(4)}(x)$ is uniformly continuous on $[a, b]$, it follows that

$$| f^{(4)}(x) | \leqslant | f^{(4)}(x) - f^{(4)}(x_{iN}) | + | f^{(4)}(x_{iN}) | < 2\epsilon$$

for $\| \Delta_N \|$ sufficiently small. This proves the theorem.

3.13. Hilbert Space Interpretation

The class $\mathcal{K}^2(a, b)$ defined in Section 3.1 is a Hilbert space under the inner product

$$(f, g) = \int_a^b f''(x)g''(x)\,dx \tag{3.13.1}$$

if one makes allowance for the pseudo-character of the inner product. For any mesh Δ: $a = x_0 < x_1 < \cdots < x_N = b$, the family, F_Δ, of all cubic splines on Δ is clearly a linear subspace of $\mathcal{K}^2(a, b)$. Since a non-periodic cubic spline on Δ is determined by its values on Δ and the values of its first derivative at x_0 and x_N (which can be taken as its defining values*), this subspace has dimension $N + 3$, or $N + 1$ if we allow for the fact that we are actually interested in the equivalence classes modulo the two-dimensional subspace of linear functions on $[a, b]$. In this sense the subspace, P_Δ, of periodic cubic splines has dimension $N - 1$. Since both F_Δ and P_Δ are finite dimensional, they are closed subspaces of $\mathcal{K}^2(a, b)$ with respect to the norm

$$\|f\| = (f, f)^{1/2} \tag{3.13.2}$$

determined by (3.13.1). If $\Delta_1 \subset \Delta_2$, then $F_{\Delta_1} \subset F_{\Delta_2}$ and $P_{\Delta_1} \subset P_{\Delta_2}$. The Gram-Schmidt orthogonalization procedure allows us to introduce an orthonormal basis into either F_Δ or P_Δ.†

If $\Delta_N \subset \Delta_{N+1}$, we denote by $[F_{\Delta_{N+1}} - F_{\Delta_N}]$ the subset of $F_{\Delta_{N+1}}$ consisting of splines $S_{\Delta_{N+1}}(x)$ which vanish at the mesh points of Δ_N and whose first derivatives vanish at $x = a$ and $x = b$. Thus, $[F_{\Delta_{N+1}} - F_{\Delta_N}]$ is the subset of $F_{\Delta_{N+1}}$ consisting of splines whose defining values on Δ_N vanish. Similarly, $[P_{\Delta_{N+1}} - P_{\Delta_N}]$ is the subset of $P_{\Delta_{N+1}}$ consisting of splines whose defining values on Δ_N vanish. We recall that, if $\{V_i\}$ $(i = 1, 2,\ldots)$ is a sequence of mutually orthogonal subspaces of $\mathcal{K}^2(a, b)$, then the infinite direct sum

$$V_\infty = V_1 \oplus V_2 \oplus \cdots$$

is the smallest linear subspace of $\mathcal{K}^2(a, b)$ which contains all the finite direct sums

$$V_1 \oplus V_2 \oplus \cdots \oplus V_N \qquad (N = 1, 2,\ldots)$$

* We assume, here and in the remainder of Chapter III, the defining values to be the quantities $\alpha y_i' + \beta y_i''$ and y_i in the Y vector [(3.7.7.7) or (3.7.7.13)] appropriate to the spline under consideration.

† In this section we speak of splines rather than equivalence classes of splines in order to simplify the arguments.

and is closed with respect to the norm (3.13.2). An element v in V_∞ has a unique representation

$$v = \sum_{i=1}^{\infty} v_i ,$$

where v_i is in V_i $(i = 1, 2, \ldots)$.

Let $\{\Delta_N\}$ $(N = 1, 2, \ldots)$ be a sequence of meshes on $[a, b]$ with $\Delta_N \subset \Delta_{N+1}$. Then, if $N \neq \bar{N}$, $[F_{\Delta_N} - F_{\Delta_{N-1}}]$ and $[F_{\Delta_{\bar{N}}} - F_{\Delta_{\bar{N}-1}}]$ have only the zero spline in common. Assume $\bar{N} > N$; then if $S(x)$ is in $[F_{\Delta_N} - F_{\Delta_{N-1}}]$, it is a spline on Δ_N; if $S(x)$ is in $[F_{\Delta_{\bar{N}}} - F_{\Delta_{\bar{N}-1}}]$, its defining values on Δ_N vanish. Consequently, $S(x)$ is a spline on Δ_N whose defining values on Δ_N vanish; therefore, $S(x)$ vanishes identically. We observe that $\mathscr{K}_P^2(a, b)$ is not a closed subspace of $\mathscr{K}^2(a, b)$ but is dense in $\mathscr{K}^2(a, b)$ (cf. Section 6.14). We now raise the question, "Given a sequence of meshes, when are the associated sequences of linear spaces $\{F_{\Delta_N}\}$ and $\{P_{\Delta_N}]$ such that

$$F_{\Delta_\infty} \equiv F_{\Delta_1} \oplus \sum_{N=2}^{\infty} \oplus [F_{\Delta_N} - F_{\Delta_{N-1}}] = \mathscr{K}^2(a, b), \tag{3.13.3}$$

$$P_{\Delta_\infty} \equiv P_{\Delta_1} \oplus \sum_{N=2}^{\infty} \oplus [P_{\Delta_N} - P_{\Delta_{N-1}}] = \mathscr{K}^2(a, b)\text{?''} \tag{3.13.4}$$

In Section 3.14, we obtain an important set of sufficient conditions for this to be the case. We note that, since $F_{\Delta_\infty} \subseteq \mathscr{K}^2(a, b)$, it is sufficient to show that, for any $f(x)$ in $\mathscr{K}^2(a, b)$ and an orthonormal basis $\{v_i(x)\}$ for F_{Δ_∞},

$$\lim_{N\to\infty} \left\| f - \sum_{i=1}^{N} (f, v_i)v_i \right\| = 0. \tag{3.13.5}$$

Similar remarks apply to P_{Δ_∞} and $\mathscr{K}_P^2(a, b)$, since the latter is dense in $\mathscr{K}^2(a, b)$. We show in Section 3.14 that the component spaces in (3.13.3) are mutually orthogonal so that the decomposition (3.13.3) is defined; we do the same for the decomposition (3.13.4).

3.14. Convergence in Norm

In Section 3.14, we establish two important theorems, the first of which is a convergence theorem that could have been included in Section 3.8.

Theorem 3.14.1. *Let $\{\Delta_N\}$ $(N = 1, 2,...)$ be a sequence of meshes with $\Delta_N \subset \Delta_{N+1}$ and $\| \Delta_N \| \to 0$ as $N \to \infty$. Let $f(x)$ in $\mathscr{K}^2(a, b)$ be given, and let $\{S_{\Delta_N}(f; x)\}$ $(N = 1, 2,...)$ be a sequence of splines of interpolation to $f(x)$ on the meshes Δ_N such that one of the conditions,* (a) *$f(x) - S_{\Delta_N}(f; x)$ is of type I' $(N = 1, 2,...)$,* (b) *$S_{\Delta_N}(f; x)$ is of type II' $(N = 1, 2,...)$,* (c) *$f(x)$ and $S_{\Delta_N}(f; x)$ are in $\mathscr{K}_P^2(a, b)$ $(N = 1, 2,...)$, is satisfied. Then*

$$\lim_{N\to\infty} \| f - S_{\Delta_N,f} \| = 0. \tag{3.14.1}$$

Proof. If $N_1 < N_2$, then the minimum norm property implies that

$$\| S_{\Delta_{N_1},f} \| \leqslant \| S_{\Delta_{N_2},f} \|, \tag{3.14.2}$$

since $S_{\Delta_{N_2}}(f; x)$ is in $\mathscr{K}^2(a, b)$ and $S_{\Delta_{N_1}}(f; x)$ is the spline of interpolation to $S_{\Delta_{N_2}}(f; x)$ on Δ_{N_1} satisfying one of the conditions (a), (b), or (c). The sequence of real numbers $\{\| S_{\Delta_N,f} \|\}$ therefore is monotone increasing and is bounded above by $\| f \|$, the latter property again being a consequence of the minimum norm property. It follows that $\{\| S_{\Delta_N,f} \|\}$ is a Cauchy sequence of real numbers. By the same argument used to establish (3.14.2), we know that the first integral relation applies to $S_{\Delta_{N_1}}(f; x)$ and $S_{\Delta_{N_2}}(f; x)$. As a result, we have

$$\| S_{\Delta_{N+p},f} - S_{\Delta_N,f} \|^2 = \| S_{\Delta_{N+p},f} \|^2 - \| S_{\Delta_N,f} \|^2 \qquad (p = 1, 2,...), \tag{3.14.3}$$

which implies that $\{S''_{\Delta_N}(f; x)\}$ is a Cauchy sequence in $L^2(a, b)$. Since $L^2(a, b)$ is complete, we can find a function $g(x)$ in $L^2(a, b)$ such that

$$\lim_{N\to\infty} \int_a^b \{g(x) - S''_{\Delta_N}(f; x)\}^2 \, dx = 0. \tag{3.14.4}$$

Let

$$G(x) = f'(a) + \int_a^x g(x) \, dx; \tag{3.14.5}$$

then

$$| G(x) - S'_{\Delta_N}(f; x) | \leqslant \int_a^x | g(x) - S''_{\Delta_N}(f; x) | \, dx + | f'(a) - S'_{\Delta_N}(f; a) |$$

$$\leqslant \left\{ \int_a^b \{g(x) - S''_{\Delta_N}(f; x)\}^2 \, dx \cdot (b-a) \right\}^{1/2} + | f'(a) - S'_{\Delta_N}(f; a) |$$

by Schwarz's inequality. Consequently, (3.14.4) implies that for each x in [a, b]

$$\lim_{N\to\infty} | G(x) - S'_{\Delta_N}(f; x) | = 0, \tag{3.14.6}$$

since

$$\lim_{N\to\infty} |f'(x) - S'_{\Delta_N}(f; x)| = 0 \tag{3.14.7}$$

uniformly for x in $[a, b]$ by Theorem 3.8.1. Indeed, since

$$|f'(x) - G(x)| \leqslant |f'(x) - S'_{\Delta_N}(f; x)| + |G(x) - S'_{\Delta_N}(f; x)|,$$

$f'(x)$ must be identical with $G(x)$. This, however, implies that $f''(x) = g(x)$ a.e., which establishes the theorem.

Theorem 3.14.1 and Lemma 3.14.1 below provide the major tools needed to demonstrate the validity of the decompositions (3.13.3) and (3.13.4).

Lemma 3.14.1. *Let $\Delta_1 \subset \Delta_2$ be two meshes on $[a, b]$. If $S_{\Delta_1}(x)$ and $S_{\Delta_2}(x)$ are splines on Δ_1 and Δ_2, respectively, such that $S_{\Delta_2}(x)$ vanishes on Δ_1, then $(S_{\Delta_1}, S_{\Delta_2}) = 0$ if $S_{\Delta_1}(x)$ is of type II', or $S_{\Delta_2}(x)$ is of type I', or both $S_{\Delta_1}(x)$ and $S_{\Delta_2}(x)$ are periodic.*

Proof. Let Δ_1 be defined by $a = x_0 < x_1 < \cdots < x_N = b$. If we integrate $(S_{\Delta_1}, S_{\Delta_2})$ by parts twice, then

$$\begin{aligned}(S_{\Delta_1}, S_{\Delta_2}) &\equiv \int_a^b S''_{\Delta_1}(x) \cdot S''_{\Delta}(x)\, dx = \sum_{i=1}^{N} \int_{x_{i-1}}^{x_1} S''_{\Delta_1}(x) \cdot S''_{\Delta_2}(x)\, dx \\ &= \sum_{i=1}^{N} \{S''_{\Delta_1}(x) \cdot S'_{\Delta_2}(x) \,|_{x_{i-1}}^{x_i} - S'''_{\Delta_1}(x) \cdot S_{\Delta_2}(x) \,|_{x_{i-1}}^{x_i}\} \\ &= S''_{\Delta_1}(x) \cdot S'_{\Delta_2}(x) \,|_a^b = 0,\end{aligned}$$

which proves the lemma.

Theorem 3.14.2. *Let $\{\Delta_N\}$ $(N = 1, 2, \ldots)$ be a sequence of meshes with $\Delta_N \subset \Delta_{N+1}$ and $\| \Delta_N \| \to 0$ as $N \to \infty$. For each N, let F_{Δ_N} be the linear space of cubic splines on Δ_N, P_{Δ_N} the subspace of periodic splines, and F'_{Δ_N} the subspace of type II' cubic splines. Then we have*

$$\mathscr{K}^2(a, b) = F_{\Delta_1} \oplus \sum_{N=2}^{\infty} \oplus [F_{\Delta_N} - F_{\Delta_{N-1}}] \equiv F_{\Delta_\infty}, \tag{3.14.8}$$

$$\mathscr{K}^2(a, b) = F'_{\Delta_1} \oplus \sum_{N=2}^{\infty} \oplus [F'_{\Delta_N} - F'_{\Delta_{N-1}}] \equiv F'_{\Delta_\infty}, \tag{3.14.9}$$

$$\mathscr{K}^2(a, b) = P_{\Delta_1} \oplus \sum_{N=2}^{\infty} \oplus [P_{\Delta_N} - P_{\Delta_{N-1}}] \equiv P_{\Delta_\infty}. \tag{3.14.10}$$

Proof. We prove only (3.14.8), since the proof of (3.14.9) and (3.14.10) are completely analogous. By definition, F_{Δ_∞} is closed, and consequently we have the decomposition

$$\mathscr{K}^2(a, b) = F_{\Delta_\infty} \oplus G_{\Delta_\infty}, \qquad (3.14.11)$$

where G_{Δ_∞} denotes the orthogonal complement of F_{Δ_∞}. Since $F_{\Delta_\infty} \subseteq \mathscr{K}^2(a, b)$, we need only prove that $f(x)$ is in F_{Δ_∞} if it is in $\mathscr{K}^2(a, b)$. Let $\{S_{\Delta_N}(f; x)\}$ $(N = 1, 2, \ldots)$ be the sequence of type I splines of interpolation to $f(x)$ determined by $\{\Delta_N\}$ such that $f(x) - S_{\Delta_N}(f; x)$ is of type I' for each N. Then, by Theorem 3.14.1,

$$\lim_{N\to\infty} \| f - S_{\Delta_N,f} \| = 0. \qquad (3.14.12)$$

This proves the theorem, since F_{Δ_∞} is closed, and Lemma 3.14.1 establishes the orthogonality of the component spaces.

REMARK 3.14.1. In establishing (3.14.9) and (3.14.10), we choose the sequence $\{S_{\Delta_N}(f; x)\}$ to consist of type II′ splines or periodic splines, respectively. In (3.14.9), for each N, $[F'_{\Delta_N} - F'_{\Delta_{N-1}}]$ is the family of type II′ splines on Δ_N whose defining values on Δ_{N-1} vanish. In the periodic case we also use the fact that $\mathscr{K}_p^2(a, b)$ is dense in $\mathscr{K}^2(a, b)$. We consider this in greater detail in Section 6.14.

3.15. Canonical Mesh Bases and Their Properties

Let $\{\Delta_N\}$ $(N = 1, 2, \ldots)$ be a sequence of meshes on $[a, b]$ with $\Delta_N \subset \Delta_{N+1}$. We assume that we are given an orthonormal basis for F_{Δ_1}, and we extend this to an orthonormal basis for F_{Δ_∞} by constructing an orthonormal basis for the orthogonal complement, $[F_{\Delta_\infty} - F_{\Delta_1}]$, of F_{Δ_1} with respect to F_{Δ_∞}. The construction yields for every N an orthonormal basis for $[F_{\Delta_N} - F_{\Delta_1}]$. The same method yields with slight modifications orthonormal bases for $[F'_{\Delta_\infty} - F'_{\Delta_1}]$ and $[P_{\Delta_\infty} - P_{\Delta_1}]$. Theorem 3.14.2 then shows that this construction provides explicit orthonormal bases for $\mathscr{K}^2[a, b]$ if $\| \Delta_N \| \to 0$ as $N \to \infty$. We call *mesh bases* these orthonormal bases for $[F_{\Delta_\infty} - F_{\Delta_1}]$, $[F'_{\Delta_\infty} - F'_{\Delta_1}]$, and $[P_{\Delta_\infty} - P_{\Delta_1}]$.

Consider the set M of all distinct mesh points determined by the sequence of meshes $\{\Delta_N\}$ excluding those that comprise Δ_1. Since M is denumerable, let it have a specific enumeration

$$M = \{P_1, P_2, \ldots\}. \qquad (3.15.1)$$

In the case where only a mesh basis for $[F_{\Delta_N} - F_{\Delta_1}]$ is desired, M has only a finite number of elements and is denoted by M_N. Let Δ_{11} be the mesh obtained by inserting the point P_1 into the mesh Δ_1, and let $\mu_1(x)$ be the type I′ spline on Δ_{11} such that $\mu_1(P_1) = 1$ and $\mu_1(x)$ vanishes on Δ_1. If Δ_{1i} is the mesh obtained by inserting P_i into the mesh $\Delta_{1,i-1}$ ($\Delta_{1,0} = \Delta_1$), then $\mu_i(x)$ is the type I′ spline on Δ_{1i} such that $\mu_i(P_i) = 1$ and $\mu_i(x)$ vanishes on $\Delta_{1,i-1}$. Lemma 3.14.1 assures us that the sequence $\{\mu_i(x)\}$ $(i = 1, 2,...)$ consists of mutually orthogonal type I′ splines and by the manner of its construction is a basis for $[F_{\Delta_{1,\infty}} - F_{\Delta_1}]$, where

$$F_{\Delta_{1,\infty}} \equiv F_{\Delta_1} \oplus [F_{\Delta_{11}} - F_{\Delta_1}] \oplus [F_{\Delta_{12}} - F_{\Delta_{11}}] \oplus \cdots .$$

Suppose

$$\phi_i(x) = \frac{\mu_i(x)}{\| \mu_i(x) \|} \qquad (i = 1, 2,...); \tag{3.15.2}$$

the resulting sequence $\{\phi_i(x)\}$ $(i = 1, 2,...)$ of orthonormal type I′ splines is a basis for $[F_{\Delta_{1,\infty}} - F_{\Delta_1}]$. By proceeding in a similar manner, but requiring that $\mu_i(x)$ be of type II′ or periodic, we are led to mesh bases for $[F'_{\Delta_{1,\infty}} - F'_{\Delta_1}]$ and $[P_{\Delta_{1,\infty}} - P_{\Delta_1}]$, respectively, where the additional definitions needed are obvious.

These bases are not unique, since the construction depends on how M is enumerated; moreover, they are not the desired bases for $[F_{\Delta_\infty} - F_{\Delta_1}]$, $[F'_{\Delta_\infty} - F'_{\Delta_1}]$, and $[P_{\Delta_\infty} - P_{\Delta_1}]$. If, however, the process exhausts the points of Δ_N for each N before any points not in Δ_N are enumerated, then we obtain the desired mesh bases. We single out one natural way of making this type of enumeration and refer to the mesh bases generated by it as *canonical mesh bases*. The enumeration employed in their construction consists of ordering from left to right for each N the mesh points that are in Δ_N but not in Δ_{N-1}. Thus, when a mesh basis is canonical, its construction is completely defined and depends on a given sequence of meshes. Any mesh basis is canonical, however, with respect to the auxiliary sequence of meshes $\{\Delta_{1,i}\}$ $(i = 0, 1,...)$ used in its construction.

Lemma 3.15.1. *Let $\{\phi_i(x)\}$ $(i = 1, 2,...)$ be a canonical mesh basis for $[F_{\Delta_\infty} - F_{\Delta_1}]$, $[F'_{\Delta_\infty} - F'_{\Delta_1}]$, or $[P_{\Delta_\infty} - P_{\Delta_1}]$ determined by a sequence of meshes $\{\Delta_N\}$ $(N = 1, 2,...)$ with $\Delta_N \subset \Delta_{N+1}$. Let $\{\Delta_{1i}\}$ $(i = 1, 2,...)$ be the related sequence of meshes used in the construction of $\{\phi_i(x)\}$. Then*

$$| \phi_i^{(\alpha)}(x) | \leqslant 2^{1/2} \| \Delta_{1i} \|^{(3-2\alpha)/2} \qquad (\alpha = 0, 1; \quad i = 1, 2,...). \tag{3.15.3}$$

Proof. Let Δ_{1i} be determined by $a = x_0^i < x_1^i < \cdots < x_{m_i}^i = b$. For any x in $[a, b]$, we can find an interval $x_{j-2}^i \leqslant x \leqslant x_j^i$ such that $\sigma_i(x_{j-2}^i) = \sigma_i(x_j^i) = 0$, since $\sigma_i(x)$ vanishes on $\Delta_{1,i-1}$. Therefore, we can find an x_{ij} in $[x_{j-2}^i, x_j^i]$ such that $\sigma_i'(x_{ij}) = 0$. It follows with the help of Schwarz's inequality that

$$| \sigma_i'(x) | \leqslant \int_{x_{ij}}^{x} | \sigma_i''(x) | \, | dx | \leqslant \| \sigma_i(x) \| \cdot | x - x_{ij} |^{1/2} \leqslant 2^{1/2} \| \Delta_{1i} \|^{1/2}.$$

If x is in $[x_{j-1}^i, x_j^i]$, then either $\sigma_i(x_{j-1}^i) = 0$ or $\sigma_i(x_j^i) = 0$. Consequently, we can assume with no loss of generality that $\sigma_i(x_{j-1}^i) = 0$. Thus,

$$| \sigma_i(x) | \leqslant \int_{x_{j-1}^i}^{x} | \sigma_i'(x) | \, dx \leqslant 2^{1/2} \| \Delta_{1i} \|^{3/2},$$

which concludes the proof.

Observe that for each N there is an i_N such that $\Delta_N = \Delta_{1,i_N}$; consequently, if $\| \Delta_N \| \to 0$ as $N \to \infty$, then $\| \Delta_{1i} \| \to 0$ as $i \to \infty$. If we assume that $\| \Delta_{1i} \| \to 0$ as $i \to \infty$ at a reasonable rate, we obtain the following theorem.

Theorem 3.15.1. *Let $\{\sigma_i(x)\}$ $(i = 1, 2, \ldots)$ be a canonical mesh basis such that $\| \Delta_{1i} \| \leqslant K/i$ for some $K > 0$ that is independent of i. Then there exists a real number $B > 0$ such that*

$$\sum_{i=1}^{\infty} \{\sigma_i(x)\}^2 < B < \infty.$$

Proof. Lemma 3.15.1 justifies the following calculation, which proves the theorem:

$$\sum_{i=1}^{\infty} \{\sigma_i(x)\}^2 \leqslant 2 \sum_{i=1}^{\infty} \| \Delta_{1i} \|^3 \leqslant 2K^3 \sum_{i=1}^{\infty} i^{-3} < \infty.$$

REMARK 3.15.1. The conditions imposed on $\{\Delta_{1i}\}$ in Theorem 3.15.1 can normally be verified from the properties of $\{\Delta_N\}$ due to the close relationship existing between the two sequences of meshes.

3.16. Remainder Formulas

Let $f(x)$ in $\mathscr{K}^2(a, b)$ and $\Delta_1 : a = x_0 < x_1 < \cdots < x_K = b$ be given. In addition, let $S_{\Delta_1}(f; x)$ be the type I spline of interpolation to $f(x)$ on

Δ_1 such that $f(x) - S_{\Delta_1}(f; x)$ is of type I'. We now investigate the remainder

$$R(x) \equiv f(x) - S_{\Delta_1}(f; x). \tag{3.16.1}$$

By adding new mesh points at the midpoints of old mesh intervals, we can define a sequence of meshes $\{\Delta_N\}$ ($N = 1, 2,\ldots$), where $\Delta_N \subset \Delta_{N+1}$ and $\| \Delta_N \| \to 0$ as $N \to \infty$. In each Δ_N there will be $(2^{N-1} \cdot K) + 1$ mesh points. If we form the canonical mesh basis $\{\sigma_i(x)\}$ ($i = 1, 2,\ldots$) for $[F_{\Delta_\infty} - F_{\Delta_1}]$ and its associated sequence of meshes $\{\Delta_{1i}\}$ ($i = 1, 2,\ldots$), then

$$\Delta_{1,2^{N-2}K} = \Delta_N \qquad (N = 2, 3,\ldots). \tag{3.16.2}$$

Since

$$\Delta_N \subseteq \Delta_{1i} \subseteq \Delta_{N+1} \qquad (i = 2^{N-2}K, 2^{N-2}K + 1,\ldots, 2^{N-1}K),$$

it follows that

$$\| \Delta_{1i} \| \leqslant \| \Delta_N \| = \frac{1}{2^{N-1}} \cdot \| \Delta_1 \| \leqslant \frac{K \| \Delta_1 \|}{i}, \tag{3.16.3}$$

in view of the fact that $i \leqslant 2^{N-1}K$ implies that $(\frac{1}{2})^{N-1} \leqslant K/i$. Consequently, the conditions of Theorem 3.15.1 are met so that

$$S(x) = \sum_{i=1}^{\infty} \{\sigma_i(x)\}^2 < B < \infty \tag{3.16.4}$$

for some positive real number B. Let

$$K_n(x, t) = \sum_{i=1}^{n} \sigma_i(x)\sigma_i''(t) \qquad (n = 1, 2,\ldots); \tag{3.16.5}$$

then

$$\int_a^b \{K_{n+p}(x, t) - K_n(x, t)\}^2 \, dt = \sum_{i=n+1}^{n+p} \{\sigma_i(x)\}^2 \tag{3.16.6}$$

by the orthonormality of the functions $\sigma_i(t)$. In view of (3.16.6) and (3.16.4), $\{K_n(x, t)\}$ ($n = 1, 2,\ldots$) is a Cauchy sequence in $L^2(a, b)$ for each x in $[a, b]$. The Schwarz inequality shows that it is also a Cauchy sequence in $L(a, b)$ for each x in $[a, b]$. Let $K(x, t)$ denote the common limit; then, by (3.16.4) and (3.16.6), the integral $\int_a^b K(x, t)^2 \, dt$ is uniformly bounded with respect to x. Thus, $K(x, t)$ is in $L^2([a, b] \times [a, b])$.

It also follows that

$$\begin{aligned}\int_a^b K(x,t)f''(t)\,dt &= \lim_{n\to\infty}\int_a^b K_n(x,t)f''(t)\,dt \\ &= \lim_{n\to\infty}\sum_{i=1}^{n}\phi_i(x)\int_a^b \phi_i''(t)f''(t)\,dt \\ &= \lim_{n\to\infty}\sum_{i=1}^{n}(\phi_i, f)\phi_i(x) \\ &= f(x) - S_{\Delta_1}(f;x) = R(x).\end{aligned}$$

We summarize these results in Theorem 3.16.1.

Theorem 3.16.1. *Let $f(x)$ in $\mathscr{K}^2(a,b)$ and Δ_1: $a = x_0 < x_1 < \cdots < x_k = b$ be given. In addition, let $S_{\Delta_1}(f;x)$ be the type I spline of interpolation to $f(x)$ on Δ_1 such that $f(x) - S_{\Delta_1}(f;x)$ is of type I′. Then there exists a kernel $K(x,t)$ in $L^2([a,b]\times[a,b])$ which is in $L(a,b)$ and $L^2(a,b)$ for every x in $[a,b]$ and*

$$R(x) = f(x) - S_{\Delta_1}(f;x) = \int_a^b K(x,t)f''(t)\,dt. \tag{3.16.7}$$

REMARK 3.16.1. Similar kernels can be obtained for type II′ and periodic spline approximations. Observe that the kernels are independent of $f(x)$.

3.17. Transformations Defined by a Mesh

Sard [1963] has used remainder formulas of the form (3.16.7) extensively in the analysis of a wide variety of approximations. The existence of kernels $K(x,t)$ for the case where $f''(x)$ in (3.16.7) is replaced by an arbitrary derivative has been established under very general conditions. The initial results date back to Peano [1913]. In Chapter V, we obtain kernels for spline approximations where derivatives other than the second derivative play the principal role. A more general point of view has been taken by Greville [1964], who has investigated the existence of such kernels when $f''(x)$ is replaced in (3.16.7) by a linear differential operator L of order n.

Greville [1964] also established, for a linear differential operator L and a family of transformations of the form

$$Tf(x) = \sum_{i=0}^{k} a_i(x)f(x_i) \tag{3.17.1}$$

defined by $k+1$ functions $a_i(x)$ in $\mathscr{K}^n(a, b)$ and a mesh Δ: $a = x_0 < x_1 < \cdots < x_k = b$, the result that if

$$R_T f(x) = f(x) - Tf(x) = \int_a^b K_T(x, t) \cdot Lf(t)\, dt, \tag{3.17.2}$$

then

$$\int_a^b \{K_T(x, t)\}^2\, dt \tag{3.17.3}$$

is minimized for each x in $[a, b]$ when the functions $a_i(x)$ in (3.17.1) are selected such that $Tf(x)$ is a generalized type II′ spline of interpolation to $f(x)$ on Δ. This is a partial extension of Schoenberg's [1964b] results on the approximation of linear functionals to the generalized setting. In Chapter VI, we give a more complete extension of Schoenberg's results to generalized splines.

A slightly more general form for the transformation T defined by (3.17.1) is given by

$$Tf(x) = \sum_{i=0}^{k} a_i(x) f(x_i) + b_0(x) f'(x_0) + b_1(x) f'(x_k), \tag{3.17.4}$$

where the additional functions $b_0(x)$ and $b_1(x)$ are also in $\mathscr{K}^n(a, b)$. We restrict ourselves to the case $n = 2$, regard $\mathscr{K}^n(a, b)$ as a Hilbert space with functions differing by a constant identified, and inner product

$$(f, g) = \int_a^b f''(x) g''(x)\, dx + f'(a) g'(a) + f'(b) g'(b), \tag{3.17.5}$$

interpret T and R_T as linear mappings of $\mathscr{K}^2(a, b)$ into itself, and ask, "Under what conditions on the functions $a_i(x)$ $(i = 0, 1, \ldots, k)$, $b_0(x)$, and $b_1(x)$ will $\| R_T \|$ be a minimum?"

We can represent $\mathscr{K}^2(a, b)$ as

$$\mathscr{K}^2(a, b) = F_\Delta \oplus G_\Delta , \tag{3.17.6.1}$$

where

$$G_\Delta = [\mathscr{K}^2(a, b) - F_\Delta] \tag{3.17.6.2}$$

is the orthogonal complement of F_Δ and is identical with the set of all functions in $\mathscr{K}^2(a, b)$ which vanish on Δ and have first derivatives that vanish at $x = a$ and $x = b$. Thus, for $f(x)$ in G_Δ,

$$R_T f(x) = f(x), \tag{3.17.7}$$

which implies $\| R_T \| \geqslant 1$ for all allowable T. A constant function $f(x)$ is equivalent to the zero function, and so we must have Tf equivalent to 0 in this case. Consequently, if we want T to be defined on $\mathscr{K}^2(a, b)$ with the indicated identifications, we must require that

$$\sum_{i=0}^{k} a_i(x)$$

be a constant function of x.

Let the functions $a_i(x)$ be chosen as the cubic type I′ splines on Δ such that $a_i(x_j) = \delta_{ij}$, $b_0(x)$ as the cubic spline on Δ which vanishes at every mesh point of Δ but has a unit first derivative at x_0 and a zero first derivative at x_k, and $b_1(x)$ as the analogous spline to $b_0(x)$ but with prescribed values of the derivatives interchanged. Then $Tf(x)$ is the projection of $f(x)$ on F_Δ. Moreover,

$$\sum_{i=0}^{k} a_i(x)$$

is a constant function of x, in fact identically 1. In this case, the linear mappings T and R_T are projections whose associated linear subspaces F_Δ and G_Δ are orthogonal complements. As a consequence,

$$\| T \| = \| R_T \| = 1. \tag{3.17.8}$$

For this choice of T, not only is T a projection, but, as a projection, it is larger than any other projection in the class of transformations under consideration, since the null space of any other projection of the form (3.17.4) must contain G_Δ. If T is not a projection, then there is a better approximation in $T[\mathscr{K}^2(a, b)]$ to $f(x)$ than $Tf(x)$. If T is a projection and $T_1 > T$ is also a projection, then $T_1 f(x)$ is at least as good an approximation to $f(x)$ as $TF(x)$. Here the measure of goodness of an approximation $Tf(x)$ to $f(x)$ is in terms of the smallness of $\| R_T f \|$.

With slight modifications of (3.17.4), we can define two related classes of transformations where type II′ splines and periodic splines, respectively, play the same role that type I splines play for this class of transformations.

3.18. A Connection with Space Technology

In order to maximize the payload delivered by a rocket, we must minimize the integral of the square of the applied acceleration (Seifert

[1959, 10-2-2]). In a gravitation-free field, this is equivalent to minimizing the integral of the square of the total acceleration. If both initial and terminal position and velocity are prescribed, as well as the time of flight, Theorem 3.4.3 tells us that the resultant trajectory has coordinates, each of which is a cubic with respect to time. This is in agreement with standard engineering analysis (Seifert [1959, 10-3-1]). If intermediate positions are prescribed for times other than the initial and terminal time, the solution is a trajectory whose coordinates are splines with respect to time. Again this follows from Theorem 3.4.3. We observe that the applied acceleration need not be assumed continuous, only square integrable. In standard analysis, the optimization is restricted to acceleration profiles that have second derivatives with respect to time in order to accommodate a double integration by parts. In the proof of Theorem 3.4.3, only the spline is differentiated, not the representative function from the class $\mathscr{K}^2(a, b)$ over which the optimization takes place.

CHAPTER IV

The Polynomial Spline

4.1. Definition and Working Equations

It is natural to attempt to extend the concept of the cubic spline to curves that are composed of segments of polynomial curves of an arbitrary given degree and to investigate extensions of the properties ascribed to the cubic spline in the previous two chapters. The purpose of this chapter is to introduce polynomial splines and to consider their algebraic properties. In the following chapter, a detailed investigation of intrinsic properties of polynomial splines of odd degree is presented.

The first significant item that one encounters in the extension to polynomial splines is that there is an essential difference between splines of even and odd degree. One finds, for example, that polynomial splines of even degree interpolating to a prescribed function at mesh points need not exist. For this reason, the definition of an odd-degree spline of interpolation which does, in fact, yield the expected extensions of cubic spline properties must be modified for splines of even degree.

We consider first the number of degrees of freedom involved. For polynomial splines of degree $2n - 1$ on a mesh Δ:

$$a = x_0 < x_1 < \cdots < x_N = b,$$

there are $2nN$ constants to be determined. Requiring derivatives of orders 0, 1,..., $2n - 2$ to be continuous at each interior mesh point accounts for $(2n - 1)(N - 1)$ degrees of freedom, leaving $N + 2n - 1$. We require interpolation at the $N + 1$ mesh points and impose $n - 1$ end conditions at $x = x_0$ and at $x = x_N$.

For splines of degree $2n$, we have $(2n + 1)N$ degrees of freedom. Requiring continuity for derivatives of orders 0, 1,..., $2n - 1$ at interior mesh points yields $2n(N - 1)$ conditions. The remaining $2n + N$ are n end conditions at $x = x_0$ and at $x = x_N$ with one condition for interpolation in each interval. A natural procedure to be used for N data points is to take mesh points midway between data points (points of interpolation) with end intervals bisected by the first and last data points.

In this chapter, no attempt is made at completeness in the discussion of even-degree splines. They are introduced principally in situations in which they combine with odd-degree splines to help clarify the total picture.

For a polynomial spline $S_\Delta(x)$ of degree k on a mesh Δ, then, we require interpolation to a prescribed function $f(x)$ at the points of the mesh if k is odd, and at interval mid-points

$$\xi_i \ (i = 1,\ldots, N; \quad x_{i-1} < \xi_i < x_i)$$

when k is even. Periodic splines of degree $2n - 1$ or $2n$ on Δ satisfy, in addition, the requirements $S_\Delta^{(q)}(x_0 +) = S_\Delta^{(q)}(x_N -)$ for $q = 0, 1,\ldots, 2n - 2$ and $q = 0, 1,\ldots, 2n - 1$, respectively.

From the Taylor theorem with integral remainder, we have

$$S_\Delta(x) = \sum_{j=0}^{k-2} \frac{1}{j!} (x - a)^j S_\Delta^{(j)}(a) + \frac{1}{(k-2)!} \int_a^x S_\Delta^{(k-1)}(t)(x - t)^{k-2}\, dt.$$

For the spline of degree $2n - 1$, we employ this expansion in the form

$$S_\Delta(x_i) = \sum_{k=0}^{2n-3} \frac{1}{k!} (x_i - a)^k S_\Delta^{(k)}(a) + \frac{1}{(2n-3)!} \int_a^b S_\Delta^{(2n-2)}(t)(x_i - t)_+^{2n-3}\, dt, \tag{4.1.1}$$

where, for $m \geqslant 0$,

$$\begin{aligned} x_+^m &= 0, & x &\leqslant 0, \\ &= x^m, & x &> 0. \end{aligned}$$

In this notation, the unit step function with step at $x = 0$ is x_+^0.

When $N \geqslant 2n - 2$ and $n - 1 \leqslant i \leqslant N - n + 1$, taking centered divided differences,

$$\delta_i^{2n-2} f(x_i) = f[x_{i-n+1}, x_{i-n+2}, \ldots, x_{i+n-1}],$$

gives

$$\delta_i^{2n-2} S_\Delta(x_i) = \frac{1}{(2n-3)!} \delta_i^{2n-2} \sum_{j=1}^{N} \int_{x_{j-1}}^{x_j} \left[S_\Delta^{(2n-2)}(x_{j-1}) \frac{x_j - t}{h_j} + S_\Delta^{(2n-2)}(x_j) \frac{t - x_{j-1}}{h_j} \right] \times (x_i - t)_+^{2n-3}\, dt, \tag{4.1.2}$$

inasmuch as $S_\Delta^{(2n-2)}(x)$ is linear on each interval (x_{j-1}, x_j), and the first term of (4.1.1) is a polynomial of degree $2n - 3$ in x_i. We have

$d(x_i - t)_+^n/dt = -n(x_i - t)_+^{n-1}$ for $n \geqslant 1$. Thus integration by parts gives, for the right-hand member of (4.1.2),

$$\frac{1}{(2n-3)!}\,\delta_i^{2n-2}\sum_{j=1}^{N}\left\{-\left[\left(M_{j-1}\frac{x_j - t}{h_j} + M_j\frac{t - x_{j-1}}{h_j}\right)\frac{(x_i - t)_+^{2n-2}}{2n-2}\right]_{x_{j-1}}^{x_j}\right.$$

$$\left. - \left[\frac{M_j - M_{j-1}}{h_j}\,\frac{(x_i - t)_+^{2n-1}}{(2n-2)(2n-1)}\right]_{x_{j-1}}^{x_j}\right\}$$

$$= \frac{1}{(2n-2)!}\,\delta_i^{2n-2}\left\{-\sum_{j=1}^{N}[M_j(x_i - x_j)_+^{2n-2} - M_{j-1}(x_i - x_{j-1})_+^{2n-2}]\right\}$$

$$- \frac{1}{(2n-1)!}\,\delta_i^{2n-2}\left\{\sum_{j=1}^{N}\frac{M_j - M_{j-1}}{h_j}[(x_i - x_j)_+^{2n-1} - (x_i - x_{j-1})_+^{2n-1}]\right\}$$

$$= \frac{1}{(2n-2)!}\,\delta_i^{2n-2}M_0\left\{(x_i - x_0)_+^{2n-2} + \frac{(x_i - x_1)_+^{2n-1} - (x_i - x_0)_+^{2n-1}}{(2n-1)h_1}\right\}$$

$$+ \frac{1}{(2n-1)!}\sum_{j=1}^{N}M_j(h_j + h_{j+1})\,\delta_i^{2n-2}\,\delta_j^2\,(x_i - x_j)_+^{2n-1}, \tag{4.1.3}$$

where $M_j = S_\Delta^{(2n-2)}(x_j)$.

The function $\delta_j^2(x - x_j)_+^{2n-1}$ is identically zero for $x \leqslant x_{j-1}$ and on $x \geqslant x_{j+1}$ coincides with a polynomial of degree $2n - 3$. Thus, $\delta_i^{2n-2}\delta_j^2(x_i - x_j)_+^{2n-1} = 0$ for $i \leqslant j - n$ and for $i \geqslant j + n$. If $i \geqslant 1$, then $(x_i - x_0)_+^{2n-2} + [(x_i - x_1)_+^{2n-1} - (x_i - x_0)_+^{2n-1}]/h_1(2n-1)$ is a polynomial of degree $2n - 3$ in x_i. Thus,

$$\delta_i^{2n-2}\{(x_i - x_0)_+^{2n-2} + [(x_i - x_1)_+^{2n-1} - (x_i - x_0)_+^{2n-1}]/h_1(2n-1)\} = 0 \quad \text{if} \quad i \geqslant n.$$

For $i = n - 1$, we may rewrite the coefficient of M_0 as

$$\frac{1}{(2n-2)!}\,\delta_i^{2n-2}\left[\frac{(x_i - x_1)_+^{2n-1} - (x_i - x_1)^{2n-1}}{(2n-1)h_1}\right]_{i=n-1}$$

$$= \frac{h_1^{2n-2}}{(2n-1)!\prod_{j=1}^{2n-2}(h_1 + \cdots + h_j)}\,. \tag{4.1.4.1}$$

We may show by simple differencing that

$$\frac{1}{(2n-2)!}\,(h_{i-n+1} + h_{i-n+2})[\delta_i^{2n-2}\,\delta_j^2(x_i - x_j)_+^{2n-1}]_{j=i-n+1}$$

$$= \frac{(h_{i-n+2})^{2n-2}}{(2n-1)!\prod_{j=i-\ +2}^{i+n-1}(h_{i-n+2} + \cdots + h_j)}\,. \tag{4.1.4.2}$$

For $n - 1 \leqslant i \leqslant N - n + 1$, we may write (4.1.2) as

$$\sum_{j=i-n+1}^{j=i+n-1} A_{ij} M_j = \delta_i^{2n-2} S_\Delta(x_i), \tag{4.1.5}$$

where

$$A_{ij} = \frac{1}{(2n-1)!} (h_j + h_{j+1})\, \delta_i^{2n-2}\, \delta_j^2 (x_i - x_j)_+^{2n-1}, \tag{4.1.6}$$

provided we define, in accordance with (4.1.4),

$$\frac{1}{(2n-1)!} (h_0 + h_1)[\delta_i^{2n-2}\, \delta_j^2 (x_i - x_j)_+^{2n-1}]_{\substack{i=n-1\\ j=0}} = \frac{h_1^{\,2n-2}}{(2n-1)! \prod_{j=1}^{2n-2} (h_1 + \cdots + h_j)}\,.$$

In the periodic case, where we designate $x_{j-N} = x_j - (b - a)$ and $x_{j+N} = x_j + (b - a)$ and employ the periodic character of $S_\Delta(x)$, the term in M_0 in (4.1.3) drops out, and (4.1.5) is valid for each point of the mesh.

We note that, since the quantities A_{ij} are independent of $S_\Delta(x)$, we may replace $S_\Delta(x)$ in (4.1.5) by the function x^{2n-2} which is itself a spline of degree $2n - 1$ on the mesh. Thus, (4.1.5) yields

$$(2n-2)! \sum_{j=i-n+1}^{i+n-1} A_{ij} = 1 \qquad (n - 1 \leqslant i \leqslant N - n + 1). \tag{4.1.7.1}$$

Similarly, if we replace $S_\Delta(x)$ by x^{2n-1}, we obtain

$$(2n-1)! \sum_{j=i-n+1}^{i+n-1} x_j A_{ij} = \sum_{j=i-n+1}^{i+n-1} x_j \qquad (n - 1 \leqslant i \leqslant N - n + 1). \tag{4.1.7.2}$$

In the periodic case, Eqs. (4.1.7) are true for all i. An additional important property is that each $A_{i,j} \geqslant 0$. In fact, if we consider the function

$$\phi(x) \equiv \frac{(x - x_{j+1})_+^{2n-1} - (x - x_j)_+^{2n-1}}{h_{j+1}} - \frac{(x - x_j)_+^{2n-1} - (x - x_{j-1})_+^{2n-1}}{h_j},$$

we find that $\phi^{(p)}(x) = 0$ $(p = 0, 1, \ldots, 2n - 2)$ for $x \leqslant x_{j-1}$, that

$$\begin{aligned} \phi^{(2n-2)}(x) &= (2n-1)!(x - x_{j-1})/h_j && \text{in} \quad x_{j-1} \leqslant x \leqslant x_j\,, \\ &= (2n-1)!(x_{j+1} - x)/h_{j+1} && \text{in} \quad x_j \leqslant x \leqslant x_{j+1}\,, \\ &= 0 \quad \text{for} \quad x \geqslant x_{j+1}\,. \end{aligned}$$

Thus, the first $2n - 2$ derivatives are nowhere negative, and all the divided differences of order $2n - 2$ in (4.1.6) are consequently nonnegative.

For periodic splines and for nonperiodic splines when

$$n - 1 \leqslant i \leqslant N - n + 1,$$

the spline equations are given by (4.1.5). For nonperiodic splines, there are, in addition, the $2n - 2$ relations resulting from spline end conditions. In determining these, we restrict our attention to splines of certain types.

By a *simple spline of degree* $2n - 1$, we mean a polynomial spline of degree $2n - 1$ which is in $C^{2n-2}[a, b]$. Furthermore, we say a polynomial spline of degree $2n - 1$ and in general a function (when the value of n is clear) is of type I′ if its first $n - 1$ derivatives vanish at $x = a$ and $x = b$. Two functions are in the same type I *equivalence class* if their difference is of type I′. In this same context (again when the value of n is clear), we say that $f(x)$ is of type II′ if $f^{(p)}(a) = f^{(p)}(b) = 0$ for $p = n, n + 1, \ldots, 2n - 2$. Two functions are in the same type II equivalence class if their difference is of type II′. Also, a spline is of type I if it is represented in a manner in which $f^{(p)}(a)$ and $f^{(p)}(b) (p = 1, 2, \ldots, n - 1)$ enter explicitly into the representation as independent parameters, and a spline is of type II if it is represented in a manner in which $f^{(p)}(a)$ and $f^{(p)}(b) (p = n, n + 1, \ldots, 2n - 2)$ enter explicitly into the representation. In these situations, the dependence upon the quantities $f^{(p)}(a)$ and $f^{(p)}(b)$ is to be linear.

In order to impose the end conditions for splines of types I and II at $x = a$, we form divided differences from (4.1.1). Let $[x_0, x_1, \ldots, x_j]^k$ and $[x_0, x_1, \ldots, x_j]_+^k$ denote the divided differences of x^k and $x_+{}^k$, respectively, over $x_0, x_1, \ldots, x_j$. Then from (4.1.1) we obtain, employing the method used in obtaining (4.1.3), the equations

$$\begin{aligned} S_\Delta[x_0, x_1, \ldots, x_q] = {} & \sum_{k=q}^{2n-3} \frac{1}{k!} S_\Delta^{(k)}(x_0) \cdot [0, x_1 \quad x_0, \ldots, x_q - x_0]^k \\ & + \frac{M_0}{(2n-2)!} \Big\{ [0, x_1 - x_0, \ldots, x_q - x_0]_+^{2n-2} \\ & + \frac{[x_0 - x_1, 0, x_2 - x_1, \ldots, x_q - x_1]_+^{2n-1} - [0, x_1 - x_0, \ldots, x_q - x_0]_+^{2n-1}}{(2n-1)h_1} \Big\} \\ & + \frac{1}{(2n-1)!} \sum_{j=1}^{q} M_j (h_j + h_{j+1})\, d_j[x_0, x_1, \ldots, x_q], \end{aligned} \tag{4.1.8}$$

$q = 1, 2, \ldots, 2n - 3$, where

$$d_j(x) = \delta_j^2 (x - x_j)_+^{2n-1}.$$

The last sum in (4.1.8) is taken over the index set $1, \ldots, q$ inasmuch as $d_j(x_k) = 0$ when $k \leqslant j - 1$.

For type I splines, we eliminate the unknown quantities $S_\Delta^{(q)}(a)$ $(q = n,\ n + 1, \ldots, 2n - 3)$ and obtain $n - 1$ equations in $M_0, M_1, \ldots, M_{2n-3}$. For type II splines, we take Eqs. (4.1.8) for $q = n, \ldots, 2n - 3$ and obtain $n - 2$ relations in $M_0, \ldots, M_{2n-3}$ which, together with the specification of M_0 under the type II condition, again constitute $n - 1$ equations. A similar set of $n - 1$ end conditions is obtained at $x = b$ using in place of (4.1.1) the relation

$$S_\Delta(x_i) = \sum_{k=0}^{2n-3} \frac{1}{k!} (x_i - b)^k S_\Delta^{(k)}(b) + \frac{1}{(2n-3)!} \int_a^b S_\Delta^{(2n-2)}(t)(x_i - t)_+^{2n-3}\, dt. \tag{4.1.9}$$

We have, then, $N + 1 - 2(n - 1)$ standard spline equations of the form (4.1.5) together with $2n - 2$ end conditions, in all $N + 1$ equations in the quantities $M_0, M_1, \ldots, M_N$.

When $N < 2n$, then the standard spline equation (4.1.5) does not apply, and the determining equations are obtained solely from (4.1.8) and its counterpart associated with (4.1.9). In this connection, we note that a necessary condition for the existence of a type II spline is $N \geqslant n - 1$. If we were to integrate

$$S_\Delta^{(2n-2)}(x) = M_0 \frac{x_1 - x}{h_1} + M_1 \frac{x - x_0}{h_1},$$

on $x_0 \leqslant x \leqslant x_1$, $n - 1$ times using $S_\Delta^{(q)}(a) = f^{(q)}(a)$ $(q = n, \ldots, 2n - 2)$, we could determine $S_\Delta^{(q)}(x_1)(q = n, \ldots, 2n - 2)$ except for the single parameter M_1. Integration of $S_\Delta^{(2n-2)}(x)$ over $x_1 \leqslant x \leqslant x_2$ would give $S_\Delta^{(q)}(x_2)(q = n, \ldots, 2n - 2)$ in terms of the parameters M_1, M_2. Finally, integration over $x_{N-1} \leqslant x \leqslant x_N$ would yield $S_\Delta^{(q)}(b)$ $(q = n, \ldots, 2n - 2)$ in terms of $M_1, \ldots, M_N$. Since the quantities $S_\Delta^{(q)}(b)$ $(q = n, \ldots, 2n - 2)$ are prescribed, there are $N - n + 1$ degrees of freedom remaining at this point, and so $N \geqslant n - 1$. Carrying out n further integrations now gives $N - n + 1 + n = N + 1$ degrees of freedom and hence, conceivably, the possibility of having $S_\Delta(x_j) = f_j$ (prescribed), $j = 0, 1, \ldots, N$.

The complete determination of the spline next requires the values of the derivatives $S_\Delta^{(q)}(x_j)(q = 1, \ldots, 2n - 3;\ j = 0, 1, \ldots, N)$ from the values of the quantities M_j and the values $S_\Delta(x_j)$ to which the spline interpolates at the points of Δ.

For $x_{j-1} \leqslant x \leqslant x_j$, direct integration of

$$S_\Delta^{(2n-2)}(x) = M_{j-1} \frac{x_j - x}{h_j} + M_j \frac{x - x_{j-1}}{h_j} \tag{4.1.10}$$

gives

$$S_\Delta^{(2n-2-p)}(x) = (-1)^p M_{j-1} \frac{(x_j - x)^{p+1}}{h_j(p+1)!} + M_j \frac{(x - x_{j-1})^{p+1}}{h_j(p+1)!}$$

$$+ \sum_{k=1}^{p} \frac{B_{kj}}{(p-k)!} (x - x_j)^{p-k} \quad (p = 1, 2, \ldots, 2n-2), \qquad (4.1.11)$$

where

$$B_{kj} = S_\Delta^{(2n-2-k)}(x_j) - M_j[h_j{}^k/(k+1)!]. \qquad (4.1.12)$$

When $n - 1 \leqslant j \leqslant N - n + 1$, taking divided differences in (4.1.1), with a replaced by x_j, gives a determining set of equations for the B_{kj}. For p even, we have

$$S_\Delta[x_{j-p/2}, \ldots, x_{j+p/2}] = \sum_{k=p}^{2n-3} \frac{1}{k!} \left\{ B_{2n-2-k,j} + M_j \frac{h_j^{2n-2-k}}{(2n-1-k)!} \right\}$$

$$\times [x_{j-p/2} - x_j, \ldots, x_{j+p/2} - x_j]^k + F_j[x_{j-p/2}, \ldots, x_{j+p/2}], \qquad (4.1.13)$$

$$F_j(x_i) = \frac{1}{(2n-3)!} \int_{x_j}^{x_i} S_\Delta^{(2n-2)}(t)(x_i - t)^{2n-3}\, dt$$

$$= \frac{1}{(2n-2)!} M_j \left\{ (x_i - x_j)^{2n-2} + \frac{(x_i - x_{j+1})^{2n-1} - (x_i - x_j)^{2n-1}}{(2n-1)h_{j+1}} \right\}$$

$$+ M_i \frac{h_i^{2n-2}}{(2n-1)!} + \frac{1}{(2n-1)!} \sum_{m=j+1}^{i-1} M_m(h_m + h_{m+1})\, \delta_m^2 (x_i - x_m)^{2n-1}$$

$$(i > j), \qquad (4.1.14)$$

$$F_j(x_i) = \frac{1}{(2n-2)!} M_j \left\{ (x_i - x_j)^{2n-2} + \frac{(x_i - x_j)^{2n-1} - (x_i - x_{j-1})^{2n-1}}{(2n-1)h_j} \right\}$$

$$+ M_i \frac{(-h_{i+1})^{2n-2}}{(2n-1)!} - \frac{1}{(2n-1)!} \sum_{m=i+1}^{j-1} M_m(h_m + h_{m+1})\, \delta_m^2 (x_i - x_m)^{2n-1}$$

$$(i < j). \qquad (4.1.15)$$

For p odd, we employ the divided difference

$$S_\Delta[x_{j-(p+1)/2}, \ldots, x_{j-1}, x_{j+1}, \ldots, x_{j+(p+1)/2}].$$

The resulting equations in the quantities $B_{k,j}(k = 1, 2, \ldots, 2n-3)$ have a triangular coefficient matrix, and the method of solution is evident.

We turn now to an alternative procedure for constructing the standard spline relation (4.1.5). Such a procedure is desirable because the algebraic evaluation of the divided differences $\delta_i^{2n-2}\delta_j^2(x_i - x_j)_+^{2n-1}$ is quite tedious.

We require first the polynomial $p(\sigma)$ of degree $2n+1$ in σ such that

$p(\sigma)$ and its first n derivatives take on prescribed values at $\sigma = 0$ and $\sigma = 1$:

$$p^{(k)}(0) = p_0^{(k)}, \qquad p^{(k)}(1) = p_1^{(k)} \qquad (k = 0, 1, \ldots, n).$$

Write $p(\sigma)$ in the form

$$p(\sigma) = p_0 + p_0'\sigma + (1/2!)p_0''\sigma^2 + \cdots + (1/n!)p_0^{(n)}\sigma^n + A_0\sigma^{n+1} + \cdots + A_n\sigma^{2n+1}.$$

Then, imposing the prescribed conditions at $\sigma = 1$ gives the system of equations

$$\begin{bmatrix} 1 & 1 & 1 & \cdots & 1 \\ n+1 & n+2 & n+3 & \cdots & 2n+1 \\ (n+1)_{(2)} & (n+2)_{(2)} & (n+3)_{(2)} & \cdots & (2n+1)_{(2)} \\ \vdots & \vdots & \vdots & & \vdots \\ (n+1)_{(n-1)} & (n+2)_{(n-1)} & (n+3)_{(n-1)} & \cdots & (2n+1)_{(n-1)} \\ (n+1)_{(n)} & (n+2)_{(n)} & (n+3)_{(n)} & \cdots & (2n+1)_{(n)} \end{bmatrix} \cdot \begin{bmatrix} A_0 \\ A_1 \\ A_2 \\ \vdots \\ A_{n-1} \\ A_n \end{bmatrix} = \begin{bmatrix} p_1 - \sum_{k=0}^{n} p_0^{(k)}/k! \\ p_1' - \sum_{k=1}^{n} p_0^{(k)}/(k-1)! \\ p_1'' - \sum_{k=2}^{n} p_0^{(k)}/(k-2)! \\ \vdots \\ p_1^{(n-1)} - p_0^{(n-1)} - p_0^{(n)} \\ p_1^{(n)} - p_0^{(n)} \end{bmatrix}, \tag{4.1.16}$$

where $k_{(j)}$ is the factorial function $k(k-1)(k-2)\cdots(k-j+1)$. Multiply on the left by the matrix

$$\mathscr{A} = \begin{bmatrix} 1 & 0 & 0 & \cdots & 0 & 0 \\ -(n+1) & 1 & 0 & \cdots & 0 & 0 \\ (n+2)_{(2)} & -(n+1)\cdot 2 & 1 & \cdots & 0 & 0 \\ -(n+3)_{(3)} & (n+2)_{(2)}\cdot 3 & -(n+1)\cdot 3 & \cdots & 0 & 0 \\ (n+4)_{(4)} & -(n+3)_{(3)}\cdot 4 & (n+2)_{(2)}\cdot 6 & \cdots & 0 & 0 \\ \vdots & \vdots & \vdots & & \vdots & \vdots \\ (-1)^n(2n)_{(n)} & (-1)^{n-1}(2n-1)_{(n-1)}\cdot {}^nC_1 & (-1)^{n-2}(2n-2)_{(n-2)}\cdot {}^nC_2 & \cdots & -(n+1)\cdot {}^nC_{n-1} & 1 \end{bmatrix}.$$

The resulting matrix on the left is

$$\begin{bmatrix} 1 & 1 & 1 & 1 & 1 & \cdots & n_{(0)} \\ 0 & 1 & 2 & 3 & 4 & \cdots & n_{(1)} \\ 0 & 0 & 2 & 6 & 12 & \cdots & n_{(2)} \\ 0 & 0 & 0 & 6 & 24 & \cdots & n_{(3)} \\ 0 & 0 & 0 & 0 & 24 & \cdots & n_{(4)} \\ \vdots & \vdots & \vdots & \vdots & \vdots & & \vdots \\ 0 & 0 & 0 & 0 & 0 & \cdots & n_{(n)} \end{bmatrix}.$$

The inverse of this matrix is

$$\mathscr{B} = \begin{bmatrix} 1 & -1 & \frac{1}{2!} & -\frac{1}{3!} & \frac{1}{4!} & \cdots & \frac{(-1)^n}{n!} \\ 0 & 1 & -1 & \frac{1}{2!} & -\frac{1}{3!} & \cdots & \frac{(-1)^{n-1}}{(n-1)!} \\ 0 & 0 & \frac{1}{2!}\cdot 1 & \frac{1}{2!}(-1) & \frac{1}{2!}\left(\frac{1}{2!}\right) & \cdots & \frac{1}{2!}\,\frac{(-1)^{n-2}}{(n-2)!} \\ 0 & 0 & 0 & \frac{1}{3!}\cdot 1 & \frac{1}{3!}(-1) & \cdots & \frac{1}{3!}\,\frac{(-1)^{n-3}}{(n-3)!} \\ 0 & 0 & 0 & 0 & \frac{1}{4!}(1) & \cdots & \frac{1}{4!}\,\frac{(-1)^{n-4}}{(n-4)!} \\ \vdots & \vdots & \vdots & \vdots & \vdots & & \vdots \\ 0 & 0 & 0 & 0 & 0 & \cdots & \frac{1}{n!} \end{bmatrix}.$$

Furthermore, we have

$$\begin{bmatrix} \sum_{k=0}^{n} \frac{p_0^{(k)}}{k!} \\ \sum_{k=0}^{n-1} \frac{p_0^{(k+1)}}{k!} \\ \\ \sum_{k=1}^{1} \frac{p_0^{(k+n-1)}}{k!} \\ p_0^{(n)} \end{bmatrix} = \mathscr{C} \begin{bmatrix} p_0 \\ p_0' \\ p_0'' \\ \vdots \\ p_0^{(n-1)} \\ p_0^{(n)} \end{bmatrix},$$

$$\mathscr{C} = \begin{bmatrix} 1 & 1 & \frac{1}{2!} & \frac{1}{3!} & \frac{1}{4!} & \cdots & & \frac{1}{n!} \\ 0 & 1 & 1 & \frac{1}{2!} & \frac{1}{3!} & \cdots & & \frac{1}{(n-1)!} \\ 0 & 0 & 1 & 1 & \frac{1}{2!} & \cdots & & \frac{1}{(n-2)!} \\ \vdots & \vdots & \vdots & \vdots & \vdots & & & \vdots \\ 0 & 0 & 0 & 0 & 0 & \cdots & 1 & 1 \\ 0 & 0 & 0 & 0 & 0 & \cdots & 0 & 1 \end{bmatrix}.$$

Thus,

$$\begin{bmatrix} A_0 \\ A_1 \\ \vdots \\ A_n \end{bmatrix} = \mathscr{B}\mathscr{A} \left\{ \begin{bmatrix} p_1 \\ p_1' \\ \vdots \\ p_1^{(n)} \end{bmatrix} - \mathscr{C} \begin{bmatrix} p_0 \\ p_0' \\ \\ p_0^{(n)} \end{bmatrix} \right\}. \tag{4.1.17}$$

We find that $\mathscr{B}\mathscr{A}$ is equal to (γ_{ij}),

$$\gamma_{ij} = \frac{(-1)^{j+k}}{k!} \sum_{i=0}^{j} \binom{n+j-i}{j-i}\binom{2n-k+1}{n-j+i-k}\binom{k}{i} \qquad (0 \leqslant j \leqslant n, 0 \leqslant k \leqslant n),$$

where $\binom{n}{m} = 0$ if $m < 0$ or $m > n$, $\binom{n}{m}$ being the binomial coefficient ${}^nC_m$, $\binom{0}{0} = 1$.

The product $\mathscr{B}\mathscr{A}\mathscr{C}$, however, is much simpler in form and suffices for the determination of the polynomial:

$$\mathscr{B}\mathscr{A}\mathscr{C} = \begin{bmatrix} +\binom{n}{0}\binom{2n+1}{n} & +\binom{n-1}{0}\binom{2n}{n} & +\frac{1}{2!}\binom{n-2}{0}\binom{2n-1}{n} & \cdots & \frac{1}{(n-1)!}\binom{1}{0}\binom{n+2}{n} & \frac{1}{n!}\binom{0}{0}\binom{n+1}{n} \\ -\binom{n+1}{1}\binom{2n+1}{n+1} & -\binom{n}{1}\binom{2n}{n-1} & -\frac{1}{2!}\binom{n-1}{1}\binom{2n-1}{n-1} & \cdots & \frac{-1}{(n-1)!}\binom{2}{1}\binom{n+2}{n-1} & \frac{-1}{n!}\binom{1}{1}\binom{n+1}{n-1} \\ +\binom{n+2}{2}\binom{2n+1}{n+2} & \binom{n+1}{2}\binom{2n}{n-2} & \frac{1}{2!}\binom{n}{2}\binom{2n-1}{n-2} & \cdots & \frac{1}{(n-1)!}\binom{3}{2}\binom{n+2}{n-2} & \frac{1}{n!}\binom{2}{2}\binom{n+1}{n-2} \\ \vdots & \vdots & \vdots & & \vdots & \vdots \\ (-1)^n\binom{2n}{n}\binom{2n+1}{0} & (-1)^n\binom{2n-1}{n}\binom{2n}{0} & (-1)^n\frac{1}{2!}\binom{2n-2}{0}\binom{2n-1}{0} & \cdots & \frac{(-1)^n}{(n-1)!}\binom{n+1}{n}\binom{n+2}{0} & \frac{(-1)^n}{n!}\binom{n}{n}\binom{n+1}{0} \end{bmatrix}. \tag{4.1.18}$$

We may write

$$\begin{aligned} p(\sigma) = {} & p_0 T_{n,0}(\sigma) + p_1 T_{n,0}(1-\sigma) \\ & + p_0' T_{n,1}(\sigma) - p_1' T_{n,1}(1-\sigma) \\ & + p_0'' T_{n,2}(\sigma) + p_1'' T_{n,2}(1-\sigma) \\ & + \cdots \\ & + p_0^{(n)} T_{n,n}(\sigma) + (-1)^n p_1^{(n)} T_{n,n}(1-\sigma), \end{aligned} \tag{4.1.19}$$

where

$$T_{n,k}(\sigma) = \frac{\sigma^k}{k!} - \frac{1}{k!} \sum_{j=0}^{n} (-1)^j \binom{n-k+j}{j}\binom{2n-k+1}{n-j} \sigma^{n+j+1}. \tag{4.1.20}$$

Consider now the component polynomial of $S_\Delta(x)$ on the interval $x_{j-1} \leqslant x \leqslant x_j$. Designate this by $S_{\Delta,j}(x)$:

$$S_{\Delta,j}(x) = \sum_{k=0}^{n-1} \left\{ S_{\Delta,j}^{(k)}(x_{j-1}) h_j^k \, T_{n-1,k}\left(\frac{x - x_{j-1}}{h_j}\right) + (-1)^k S_{\Delta,j}^{(k)}(x_j) h_j^k \, T_{n-1,k}\left(\frac{x_j - x}{h_j}\right) \right\}. \tag{4.1.21}$$

Then, for $q = n, \ldots, 2n-1$, we have

$$S_{\Delta,j}^{(q)}(x_{j-1}) = \sum_{k=0}^{n-1} \left\{ S_{\Delta,j}^{(k)}(x_{j-1}) \frac{h_j^k}{h_j^q} T_{n-1,k}^{(q)}(0) + (-1)^{k+q} S_{\Delta,j}^{(k)}(x_j) \frac{h_j^k}{h_j^q} T_{n-1,k}^{(q)}(1) \right\},$$

$$S_{\Delta,j}^{(q)}(x_j) = \sum_{k=0}^{n-1} \left\{ S_{\Delta,j}^{(k)}(x_{j-1}) \frac{h_j^k}{h_j^q} T_{n-1,k}^{(q)}(1) + (-1)^{k+q} S_{\Delta,j}^{(k)}(x_j) \frac{h_j^k}{h_j^q} T_{n-1,k}^{(q)}(0) \right\}, \tag{4.1.22}$$

where

$$T_{n-1,k}^{(q)}(0) = -\frac{1}{k!} (-1)^{q-n} \binom{q-k-1}{q-n} \binom{2n-1-k}{2n-1-q} q!,$$

$$T_{n-1,k}^{(q)}(1) = -\frac{1}{k!} \sum_{j=q-n}^{n-1} (-1)^j \binom{n-k-1+j}{j} \binom{2n-k-1}{n-j-1} (n+j)_{(q)} . \tag{4.1.23}$$

In particular,

$$T_{n-1,k}^{(2n-2)}(0) = \frac{1}{k!} \binom{2n-k-3}{n-2} \binom{2n-1-k}{1} (2n-2)!,$$

$$T_{n-1,k}^{(2n-2)}(1) = \frac{1}{k!} (-1)^{n-1} \binom{2n-k-3}{n\quad 2} \binom{2n-1-k}{1} (2n-2)! - \frac{(-1)^{n-1}}{k!} \binom{2n-k-2}{n-1} (2n-1)!. \tag{4.1.24}$$

If we now impose the condition that $S_\Delta^{(q)}(x)$ be continuous at x_j, for $q = n, n+1, \ldots, 2n-2$, we have for these values of q the relation $S_{\Delta,j}^{(q)}(x_j) = S_{\Delta,j+1}^{(q)}(x_j)$, that is,

$$h_j^q \sum_{k=0}^{n-1} \{ S_{\Delta,j}^{(k)}(x_{j-1}) \, T_{n-1,k}^{(q)}(1) + (-1)^{k+q} \, S_{\Delta,j}^{(k)}(x_j) \, T_{n-1,k}^{(q)}(0) \}$$

$$= h_{j+1}^q \sum_{k=0}^{n-1} \{ S_{\Delta,j}^{(k)}(x_j) \, T_{n-1,k}^{(q)}(0) + (-1)^{k+q} \, S_{\Delta,j}^{(k)}(x_{j+1}) \, T_{n-1,k}^{(q)}(1) \}. \tag{4.1.25}$$

Denote $S_\Delta^{(q)}(x_j)$ by $S_j^{(q)}$. Then there are $n-1$ equations ($q = n,\dots, 2n-2$)

$$\begin{aligned} &h_j^q T_{n-1,n-1}^{(q)}(1)\, S_{j-1}^{(n-1)} + T_{n-1,n-1}^{(q)}(0)[(-1)^{n+q-1}h_j^q + h_{j+1}^q]\, S_j^{(n-1)} \\ &- (-1)^{n+q-1}h_{j+1}^q\, T_{n-1,n-1}^{(q)}(1)\, S_{j+1}^{(n-1)} \\ &\quad = -\sum_{k=0}^{n-2} \{h_j^q T_{n-1,k}^{(q)}(1)\, S_{j-1}^{(k)} + T_{n-1,k}^{(q)}(0)[(-1)^{k+q}h_j^q + h_{j+1}^q]\, S_j^{(k)} \\ &\qquad - (-1)^{k+q}h_{j+1}^q\, T_{n-1,k}^{(q)}(1)\, S_{j+1}^{(k)}\}, \end{aligned} \tag{4.1.26}$$

at each point x_j. When $n-1 \leqslant i \leqslant N-n+1$, Eqs. (4.1.26) taken at the points $x_{i-n+2}, x_{i-n+3}, \dots, x_{i+n-2}$ give $(2n-3)(n-1)$ relations in the $(2n-1)(n-1)$ variables

$$S_j^{(q)} (j = i-n+1,\dots, i+n-1; \quad q = 1, 2,\dots, n-1).$$

Elimination of $S_j^{(q)}(j = i-n+1,\dots, i+n-1,\ q = 1, 2,\dots, n-2)$ from these gives the spline equation in terms of

$$S_j^{(n-1)}(j = i-n+1,\dots, i+n-1).$$

For the spline equation in terms of the quantities M_j, we form by means of (4.1.16) the expressions for $S_{j-1}^{(n-1)}$ and $S_j^{(n-1)}$ in terms of M_{j-1}, M_j, and $S_{j-1}^{(q)}$ and $S_j^{(q)}(q = 0, 1,\dots, n-2)$. We substitute these into (4.1.26) and then carry out the elimination process as before. A relation equivalent to (4.1.5) results.

We carry through this construction for the quintic spline as an illustration. The functions $T_{2,0}(\sigma)$, $T_{2,1}(\sigma)$, $T_{2,2}(\sigma)$ are found here to be

$$T_{2,0}(\sigma) = 1 - \sum_{j=0}^{2} (-1)^j \binom{2+j}{j}\binom{5}{2-j} \sigma^{3+j} = 1 - 10\sigma^3 + 15\sigma^4 - 6\sigma^5,$$

$$T_{2,1}(\sigma) = \sigma - \sum_{j=0}^{2} (-1)^j \binom{1+j}{j}\binom{4}{2-j} \sigma^{3+j} = \sigma - 6\sigma^3 + 8\sigma^4 - 3\sigma^5,$$

$$T_{2,2}(\sigma) = \frac{\sigma^2}{2} - \frac{1}{2}\sum_{j=0}^{2} (-1)^j \binom{j}{j}\binom{3}{2-j} \sigma^{3+j} = \frac{\sigma^2}{2!} - \frac{1}{2}(3\sigma^3 - 3\sigma^4 + \sigma^5),$$

so that

$$\begin{aligned} T_{2,0}'''(0) &= -60, & T_{2,1}'''(0) &= -36, & T_{2,2}'''(0) &= -9, \\ T_{2,0}'''(1) &= -60, & T_{2,1}'''(1) &= -24, & T_{2,2}'''(1) &= -3, \\ T_{2,0}^{(4)}(0) &= 360, & T_{2,1}^{(4)}(0) &= 192, & T_{2,2}^{(4)}(0) &= 36, \\ T_{2,0}^{(4)}(1) &= -360, & T_{2,1}^{(4)}(1) &= -168, & T_{2,2}^{(4)}(1) &= -24. \end{aligned}$$

We have from (4.1.22)

$$M_{j-1} = 360 \frac{S_{j-1}}{h_j^4} - 360 \frac{S_j}{h_j^4} + 192 \frac{S'_{j-1}}{h_j^3} + 168 \frac{S'_j}{h_j^3} + 36 \frac{S''_{j-1}}{h_j^2} - 24 \frac{S''_j}{h_j^2},$$

$$M_j = -360 \frac{S_{j-1}}{h_j^4} + 360 \frac{S_j}{h_j^4} - 168 \frac{S'_{j-1}}{h_j^3} - 192 \frac{S'_j}{h_j^3} - 24 \frac{S''_{j-1}}{h_j^2} + 36 \frac{S''_j}{h_j^2}, \tag{4.1.27}$$

so that

$$S''_{j-1} = \frac{6}{h_j} \frac{S_j - S_{j-1}}{h_j} - \frac{1}{h_j}(4S'_{j-1} + 2S'_j) + h_j^2 \frac{3M_{j-1} + 2M_j}{60},$$

$$S''_j = -\frac{6}{h_j} \frac{S_j - S_{j-1}}{h_j} + \frac{1}{h_j}(2S'_{j-1} + 4S'_j) + h_j^2 \frac{2M_{j-1} + 3M_j}{60}. \tag{4.1.28}$$

Thus,

$$S'''_{\Delta,j}(x_{j-1}) = \frac{S_j - S_{j-1}}{h_j}\left(-\frac{12}{h_j^2}\right) + 6\frac{S'_{j-1} + S'_j}{h_j^2} - \frac{h_j}{60}(9M_j + 21M_{j-1}),$$

$$S'''_{\Delta,j}(x_j) = \frac{S_j - S_{j-1}}{h_j}\left(-\frac{12}{h_j^2}\right) + 6\frac{S'_{j-1} + S'_j}{h_j^2} + \frac{h_j}{60}(9M_{j-1} + 21M_j). \tag{4.1.29}$$

Continuity of $S'''_\Delta(x)$ at x_j gives

$$\tfrac{3}{20} h_j M_{j-1} + \tfrac{7}{20}(h_j + h_{j+1}) M_j + \tfrac{3}{20} h_{j+1} M_{j+1}$$
$$= -6\left\{\frac{S'_{j-1}}{h_j^2} + \left(\frac{1}{h_j^2} - \frac{1}{h_{j+1}^2}\right) S'_j - \frac{S'_{j+1}}{h_{j+1}^2}\right\}$$
$$- \frac{12}{h_{j+1}^2} \frac{S_{j+1} - S_j}{h_{j+1}} + \frac{12}{h_j^2} \frac{S_j - S_{j-1}}{h_j}. \tag{4.1.30}$$

Continuity of $S''_\Delta(x)$ at x_j by (4.1.28) gives

$$\frac{h_j^2}{30} M_{j-1} + \frac{1}{20}(h_j^2 - h_{j+1}^2) M_j - \frac{h_{j+1}^2}{30} M_{j+1}$$
$$= -\frac{2}{h_j} S'_{j-1} - \left(\frac{4}{h_j} + \frac{4}{h_{j+1}}\right) S'_j - \frac{2}{h_{j+1}} S'_{j+1}$$
$$+ \frac{6}{h_{j+1}} \frac{S_{j+1} - S_j}{h_{j+1}} + \frac{6}{h_j} \frac{S_j - S_{j-1}}{h_j}. \tag{4.1.31}$$

We write Eqs. (4.1.25) and (4.1.26) at x_{j-1}, x_j, x_{j+1} and eliminate S'_{j-2}, S'_{j-1}, S'_j, S'_{j+1}, S'_{j+2} from these six equations. There results

$$
\begin{aligned}
&\frac{1}{120}\frac{h_{j-1}^3}{(h_{j-1}+h_j)(h_{j-1}+h_j+h_{j+1})}M_{j-2}\\
&+\frac{1}{120}\left\{\left[4h_{j-1}+3h_j+\frac{h_{j-1}+h_j}{h_{j-1}}\left(\frac{h_jh_{j+1}}{h_j+h_{j+1}}+2h_j\right)\right]\frac{h_{j-1}}{h_{j-1}+h_j+h_{j+1}}\right.\\
&\left.+\frac{h_j^2(h_{j+1}+h_{j+2})}{(h_j+h_{j+1})(h_j+h_{j+1}+h_{j+2})}\right\}M_{j-1}\\
&+\frac{1}{120}\left\{\left[\frac{h_jh_{j-1}}{h_{j-1}+h_j}+2h_j+\frac{h_{j-1}+h_j}{h_{j-1}}(3h_j+4h_{j+1})\right]\frac{h_{j-1}}{h_{j-1}+h_j+h_{j+1}}\right.\\
&\left.+\left[\frac{h_{j+1}h_{j+2}}{h_{j+1}+h_{j+2}}+2h_{j+1}+(4h_j+3h_{j+1})\frac{h_{j+1}+h_{j+2}}{h_{j+2}}\right]\frac{h_{j+2}}{h_j+h_{j+1}+h_{j+2}}\right\}M_j\\
&+\frac{1}{120}\left\{\frac{(h_{j-j}+h_j)\,h_{j+1}^2}{(h_j+h_{j+1})(h_{j-1}+h_j+h_{j+1})}\right.\\
&\left.+\left[3h_{j+1}+4h_{j+2}+\frac{h_{j+1}+h_{j+2}}{h_{j+2}}\left(\frac{h_jh_{j+1}}{h_j+h_{j+1}}+2h_{j+1}\right)\right]\frac{h_{j+2}}{h_j+h_{j+1}+h_{j+2}}\right\}M_{j+1}\\
&+\frac{1}{120}\frac{h_{j+2}^3}{(h_{j+1}+h_{j+2})(h_j+h_{j+1}+h_{j+2})}M_{j+2}\\
&=(h_{j-1}+h_j+h_{j+1}+h_{j+2})\,S_\Delta[x_{j-2},x_{j-1},x_j,x_{j+1},x_{j+2}].
\end{aligned}
$$

We have next to exhibit the end condition for the quintic spline. We write these for type I splines, although the methods employed apply equally well to type II splines. For $x = a$, Eqs. (4.1.25) and (4.1.26) are employed to impose continuity on $S''_\Delta(x)$ and $S'''_\Delta(x)$ at x_1 and x_2. A fifth equation is obtained from the first of Eqs. (4.1.23) (S''_0 is specified). Elimination of S'_1, S'_2, and S'_j now gives two conditions in M_0, M_1, M_2, M_3:

$$
\begin{aligned}
&\frac{h_1^2}{h_1+h_2}\frac{M_0}{120}\left[\frac{h_2+h_3}{h_1+h_2+h_3}+\frac{3h_2+2h_1}{h_1+h_2}\right]\\
&+\frac{M_1}{120}\left[\frac{(4h_1+3h_2)(h_2+h_3)}{h_1+h_2+h_3}+\frac{h_1(4h_2+3h_1)}{h_1+h_2}+\frac{h_2h_3(3h_2+2h_3)}{(h_2+h_3)(h_1+h_2+h_3)}\right]\\
&+\frac{M_2}{120}\left[\frac{h_2(3h_1+2h_2)}{h_1+h_2}\frac{h_2+h_3}{h_1+h_2+h_3}+\frac{h_3(4h_3+3h_2)}{h_1+h_2+h_3}+\frac{h_2^2h_1}{(h_1+h_2)^2}\right]\\
&+\frac{M_3}{120}\frac{h_2h_3^2}{(h_2+h_3)(h_1+h_2+h_3)}\\
&=S_\Delta[x_0,x_1,x_2,x_3]-\frac{1}{h_1(h_1+h_2)}\left[S'_0-\frac{2h_1+h_2}{h_1+h_2}\frac{S_1-S_0}{h_1}+\frac{h_1}{h_1+h_2}\frac{S_2-S_1}{h_2}\right],
\end{aligned}
$$

$$\frac{M_0}{120} h_1^2\left[3 + \frac{h_2(3h_2 + 2h_1)}{(h_1 + h_2)^2}\right] + \frac{M_1}{120} h_1\left[2h_1 + \frac{h_2(4h_2 + 3h_1)}{h_1 + h_2}\right] + \frac{M_2}{120} \frac{h_2^3 h_1}{(h_1 + h_2)^2}$$

$$= -\frac{h_2}{h_1 + h_0}\frac{1}{h_1}\left[S_0' - \frac{2h_1 + h_2}{h_1 + h_2}\frac{S_1 - S_0}{h_1} + \frac{h_1}{h_1 + h_2}\frac{S_2 - S_1}{h_2}\right]$$

$$- \left[\frac{S_0''}{2} - \frac{1}{h_1 + h_2}\left(\frac{S_2 - S_1}{h_2} - \frac{S_1 - S_0}{h_1}\right)\right]$$

$$- 2\left[\frac{1}{h_1}\left(\frac{S_1 - S_0}{h_1} - S_0'\right) - \frac{S_0''}{2}\right].$$

The corresponding end conditions at $x = b$ may be obtained directly from these by symmetry.

In order to represent the spline over the interval (x_{j-1}, x_j) once the quantities M_j have been determined, it is necessary to determine $S_{j-1}', S_j', S_{j-1}'', S_j''$. Then (4.1.21) gives $S_\Delta(x)$. If we eliminate S_{j-2}' from the two continuity relations at x_{j-1} and then S_{j+1}' from those at x_j, we obtain two equations in S_{j-1}' and S_j' which yield

$$S_{j-1}'\left(\frac{1}{h_{j-1}} + \frac{1}{h_j}\right) = \frac{1}{h_j}\frac{S_j - S_{j-1}}{h_j} + \frac{1}{h_{j-1}}\frac{S_{j-1} - S_{j-2}}{h_{j-1}}$$

$$- (h_{j-1} + h_j)\, h_j^2 S_\Delta[x_{j-2}, x_{j-1}, x_j, x_{j+1}] + \frac{h_{j-1}^2(h_j + h_{j+1})}{h_{j-1} + h_j + h_{j+1}}\frac{M_{j-2}}{120}$$

$$+ \frac{(4h_{j-1} + 3h_j)(h_j + h_{j+1})^2 + h_j h_{j+1}(3h_{j+1} + 2h_j)}{(h_j + h_{j+1})(h_{j-1} + h_j + h_{j+1})}(h_{j-1} + h_j)\frac{M_{j-1}}{120}$$

$$+ \frac{(4h_{j+1} + 3h_j)\, h_{j+1}(h_{j-1} + h_j) + (h_{j+1} + h_j)\, h_j(3h_{j-1} + 2h_j)}{h_{j-1} + h_j + h_{j+1}}\frac{M_j}{120}$$

$$+ \frac{h_{j+1}^3(h_{j-1} + h_j)}{(h_j + h_{j+1})(h_{j-1} + h_j + h_{j+1})}\frac{M_{j+1}}{120}.$$

Finally, S_{j-1}' and S_j' are obtained from (4.1.28).

It is apparent that polynomial splines for unequal intervals are cumbersome to work with. Most of the complexity is attributable to the fact that the quantities M_j are implicitly determined by the spline equations. We introduce in Section 4.5 quintic splines of maximum deficiency, which on the other hand exhibit little of this complexity and are quite convenient to work with.

4.2. Equal Intervals

Polynomial splines on meshes whose intervals are of equal length are of central importance in the theory of polynomial splines. In this case, let $h = (b - a)/N$ be the interval length, and let $\Delta \equiv E - 1$ be the difference operator associated with this displacement, $Ef(x) = f(x + h)$. We write Eqs. (4.1.5) and (4.1.6) as

$$\sum_{j=-(n-1)}^{n-1} A_j^{(2n-1)} M_{k-j} = \Delta^{2(n-1)} E^{-(n-1)} S_\Delta(kh), \tag{4.2.1}$$

$$A_j^{(2n-1)} = \frac{2h}{(2n-1)!} \delta_k^{2n-2}\, \delta_j^2[(i-j)h]_+^{2n-1}(2n-2)!h^{2n-2}.$$

(Note that δ_j indicates divided difference as heretofore.) Since $\delta_j^2[(i-j)h]_+^{2n-1} = \delta_i^2[(i-j)h]_+^{2n-1}$, we can write this equation as

$$A_j^{(2n-1)} = \frac{1}{(2n-1)!h} \Delta^{2n} E^{-n} (jh)_+^{2n-1}. \tag{4.2.2}$$

If we use now unit intervals for differencing and set

$$\phi_k^{(n)} = \Delta^{n+1} E^{-n} (k)_+^n \qquad (k = 0, 1, 2, \ldots, n-1), \tag{4.2.3}$$

we have

$$A_j^{(2n-1)} = \frac{h^{2n-2}}{(2n-1)!} \phi_{j+n-1}^{(2n-1)}. \tag{4.2.4}$$

Thus,

$$\frac{1}{(2n-1)!} \sum_{k=0}^{2n-2} \phi_k^{(2n-1)} M_{j-n+1+k} = \delta^{2n-2} S_\Delta(x_j)/h^{2n-2}, \tag{4.2.5}$$

where δ^2 signifies the central difference operator $E^{-1}\Delta^2$.

The quantities $\phi_k^{(n)}$ for n even are associated with even-degree splines interpolating at mesh points. It is convenient, however, to consider the entire set of these quantities. We note the relationship between advancing differences of x^n at $x = 0$ ("differences of zero"; cf. Freeman [1949, p. 123]) and the $(n-1)$th differences of $(x)_+^n$. If we denote $\Delta^k x^m |_{x=0}$ by $\Delta^k 0^m$, then with unit differencing interval we have

$$\phi_k^{(m)} = \Delta^{m+1} E^{-m} (k)_+{}^m = \sum_{j=0}^{k} (-1)^j \binom{m-k-1+j}{j} \Delta^{k+1-j} 0^m \quad (k = 0, \ldots, m-1). \tag{4.2.6}$$

This relationship is evident in the case $m = 3$, which serves as an illustration:

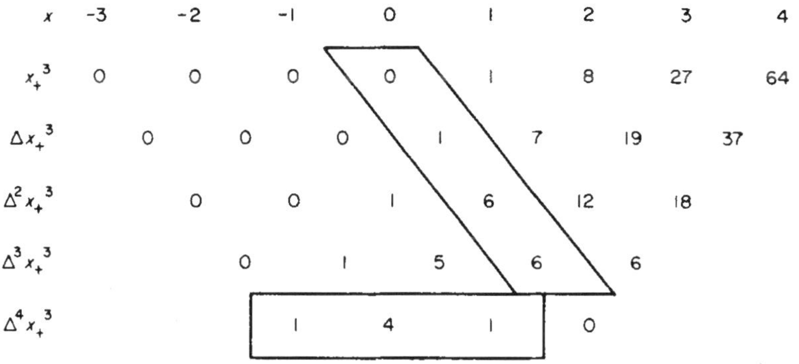

In the horizontal box are $\phi_0^{(3)}$, $\phi_1^{(3)}$, $\phi_2^{(3)}$, whereas in the diagonal box are 0^3, $\Delta 0^3$, $\Delta^2 0^3$, $\Delta^3 0^3$.

Evidently we have

$$\Delta 0^m = \phi_0^{(m)} = 1,$$

$$\Delta^2 0^m = \phi_1^{(m)} + (m-1)\,\phi_0^{(m)},$$

$$\begin{aligned}\Delta^3 0^m &= \phi_2^{(m)} + (\phi_1^{(m)} + \phi_0^{(m)}) + (\phi_1^{(m)} + 2\phi_0^{(m)}) + \cdots + (\phi_1^{(m)} + (m-2)\,\phi_0^{(m)}) \\ &= \phi_2^{(m)} + \binom{m-2}{1}\phi_1^{(m)} + \binom{m-1}{2}\phi_0^{(m)},\end{aligned}$$

$$\begin{aligned}\Delta^4 0^m &= \phi_3^{(m)} + (\phi_2^{(m)} + \phi_1^{(m)} + \phi_0^{(m)}) + (\phi_2^{(m)} + 2\phi_1^{(m)} + 3\phi_0^{(m)}) \\ &\quad + \cdots + \left(\phi_2^{(m)} + (m-3)\,\phi_1^{(m)} + \binom{m-2}{2}\phi_0^{(m)}\right) \\ &= \phi_3^{(m)} + \binom{m-3}{1}\phi_2^{(m)} + \binom{m-2}{2}\phi_1^{(m)} + \binom{m-1}{3}\phi_0^{(m)},\end{aligned}$$

$$\cdots \qquad \cdots$$

$$\Delta^m 0^m = \phi_{m-1}^{(m)} + \phi_{m-2}^{(m)} + \cdots + \phi_0^{(m)}.$$

Solving these equations for the quantities $\phi_k^{(m)}$ gives directly (4.2.6).

The differences of zero satisfy the recurrence relationship

$$\Delta^k 0^{m+1} = k(\Delta^k 0^m + \Delta^{k-1} 0^m). \tag{4.2.7}$$

We show that the quantities $\phi_k^{(m)}$ satisfy the recurrence relation

$$\phi_k^{(m)} = (k+1)\,\phi_k^{(m-1)} + (m-k)\,\phi_{k-1}^{(m-1)}. \tag{4.2.8}$$

Using (4.2.6), we have

$$(k+1)\,\phi_k^{(m-1)} + (m-k)\,\phi_{k-1}^{(m-1)}$$
$$= (k+1)\,\Delta^{k+1}0^{m-1} - (k+1)\sum_{j=0}^{k-1}(-1)^j\binom{m-k-1+j}{j+1}\Delta^{k-j}0^{m-1}$$
$$+ (m-k)\sum_{j=0}^{k-1}(-1)^j\binom{m-k-1+j}{j}\Delta^{k-j}0^{m-1}. \tag{4.2.9}$$

Now

$$-(k+1)\binom{m-k-1+j}{j+1} + (m-k)\binom{m-k-1+j}{j}$$
$$= -(k-j)\binom{m-k-1+j}{j+1} + \binom{m-k-1+j}{j}$$
$$+\left[-(j+1)\binom{m-k-1+j}{j+1} + (m-k-1)\binom{m-k-1+j}{j}\right], \tag{4.2.10}$$

and the term in brackets vanishes, since $k\binom{k+j}{j} = (j+1)\binom{k+j}{j+1}$. Also, $\binom{m}{j} + \binom{m}{j+1} = \binom{m+1}{j+1}$. Hence, the left-hand member of (4.2.10) is equal to

$$-(k-j)\left[\binom{m-k-1+j}{j+1} + \binom{m-k-1+j}{j}\right] + (k+1-j)\binom{m-k-1+j}{j}$$
$$= -(k-j)\binom{m-k+j}{j} + (k+1-j)\binom{m-k-1+j}{j}. \tag{4.2.11}$$

Thus, the right-hand member of (4.2.8) is equal to

$$(k+1)\,\Delta^{k+1}0^{m-1} + \sum_{j=0}^{k-1}(-1)^j\left[-(k-j)\binom{m-k+j}{j}\right.$$
$$\left.+(k+1-j)\binom{m-k-1+j}{j}\right]\Delta^{k-j}0^{m-1}. \tag{4.2.12}$$

On the other hand, by (4.2.7), we have

$$\phi_k^{(m)} = \sum_{j=0}^{k}(-1)^j\binom{m-k-1+j}{j}\Delta^{k+1-j}0^m$$
$$= \sum_{j=0}^{k}(-1)^j\binom{m-k-1+j}{j}(k+1-j)[\Delta^{k+1-j}0^{m-1} + \Delta^{k-j}0^m]$$

$$= (k+1)\,\Delta^{k+1}0^{m-1} + \sum_{j=0}^{k-1} (-1)^j \Big[-(k-j) \sum_{j+1}^{m-k+j}$$

$$+(k+1-j)\binom{m-k-1+j}{j}\Big]\,\Delta^{k-j}0^{m-1} + (-1)^k \binom{m-1}{k}\Delta^0 0^{m-1}.$$

Here the last term is equal to zero, and (4.2.8) follows.

The initial part of the array of coefficients $\phi_k^{(m)}$ is given in the following table (m refers to row, k to diagonal):

$m = 1$							1							$k = 0$
$m = 2$						1		1						$k = 1$
$m = 3$					1		4		1					$k = 2$
$m = 4$				1		11		11		1				$k = 3$
$m = 5$			1		26		66		26		1			$k = 4$
$m = 6$		1		57		302		302		57		1		$k = 5$
$m = 7$	1		120		1191		2416		1191		120		1	$k = 6$

For equal intervals, the spline relation for quintic splines, (4.1.27), is seen to collapse to

$$\tfrac{1}{120}\,[M_{j-2} + 26M_{j-1} + 66M_j + 26M_{j+1} + M_{j+2}]$$

$$= \frac{S_{j+2} - 4S_{j+1} + 6S_j - 4S_{j-1} + S_{j-2}}{h^4}. \tag{4.2.13}$$

We illustrate also the application to quartic splines on equal intervals. By returning to (4.1.1), we obtain

$$S_\Delta(x_j) = \sum_{k=0}^{2} \frac{1}{k!}(x_j - a)^k + \frac{1}{2!}\int_a^b S_\Delta'''(t)(x_j - t)_+{}^2\,dt$$

and by a derivation similar to that used for (4.1.5) derive

$$\tfrac{1}{24}\,(M_{j-2} + 11M_{j-1} + 11M_j + M_{j+1}) = \frac{S_{j+1} - 3S_j + 3S_{j-1} - S_{j-2}}{h^3}. \tag{4.2.14}$$

In order to formulate the complete equation system for type I and type II splines, it is desirable to express (4.1.8) in simplified form.

For uniform meshes, Eqs. (4.1.8) ($q = 1, 2, \ldots, 2n-3$) become

$$\Delta^q S_j\big|_{j=0} = \sum_{k=q}^{2n-3} \frac{h^k}{k!} S_\Delta^{(k)}(a) \cdot \Delta^q 0^k + \frac{M_0 h^{2n-2}}{(2n-2)!}\left[\Delta^q(i)_+^{2n-2} - \frac{\Delta^{q+1}(i-1)_+^{2n-1}}{2n-1}\right]_{i=0} + \frac{h^{2n-2}}{(2n-1)!}\sum_{j=1}^{q} M_j \Delta^{q+2}(i-1-j)_+^{2n-1}\Big|_{i=0}. \quad (4.2.15)$$

(In the second and third terms on the right, Δ operates on the index i. Of course, $\Delta^q(i)_+^{2n-2} = \Delta^q 0^{2n-2}$.)

For the representation of $S_\Delta(x)$ and its derivatives on $[x_{j-1}, x_j]$, it is much more convenient in the present situation to replace (4.1.11) by the following:

$$\left.\begin{aligned} S_\Delta^{(2n-2p-1)}(x) &= -M_{j-1}\frac{(x_j-x)^{2p}}{(2p)!h} + M_j\frac{(x-x_{j-1})^{2p}}{(2p)!h} \\ &\quad - \sum_{k=1}^{p} A_{k,j-1}\frac{(x_j-x)^{2p-2k}}{(2p-2k)!} + \sum_{k=1}^{p} B_{kj}\frac{(x-x_{j-1})^{2p-2k}}{(2p-2k)!}, \\ S_\Delta^{(2n-2p-2)}(x) &= M_{j-1}\frac{(x_j-x)^{2p+1}}{(2p+1)!h} + M_j\frac{(x-x_{j-1})^{2p+1}}{(2p+1)!h} \\ &\quad + \sum_{k=1}^{p} A_{k,j-1}\frac{(x_j-x)^{2p-2k+1}}{(2p-2k+1)!} + \sum_{k=1}^{p} B_{k,j}\frac{(x-x_{j-1})^{2p-2k+1}}{(2p-2k+1)!}, \end{aligned}\right\} \quad (4.2.16)$$

for $p = 0, 1, 2, \ldots, n-1$.

By the continuity of $S_\Delta^{(2n-3)}(x)$ and $S_\Delta^{(2n-4)}(x)$ at x_j, it follows that

$$A_{1,j} = B_{1,j}, \qquad \frac{h}{2!} M_j = \frac{\delta^2}{2} A_{1,j}. \quad (4.2.17)$$

It is immediately seen by induction that, for $p = 1, 2, \ldots n-1$,

$$\begin{gathered} A_{p,j} = B_{p,j}, \\ \frac{h^{2p}}{(2p)!}\frac{M_j}{h} + \frac{h^{2p-2}}{(2p-2)!}A_{1,j} + \cdots + \frac{h^2}{a!}A_{p-1,j} = \frac{\delta^2}{2}A_{p,j}. \end{gathered} \quad (4.2.18)$$

For $p = n$, we have also

$$\frac{h^{2n-1}}{(2n-1)!}\frac{M_j}{h} + \frac{h^{2n-3}}{(2n-3)!}A_{1,j} + \cdots + hA_{n-1,j} = S_j. \quad (4.2.19)$$

Write this system of difference equations as

$$\mathscr{P}\begin{bmatrix} M_j/h \\ A_{1,j} \\ A_{2,j} \\ \vdots \\ A_{n-1,j} \end{bmatrix} = \begin{bmatrix} 0 \\ 0 \\ 0 \\ \vdots \\ S_j \end{bmatrix}, \tag{4.2.20}$$

where

$$\mathscr{P} = \begin{bmatrix} \frac{h^2}{2!} & -\frac{\delta^2}{2} & 0 & \cdots & 0 \\ \frac{h^4}{4!} & \frac{h^2}{2!} & -\frac{\delta^2}{2} & \cdots & 0 \\ \vdots & \vdots & & & \vdots \\ \frac{h^{2n-2}}{(2n-2)!} & \frac{h^{2n-4}}{(2n-4)!} & \cdots & \frac{h^2}{2!} & -\frac{\delta^2}{2} \\ \frac{h^{2n-1}}{(2n-1)!} & \frac{h^{2n-3}}{(2n-3)!} & \cdots & \frac{h^3}{3!} & h \end{bmatrix}. \tag{4.2.21}$$

For periodic splines and for nonperiodic splines when

$$n - 1 \leqslant j \leqslant N - n + 1,$$

premultiply both sides of (4.2.20) by the adjoint $\mathscr{P}^*$ of $\mathscr{P}$, considered as a matrix. Let $|\mathscr{P}|$ be the determinant of $\mathscr{P}$, and denote the elements of $\mathscr{P}^*$ by $P_{k,i}^*$. Then there results

$$\begin{bmatrix} |\mathscr{P}| & & & \\ & |\mathscr{P}| & & \\ & & \ddots & \\ & & & |\mathscr{P}| \end{bmatrix} \begin{bmatrix} M_j/h \\ A_{1,j} \\ \vdots \\ A_{n-1,j} \end{bmatrix} = \begin{bmatrix} P_{1,n}^* S_j \\ P_{2,n}^* S_j \\ \vdots \\ P_{n,n}^* S_j \end{bmatrix}. \tag{4.2.22}$$

Thus we have

$$|\mathscr{P}| M_j/h = P_{1,n}^* S_j, \tag{4.2.23}$$

$$|\mathscr{P}| A_{i,j} = P_{i+1,n}^* S_j \qquad (i = 1, 2, \ldots, n-1). \tag{4.2.24}$$

Let us now compare (4.2.23) with (4.2.5). We have

$$P_{n,1}^* = \left(-\frac{\delta^2}{2}\right)^{n-1}$$

and so

$$2^{n-1}|\mathscr{P}| M_j = \frac{h^{2n-1}}{(2n-1)!} \sum_{k=0}^{2n-2} \phi_k^{(2n-1)} M_{j-n+1+k}. \tag{4.2.25}$$

This identity can, of course, be established directly from the expansion of $|\mathscr{P}|$. The derivation, however, is somewhat lengthy.

The operator in the right-hand member of (4.2.24) may be written as

$$P^*_{i+1,n} = \begin{vmatrix} \frac{h^2}{2!} & -\frac{\delta^2}{2} & 0 & \cdots & & & & & 0 \\ \frac{h^4}{4!} & \frac{h^2}{2!} & -\frac{\delta^2}{2} & 0 & \cdots & & & & 0 \\ \vdots & \vdots & & & & & & & \vdots \\ \frac{h^{2i-2}}{(2i-2)!} & \frac{h^{2i-4}}{(2i-4)!} & \cdots & \frac{h^2}{2!} & -\frac{\delta^2}{2} & 0 & \cdots & & 0 \\ \frac{h^{2i}}{(2i)!} & \frac{h^{2i-2}}{(2i-2)!} & \cdots & \frac{h^4}{4!} & \frac{h^2}{2!} & 0 & \cdots & & 0 \\ \frac{h^{2i+2}}{(2i+2)!} & \frac{h^{2i}}{(2i)!} & \cdots & \frac{h^6}{6!} & \frac{h^4}{4!} & -\frac{\delta^2}{2} & 0 & \cdots & 0 \\ \vdots & \vdots & & & & & & & \vdots \\ \frac{h^{2n-4}}{(2n-4)!} & \frac{h^{2n-6}}{(2n-6)!} & \cdots & & & & -\frac{\delta^2}{2} & & 0 \\ \frac{h^{2n-2}}{(2n-2)!} & \frac{h^{2n-4}}{(2n-4)!} & \cdots & & & & \frac{h^2}{2!} & & -\frac{\delta^2}{2} \end{vmatrix}$$

$$= \begin{vmatrix} \frac{h^2}{2!} & -\frac{\delta^2}{2} & 0 & \cdots & & 0 \\ \frac{h^4}{4!} & \frac{h^2}{2!} & -\frac{\delta^2}{2} & \cdots & & 0 \\ \vdots & \vdots & & & & \vdots \\ \frac{h^{2i-2}}{(2i-2)!} & \frac{h^{2i-4}}{(2i-4)!} & \cdots & \frac{h^2}{2} & & -\frac{\delta^2}{2} \\ \frac{h^{2i}}{(2i)!} & \frac{h^{2i-2}}{(2i-2)!} & \cdots & \frac{h^4}{4!} & & \frac{h^2}{2!} \end{vmatrix} \left(-\frac{\delta^2}{2}\right)^{n-i-1}. \qquad (4.2.26)$$

We note that, if we define

$$Q_n(x) = \begin{vmatrix} \frac{1}{2!} & -x & 0 & 0 & \cdots & 0 \\ \frac{1}{4!} & \frac{1}{2!} & -x & 0 & \cdots & 0 \\ \frac{1}{6!} & \frac{1}{4!} & \frac{1}{2!} & -x & \cdots & 0 \\ \vdots & \vdots & & & & \vdots \\ \frac{1}{(2n-2)!} & \frac{1}{(2n-4)!} & \cdots & & \frac{1}{2!} & -x \\ \frac{1}{(2n)!} & \frac{1}{(2n-2)!} & \cdots & & \frac{1}{4!} & \frac{1}{2!} \end{vmatrix}, \qquad (4.2.27)$$

then expanding in terms of minors of the first column gives

$$Q_n(x) = \frac{1}{2!} Q_{n-1}(x) + \frac{x}{4!} Q_{n-2}(x) + \cdots + \frac{x^{n-2}}{(2n-2)!} Q_1(x) + \frac{x^{n-1}}{(2n)!}.$$

This is valid for $n \geqslant 2$ if we define $Q_1 = 1/(2!)$. If we express $Q_n(x)$ as

$$Q_n(x) = \alpha_{n,0} + \alpha_{n,1}x + \cdots + \alpha_{n,n-1}x^{n-1}, \tag{4.2.28}$$

then we have

$$\sum_{k=0}^{n-2} \alpha_{nk} x^k = \sum_{k=1}^{n-1} \frac{x^{k-1}}{(2k)!} \sum_{j=0}^{n-k-1} \alpha_{n-k,j} x^j$$

$$= \sum_{u=1}^{n-1} x^{u-1} \sum_{k=1}^{u} \frac{\alpha_{n-k,u-k}}{(2k)!}.$$

Thus,

$$\alpha_{n,j} = \sum_{k=1}^{j+1} \frac{\alpha_{n-k,j+1-k}}{(2k)!} \quad (j = 0,\ldots, n-2); \qquad \alpha_{n,n-1} = \frac{1}{(2n)!}. \tag{4.2.29}$$

In particular,

$$\alpha_{n,0} = 1/(2!)^n. \tag{4.2.30}$$

We see further that

$$h^2/2! = h^2 Q_1(x), \qquad \begin{vmatrix} \frac{h^2}{2!} & x \\ \frac{h^4}{4!} & \frac{h^2}{2!} \end{vmatrix} = h^4 Q_2(x),$$

and by induction that

$$\begin{vmatrix} h^2/2! & -x & 0 & \cdots & 0 & 0 \\ h^4/4! & h^2/2! & -x & \cdots & 0 & 0 \\ h^6/6! & h^4/4! & h^2/2! & \cdots & 0 & 0 \\ \vdots & \vdots & \vdots & & \vdots & \vdots \\ h^{2n-2}/(2n-2)! & h^{2n-4}/(2n-4)! & h^{2n-6}/(2n-6)! & \cdots & h^2/2! & -x \\ h^{2n}/(2n)! & h^{2n-2}/(2n-2)! & h^{2n-4}/(2n-4)! & \cdots & h^4/4! & h^2/2! \end{vmatrix} = h^{2n} Q_n(x).$$

Thus,

$$P^*_{i+1,n} = h^{2i} Q_i(\delta^2/2)(-\delta^2/2)^{n-i-1}. \tag{4.2.31}$$

We turn now to the determination of the quantities $A_{k.j}$ in the case of type I and type II splines. From (4.2.16), we have

$$\begin{aligned} S_\Delta^{(2n-2p-1)}(x_{j-1}) &= -M_{j-1}\frac{h^{2p-1}}{(2p)!} - \sum_{k=1}^{p} A_{k,j}\frac{h^{2p-2k}}{(2p-2k)!}, \\ S_\Delta^{2n-2p-2}(x_{j-1}) &= M_{j-1}\frac{h^{2p}}{(2p+1)} + \sum_{k=1}^{p} A_{k,j}\frac{h^{2p-2k+1}}{(2p-2k+1)!}. \end{aligned} \tag{4.2.32}$$

For type I splines, when the quantities M_j have been found, we may determine $S_\Delta^{(q)}(a)$ ($q = 2n-3,\ldots, N$) from (4.2.15) rewritten as

$$\begin{aligned} S_\Delta^{(q)}(a) = \frac{1}{h^q}\Delta^q S_j\Big|_{j=0} &- \sum_{k=q+1}^{2n-3}\frac{h^{k-q}}{k!}S_\Delta^{(k)}(a)\,\Delta^q 0^k \\ &- \frac{M_0 h^{2n-q-2}}{(2n-2)!}\left[\Delta^q(i)_+^{2n-2} - \frac{\Delta^{q+1}(i-1)^{2n-1}}{2n-1}\right]_{i=0} \\ &- \frac{h^{2n-q-2}}{(2n-1)!}\sum_{j=1}^{q} M_j\,\Delta^{q+2}(i-1-j)_+^{2n-1}\Big|_{i=0}. \end{aligned}$$

For type II splines, we similarly determine $S_\Delta^{(q)}(a)$ ($q = 1, 2,\ldots, n-1$). Once all the quantities $S_\Delta^{(q)}(a)$ ($q = 1,\ldots, 2n-3$) have been found, we may determine the quantities $S_\Delta^{(q)}(x_j)$ by integration. Thus,

$$\begin{aligned} S_\Delta^{(2n-2p-1)}(x_j) &= \sum_{k=0}^{2p-2}\frac{h^k}{k!}S_\Delta^{(2n-p-1+k)}(a) \\ &\quad + \frac{1}{(2p-2)!}\sum_{k=1}^{j}\int_{x_{k-1}}^{x_k} S_\Delta^{(2n-2)}(t)(x_k - t)^{2p-2}\,dt \\ &= \sum_{k=0}^{2p-2}\frac{h^k}{k!}S_\Delta^{(2n-p-1+k)}(a) \\ &\quad + \frac{h^{2p-1}}{(2p-1)!}\left[\frac{2p-1}{2p}M_0 + M_1 + \cdots + M_{j-1} + \frac{1}{2p}M_j\right], \end{aligned}$$

as may be seen by integrating by parts twice.

4.3. Existence

For polynomial splines on nonuniform meshes, existence proofs based directly upon the properties of the coefficient matrix are quite difficult to construct. We note that, even for the case of equal intervals, the coefficient matrix for the splines of degree 7 does not have dominant main diagonal (cf. coefficient table in Section 4.2).

For polynomial splines of odd degree which are of best approximation or of minimum norm, the existence is a consequence of the first integral relation, as in the case of the cubic spline. These properties are explained in detail in Chapter V.

In the case of periodic polynomial splines on equal-interval meshes, nevertheless, existence may be handled directly. The proof leads, moreover, to several properties of the coefficient matrix which are of importance in themselves. The coefficient matrix in (4.2.1) is the circulant matrix of order N,

$$A = \begin{bmatrix} a_1 & a_2 & a_3 & \cdots & a_N \\ a_N & a_1 & a_2 & \cdots & a_{N-1} \\ a_{N-1} & a_N & a_1 & \cdots & a_{N-2} \\ \vdots & \vdots & \vdots & & \vdots \\ a_2 & a_3 & a_4 & & a_1 \end{bmatrix} = C(a_1, a_2, \ldots, a_N), \tag{4.3.1}$$

$$a_1 = A_0^{(2n-1)}, \qquad a_k = a_{N+2-k} = A_k^{2n-1} = A_{-k}^{2n-1} \qquad (k = 1, 2, \ldots, n);$$
$$a_k = 0 \text{ otherwise.}$$

It is well known (cf. Aitken [1958] or Muir [1960]) that the eigenvalues of the matrix A in (4.3.1) are

$$\theta_k = a_1 + a_2\omega_k + \cdots + a_N\omega_k^{N-1} \qquad (k = 1, 2, \ldots, N), \tag{4.3.2}$$

where $\omega_k = e^{2\pi ki/N}$. The corresponding eigenvectors are

$$(1, \omega_k, \omega_k^2, \ldots, \omega_k^{N-1}). \tag{4.3.3}$$

Thus we may represent the matrix A as $A = \Omega\Theta\Omega^{-1}$, where

$$\Omega = \begin{bmatrix} 1 & 1 & \cdots & 1 \\ \omega_1 & \omega_2 & \cdots & \omega_N \\ \omega_1^2 & \omega_2^2 & \cdots & \omega_N^2 \\ \vdots & \vdots & & \vdots \\ \omega_1^{N-1} & \omega_2^{N-1} & \cdots & \omega_N^{N-1} \end{bmatrix}, \tag{4.3.4}$$

$$\Theta = \begin{bmatrix} \theta_1 & 0 & 0 & \cdots & 0 \\ 0 & \theta_2 & 0 & \cdots & 0 \\ 0 & 0 & \theta_3 & \cdots & 0 \\ \vdots & \vdots & \vdots & & \vdots \\ 0 & 0 & 0 & \cdots & \theta_N \end{bmatrix}. \tag{4.3.5}$$

We have

$$\Omega^{-1} = \begin{bmatrix} 1/N & \omega_1^{-1}/N & \omega_1^{-2}/N & \cdots & \omega_1^{1-N}/N \\ 1/N & \omega_2^{-1}/N & \omega_2^{-2}/N & \cdots & \omega_2^{1-N}/N \\ 1/N & \omega_3^{-1}/N & \omega_3^{-2}/N & \cdots & \omega_3^{1-N}/N \\ \vdots & \vdots & \vdots & & \vdots \\ 1/N & \omega_N^{-1}/N & \omega_N^{-2}/N & \cdots & \omega_N^{1-N}/N \end{bmatrix}, \tag{4.3.6}$$

and, if none of the eigenvalues is equal to zero,

$$A^{-1} = \Omega\Theta^{-1}\Omega^{-1} = C\left(\sum_{k=1}^{N} \theta_k^{-1}/N, \sum_{k=1}^{N} (\omega_k\theta_k)^{-1}/N, \ldots, \sum_{k=1}^{N} (\omega_k^{N-1}\theta_k)^{-1}/N\right). \tag{4.3.7}$$

The difference equation (4.2.6) has been studied by Hille [1962, p. 47] in respect to its association with the differential operator $\theta \equiv zd/dz$ in the complex plane. Let

$$P_m(z) = z \sum_{k=0}^{m-1} \phi_k^{(m)} z^k, \tag{4.3.8}$$

where the quantities $\phi_k^{(m)}$ are as defined in (4.2.3). We show by induction that

$$\theta^m \frac{1}{1-z} = \frac{P_m(z)}{(1-z)^{m+1}}. \tag{4.3.9}$$

First,

$$\theta \frac{1}{1-z} = \frac{z}{(1-z)^2} = \frac{z\phi_0^{(1)}}{(1-z)^2}.$$

Then, assuming

$$\theta^{m-1} \frac{1}{1-z} = \frac{z \sum_{k=0}^{m-2} \phi_k^{(m-1)} z^k}{(1-z)^m},$$

where $\phi_0^{(m)} = \phi_{m-1}^{(m)} = 1$ for all $m \geqslant 1$, we obtain

$$\begin{aligned} \theta^m \frac{1}{1-z} &= \frac{z\{mP_{m-1}(z) + (1-z)\, P'_{m-1}(z)\}}{(1-z)^{m+1}} \\ &= \frac{z\{mz \sum_{k=0}^{m-2} \phi_k^{(m-1)} z^k + (1-z) \sum_{k=0}^{m-1} (k+1)\, \phi_k^{(m-1)} z^k\}}{(1-z)^{m+1}} \\ &= \frac{z\{\phi_0^{(m-1)} + \sum_{k=1}^{m-2} [m\phi_{k-1}^{(m-1)} + (k+1)\phi_k^{(m-1)} - k\phi_{k-1}^{(m-1)}] z^k + \phi_{m-2}^{(m-1)} z^{m-1}}{(1-z)^{m+1}} \\ &= \frac{zP_m(z)}{(1-z)^{m+1}}, \end{aligned} \tag{4.3.10}$$

since $\phi_k^{(m)} = (k+1)\phi_k^{(m-1)} + (m-k)\phi_{k-1}^{(m-1)}$. From (4.3.10), we see that we have

$$P_1(z) = z, \qquad P_m(z) = z[mP_{m-1}(z) + (1-z)P'_{m-1}(z)] \qquad (m > 1). \tag{4.3.11}$$

We show also by induction that $P_m(z)$ has $n-1$ distinct real negative zeros.

We note that $P_2(z) = z(z+1)$, so that -1 is a zero of $P_2(z)$. Assume that $P_{m-1}(z)$ has $m-2$ distinct negative real zeros in addition to vanishing at $z = 0$. Since $P_{m-1}(x)$ is real $(x = \Re z)$, there must be a zero of $P'_{m-1}(x)$ between two successive zeros of $P_{m-1}(x)$. Thus, $P_{m-1}(x)$ and $P_m(x)$ do not simultaneously vanish except at $x = 0$. At a zero of $P'_{m-1}(x)$, $P_m(x)$ and $P_{m-1}(x)$ have opposite sign. $P_m(x)$ is monic so that, as $x \to -\infty$, $P_m(x) \to -\infty$ or $+\infty$ according as m is odd or even. Thus $P_m(x)$ has a zero between each two consecutive zeros of $P'_{m-1}(x)$ and a zero to the left of the left-most zero of $P_{m-1}(x)$. In addition, $P_m(0) = 0$, and, since $P'_m(0) > 0$, there is a zero of $P_m(x)$ between 0 and the right-most zero of $P'_{m-1}(x)$. Consequently, $P_m(x)$ has $n-1$ distinct negative real roots in addition to the zero root. This completes the inductive proof.

Now $\phi_k^{(m)} = \phi_{m-1-k}^{(m)}$, as may be easily shown in a variety of ways. Thus, the reciprocal of each zero of $P_m(z)/z$ is again a zero, and $P_{2n}(-1) = 0$. Thus, for periodic splines of odd degree, the eigenvalues θ_k are all different from zero. [Indeed, they are all real, as may be seen from (4.3.2), where $a_k = a_{N+2-k}(1 < k \leqslant N)$.] The matrix A is therefore nonsingular in this case.

We note that (-1) is an Nth root of unity only if N is even. Thus for even-degree splines the matrix A is nonsingular if N is odd. This concludes the proof of the following theorem.

Theorem 4.3.1. *Periodic polynomial splines of interpolation of odd degree $\leqslant N$ on a uniform mesh always exist. Periodic polynomial splines of even degree $\leqslant N$ exist if the number N of mesh intervals is odd.*

4.4. Convergence

A complete array of convergence properties analogous to those presented for cubic splines in Chapters II and III is not yet available for polynomial splines in general. If $f(x)$ is of class $C^q[a, b]$ $(0 \leqslant q \leqslant 2n-1)$ and $S_{\Delta_k}(x)$ is the spline of interpolation to $f(x)$ on Δ_k satisfying certain rather general end conditions and the sequence of meshes $\{\Delta_k\}$ has $\lim_{k\to\infty} \| \Delta_k \| = 0$, we might expect that

$$f^{(p)}(x) - S^{(p)}_{\Delta_k}(x) = o(\| \Delta_k \|^{q-p}) \qquad (0 \leqslant p \leqslant q \leqslant 2n - 1), \qquad (4.4.1)$$

provided in the case of derivatives of order $2n - 1$ that the quantities $R_{\Delta_k} = \{\max_i \| \Delta_k \| / (x_{k,i} - x_{k,i-1})]$ are bounded.

The authors have demonstrated convergence of sequences of periodic polynomial splines for asymptotically uniform meshes (Ahlberg *et al.* [1965]) for functions of class $C^{2n-2}[a, b]$. More recently, Ziegler [1965] has announced a proof of convergence for periodic splines without the restriction of asymptotic uniformity on the meshes. A recent result for generalized splines (Ahlberg *et al.* [1965a]) gives estimates of the order of convergence when $f(x)$ is in $C^n[a, b]$ and when $f(x)$ is in $C^{2n}[a, b]$ provided in the latter case the meshes satisfy (2.3.7) (see Chapters V and VI).

In Chapter V, we establish the fact that, if $f(x)$ is in $\mathscr{K}^n(a, b)$, then

$$f^{(p)}(x) - S^{(p)}_{\Delta_k}(x) = O(\| \Delta_k \|^{n-p-1/2}) \qquad (0 \leqslant p \leqslant n - 1).$$

Furthermore, if the quantities R_{Δ_k} are bounded as $k \to \infty$ and if $f(x)$ is in $\mathscr{K}^n(a, b)$, then

$$f^{(p)}(x) - S^{(p)}_{\Delta_k}(x) = O(\| \Delta_k \|^{2n-p-1}) \qquad (0 \leqslant p \leqslant 2n - 1).$$

As in the case of the cubic spline, the apparent defect in the rate of convergence arises from the method of proof employed.

In order to get at the more precise relation (4.4.1) as for cubics, it appears necessary to use properties of the inverse of the coefficient matrix for the equation system determining the spline. As of the present time, these properties have not been demonstrated except in certain special cases.

In this section, we prove some convergence results for general polynomial splines of odd degree which anticipate properties of the inverse coefficient matrix A for the spline equations described in Section 4.1. This is followed in the next section by a detailed discussion for periodic polynomial splines on uniform meshes.

Theorem 4.4.1. *Let $\{\Delta_k\}$ be a sequence of meshes on $[a, b]$ with $\| \Delta_k \| \to 0$ as $k \to \infty$. Let $f(x)$ be of class $C^{2n-2}[a, b]$. Let S_{Δ_k} be the polynomial spline of degree $2n - 1$ of interpolation to $f(x)$ on Δ_k such that $f(x) - S_{\Delta_k}(x)$ is of type I′ or type II′ or such that $S_{\Delta_k}(x)$ is periodic [provided $f(x)$ is periodic and of class $C^{2n-2}(-\infty, \infty)$]. If the coefficient matrix A_k*

associated with the spline equations (4.1.5) and the end conditions has an inverse A_k^{-1} *which is bounded with respect to* k, *then uniformly on* $[a, b]$

$$f^{(p)}(x) - S_{\Delta_k}^{(p)}(x) = o(\|\Delta_k\|^{2n-2-p}) \qquad (p = 0, 1,..., 2n-2). \qquad (4.4.2)$$

If $f^{2n-2}(x)$ *satisfies a Hölder condition of order* α $(0 < \alpha \leqslant 1)$ *on* $[a, b]$, *then*

$$f^{(p)}(x) - S_{\Delta_k}^{(p)}(x) = O(\|\Delta_k\|^{2n-2+\alpha-p}) \qquad (p = 0, 1,..., 2n-2). \qquad (4.4.3)$$

uniformly with respect to x *in* $[a, b]$.

Proof. Let us drop the mesh index k, denote by M the vector $(M_0, M_1,..., M_N)^T$, and let A represent the coefficient matrix of the spline equation system. Write the spline equations as

$$AM = d. \qquad (4.4.4)$$

If $S_\Delta(x)$ is periodic, then (4.4.4) is precisely the system of equations (4.1.5) $(i = 1, 2,..., N)$. Here d is the vector $(d_1,..., d_N)$ with

$$d_i = \delta_i^{2n-2} f(x_i). \qquad (4.4.5)$$

Thus we have

$$A[M - (2n-2)!\, d] = [I - (2n-2)!\, A]\, d, \qquad (4.4.6)$$

where I is the unit matrix of order N. In view of (4.1.7), the elements of the vector on the right may be rearranged as

$$\begin{bmatrix} (2n-2)! \sum_{j=1}^{N} A_{1j}(d_1 - d_j) \\ (2n-2)! \sum_{j=1}^{N} A_{2j}(d_2 - d_j) \\ \vdots \\ (2n-2)! \sum_{j=1}^{N} A_{Nj}(d_N - d_j) \end{bmatrix}.$$

The quantities A_{ij} are nonnegative and consequently, in view of (4.1.7), are bounded uniformly with respect to the mesh index k. Moreover, $A_{i,j} = 0$ for $j < i - n + 1$ and $j > i + n - 1$. For $i - n + 1 \leqslant j \leqslant i + n - 1$,

$$|d_j - d_i| \leqslant \mu(f^{(2n-2)}; (2n-2)\|\Delta\|). \qquad (4.4.7)$$

Thus, we write

$$\| M - (2n-2)!\, d \| \leqslant \| A^{-1} \| \, \mu(f^{(2n-2)}; (2n-2)\| \Delta \|). \tag{4.4.8}$$

From this point, the proof for the periodic case proceeds in a familiar fashion. By a $(2n-3)$-fold application of Rolle's theorem and the fact that $S_\Delta(x)$ interpolates to $f(x)$ at the points of Δ, we find that in any $(2n-2)$ consecutive intervals there is at least one point ξ at which $S_\Delta^{(2n-3)}(\xi) = f^{(2n-3)}(\xi)$. By writing

$$f^{(2n-3)}(x) - S_\Delta^{(2n-3)}(x) = \int_\xi^x [f^{(2n-2)}(t) - S_\Delta^{(2n-2)}(t)]\, dt,$$

we find that

$$\max_{[a,b]} | f^{(2n-3)}(x) - S_\Delta^{(2n-3)}(x) | \leqslant (2n-3) \| A^{-1} \| \, \mu(f^{(2n-2)}; (2n-2)\| \Delta \|) \cdot \| \Delta \|.$$

Relations (4.4.2) and (4.4.3) now follow for the periodic case.

Consider next the type II splines. Here the proof differs from that employed in the periodic case because of the $n-1$ end conditions to be imposed at each end. Since we have explicitly assumed the uniform boundedness of $\| A^{-1} \|$ (the *existence* of A^{-1} is shown in Chapter V), we need only show that the right-hand member of (4.4.6) approaches zero as before.

We take Eqs. (4.1.5) for $i = n-1, n, \ldots, N-n+1$. In addition to these we have the $n-1$ relations consisting of

$$M_0 = f^{(2n-2)}(0) \tag{4.4.9.1}$$

and Eqs. (4.1.8) ($q = n, n+1, \ldots, 2n-3$) written in the form

$$\sum_{j=1}^{q} A_{q-n+1,j} M_j = \left\{ f[x_0, x_1, \ldots, x_q] - \sum_{k=q}^{2n-3} \frac{1}{k!} f^{(k)}(a)[0, x_1 - a, \ldots, x_q - a]^k \right\}$$
$$\cdot \{[0, x_1 - a, \ldots, x_q - a]^{2n-2}\}^{-1}. \tag{4.4.9.2}$$

For a polynomial $p(x)$ of degree not greater than $2n-2$, the right-hand member of (4.4.9.2) is precisely $p^{(2n-2)}(x_0)/(2n-2)!$. Since (4.1.8) is an identity for polynomials of degree $\leqslant 2n-2$, set $p(x) = x^{2n-2}/(2n-2)!$. Then each $M_j = 1$ in (4.1.8). Also, we have represented the coefficient of M_j in (4.1.8) as $A_{q-n+1,j}\ [0, x_1 - a, \ldots, x_q - a]^{2n-2}$. Thus, $\sum_{j=0}^{q} A_{q-n+1,j} = 1/(2n-2)!$.

It remains to show that the right-hand member of (4.4.9.2) approaches

$S_\Delta^{(2n-2)}(x_0)/(2n-2)!$ as $\|\Delta\| \to 0$. Let $p(x)$ be the polynomial of degree $2n-2$ defined by $p^{(\alpha)}(x_0) = S_\Delta^{(\alpha)}(x_0)$, $\alpha = 0, 1, \ldots, 2n-2$. Then from

$$p(x) = \sum_{k=0}^{2n-2} \frac{1}{k!} S_\Delta^{(k)}(a)(x-a)^k$$

it follows that

$$p[x_0, \ldots, x_q] - \sum_{k=q}^{2n-3} \frac{1}{k!} S_\Delta^{(k)}(a) \cdot [0, x_1 - a, \ldots, x_q - a]^k$$
$$= \frac{1}{(2n-2)!} S_\Delta^{(2n-2)}(a) \quad [0, x_1 - a, \ldots, x_q - a]^{2n-2}$$

and that the right-hand member of (4.4.9.2) may be written in the form

$$\frac{S_\Delta[x_0, \ldots, x_q] - p[x_0, \ldots, x_q]}{[0, x_1 - a, \ldots, x_q - a]^{2n-2}} + \frac{1}{(2n-1)!} S_\Delta^{(2n-2)}(a). \tag{4.4.10}$$

The first term in the last expression is the quotient of qth divided differences, over $x_0, x_1, \ldots, x_q$, of a function $F = S_\Delta - p$ whose first $2n-2$ derivatives vanish at x_0 and of the function x^{2n-2}.

Consider the more general problem of evaluating the quotient of divided differences of two k-fold differentiable functions,

$$\frac{F[x_0, x_1, \ldots, x_k]}{G[x_0, x_1, \ldots, x_k]}. \tag{4.4.11}$$

We note that we can write the kth divided difference in the form (cf. Davis [1963, p. 46])

$$F[x_0, x_1, \ldots, x_k] = \begin{vmatrix} 1 & x_0 & x_0^2 & \cdots & x_0^{k-1} & F(x_0) \\ 1 & x_1 & x_1^2 & \cdots & x_1^{k-1} & F(x_1) \\ \vdots & \vdots & \vdots & & \vdots & \vdots \\ 1 & x_k & x_k^2 & \cdots & x_k^{k-1} & F(x_k) \end{vmatrix} \div \begin{vmatrix} 1 & x_0 & x_0^2 & \cdots & x_0^k \\ 1 & x_1 & x_1^2 & \cdots & x_1^k \\ \vdots & \vdots & \vdots & & \vdots \\ 1 & x_k & x_k^2 & \cdots & x_k^k \end{vmatrix}. \tag{4.4.12}$$

Consider then (cf. Goursat-Hedrick [1904, p. 10])

$$\phi(x) = \begin{vmatrix} 1 & x_0 & x_0^2 & \cdots & x_0^{k-1} & F(x_0) \\ 1 & x_1 & x_1^2 & \cdots & x_1^{k-1} & F(x_1) \\ \vdots & \vdots & \vdots & & \vdots & \vdots \\ 1 & x_{k-1} & x_{k-1}^2 & \cdots & x_{k-1}^{k-1} & F(x_{k-1}) \\ 1 & x & x^2 & \cdots & x^{k-1} & F(x) \end{vmatrix} - K \begin{vmatrix} 1 & x_0 & x_0^2 & \cdots & x_0^{k-1} & G(x_0) \\ 1 & x_1 & x_1^2 & \cdots & x_1^{k-1} & G(x_1) \\ \vdots & \vdots & \vdots & & \vdots & \vdots \\ 1 & x_{k-1} & x_{k-1}^2 & \cdots & x_{k-1}^{k-1} & G(x_{k-1}) \\ 1 & x & x^2 & \cdots & x^{k-1} & G(x) \end{vmatrix}.$$

The function $\phi(x)$ vanishes at $x = x_0, x_1, \ldots, x_{k-1}$. If K is set equal to (4.4.11), then $\phi(x_q) = 0$ also. Thus $\phi'(x)$ vanishes k times in (x_0, x_q),

$\phi''(x)$ vanishes $k-1$ times,..., $\phi^{(k)}(x)$ vanishes once in (x_0, x_q): at ξ, say. But

$$\phi^{(k)}(x) = \begin{vmatrix} 1 & x_0 & x_0^2 & \cdots & x_0^{k-1} \\ 1 & x_1 & x_1^2 & \cdots & x_1^{k-1} \\ \vdots & \vdots & \vdots & & \vdots \\ 1 & x_{k-1} & x_{k-1}^2 & \cdots & x_{k-1}^{k-1} \end{vmatrix} [F^{(k)}(x) - KG^{(k)}(x_1)].$$

Thus, for some ξ, $x_0 < \xi < x_k$, we have

$$\frac{F[x_0, x_1, ..., x_k]}{G[x_0, x_1, ..., x_k]} = \frac{F^{(k)}(\xi)}{G^{(k)}(\xi)}.$$

Hence the first member of (4.4.10) is equal to

$$\frac{S_\Delta^{(q)}(\xi) - p^{(q)}(\xi)}{(2n-2)(2n-3)\cdots(2n-q-1)\,\xi^{2n-q-2}},$$

the limit of which, as $\| \Delta \| \to 0$, is 0. It follows from (4.4.10) now that the limit of the right-hand member of (4.4.9b) as $\| \Delta \| \to 0$ is $S_\Delta^{(2n-2)}(x_0)/(2n-2)!$ The remainder of the proof for type II splines proceeds as in the previous case.

The proof for type I splines is omitted. No new ideas are introduced, and the proof is largely involved with the elimination of the quantities $S_\Delta^{(n)}(a)$, $S_\Delta^{(n+1)}a$,..., $S_\Delta^{(2n-3)}(a)$ from Eqs. (4.1.8)—a straightforward but somewhat tedious process.

We point out certain important cases in which the uniform boundedness of $\| A^{-1} \|$ has been established and to which the theorem applies. The authors have shown (Ahlberg *et al.* [1965, Theorem 4]) that this is the case for periodic splines on a sequence of asymptotically uniform meshes $\{\Delta_k\}$: $\| \Delta_k \| \to 0$ and $[\max_j | \frac{1}{2} - h_{k,j+1}/(h_{k,j} + h_{k,j+1})|] \to 0$. In particular, periodic splines on uniform meshes will be considered subsequently.

A second general result may be demonstrated for the case in which continuity requirements on the approximated function are relaxed but the additional mesh requirement (2.3.7) imposed.

Theorem 4.4.2. *Let* $\{\Delta_k\}$ *be a sequence of meshes on* $[a, b]$ *with* $\| \Delta_k \| \to 0$ *as* $k \to \infty$ *and* $R_{\Delta_k} = [max_j \| \Delta_k \|/(x_{k,j+1} - x_{k,j})] \leqslant \beta < \infty$. *Let* $f(x)$ *be of class* $C^q[a, b]$ $(0 \leqslant q \leqslant 2n-3)$. *Let the norms* $\| A_k^{-1} \|$ *of the inverses of the coefficient matrices be bounded as* $k \to \infty$. *Then for the polynomial splines* $S_{\Delta_k}(x)$ *of degree* $2n-1$ *of interpolation to* $f(x)$ *on* Δ_k

such that $f(x) - S_{\Delta_k}(x)$ is of type I', type II', or such that $S_{\Delta_k}(x)$ is periodic [if $f(x)$ is periodic and of class $C^q(-\infty, \infty)$], we have

$$[f^{(p)}(x) - S_{\Delta_k}^{(p)}(x)] = o(\| \Delta_k \|^{q-p}) \qquad (p = 0, 1,..., q). \tag{4.4.13}$$

If $f^{(m)}(x)$ satisfies a Hölder condition of order $\alpha(0 < \alpha \leqslant 1)$ on $[a, b]$, then

$$[f^{(p)}(x) - S_{\Delta_k}^{(p)}(x)] = O(\| \Delta_k \|^{q+\alpha-p}) \qquad (p = 0, 1,..., q). \tag{4.4.14}$$

Proof. We limit our arguments to the cases of periodic splines and type II splines, as in the case of the preceding proof. For $q < 2n - 2$, the divided difference (dropping the mesh index) $f[x_{j-n+1},..., x_{j+n-1}]$ satisfies

$$| f[x_{j-n+1},..., x_{j+n-1}] | \leqslant \frac{2^{2n-q-2}\beta^{2n-q-2}}{(2n-2)! \, \| \Delta \|^{2n-q-2}} \mu[f^{(q)}; (q+1)\| \Delta \|]. \tag{4.4.15}$$

The right-hand members of (4.4.9.2) can be shown to satisfy a similar inequality involving a constant multiple of

$$\mu[f^{(q)}; (q+1)\| \Delta \|]/\| \Delta \|^{2n-q-2}.$$

It then follows from the uniform boundedness of $\| A^{-1} \|$ that the spline equations (4.1.5) augmented by (4.4.9), etc., give, for some K_0 independent of the mesh index, the inequality

$$[\max \| \Delta \|^{2n-q-2} | M_j |] \leqslant K_0\mu[f^{(q)}; (q+1)\| \Delta \|] \leqslant K_0(q+1)\, \mu(f^{(q)}; \| \Delta \|). \tag{4.4.16}$$

Hence,

$$[\max_x \| \Delta \|^{2n-q-2} | S_{\Delta}^{(2n-2)}(x) |] \leqslant K_0(q+1)\, \mu(f^{(q)}; \| \Delta \|).$$

From (4.1.13), it may be concluded in the periodic case for K_p independent of the mesh index that

$$\| \Delta \|^{2n-2-p-q} | B_{p,j} | \leqslant K_p\mu(f^{(q)}; \| \Delta \|) \qquad (p = 1, 2,..., q+1);$$

this inequality is valid as well in the nonperiodic case when $n - 1 \leqslant j \leqslant N - n + 1$, and a similar inequality results for $0 \leqslant j < n - 1$, $N - n + 1 < j \leqslant N$ if we employ the boundary conditions.

It now follows from (4.1.11) that for modified constants K_p^*

$$\| \Delta \|^{2n-p-q-2} | S_{\Delta}^{(p)}(x) | \leqslant K_p^* \mu(f^{(q)}; \| \Delta \|)$$

and hence that

$$| S_\Delta^{(q)}(x) - S_\Delta^{(q)}(x_j) | = \left| \int_{x_j}^{x} S_\Delta^{(q+1)}(x)\, dx \right|$$
$$\leqslant \frac{K_{q+1}^* \mu(f^{(q)}; \| \Delta \|)}{\| \Delta \|} | x - x_j |.$$

Also $S_\Delta(x_j) = f(x_j)$, and we have $f[x_{j-q}, \ldots, x_j] = S_\Delta^{(q)}(\xi_1) = f^{(q)}(\xi_2)$ for some ξ_1 and ξ_2 in (x_{j-q+1}, x_{j+q-1}). Thus, on $[x_{j-1}, x_j]$,

$$[S_\Delta^{(q)}(x) - f^{(q)}(x)] = [S_\Delta^{(q)}(x) - S_\Delta^{(q)}(x_j)] + [S_\Delta^{(q)}(x_j) - S_\Delta^{(q)}(\xi_1)]$$
$$+ [f^{(q)}(\xi_2) - f^{(q)}(x)],$$
$$| S_\Delta^{(q)}(x) - f^{(q)}(x) | \leqslant [K_{q+1}^*(1 + q) + q]\, \mu(f^{(q)}; \| \Delta \|).$$

Relations (4.4.13) and (4.4.14) are now a direct consequence for $p = q$. The relations for $p < q$ follow again by integration and the use of the interpolation property.

It may be seen that the proofs of the preceding theorems rest upon certain boundedness properties of the quantities M_j rather than directly upon the boundedness of the inverse matrix norms $\| A_k^{-1} \|$. Let $f(x)$ be of class $C^{2n-2}[a, b]$. If $| M_{k,j} | \leqslant B$ ($j = 0, 1, \ldots, N_k$; $k = 1, 2, \ldots$) and if the sequence of meshes is nested, it may be shown for the polynomial splines of interpolation $S_{\Delta_k}(x)$ that $\{S_{\Delta_k}^{(2n-2)}(x)\}$ converges uniformly to $f^{(2n-2)}(x)$ on $[a, b]$ (see Ahlberg *et al.* [1965], Theorem 3). On the other hand, we can remove the requirement of being nested if we assume that the $S_{\Delta_k}^{(2n-2)}(x)$ are equicontinuous. For, by the interpolation property, $S_{\Delta_k}^{(2n-2)}(x) = f^{(2n-2)}(x)$ at least once in any $2n - 2$ consecutive intervals, and so

$$| S_{\Delta_k}^{(2n-2)}(x) - f^{(2n-2)}(x) | \leqslant \mu[f^{(2n-2)}; (n-1)\| \Delta_k \|] + \mu[S_{\Delta_k}^{(2n-2)}; (n-1)\| \Delta_k \|].$$

We may further show (see Ahlberg *et al.* [1965], p.237) that, if the meshes are nested and $\{S_{\Delta_k}(x)\}$ is a sequence of splines interpolating to an arbitrary function $f(x)$ defined on $[a, b]$ with $S_{\Delta_k}^{(2n-2)}(x)$ equicontinuous and bounded at one point, then $f^{(2n-2)}(x)$ exists, and $S_{\Delta_k}^{(2n-2)}(x) \to f^{(2n-2)}(x)$ uniformly on $[a, b]$.

Theorem 4.4.2 may be modified as follows.

Theorem 4.4.3. *Let $\{\Delta_k\}$ be a sequence of meshes on $[a, b]$ with $\| \Delta_k \| \to 0$ as $k \to \infty$. Let $f(x)$ be of class $C^q[a, b]$ $(0 \leqslant q \leqslant 2n - 3)$. Assume for the polynomial splines $S_{\Delta_k}(x)$ of interpolation to $f(x)$ on Δ_k that*

$$\lim_{k \to \infty} \{ \max_j [| M_{k,j} | \, \| \Delta_k \|^{2n-q-2}] \} = 0.$$

Then on $[a, b]$

$$[f^{(p)}(x) - S_\Delta^{(p)}(x)] = o(\| \Delta_k \|^{q-p}) \qquad (0 \leqslant p \leqslant q).$$

Proof. The proof is merely an obvious modification of the proof of Theorem 4.4.2 beginning at (4.4.16).

4.5. Quintic Splines of Deficiency 2, 3

The first integral relation developed in Chapter III for cubic splines is extended in Chapter V to include splines of odd degree. As we shall see there the condition for the validity of this relation for a function $f(x)$ of class $C^n[a, b]$ and a polynomial spline of degree $2n - 1$ is that

$$\sum_{j=1}^{N} \sum_{p=1}^{n} [f^{(n-p)}(x) - S_\Delta^{(n-p)}(x)]\, S_\Delta^{(n+p-1)}(x) \Big|_{x_{j-1}}^{x_j} = 0.$$

We pass over, for the time being, the spline end conditions that are relevant to this constraint and observe that for a simple spline (i.e., of class $C^{2n-2}[a, b]$) the terms for $j = 1,..., N - 1$, $p = 1, 2,..., n - 1$ drop out because of the continuity of $S_\Delta^{(n+p-1)}(x)$ at x_j. The terms involving $S_\Delta^{2n-1}(x_j)$ vanish because $f(x_j) - S(x_j) = 0$.

We discuss in Chapter V the fact that it is possible to replace the requirement of continuity on $S_\Delta^{(n+p-1)}(x)$ by the condition

$$S_\Delta^{(n-p)}(x_j) = f^{(n-p)}(x_j)$$

for all p satisfying $1 \leqslant q \leqslant p \leqslant n - 1$ (q prescribed). In the case of the quintic spline, the maximum deficiency permitted is 3 ($q = 1$). Here

$$S_\Delta^{(p)}(x_j) = f_\Delta^{(p)}(x_j) \qquad (p = 0, 1, 2; \;\; j = 1,..., N - 1).$$

In setting up procedures for approximating a given analytic function in numerical integration, differentiation, or interpolation, it is frequently practical to use such higher-order interpolation. This is an important application of splines with deficiency greater than 1.

A different application of this concept which is of considerable interest, however, involves the use of splines of maximum deficiency when only the function $f(x)$ itself is known or can conveniently be determined at mesh points. Here we first approximate the derivatives required by some auxiliary device, such as by using polynomials of interpolation.*

* The effectiveness of this quintic spline in curve-fitting together with its relation to Simpson's rule and the three-eighth's rule was pointed out by S. Auslender.

For quintic splines of deficiency 3, we take the approximations to f_j' and f_j'' from parabolas of interpolation. For $0 < j < N$, let $u_j = u_j(x)$ represent the parabola passing through (x_{j-1}, f_{j-1}), (x_j, f_j), and (x_{j+1}, f_{j+1}). Thus,

$$\left.\begin{aligned} u_j(x_j) &= f_j, \\ u_j'(x_j) &= \lambda_j \frac{f_j - f_{j-1}}{h_j} + \mu_j \frac{f_{j+1} - f_j}{h_{j+1}}, \\ u_j''(x_j) &= 2f[x_{j-1}, x_j, x_{j+1}]. \end{aligned}\right\} \tag{4.5.1}$$

Here, as in Chapter II, $\lambda_j = 1 - \mu_j = h_{j+1}/(h_j + h_{j+1})$.

The quintic spline $\hat{S}_\Delta(x)$ of deficiency 3 is defined over the interval $[x_{j-1}, x_j]$ by

$$\hat{S}_\Delta^{(p)}(x_{j-1}) = u_{j-1}^{(p)}(x_{j-1}), \qquad \hat{S}_\Delta^{(p)}(x_j) = u_j^{(p)}(x_j) \qquad (p = 0, 1, 2). \tag{4.5.2}$$

Now we have the equations

$$\left.\begin{aligned} u_j(x) &= f_j + (x - x_j)\, u_j'(x_j) + (x - x_j)^2 u_j''(x_j)/2!, \\ u_j(x_{j-1}) &= f_j - h_j u_j'(x_j) + h_j^2 u_j''(x_j)/2, \\ u_j(x_{j+1}) &= f_j + h_{j+1} u_j'(x_j) + h_{j+1}^2 u_j''(x_j)/2. \end{aligned}\right\} \tag{4.5.3}$$

Let $\alpha(\sigma)$ be the cubic satisfying $\alpha(0) = \alpha'(0) = \alpha'(1) = 0$, $\alpha(1) = 1$. Then

$$\alpha(\sigma) = 3\sigma^2 - 2\sigma^3, \tag{4.5.4}$$

and we may express the quintic with which $\hat{S}_\Delta(x)$ coincides on $[x_{j-1}, x_j]$ as

$$u_{j-1}(x)[1 - \alpha_j(x)] + u_j(x)\, \alpha_j(x), \tag{4.5.5}$$

where $\alpha_j(x) = \alpha[(x - x_{j-1})/h_j]$.

We note at this juncture that the first and second derivatives at x_j are weighted means of the slopes m_{j-1}, m_j, m_{j+1} and moments M_{j-1}, M_j, M_{j+1} of the simple cubic spline [see (2.1.15) and (2.1.7)]. For equal intervals this represents a smoothing, in the sense of Schoenberg, of the first and second derivatives of the cubic spline. It has been found in practice that there is occasionally an advantage in curve-fitting in using this quintic spline instead of the simple cubic spline.

It is also important to observe that the quintic spline of deficiency 3 is locally completely determined from the approximated function and its first and second divided differences. Thus, no simultaneous system of equations need be solved for the determination of these quintics. In addition, four parameters suffice to describe the quintic on $[x_{j-1}, x_j]$. We have

$$\hat{S}_\Delta(x) = \{f_{j-1} + (x - x_{j-1})\, u'_{j-1}(x_{j-1}) + (x - x_{j-1})^2 u''_{j-1}(x_{j-1})/2!\}[1 - \alpha_j(x)]$$
$$+ \{f_j + (x - x_j)u'_j(x_j) + (x - x_j)^2 u''_j(x_j)/2!\}\, \alpha_j(x). \quad (4.5.6)$$

Since

$$u'_j(x_j) = \frac{f_j - f_{j-1}}{h_j} + \frac{h_j}{2} u''_j(x_j),$$

$$u'_{j-1}(x_{j-1}) = \frac{f_j - f_{j-1}}{h_j} - \frac{h_j}{2} u''_{j-1}(x_{j-1}),$$

we have

$$\hat{S}_\Delta(x) = f_{j-1} \frac{x_j - x}{h_j} + f_j \frac{x - x_{j-1}}{h_j}$$
$$- \frac{(x_j - x)(x - x_{j-1})}{2} \{u''_{j-1}(x_{j-1})[1 - \alpha_j(x)] + u''_j(x_j)\, \alpha_j(x)\}. \quad (4.5.7)$$

There are significant relations of this type of spline to numerical integration. We obtain

$$\int_{x_{j-1}}^{x_j} \hat{S}_\Delta(x)\, dx = h_j \frac{f_{j-1} + f_j}{2} - \frac{h_j^3}{24} [u''_{j-1}(x_{j-1}) + u''_j(x_j)],$$

noting that we have employed $f_{j-2}, f_{j-1}, f_j, f_{j+1}$ in this approximation. Let us set $x_j - x_{j-1} = h$, $x_{j-1} - x_{j-2} = x_{j+1} - x_j = \lambda h$. Then the approximation becomes

$$\int_{x_{j-1}}^{x_j} f(x)\, dx = \frac{h}{12\lambda(1 + \lambda)} \{-f_{j-2} + [6\lambda(1 + \lambda) + 1](f_{j-1} + f_j) - f_{j+1}\}. \quad (4.5.8)$$

If we take $\lambda = -\frac{1}{3}$, the effect is to integrate over three intervals with the abscissas arranged in the order $x_{j-1}, x_{j-2}, x_{j+1}, x_j$ with common interval of spacing $H = h/3$. The result is

$$\tfrac{3}{8}H(f_{j-1} + 3f_{j-2} + 3f_{j+1} + f_j),$$

which is the three-eighth's rule.

If we take $\lambda = -\frac{1}{2}$, the effect is to integrate over two intervals with abscissas arranged as x_{j-1}, $x_{j-2} = x_{j+1}$, x_j with interval $H = h/2$. Here we obtain

$$(H/6)(f_{j-1} + 4f_{j+1} + f_j),$$

which is Simpson's rule.

Suppose we choose λ in such a way that the coefficients of f_{j-1} and f_j vanish. We obtain

$$6\lambda^2 + 6\lambda + 1 = 0, \qquad \lambda = (-3 \pm 3^{1/2})/6.$$

Thus we have

$$\int_{x_{j-1}}^{x_j} f(x)\,dx \doteq \frac{h}{2}\left\{f\left(x_{j-1} + h\frac{3 - 3^{1/2}}{6}\right) + f\left(x_{j+1} - h\frac{3 - 3^{1/2}}{6}\right)\right\}, \tag{4.5.9}$$

which is Gaussian integration of second order.

As may be expected, the convergence is effectively comparable to that of the cubic spline. On $[x_{j-1}, x_j]$ we have from (4.5.7)

$$\begin{aligned} | \hat{S}_\Delta''(x) - f''(x) | &= | [u_{j-1}''(x_{j-1})(1 - \sigma) + u_j''(x_j)\,\sigma - f''(x)] \\ &\quad + 10\sigma(1 - \sigma)(1 - 2\sigma)[u_{j-1}''(x_{j-1}) - u_j''(x_j)] | \\ &\leqslant \mu(f''; \| \Delta \|) \cdot [2 + 1/6(3)^{1/2}]. \end{aligned} \tag{4.5.10}$$

If $f(x)$ is of class $C'[a, b]$, we have on $[x_{j-1}, x_j]$

$$\begin{aligned} \hat{S}_\Delta'(x) - f'(x) &= \left[\frac{f_j - f_{j-1}}{h_j} - f'(x)\right] + \left\{\frac{2\sigma - 1}{2} h_j\, [u_{j-1}''(x_{j-1})(1 - \alpha_j(x)) \right. \\ &\quad \left. + u_j''(x_j)\,\alpha_j(x)] - \frac{\sigma(1 - \sigma)}{2} h_j[u_j''(x_j) - u_{j-1}''(x_{j-1})]\,\alpha_j'(x)\right\}. \end{aligned}$$

If $0 < \beta^{-1} < h_j/h_{j+1} < \beta$ for all meshes Δ (fixed β), then

$$| h_j u_{j-1}''(x_{j-1}) | < \frac{\beta}{\beta + 1}\,\mu(f'; 2\| \Delta \|),$$

$$| h_j u_j''(x_j) | < \frac{\beta}{\beta + 1}\,\mu(f'; 2\| \Delta \|).$$

Thus there follows

$$| \hat{S}_\Delta'(x) - f'(x) | \leqslant \text{const} \cdot \mu(f'; \| \Delta \|). \tag{4.5.11}$$

Finally, if $f(x)$ is of class $C[a, b]$, then

$$\hat{S}_\Delta(x) - f(x) = \left[\left(f_{j-1}\frac{x_j - x}{h_j} + f_j\frac{x - x_{j-1}}{h_j}\right) - f(x)\right]$$
$$- \frac{\sigma(1-\sigma)}{2} h_j^2\{u''_{j-1}(x_{j-1})[1 - \alpha_j(x)] + u''_j(x_j)\,\alpha_j(x)\},$$

and, if again $0 < \beta^{-1} < h_j/h_{j+1} < \beta$ for all meshes Δ, we have

$$|\,h_j^2 u''_{j-1}(x_{j-1})\,| \leqslant \beta\mu(f; \|\Delta\|).$$

Thus, it follows that

$$|\,\hat{S}_\Delta(x) - f(x)\,| \leqslant \text{const}\cdot\mu(f; \|\Delta\|). \tag{4.5.12}$$

In another direction, we consider the extension to quintic splines of the ideas of Fejér introduced in connection with the proof of Theorem 2.3.1. Let us study the quintic spline of deficiency 2 which interpolates to a function $f(x)$ of class $C[a, b]$ at the points of a mesh Δ on $[a, b]$ and has zero derivative at each of these points. We confine our attention here to periodic quintic splines with $f(x)$ in $C(-\infty, \infty)$ and of period $b - a$.

Again designate this spline by $\hat{S}_\Delta(x)$, and, for convenience, set $N_j = \hat{S}''_\Delta(x_j)$. From (4.1.22), we have the relations

$$\begin{aligned}\hat{S}'''_\Delta(x_j\,-) &= \frac{f_j - f_{j-1}}{h_j}\cdot\frac{60}{h_j^2} + \frac{9N_j - 3N_{j-1}}{h_j},\\ \hat{S}'''_\Delta(x_j\,+) &= \frac{f_{j+1} - f_j}{h_{j+1}}\cdot\frac{60}{h_{j+1}^2} + \frac{3N_{j+1} - 9N_j}{h_{j+1}};\end{aligned} \tag{4.5.13}$$

continuity of $\hat{S}'''_\Delta(x)$ at x_j gives the condition

$$-\frac{1}{h_j}N_{j-1} + 3\left(\frac{1}{h_j} + \frac{1}{h_{j+1}}\right)N_j - \frac{1}{h_{j+1}}N_{j+1}$$
$$= 20\left(\frac{f_{j+1} - f_j}{h_{j+1}}\cdot\frac{1}{h_{j+1}^2} - \frac{f_j - f_{j-1}}{h_{j+1}}\cdot\frac{1}{h_j^2}\right)$$

or, alternatively, in the notation of Chapter II,

$$\lambda_j N_{j-1} - 3N_j + \mu_j N_{j+1}$$
$$= 20\,\frac{[(f_{j+1} - f_j)/h_{j+1}](h_j/h_{j+1}) - [(f_j - f_{j-1})/h_j](h_{j+1}/h_j)}{h_j + h_{j+1}}. \tag{4.5.14}$$

Here the norm of the inverse of the coefficient matrix is bounded independently of Δ. If $f(x)$ is continuous, then $|N_j| \, \|\Delta\|^2 \leqslant \frac{1}{2}20\beta^2(2\beta - 1)\mu(f; \|\Delta\|)$ if $[\max_j \|\Delta\|/h_j] \leqslant \beta$. From (4.6.13), it may be concluded that the quantities $\hat{S}'''_\Delta(x_j) \, \|\Delta\|^3$ have similar bounds independent of Δ, and from (4.1.27) that the same is true of $\hat{S}^{(4)}_\Delta(x_j -) \, \|\Delta\|^4$ and $\hat{S}^{(4)}_\Delta(x_j +) \, \|\Delta\|^4$. Since on $[x_{j-1}, x_j]$ we have

$$\begin{aligned}
\hat{S}_\Delta(x) &= \hat{S}^{(4)}_\Delta(x_{j-1}) \frac{(x_j - x)^5}{5! \, h_j} + \hat{S}^{(4)}_\Delta(x_j) \frac{(x - x_{j-1})^5}{5! \, h_j} \\
&+ \left[\hat{S}'''_\Delta(x_{j-1}) + \hat{S}^{(4)}_\Delta(x_{j-1}) \frac{h_j}{2}\right] \frac{(x - x_{j-1})^3}{3!} \\
&+ \left[\hat{S}''_\Delta(x_{j-1}) - \hat{S}^{(4)}_\Delta(x_{j-1}) \frac{h_j^2}{3!}\right] \frac{(x - x_{j-1})^2}{2!} \\
&+ \left[\hat{S}_\Delta'(x_{j-1}) + S^{(4)}_\Delta(x_{j-1}) \frac{h_j^3}{4!}\right] (x - x_{j-1}) + \left[\hat{S}_\Delta(x_{j-1}) - \hat{S}^{(4)}_\Delta(x_{j-1}) \frac{h_j^4}{5!}\right],
\end{aligned}$$

we may conclude that $\hat{S}_\Delta(x) - f(x)$ may be made arbitrarily small by taking $\|\Delta\|$ sufficiently small, provided (2.3.7) is satisfied. We have thus proved the following theorem.

Theorem 4.5.1. *Let $\{\Delta_k\}$ be a sequence of meshes on $[a, b]$ with $\|\Delta_k\| \to 0$ as $k \to \infty$ and satisfying (2.3.7). Let $f(x)$ be of class $C(-\infty, \infty)$ and of period $b - a$. Let $\hat{S}_{\Delta_k}(x)$ be the periodic quintic spline of deficiency 2 interpolating to $f(x)$ and with $S'_{\Delta_k}(x) = 0$ at the points of Δ_k. Then $\{S_{\Delta_k}(x)\}$ converges uniformly to $f(x)$ as $k \to \infty$.*

4.6. Convergence of Periodic Splines on Uniform Meshes

The coefficient matrix in (4.2.5), which after multiplication by $(2n - 1)!$ becomes the circulant of order N,

$$C(\phi_{n-1}^{(2n-1)}, \phi_n^{(2n-1)}, \ldots, \phi_{2n-2}^{(2n-1)}, 0, \ldots, 0, \phi_0^{(2n-1)}, \phi_1^{(2n-1)}, \ldots, \phi_{n-2}^{(2n-1)}), \tag{4.6.1}$$

has been shown in Section 4.3 to be nonsingular. We want to show also that the norms of its inverse, for fixed n, are bounded with respect to N.

It was established in Section 4.3 that the function

$$q(z) = z \sum_{i=0}^{2n-2} \phi_k^{(2n-1)} z^k \tag{4.6.2}$$

has only real negative roots different from -1. The eigenvalues of (4.6.1) are the numbers $q(w_k)/\omega_k^{n-1}$, where $\omega_k = \exp(2k\pi i/N)$. Thus the eigenvalues are bounded away from zero. The following theorem on circulants now gives us the property needed.

Theorem 4.6.1. *Let C_k be a sequence of circulants $C(a_1^{(k)}, a_2^{(k)},..., a_{N_k}^{(k)})$, $k = 1, 2,...,$. Let a_j $(j = -m + 2, -m + 3,..., m)$ be given, real or complex, and suppose that $a_j^{(k)} = a_j$ $(j = 1,..., m)$, $a_j^{(k)} = a_{j-N_k}$ $(j = N_k - m + 2,..., N_k)$, $a_j^{(k)} = 0$ otherwise. If the polynomial $q(z) = \sum_{j=-m+2}^{m} a_j z^{j+m-2}$ has no roots of modulus unity, then C_k^{-1} exists, and $\| C_k^{-1} \|$ is bounded as $k \to \infty$.*

Proof. Let P_k be the permutation matrix of order N_k:

$$P_k = C(0, 1, 0,..., 0, 0).$$

Then $P_k \cdot C(a_1^{(k)}, a_2^{(k)},..., a_{N_k}^{(k)}) = C(a_{N_k}^{(k)}, a_1^{(k)},..., a_{N_{k-1}}^{(k)})$. Thus

$$\begin{aligned} C_k &= a_1^{(k)} I_k + a_2^{(k)} P_k + \cdots + a_{N_k}^{(k)} P_k^{N_k - 1} \\ &= P_k^{-m+1}\{a_{-m+2} I_k + a_{-m+3} P_k + \cdots + a_m P_k^{(2m-1)}\} \\ &= P_k^{-m+1} q(P_k), \end{aligned}$$

where I_k is the unit matrix of order N_k. Since the polynomial $q(z)$ has no zeros of modulus unity, there exists an annulus containing $|z| = 1$, $r_1 < |z| < r_2$, in which $q(z) \neq 0$. In this annulus, $[z^{-m+1} q(z)]^{-1}$ may be expanded in a power series $\sum_{j=-\infty}^{\infty} b_j z^j$ which converges absolutely. Since $\| P_k \| = 1$ (row-max norm), the series $\sum_{j=-\infty}^{\infty} b_j P_k^j$ converges in this norm to the inverse C_k^{-1} of C_k. Furthermore,

$$\| C_k^{-1} \| \leqslant \sum_{j=-\infty}^{\infty} | b_j |,$$

where the right-hand member depends only upon $a_{-m+2},..., a_m$.

The following theorem is now an immediate consequence of Theorem 4.4.1.

Theorem 4.6.2. *Let $f(x)$ be of class $C^{2n-2}(-\infty, \infty)$ and have period $b - a$. Let $\{\Delta_k\}$ be a sequence of uniform meshes on $[a, b]$ with $\lim_{k \to \infty} \| \Delta_k \| = 0$. For a given $n > 1$, let $S_{\Delta_k}(x)$ be the periodic polynomial spline of degree $2n - 1$ on Δ_k interpolating to $f(x)$ at the mesh points. Then*

$$[f^{(p)}(x) - S_{\Delta_k}^{(p)}(x)] = o(\| \Delta_k \|^{2n-2-p}) \qquad (p = 0, 1, 2,..., 2n - 2)$$

uniformly with respect to x *in* $[a, b]$. *If* $f^{2n-2}(x)$ *satisfies a Hölder condition of order* α *on* $[a, b]$ $(0 < \alpha \leqslant 1)$, *then*

$$[f^{(p)}(x) - S_{\Delta_k}^{(p)}(x)] = O(\| \Delta_k \|^{2n-2+\alpha-p}) \qquad (p = 0, 1, \ldots, 2n-2)$$

uniformly with respect to x *in* $[a, b]$.

We consider next the strengthening of the differentiability properties of $f(x)$.

Theorem 4.6.3. *Let* $f(x)$ *be of class* $C^{2n-1}(-\infty, \infty)$ *and have period* $b - a$. *Let* $\{\Delta_k\}$ *be a sequence of uniform meshes on* $[a, b]$ *with* $\lim_{k\to\infty} \| \Delta_k \| = 0$. *For a given* $n > 1$, *let* $S_{\Delta_k}(x)$ *be the periodic polynomial spline of degree* $2n - 1$ *on* Δ_k *interpolating to* $f(x)$ *at the mesh points. Then, uniformly on* $[a, b]$,

$$[f^{(p)}(x) - S_{\Delta_k}^{(p)}(x)] = o(\| \Delta_k \|^{2n-1-p}) \qquad (p = 0, 1, \ldots, 2n-1), \qquad (4.6.3)$$

where $S_{\Delta_k}^{(2n-1)}(x_j)$ *may be taken either as the right-hand or left-hand limit at the mesh point* x_j. *If* $f^{(2n-1)}(x)$ *satisfies a Hölder condition of order* α *on* $[a, b]$ $(0 < \alpha \leqslant 1)$, *then*

$$[f^{(p)}(x) - S_{\Delta_k}^{(p)}(x)] = O(\| \Delta_k \|^{2n-1+\alpha-p}) \qquad (p = 0, 1, \ldots, 2n-1). \qquad (4.6.4)$$

uniformly with respect to x *in* $[a, b]$.

Proof. We set (dropping mesh index k)

$$\sigma_j = (M_j - M_{j-1})/h$$

and obtain from (4.2.5) by subtracting members of each equation from corresponding members of its successor

$$\begin{aligned} \frac{1}{(2n-1)!} \sum_{k=0}^{2n-2} \phi_k^{2n-1} \sigma_{j-n+1+k} &= (\delta^{2n-2} f_j - \delta^{2n-2} f_{j-1})/h^{2n-1} \\ &= (2n-1)!\, [f_{j-n}, f_{j-n+1}, \ldots, f_{j+n-1}]. \qquad (4.6.5) \end{aligned}$$

Thus, if C is the circulant (4.6.1), σ the vector $(\sigma_1, \ldots, \sigma_{N_k})$, and r the vector representing the right-hand members of (4.6.5), we have

$$\frac{1}{(2n-1)!} C \cdot (\sigma - r) = \left(I - \frac{1}{(2n-1)!} C\right) r. \qquad (4.6.6)$$

Here the right-hand member may be put into the form

$$\begin{bmatrix} \sum_{k=0}^{2n-2} \dfrac{\phi_k^{(2n-1)}}{(2n-1)!}(r_1 - r_{k-n+2}) \\ \sum_{k=0}^{2n-2} \dfrac{\phi_k^{(2n-1)}}{(2n-1)!}(r_2 - r_{k-n+3}) \\ \vdots \\ \sum_{k=0}^{2n-2} \dfrac{\phi_k^{(2n-1)}}{(2n-1)!}(r_{N_k} - r_{k-n+N_k+1}) \end{bmatrix},$$

where we have used $r_{-j} = r_{N_k-j}$, $r_{N_k+j} = r$.

The norm of the right-hand vector of (4.6.6) is, therefore, not greater than $(3n-3)\mu(f^{(2n-1)}; \| \Delta_k \|)$. Thus,

$$\| \sigma - r \| \leqslant (2n-1)! \, \| C^{-1} \| (3n-3) \, \mu(f^{(2n-1)}; \| \Delta_k \|).$$

On the other hand, on $[x_{j-1}, x_j]$,

$$\begin{aligned} | f^{(2n-1)}(x) - r_j | &\leqslant \mu(f^{(2n-1)}; (2n-1)\| \Delta_k \|) \\ &\leqslant (2n-1) \, \mu(f^{(2n-1)}; \| \Delta_k \|). \end{aligned}$$

On $[x_{j-1}, x_j]$, $S_\Delta^{(2n-1)}(x) = \sigma_j$. Thus,

$$\Big[\sup_{x \text{ on } [a,b]} | S_\Delta^{(2n-1)}(x) - f^{(2n-1)}(x) | \Big] \leqslant [(2n-1) + (2n-1)! \, \| C^{-1} \| (3n-3)] \cdot \mu(f^{(2n-1)}; \| \Delta_k \|).$$

This establishes (4.6.3) and (4.6.4) for $p = 2n - 1$. By integration and the interpolation property of $S_\Delta(x)$, these relationships may be established for the smaller values of p in the usual manner (cf. Theorem 2.3.3).

Similar methods yield the extension of Theorem 2.9.5. We merely state the result.

Theorem 4.6.4. *Let $f(x)$ be of class $C^{2n}(-\infty, \infty)$ and of period $b - a$. Let $\{\Delta_k\}$ be a sequence of uniform meshes on $[a, b]$ with $lim_{k\to\infty} \| \Delta_k \| = 0$. If $S_{\Delta_k}(x)$ is the periodic polynomial spline of degree $2n - 1$ of interpolation to $f(x)$ on Δ_k, then*

$$\lim_{k\to\infty} \left[\max \left| \frac{S_{\Delta_k}^{(2n-1)}(x_{k,j}+) - S_{\Delta_k}^{(2n-1)}(x_{k,j}-)}{h_{k,j}} - \frac{f^{(2n)}(x_{k,j})}{2} \right| \right] = 0.$$

Other convergence results relate to the weakening of the requirements on $f(x)$. We state these in the following theorem, which follows in consequence of Theorem 4.4.2.

Theorem 4.6.5. *Let $f(x)$ be of class $C^q(-\infty, \infty)$ $(0 \leqslant q \leqslant 2n-2)$ and of period $b-a$. Let $\{\Delta_k\}$ be a sequence of uniform meshes on $[a, b]$ with $\lim_{k\to\infty} \|\Delta_k\| = 0$. Let $S_\Delta(x)$ be the periodic polynomial spline of degree $2n-1$ of interpolation to $f(x)$ on Δ_k. Then, uniformly on $[a, b]$,*

$$[f^{(p)}(x) - S_{\Delta_k}^{(p)}(x)] = o(\|\Delta_k\|^{q-p}) \qquad (0 \leqslant p \leqslant q). \tag{4.6.7}$$

If $f^{(q)}(x)$ satisfies a Hölder condition of order α on $[a, b]$ $(0 < \alpha \leqslant 1)$, then

$$[f^{(p)}(x) - S_{\Delta_k}^{(p)}(x)] = O(\|\Delta_k\|^{q+\alpha-p}) \qquad (0 \leqslant p \leqslant q). \tag{4.6.8}$$

uniformly with respect to x in $[a, b]$.

CHAPTER V

Intrinsic Properties of Polynomial Splines of Odd Degree

5.1. Introduction

To a large extent, this chapter parallels Chapter III, and almost every theorem obtained for cubic splines in Chapter III has its analog here. The major change that occurs is that, when considering a polynomial spline of degree $2n - 1$ ($n > 1$), we replace the function space $\mathscr{K}^2(a, b)$ by the function space $\mathscr{K}^n(a, b)$ and the inner product

$$(f, g) = \int_a^b f''(x)g''(x)\,dx \tag{5.1.1}$$

by the inner product

$$(f, g) = \int_a^b f^{(n)}(x)\,g^{(n)}(x)\,dx. \tag{5.1.2}$$

Chapter IV already has brought to light some of the problems that occur with splines of even degree and has indicated several ways of circumventing part of these difficulties. In this chapter, the requirement that the splines under consideration be of odd degree is of paramount importance, and the requirement cannot be relaxed.

The development of the intrinsic properties for generalized splines, which include polynomial splines of odd degree as a special case, again requires the introduction of an inner product (f, g) into $\mathscr{K}^n(a, b)$. This can be done when the splines satisfy, except at mesh points, a self adjoint differential equation

$$AS_\Delta = 0 \tag{5.1.3}$$

of order $2n$. In this case, A has a factorization

$$A = L^*L \tag{5.1.4}$$

where L is a linear operator of order n and L^* is its formal adjoint. We then are able to define (f, g) as

$$(f, g) = \int_a^b (Lf)(x) \cdot (Lg)(x)\, dx. \tag{5.1.5}$$

In Chapter VI, we adopt this very general point of view. It is necessary, however, that L have real coefficients and no singularities.*

When a proof in this chapter essentially repeats the proof for the cubic case given in Chapter III, we only state the theorem. In general, we limit the discussion to the differences in the argument. The uniqueness and existence theorems that we obtain in particular require some further elaboration.

5.2. The Fundamental Identity

Let $S_\Delta(x)$ be a polynomial spline of degree $2n - 1$ on a mesh Δ: $a = x_0 < x_1 < \cdots < x_N = b$, and let $f(x)$ be in $\mathscr{K}^n(a, b)$. We have the identity

$$\int_a^b \{f^{(n)}(x) - S_\Delta^{(n)}(x)\}^2\, dx$$
$$= \int_a^b \{f^{(n)}(x)\}^2\, dx - 2\int_a^b \{f^{(n)}(x) - S_\Delta^{(n)}(x)\} \cdot S_\Delta^{(n)}(x)\, dx - \int_a^b \{S_\Delta^{(n)}(x)\}^2\, dx \tag{5.2.1}$$

in which the second integral of the right-hand member may be written as

$$\int_a^b \{f^{(n)}(x) - S_\Delta^{(n)}(x)\}\, S_\Delta^{(n)}(x)\, dx$$
$$= \sum_{j=1}^{N} \int_{x_{j-1}}^{x_j} \{f^{(n)}(x) - S_\Delta^{(n)}(x)\} \cdot S_\Delta^{(n)}(x)\, dx.$$

In each mesh interval $[x_{j-1}, x_j]$ we can integrate by parts n times; thus

$$\int_{x_{j-1}}^{x_j} \{f^{(n)}(x) - S_\Delta^{(n)}(x)\}\, S_\Delta^{(n)}(x)\, dx$$
$$= \sum_{\alpha=1}^{n} (-1)^{\alpha+1} \{f^{(n-\alpha)}(x) - S_\Delta^{(n-\alpha)}(x)\}\, S_\Delta^{(n+\alpha-1)}(x) \Big|_{x_{j-1}}^{x_j}.$$

* A similar theory for complex-valued splines on $[a, b]$ is possible. The definitions of (f, g) and L^*, however, require slight modifications.

It follows that

$$\int_a^b \{f^{(n)}(x) - S_\Delta^{(n)}(x)\}^2\,dx$$

$$= \int_a^b \{f^{(n)}(x)\}^2\,dx - 2\sum_{\alpha=1}^{n-1} (-1)^{\alpha+1}\{f^{(n-\alpha)}(x) - S_\Delta^{(n-\alpha)}(x)\}\,S_\Delta^{(n+\alpha-1)}(x)\Big|_a^b$$

$$- 2\sum_{j=1}^{N} (-1)^{n+1}\{f(x) - S_\Delta(x)\}\,S_\Delta^{(2n-1)}(x)\Big|_{x_{j-1}}^{x_j} - \int_a^b \{S_\Delta^{(n)}(x)\}^2\,dx. \tag{5.2.2}$$

In obtaining (5.2.2), we have used the continuity of

$$\{f^{(n-\alpha)}(x) - S_\Delta^{(n-\alpha)}(x)\}\,S_\Delta^{(n+\alpha-1)}(x) \quad \text{on} \quad [a, b] \quad \text{for} \quad \alpha = 1, 2, \ldots, n-1$$

but have imposed no requirement other than that $S_\Delta(x)$ is a simple polynomial spline of degree $2n - 1$ on Δ and that $f(x)$ is in $\mathcal{K}^n(a, b)$. Equation (5.2.2) is the *fundamental identity* for a simple polynomial spline of degree $2n - 1$ on a mesh Δ.

5.3. The First Integral Relation

It follows immediately from the fundamental identity that, if $S_\Delta(f; x)$ is a spline of interpolation to $f(x)$ on Δ satisfying any of a variety of end conditions, we have the relation

$$\int_a^b \{f^{(n)}(x)\}^2\,dx = \int_a^b \{S_\Delta^{(n)}(f; x)\}^2\,dx + \int_a^b \{f^{(n)}(x) - S_\Delta^{(n)}(f; x)\}^2\,dx,$$

which constitutes the *first integral relation* for a polynomial spline of degree $2n - 1$ interpolating to a function $f(x)$ in $\mathcal{K}^n(a, b)$ on a mesh Δ. We have the following theorem.

Theorem 5.3.1. *Let* Δ: $a = x_0 < x_1 < \cdots < x_N = b$ *and* $f(x)$ *in* $\mathcal{K}^n(a, b)$ *be given. If* $S_\Delta(f; x)$ *is a spline of interpolation to* $f(x)$ *on* Δ *and one of the conditions,* (a) $f(x) - S_\Delta(f; x)$ *is of type I′,* (b) $S_\Delta(f; x)$ *is of type II′,* (c) $S_\Delta(f; x)$ *and* $f(x)$ *are periodic, is satisfied, then*

$$\int_a^b \{f^{(n)}(x)\}^2\,dx = \int_a^b \{S_\Delta^{(n)}(f; x)\}^2\,dx + \int_a^b \{f^{(n)}(x) - S_\Delta^{(n)}(f; x)\}^2\,dx. \tag{5.3.1}$$

Clearly, we also can employ end conditions of mixed type; we can as indicated in Chapter III even relax the continuity requirements imposed on $S_\Delta(f; x)$ and its derivatives and still obtain the first integral relation by requiring that certain derivatives of $S_\Delta(f; x)$ interpolate to corresponding derivatives of $f(x)$ on Δ. These extra interpolation requirements replace the continuity of $\{f^{(n-\alpha)}(x) - S_\Delta^{(n-\alpha)}(f; x)\} \cdot S_\Delta^{(n+\alpha-1)}(f; x)$ on $[a, b]$. The following theorem expresses this possibility.

Theorem 5.3.2. *Let Δ: $a = x_0 < x_1 < \cdots < x_N = b$ and $f(x)$ in $\mathscr{K}^n(a, b)$ be given. Let $S_\Delta(x)$ be in $\mathscr{K}^{2n-k}(a, b)$ $(k \leqslant n)$ and $S_\Delta^{(2n)}(x) \equiv 0$ on each open mesh interval of Δ. If $S_\Delta^{(\alpha)}(x)$ interpolates on Δ to $f^{(\alpha)}(x)$ $(\alpha = 0, 1, \ldots, k-1$; when $\alpha \neq 0$, $x \neq a$, $x \neq b)$, then we have*

$$\int_a^b \{f^{(n)}(x)\}^2\,dx = \int_a^b \{S_\Delta^{(n)}(x)\}^2\,dx + \int_a^b \{f^{(n)}(x) - S_\Delta^{(n)}(x)\}^2\,dx$$

provided that one of the conditions, (a) *$f(x) - S_\Delta(x)$ is of type I′,* (b) *$S_\Delta(x)$ is of type II′,* (c) *$S_\Delta(x)$ and $f(x)$ are periodic, is satisfied.*

Remark 5.3.1. In the periodic case this theorem, as well as a number of other theorems in this chapter, requires that $S_\Delta(f; a) = f(a)$ and $S_\Delta^{(\alpha)}(f; a) = S_\Delta^{(\alpha)}(f; b)$ $(\alpha = 0, 1, \ldots, 2n-2)$. The conditions $S_\Delta^{(\alpha)}(f; a) = f^{(\alpha)}(a)$ $(\alpha = 0, 1, \ldots, k-1)$ and $S_\Delta^{(\alpha)}(f; a) = S_\Delta^{(\alpha)}(f; b)$ $(\alpha = 0, 1, \ldots, 2n-k-1)$ can also be used.

5.4. The Minimum Norm Property

The establishment of the first integral relation for polynomial splines of degree $2n - 1$ has as an immediate consequence the analog of the minimum norm property of cubic splines. In Theorem 5.4.1, which follows, we express this property for three principal sets of conditions under which it is valid.

Theorem 5.4.1. *Let Δ: $a = x_0 < x_1 < \cdots < x_N = b$ and $f(x)$ be given, where $f(x)$ is an arbitrary function on $[a, b]$ having $n - 1$ derivatives at both $x = a$ and $x = b$. Then, of all functions $g(x)$ in $\mathscr{K}^n(a, b)$ which interpolate to $f(x)$ on Δ, the type II′ spline $S_\Delta(f; x)$ minimizes*

$$\int_a^b \{g^{(n)}(x)\}^2\,dx. \tag{5.4.1}$$

If the functions $g(x)$ are restricted so that $f(x) - g(x)$ is of type I′, or if $f(x)$ and $g(x)$ are required to be periodic functions, then (5.4.1) is minimized by the spline of interpolation to $f(x)$ on Δ satisfying the same restriction.

As in Theorem 5.3.2, we can relax the continuity requirements imposed on $S_\Delta(f; x)$. In order to facilitate the discussion, we introduce the following terminology. Let a mesh Δ: $a = x_0 < x_1 < \cdots < x_N = b$ be given, and let $S_\Delta(x)$ be a function in $\mathscr{K}^{2n-k}(a, b)$ with the property that $S_\Delta^{(2n)}(x)$ vanishes identically in each open mesh interval of Δ. If $S_\Delta(x)$ satisfies these conditions, we call $S_\Delta(x)$ a polynomial spline of degree $2n - 1$ with *deficiency k*. We impose the restriction $0 \leqslant k \leqslant n$. In this terminology, a simple spline on Δ has deficiency one, and a polynomial of degree $2n - 1$ has deficiency zero.

Theorem 5.4.2. *Let Δ: $a = x_0 < x_1 < \cdots < x_N = b$ and $f(x)$ be given, where $f(x)$ is an arbitrary function on $[a, b]$ having $n - 1$ derivatives at $x = a$ and $x = b$ and $k - 1$ $(k \leqslant n)$ derivatives at the interior mesh points of Δ. Then, of all functions $g(x)$ in $\mathscr{K}^n(a, b)$ interpolating to $f(x)$ on Δ and with $g^{(\alpha)}(x)$ interpolating to $f^{(\alpha)}(x)(\alpha = 1, 2,..., k - 1)$ at the interior mesh points of Δ, the type II′ spline of deficiency k minimizes (5.4.1). If the functions $g(x)$ are further restricted so that $f(x) - g(x)$ is of type I′ or that $f(x)$ and $g(x)$ are required to be periodic functions, then (5.4.1) is minimized by the spline of interpolation of deficiency k satisfying the same restrictions.*

Let $g(x)$ be a function satisfying the conditions of either Theorem 5.4.1 or Theorem 5.4.2, and let $g(x)$ minimize (5.4.1). Then $g(x)$ must differ from the corresponding spline of interpolation $S_\Delta(f; x)$ by a solution of $D^n f = 0$; this follows directly from the first integral relation. In addition, $g(x) - S_\Delta(f; x)$ must vanish on Δ, and, depending on the auxiliary conditions imposed, at certain points of Δ some of its derivatives must also vanish. If the number of these interpolation requirements is n or greater, then we can expect that $g(x) = S_\Delta(f; x)$. When, in particular, Δ contains at least n points, this is true. Moreover, if $g(x)$ is required to be periodic, then $g(x) - S_\Delta(f; x)$ is periodic and consequently a constant; but the constant is zero, since $g(a) = S_\Delta(f; a)$. In Section 5.6, we examine this question in more detail.

5.5. The Best Approximation Property

A polynomial spline $S_\Delta(x)$ on a mesh Δ depends linearly on its values at mesh points and linearly on its prescribed derivatives. Moreover, $S_\Delta(x)$ is completely determined by these quantities. These statements hold whether or not the deficiency of the spline is one. In particular, Eqs. (4.1.5), (4.1.8), and (4.1.11)–(4.1.13) of Chapter IV and Eqs.

(5.7.3), (5.7.4), and (5.12.3) of this chapter exhibit this linear dependence. Consequently, we have decompositions of the form

$$S_\Delta(f+g;x) = S_\Delta(f;x) + S_\Delta(g;x), \tag{5.5.1}$$

subject to appropriate selection of end conditions. These decompositions extend those obtained earlier for cubic splines, and here, as in Chapter III, the most useful of these decompositions occur when one of the following conditions is satisfied:

(a) $S_\Delta(f+g;x) - (f+g)(x)$, $S_\Delta(f;x) - f(x)$, and $S_\Delta(g;x) - g(x)$ are all of type I′.

(b) $S_\Delta(f+g;x)$ and $S_\Delta(f;x) + S_\Delta(g;x)$ are both of type II′.

(c) $S_\Delta(f+g;x)$, $S_\Delta(f;x)$, and $S_\Delta(g;x)$ are all periodic splines.

One of the most important consequences of the decomposition (5.5.1) is that, if $g(x)$ is identical with a spline $-S_\Delta(x)$, then (5.5.1) becomes

$$S_\Delta(f - S_\Delta\,; x) = S_\Delta(f;x) - S_\Delta(x) \tag{5.5.2}$$

when any of the conditions (a), (b), or (c) is met.* Again (5.5.2) is valid under these conditions even when the deficiency of $S_\Delta(f - S_\Delta\,;x)$, $S_\Delta(f;x)$, and $S_\Delta(x)$ is $k > 1$. If we determine $S_\Delta(f - S_\Delta\,;x)$ such that the first integral relation holds, it follows, just as in Chapter III, that

$$\begin{aligned}\int_a^b \{f^{(n)}(x) - S_\Delta^{(n)}(x)\}^2\,dx &= \int_a^b \{S_\Delta^{(n)}(f - S_\Delta\,;x)\}^2\,dx \\ &\quad + \int_a^b \{f^{(n)}(x) - S_\Delta^{(n)}(x) - S_\Delta^{(n)}(f - S_\Delta\,;x)\}^2\,dx \\ &= \int_a^b \{S_\Delta^{(n)}(f;x) - S_\Delta^{(n)}(x)\}^2\,dx \\ &\quad + \int_a^b \{f^{(n)}(x) - S_\Delta^{(n)}(f;x)\}^2\,dx. \end{aligned} \tag{5.5.3}$$

The two theorems that follow are immediate from (5.5.3).

Theorem 5.5.1. *Let Δ: $a = x_0 < x_1 < \cdots < x_N = b$ and $f(x)$ in $\mathscr{K}^n(a,b)$ be given. Let $S_\Delta(x)$ be a spline on Δ, and let $S_\Delta(f;x)$ be the spline of interpolation to $f(x)$ on Δ such that $f(x) - S_\Delta(f;x)$ is of type I′. Then*

$$\int_a^b \{f^{(n)}(x) - S_\Delta^{(n)}(x)\}^2\,dx \geqslant \int_a^b \{f^{(n)}(x) - S_\Delta^{(n)}(f;x)\}^2\,dx. \tag{5.5.4}$$

* Both $S_\Delta(f;x)$ and $-S_\Delta(g;x)$ are assumed to be in the same type II equivalence class as $S_\Delta(x)$ when condition (b) pertains.

If $S_\Delta(x)$ is restricted to a prescribed type II equivalence class, the integral

$$\int_a^b \{f^{(n)}(x) - S_\Delta^{(n)}(x)\}^2\, dx \tag{5.5.5}$$

is minimized by the spline of interpolation to $f(x)$ on Δ in the same equivalence class; if $f(x)$ and $S_\Delta(x)$ are required to be periodic functions, (5.5.5) again is minimized by the spline of interpolation to $f(x)$ on Δ.

Theorem 5.5.2. *Let Δ: $a = x_0 < x_1 < \cdots < x_N = b$ and $f(x)$ in $\mathscr{K}^n(a, b)$ be given. Let $S_\Delta(x)$ be a spline on Δ of deficiency k $(k \leqslant n)$, and let $S_\Delta(f; x)$ be the spline of interpolation to $f(x)$ on Δ of deficiency k such that $f(x) - S_\Delta(f; x)$ is of type I′ and such that $S_\Delta^{(\alpha)}(f; x)$ interpolates to $f^{(\alpha)}(x)$ $(\alpha = 1, 2,..., k - 1)$ at the interior mesh points of Δ. Then (5.5.4) holds. Moreover, if $S_\Delta(x)$ is restricted to a prescribed type II equivalence class, or if $f(x)$ and $S_\Delta(x)$ are restricted to periodic functions, then (5.5.5) is minimized by the corresponding splines $S_\Delta(f; x)$ of deficiency k, which interpolate to $f(x)$ on Δ and have derivatives $S_\Delta^{(\alpha)}(f; x)$ which interpolate to $f^{(\alpha)}(x)$ $(\alpha = 1, 2,..., k - 1)$ at interior mesh points of Δ.*

If $S_\Delta(x)$ also minimizes (5.5.5) and otherwise satisfies the requirements imposed on $S_\Delta(x)$ in Theorem 5.5.1 or Theorem 5.5.2, then $S_\Delta(x) - S_\Delta(f; x)$ satisfies $D^n y = 0$. In the periodic case, $S_\Delta(x) - S_\Delta(f; x)$ is a constant.

5.6. Uniqueness

The question of the uniqueness of a polynomial spline of degree $2n - 1$ on a mesh Δ: $a = x_0 < x_1 < \cdots < x_N = b$ is easily reduced to the question of whether or not a polynomial $P(x)$ of degree $n - 1$ which vanishes on Δ and has certain other properties vanishes identically. If $P(x)$ is of type I′ or if $P(x)$ is periodic, $P(x)$ vanishes identically. In these two instances, Δ may consist of just the two points $x = a$ and $x = b$. When $P(x)$ is of type II′, the situation is different, since requiring that derivatives of order α $(\alpha = n, n + 1,..., 2n - 2)$ vanish at $x = a$ and $x = b$ imposes no additional constraint on $P(x)$. In this case, Δ must contain at least n points to ensure that $P(x)$ vanishes identically whenever it vanishes on Δ. If, however, $P^{(\alpha)}(x)$ $(\alpha = 0, 1,..., k - 1)$ is required to vanish at the interior mesh points of Δ, then $P(x)$ vanishes identically when $k(N - 1) \geqslant n - 2$ and $P(a) = P(b) = 0$.

We observe that the zero function $z(x)$ is a polynomial spline of degree $2n - 1$ for any integral value of n greater than zero. Not only is $z(x)$ of type I′, but it is of type II′ and is periodic as well. Moreover, $z(x)$ can be interpreted as a spline of degree $2n - 1$ on Δ of deficiency k

whose $k - 1$ derivatives interpolate to zero at interior mesh points of Δ. Finally, $z(x)$ minimizes the integral

$$\int_a^b \{f^{(n)}(x)\}^2 \, dx. \tag{5.6.1}$$

Consider now any two splines $S_\Delta(x)$ and $\bar{S}_\Delta(x)$ on Δ such that $\bar{S}_\Delta(x) - S_\Delta(x)$ vanishes on Δ and is of type I′, type II′, or periodic. Since $\bar{S}_\Delta(x) - S_\Delta(x)$ is a spline interpolating to $z(x)$ on Δ, we must have

$$\int_a^b \{\bar{S}_\Delta^{(n)}(x) - S_\Delta^{(n)}(x)\}^2 \, dx = 0. \tag{5.6.2}$$

From the continuity of the integrand, we infer that $S_\Delta(x)$ and $\bar{S}_\Delta(x)$ differ by a polynomial of degree $n - 1$ which vanishes on Δ and is of type I′, type II′, or is periodic. We have the following theorem.

Theorem 5.6.1. *Let Δ: $a = x_0 < x_1 < \cdots < x_N = b$ and $f(x)$ be given. Then in each type I equivalence class there is at most one spline of interpolation to $f(x)$ on Δ. If $f(a) = f(b)$, then there is at most one periodic spline of interpolation to $f(x)$ on Δ. Finally, if $N > n - 2$, then in each type II equivalence class there is at most one spline of interpolation to $f(x)$ on Δ.*

Also, if $S_\Delta(x)$ and $\bar{S}_\Delta(x)$ are two polynomial splines of degree $2n - 1$ on Δ both of deficiency $k (k \leqslant n)$ such that $S_\Delta(x_i) = \bar{S}_\Delta(x_i) (i = 0, 1, \ldots, N)$, $S_\Delta^{(\alpha)}(x_i) = \bar{S}_\Delta^{(\alpha)}(x_i) (i = 1, 2, \ldots, N - 1;\ \alpha = 1, 2, \ldots, k - 1)$ and if $S_\Delta(x) - \bar{S}_\Delta(x)$ is of type I′, type II′, or periodic, then we can argue just as before that (5.6.2) holds. This establishes Theorem 5.6.2, of which Theorem 5.6.1 is a special case.

Theorem 5.6.2. *Let Δ: $a = x_0 < x_1 < \cdots < x_N = b$ and $f(x)$ be given, where $f(x)$ has $k - 1$ derivatives at each interior mesh point of Δ. Then in each type I equivalence class there is at most one polynomial spline $S_\Delta(f; x)$ of degree $2n - 1$ and deficiency $k (k \leqslant n)$ which interpolates to $f(x)$ on Δ and such that $S_\Delta^{(\alpha)}(f; x) = f^{(\alpha)}(x)$ $(\alpha = 1, 2, \ldots, k - 1)$ at the interior mesh points of Δ. Similarly, if $f(a) = f(b)$, then there is at most one periodic spline of deficiency k satisfying these interpolation requirements. Finally, in each type II equivalence class there is at most one such spline provided $k(N - 1) \geqslant n - 2$.*

5.7. Defining Equations

The representation obtained for polynomial splines of odd degree in Chapter IV is complex, as Eqs. (4.1.5)–(4.1.13) reveal. We now proceed to replace these equations by a system of equations analogous to those obtained in Section 3.7.

Let $u_j(x) = (1/(j-1)!)x^{j-1}$ $(j = 1, 2,..., 2n)$. Then $u_j^{(\alpha)}(0) = \delta_{j-1,\alpha}$, and the functions $u_j(x)$ constitute a fundamental system of solutions of the differential equation

$$D^{2n}f = 0. \tag{5.7.1}$$

Thus, any solution of (5.7.1) is of the form

$$f(x) = \sum_{j=1}^{2n} c_j u_j(x). \tag{5.7.2}$$

Since, for a given mesh Δ, a polynomial spline $S_\Delta(x)$ satisfies (5.7.1) on each open mesh interval $x_{i-1} \leqslant x \leqslant x_i$ $(i = 1, 2,..., N)$, we have

$$S_\Delta(x) = \sum_{j=1}^{2n} c_{ij} u_j(x - x_{i-1}).$$

This representation is unique, since the functions $u_j(x)$ are linearly independent. Consequently, such a set of c_{ij} $(i = 1, 2,..., N; j = 1, 2,..., 2n)$ uniquely defines a spline $S_\Delta(x)$, and, conversely, $S_\Delta(x)$ uniquely defines a set of c_{ij} if $S_\Delta(x)$ exists.

Utilizing the representation (5.7.2) together with both the continuity and interpolation requirements imposed on type I, type II, and periodic splines, respectively, we are led to the following system of equations for determining the c_{ij} and consequently $S_\Delta(Y; x)$.

$$A_\Omega \cdot C = Y_\Omega \qquad (\Omega = \mathrm{I}, \mathrm{II}, P),$$

$$A_\Omega = \begin{bmatrix} C^\Omega_{0,n} & 0 & & & & 0 \\ A_{1,n} & B_n & 0 & & & 0 \\ 0 & A_{2,n} & B_n & & & 0 \\ \cdots & & & \cdots & & \cdots \\ 0 & & & 0 & A_{N-2,n} & B_n \\ 0 & & & & 0 & C^\Omega_{1,n} \end{bmatrix}_{(\Omega=\mathrm{I},\mathrm{II})}, \tag{5.7.3.1}$$

$$A_P = \begin{bmatrix} A_{1,n} & B_n & 0 & & & 0 \\ 0 & A_{2,n} & B_n & 0 & & 0 \\ \cdots & & & & & \cdots \\ \cdots & & & & & \cdots \\ 0 & & & 0 & A_{N-1,n} & B_n \\ B_n & & & & 0 & A_{N,n} \end{bmatrix}, \tag{5.7.3.2}$$

$$A_{i,n} = \begin{bmatrix} 0 & 0 & \cdots & \cdots & 0 \\ u_1(h_i) & u_2(h_i) & \cdots & \cdots & u_{2n}(h_i) \\ u_1^{(1)}(h_i) & u_2^{(1)}(h_i) & \cdots & \cdots & u_{2n}^{(1)}(h_i) \\ \cdots & & & & \cdots \\ \cdots & & & & \cdots \\ u_1^{(2n-2)}(h_i) & u_2^{(2n-2)}(h_i) & \cdots & \cdots & u_{2n}^{(2n-2)}(h_i) \end{bmatrix}_{h_i = x_i - x_{i-1}}, \tag{5.7.3.3}$$

$$B_n = \underbrace{\begin{bmatrix} 1 & 0 & 0 \cdots & \cdots & 0 & 0 & 0 \\ -1 & 0 & 0 \cdots & \cdots & 0 & 0 & 0 \\ 0 & -1 & 0 \cdots & \cdots & 0 & 0 & 0 \\ \cdots & & & & & & \cdots \\ \cdots & & & & & & \cdots \\ 0 & 0 & 0 \cdots & \cdots & -1 & 0 & 0 \\ 0 & 0 & 0 \cdots & \cdots & 0 & -1 & 0 \end{bmatrix}}_{2n}, \tag{5.7.3.4}$$

$$C_{0,n}^{\mathrm{I}} = \underbrace{\begin{bmatrix} 1 & 0 & 0 \cdots & & & & & \cdots 0 \\ 0 & 1 & 0 \cdots & & & & & \cdots 0 \\ \cdots & & & & & & & \cdots \\ \cdots & & & & & & & \cdots \\ 0 \cdots & & \cdots 0 & 1 & 0 & 0 \cdots & & \cdots 0 \\ 0 \cdots & & \cdots 0 & 0 & 1 & 0 \cdots & & \cdots 0 \end{bmatrix}}_{2n}, \tag{5.7.3.5}$$

(the first n columns are marked by a brace labelled n)

$$C_{0,n}^{\mathrm{II}} = \underbrace{\begin{bmatrix} 1 & 0 & 0 \cdots & \cdots 0 & 0 & 0 & 0 \cdots & \cdots 0 \\ 0 & 0 \cdots & & \cdots 0 & 1 & 0 & 0 \cdots & \cdots 0 \\ 0 \cdots & & & \cdots 0 & 0 & 1 & 0 \cdots & \cdots 0 \\ \cdots & & & & & & & \cdots \\ \cdots & & & & & & & \cdots \\ 0 \cdots & & & & & \cdots 0 & 1 & 0 \\ 0 \cdots & & & & & \cdots 0 & 0 & 1 \end{bmatrix}}_{2n}, \tag{5.7.3.6}$$

(the last n columns are marked by a brace labelled n)

$$C_{1,n}^{\mathrm{I}} = \begin{bmatrix} u_1(h_N) & u_2(h_N) & \cdots & \cdots & u_{2n}(h_N) \\ u_1^{(1)}(h_N) & u_2^{(1)}(h_N) & \cdots & \cdots & u_{2n}^{(1)}(h_N) \\ \cdots & & & & \cdots \\ \cdots & & & & \cdots \\ u_1^{(n-1)}(h_N) & u_2^{(n-1)}(h_N) & \cdots & \cdots & u_{2n}^{(n-1)}(h_N) \end{bmatrix}_{h_N = x_N - x_{N-1}}, \tag{5.7.3.7}$$

$$C_{1,n}^{\mathrm{II}} = \begin{bmatrix} u_1(h_N) & u_2(h_N) & \cdots & \cdots & u_{2n}(h_N) \\ u_1^{(n)}(h_N) & u_2^{(n)}(h_N) & \cdots & \cdots & u_{2n}^{(n)}(h_N) \\ \cdots & & & & \cdots \\ \cdots & & & & \cdots \\ u_1^{(2n-2)}(h_N) & u_2^{(2n-2)}(h_N) & \cdots & \cdots & u_{2n}^{(2n-2)}(h_N) \end{bmatrix}_{h_N = x_N - x_{N-1}}, \tag{5.7.3.8}$$

$$
C = \begin{bmatrix} c_{11} \\ c_{12} \\ \cdot \\ \cdot \\ \cdot \\ c_{1,n+1} \\ \cdot \\ \cdot \\ c_{1,2n} \\ c_{21} \\ c_{22} \\ \cdot \\ \cdot \\ \cdot \\ c_{2,2n} \\ c_{31} \\ c_{32} \\ \cdot \\ \cdot \\ \cdot \\ c_{N-1,n+1} \\ \cdot \\ \cdot \\ c_{N-1,2n} \\ c_{N,1} \\ \cdot \\ \cdot \\ c_{N,n+1} \\ c_{N,n+2} \\ \cdot \\ \cdot \\ c_{N,2n} \end{bmatrix}, \quad
Y_{\mathrm{I}} = \begin{bmatrix} y_0 \\ y_0^{(1)} \\ \cdot \\ \cdot \\ y_0^{(n-1)} \\ y_1 \\ 0 \\ \cdot \\ \cdot \\ \cdot \\ \cdot \\ 0 \\ y_2 \\ 0 \\ \cdot \\ \cdot \\ \cdot \\ \cdot \\ \cdot \\ 0 \\ y_{N-1} \\ 0 \\ \cdot \\ \cdot \\ \cdot \\ \cdot \\ 0 \\ y_N \\ y_N^{(1)} \\ \cdot \\ \cdot \\ y_N^{(n-1)} \end{bmatrix}, \quad
Y_{\mathrm{II}} = \begin{bmatrix} y_0 \\ y_0^{(n)} \\ \cdot \\ \cdot \\ y_0^{(2n-2)} \\ y_1 \\ 0 \\ \cdot \\ \cdot \\ \cdot \\ \cdot \\ 0 \\ y_2 \\ 0 \\ \cdot \\ \cdot \\ \cdot \\ \cdot \\ \cdot \\ 0 \\ y_{N-1} \\ 0 \\ \cdot \\ \cdot \\ \cdot \\ \cdot \\ 0 \\ y_N \\ y_N^{(n)} \\ \cdot \\ \cdot \\ y_N^{(2n-2)} \end{bmatrix}, \quad
Y_P = \begin{bmatrix} y_1 \\ 0 \\ \cdot \\ \cdot \\ \cdot \\ \cdot \\ \cdot \\ \cdot \\ 0 \\ y_2 \\ 0 \\ \cdot \\ \cdot \\ \cdot \\ 0 \\ y_3 \\ 0 \\ \cdot \\ \cdot \\ \cdot \\ \cdot \\ \cdot \\ \cdot \\ 0 \\ y_N \\ 0 \\ \cdot \\ \cdot \\ \cdot \\ \cdot \\ \cdot \\ 0 \end{bmatrix}.
$$

(5.7.3.9) (5.7.3.10) (5.7.3.11) (5.7.3.12)

When the spline $S_\Delta(Y; x)$ is of deficiency k, the preceding system of equations should be modified as follows:

$$
A_{i,n} = \begin{bmatrix} 0 & \cdots & & \cdots & 0 \\ \vdots & & & & \vdots \\ 0 & \cdots & & \cdots & 0 \\ u_1(h_i) & & & & u_{2n}(h_i) \\ \vdots & & & & \vdots \\ \cdots & & & & \\ u_1^{(2n-k-1)}(h_i) & \cdots & & \cdots & u_{2n}^{(2n-k-1)}(h_i) \end{bmatrix}_{h_i = x_i - x_{i-1}} \left.\vphantom{\begin{matrix}0\\0\\0\end{matrix}}\right\} k, \qquad (5.7.4.1)
$$

$$
B_n = \begin{bmatrix}
\overbrace{1 & 0 & 0 & & & & 0}^{k} & & & & & 0 & 0 & 0 \\
0 & 1 & 0 & & & & 0 & & & & & & \cdots & \\
& \cdots & & & & & & & & & & & & \\
& \cdots & & & 0 & 0 & 1 & & & & & 0 & 0 & 0 \\
-1 & 0 & 0 & & & & & & & & & & & \\
0 & -1 & 0 & & & & & & & & & & \cdots & \\
\underbrace{0 & 0 & 0 & & & & & 0 & 0 & -1}_{2n-k} & 0 & 0 & 0 & 0
\end{bmatrix}, \tag{5.7.4.2}
$$

$$
C = \begin{bmatrix} c_{11} \\ c_{12} \\ \cdot \\ \cdot \\ \cdot \\ c_{1,n+1} \\ \cdot \\ \cdot \\ c_{1,2n} \\ c_{21} \\ c_{22} \\ \cdot \\ \cdot \\ \cdot \\ c_{2,2n} \\ c_{31} \\ c_{32} \\ \cdot \\ \cdot \\ \cdot \\ c_{N-1,n+1} \\ \cdot \\ \cdot \\ c_{N-1,2n} \\ c_{N,1} \\ \cdot \\ \cdot \\ c_{N,n+1} \\ c_{N,n+2} \\ \cdot \\ c_{N,2n} \end{bmatrix}, \quad
Y_{\mathrm{I}} = \begin{bmatrix} y_0 \\ y_0^{(1)} \\ \cdot \\ \cdot \\ y_0^{(n-1)} \\ y_1 \\ \cdot \\ y_1^{(k-1)} \\ 0 \\ \cdot \\ \cdot \\ 0 \\ y_2 \\ \cdot \\ y_2^{(k-1)} \\ 0 \\ \cdot \\ \cdot \\ \cdot \\ 0 \\ y_{N-1} \\ \cdot \\ y_{N-1}^{(k-1)} \\ 0 \\ \cdot \\ \cdot \\ 0 \\ y_N \\ y_N^{(1)} \\ \cdot \\ y_N^{(n-1)} \end{bmatrix}, \quad
Y_{\mathrm{II}} = \begin{bmatrix} y_0 \\ y_0^{(n)} \\ \cdot \\ \cdot \\ y_0^{(2n-2)} \\ y_1 \\ \cdot \\ y_1^{(k-1)} \\ 0 \\ \cdot \\ \cdot \\ 0 \\ y_2 \\ \cdot \\ y_2^{(k-1)} \\ 0 \\ \cdot \\ \cdot \\ \cdot \\ 0 \\ y_{N-1} \\ \cdot \\ y_{N-1}^{(k-1)} \\ 0 \\ \cdot \\ \cdot \\ 0 \\ y_N \\ y_N^{(n)} \\ \cdot \\ y_N^{(2n-2)} \end{bmatrix}, \quad
Y_P = \begin{bmatrix} y_1 \\ y_1^{(1)} \\ \cdot \\ y_1^{(k-1)} \\ 0 \\ \cdot \\ \cdot \\ \cdot \\ 0 \\ y_2 \\ \cdot \\ y_2^{(k-1)} \\ 0 \\ \cdot \\ 0 \\ y_3 \\ \cdot \\ y_3^{(k-1)} \\ 0 \\ \cdot \\ \cdot \\ \cdot \\ \cdot \\ 0 \\ y_N \\ y_N^{(1)} \\ \cdot \\ y_N^{(k-1)} \\ \cdot \\ \cdot \\ \cdot \\ 0 \end{bmatrix}.
$$

(5.7.4.3) (5.7.4.4) (5.7.4.5) (5.7.4.6)

In the next section, we investigate the invertibility of the matrix A_Ω upon which the existence of $S_\Delta(Y;\ x)$ depends. The equations for the periodic spline are for the case: $S_\Delta^{(\alpha)}(f;\ a) = f^{(\alpha)}(a)$ $(\alpha = 0, 1,..., k-1)$, $S_\Delta^{(\alpha)}(f;\ a) = S_\Delta^{(\alpha)}(f;\ b)$ $(\alpha = 0, 1,..., 2n - k - 1)$.

5.8. Existence

In Section 5.6 we established the uniqueness of polynomial splines of odd degree, and in Section 5.7 we established that to every polynomial spline of odd degree $S_\Delta(x)$ there corresponds a unique set of coefficients c_{ij} $(i = 1, 2,..., N;\ j = 0, 1,... 2n - 1)$. Consequently, if the equation

$$A_\Omega C = 0 \tag{5.8.1}$$

has more than the null solution, there are two distinct null splines; this would contradict Theorem 5.6.1 or Theorem 5.6.2. Thus, A_Ω^{-1} exists, and we have Theorems 5.8.1 and 5.8.2, which supplement Theorems 5.6.1 and 5.6.2, respectively.

Theorem 5.8.1. *Let Δ: $a = x_0 < x_1 < \cdots < x_N = b$ and $f(x)$ be given. Then in each type I equivalence class there is a unique spline of interpolation to $f(x)$ on Δ. If $f(a) = f(b)$, then there is a unique periodic spline of interpolation to $f(x)$ on Δ. Finally, if $N > n - 2$, then in each type II equivalence class there is a unique spline of interpolation to $f(x)$ on Δ.*

Theorem 5.8.2. *Let Δ: $a = x_0 < x_1 < \cdots < x_N = b$ and $f(x)$ be given, where $f(x)$ has $k - 1$ derivatives at each interior mesh point of Δ. Then in each type I equivalence class there is a unique polynomial spline $S_\Delta(f; x)$ of degree $2n - 1$ and deficiency k $(k \leqslant n)$ which interpolates to $f(x)$ on Δ and such that $S_\Delta^{(\alpha)}(f;\ x) = f^{(\alpha)}(x)$ $(\alpha = 1, 2,..., k - 1)$ at the interior mesh points of Δ. Similarly, if $f(a) = f(b)$, then there is a unique periodic spline of deficiency k satisfying these interpolation requirements. Finally, in each type II equivalence class there is a unique spline provided $k(N - 1) \geqslant n - 2$.*

The uniqueness theorems and the existence theorems obtained in this chapter follow directly from the minimum norm property and could have been established prior to the proof of the best approximation property. This is important, since the proof given in Section 5.5 of the latter property requires the existence of the auxiliary spline $S_\Delta(f - S_\Delta\ ;\ x)$. An alternative proof of the best approximation property could be given, however, which would not use the auxiliary spline, but there would be a definite loss in simplicity of presentation.

In the case of the cubic spline, the existence theorem of Chapter III is not so strong as that obtained in Chapter II by other methods; in the case of polynomial splines of odd degree, however, these methods, as pursued in Chapter IV, lead to an existence theorem requiring a nearly uniform mesh. Consequently, Theorems 5.8.1 and 5.8.2 are of major importance.

5.9. Convergence of Lower-Order Derivatives

Let $f(x)$ be a function in $\mathscr{K}^n(a, b)$, and let $S_\Delta(f; x)$ be a spline of interpolation to $f(x)$ on a mesh Δ: $a = x_0 < x_1 < \cdots < x_N = b$. Repeated application of Rolle's theorem tells us that at least once in every α consecutive intervals $S_\Delta^{(\alpha)}(f; x)$ interpolates to $f^{(\alpha)}(x)$ $(0 \leqslant \alpha < n)$. If $\bar{x}_\alpha$ is such a point of interpolation,

$$f^{(\alpha)}(x) - S_\Delta^{(\alpha)}(f; x) = \int_{\bar{x}_\alpha}^{x} \{f^{(\alpha+1)}(x) - S_\Delta^{(\alpha+1)}(f; x)\}\, dx. \tag{5.9.1}$$

Here the interval of integration can be chosen so that $|\bar{x}_\alpha - x| \leqslant \frac{1}{2}(\alpha + 1) \cdot \|\Delta\|$ whenever such interpolation points lie both to the left and to the right of x, since $\bar{x}_\alpha$ can be selected on either side of x. If this is not the case, the factor $\frac{1}{2}$ generally must be omitted. When considering a sequence $\{\Delta_N\}$ of meshes with $\|\Delta_N\| \to 0$ as $N \to \infty$ and when x is not either a or b, the factor of $\frac{1}{2}$ can be included as soon as N is sufficiently large so that x lies between such interpolation points. When, in particular, $f(x) - S_\Delta(f; x)$ is of type I′ or both $f(x)$ and $S_\Delta(f; x)$ are in $\mathscr{K}_P{}^n(a, b)$, the factor $\frac{1}{2}$ need never be omitted.

Let $\alpha = n - 1$. Then we have

$$\begin{aligned} |f^{(n-1)}(x) - S_\Delta^{(n-1)}(f; x)| &\leqslant \int_{\bar{x}_{n-1}}^{x} |f^{(n)}(x) - S_\Delta^{(n)}(f; x)|\, |dx| \\ &\leqslant J\{B \cdot n \cdot \|\Delta\|\}^{1/2}, \end{aligned} \tag{5.9.2.1}$$

where

$$J^2 = \int_a^b \{f^{(n)}(x) - S_\Delta^{(n)}(f; x)\}^2\, dx \tag{5.9.2.2}$$

and B is either $\frac{1}{2}$ or 1. Repeating this argument, we obtain the general result that

$$\begin{aligned} |f^{(\alpha)}(x) - S_\Delta^{(\alpha)}(f; x)| \leqslant J \cdot n^{1/2}(n-1) \cdots (\alpha+1) \\ \cdot B^{(2n-2\alpha-1)/2} \cdot \|\Delta\|^{(2n-2\alpha-1)/2} \end{aligned} \tag{5.9.3}$$

for $0 \leqslant \alpha < n$. Theorem 5.9.1, which follows, is now immediate if one observes that Minkowski's inequality, together with the minimum norm property (Theorem 5.4.1), implies that

$$\left\{\int_a^b \{f^{(n)}(x) - S_{\Delta_N}^{(n)}(f; x)\}^2 \, dx\right\}^{1/2} \leqslant 2\left\{\int_a^b \{f^{(n)}(x)\}^2 \, dx\right\}^{1/2}. \qquad (5.9.4)$$

Theorem 5.9.1. *Let $f(x)$ be in $\mathscr{K}^n(a, b)$, and let $\{\Delta_N : a = x_0^N < \cdots < x_{m_N}^N = b\}$ be a sequence of meshes with $\| \Delta_N \| \to 0$ as $N \to \infty$. Let $S_{\Delta_N}(f; x)$ be a spline of interpolation to $f(x)$ on Δ_N ($N = 0, 1,\ldots$) satisfying one of the conditions* (a) *$f(x) - S_{\Delta_N}(f; x)$ is of type I' ($N = 0, 1,\ldots$),* (b) *$f(x)$ and $S_{\Delta_N}(f; x)$ are periodic ($N = 0, 1,\ldots$),* (c) *$S_{\Delta_N}(f; x)$ is of type II' ($N = 0, 1,\ldots$).*
Then we have

$$f^{(\alpha)}(x) = S_{\Delta_N}^{(\alpha)}(f; x) + \eta_\alpha(x) \qquad (\alpha = 0, 1,\ldots, n-1), \qquad (5.9.5.1)$$

$$| \eta_\alpha(x) | \leqslant (n)^{1/2}(n-1) \cdots (\alpha+1) \cdot 2^{-(2n-2\alpha-1)/2} \cdot \| \Delta_N \|^{(2n-2\alpha-1)/2} \cdot 2\left\{\int_a^b \{f^{(n)}(x)\}^2 \, dx\right\}^{1/2}. \qquad (5.9.5.2)$$

When condition (c) *is assumed, the factor $2^{-(2n-2\alpha-1)/2}$ must be omitted for $x = a$ and $x = b$. Finally, if the condition* (d) *$\Delta_0 \subset \Delta_N$ and $S_{\Delta_N}(f; x) - S_{\Delta_0}(f; x)$ is of type II' ($N = 1, 2,\ldots$), is satisfied, then (5.9.5.1) and (5.9.5.2) are valid if*

$$2\left\{\int_a^b \{f^{(n)}(x)\}^2 \, dx\right\}^{1/2}$$

is replaced by

$$\left\{\int_a^b \{f^{(n)}(x) - S_{\Delta_0}^{(n)}(f; x)\}^2 \, dx\right\}^{1/2}.$$

We could easily formulate an analog of Theorem 5.9.1 for the case of type I or type II splines of deficiency k. It is perhaps somewhat more illuminating, however, to consider polynomial splines of deficiency k such that $f^{(\alpha)}(x_i) = S_\Delta^{(\alpha)}(f; x_i)$ ($\alpha = 0, 1,\ldots, k-1$) not only at the interior mesh points of Δ but at a and b as well. In order to define the spline completely in the nonperiodic case, we require in addition

$$S_\Delta^{(\alpha)}(f; x_i) = 0 \qquad (\alpha = n, n+1,\ldots, 2n-k-1; \ i = 0, N). \qquad (5.9.6)$$

In the periodic case we require $S_\Delta^{(\alpha)}(f; a) = S_\Delta^{(\alpha)}(f; b)$ for $\alpha = 0, 1,\ldots, 2n-k-1$. We refer to these splines, both nonperiodic and periodic, as splines of interpolation of *type k*.

For splines of interpolation of type k the first integral relation is valid, and, consequently, we have the minimum norm property, uniqueness, existence, and the best approximation property. These four properties allow us to obtain the counterpart of Theorem 5.9.1 by a parallel argument, which we omit.

Theorem 5.9.2. *Let $f(x)$ be in $\mathscr{K}^n(a, b)$, and let $\{\Delta_N : a = x_0^N < \cdots < x_{m_N}^N = b\}$ be a sequence of meshes with $\| \Delta_N \| \to 0$ as $N \to \infty$. Let $S_{\Delta_N}(f; x)$ be a spline of interpolation to $f(x)$ on Δ_N satisfying one of the conditions,* (a) *$S_{\Delta_N}(f; x)$ is of type k ($N = 0, 1,\ldots$),* (b) *$f(x)$ is in $\mathscr{K}_P{}^n(a, b)$, and $S_{\Delta_N}(f; x)$ is a periodic spline of type k ($N = 0, 1,\ldots$). Then*

$$f^{(\alpha)}(x) = S_{\Delta_N}^{(\alpha)}(f; x) + \eta_\alpha(x) \qquad (\alpha = 0, 1,\ldots, n-1), \tag{5.9.7.1}$$

where

$$| \eta_\alpha(x) | \leqslant (n - 2k + 2)^{1/2} \frac{(n - 2k + 1)!}{(\alpha - 2k + 2)!} 2^{-(2n-2\alpha-1)/2} \| \Delta_N \|^{(2n-2\alpha-1)/2}$$
$$\cdot 2 \left\{ \int_a^b \{f^{(n)}(x)\}^2 \, dx \right\}^{1/2}. \tag{5.9.7.2}$$

When condition (a) *is assumed, the factor $2^{-(2n-2\alpha-1)/2}$ must be omitted for $x = a$ and $x = b$ if $\alpha > k - 1$. If $n - 2k + 2 < 1$ in (5.9.7.2), it is replaced by* 1.

The reason that the factor $(n)^{1/2}(n - 1) \cdots (\alpha + 1)$ in (5.9.5.2) is replaced by the factor $(n - 2k + 2)^{1/2}(n - 2k + 1)!/(\alpha - 2k + 2)!$ in (5.9.7.2) is that $S_\Delta^{(2k-1)}(f; x)$ interpolates to $f^{(2k-1)}(x)$ at least once in every mesh interval when $S_\Delta(f; x)$ is a spline of type k. Thus, $S_\Delta^{(2k-1)}(f; x)$ in this situation possesses interpolation properties normally associated with the first derivative. In interpreting (5.9.7.2), we interpret $m!$ as 1 when m is a nonpositive integer.

5.10. The Second Integral Relation

The relations obtained in Sections 3.9 and 3.10 can be extended to polynomial splines of degree $2n - 1$ in a straightforward manner. Let

$$(f, g) = \int_a^b D^n f \cdot D^n g \, dx \tag{5.10.1}$$

and

$$\| f \| = (f, f)^{1/2}. \tag{5.10.2}$$

In addition, let Δ: $a = x_0 < x_1 < \cdots < x_N = b$ be given, and let $S_\Delta(x)$ be a polynomial spline of degree $2n - 1$ on Δ. If $f(x)$ is in $\mathscr{K}^{2n}(a, b)$, we may write

$$\int_a^b \{f^{(n)}(x) - S_\Delta^{(n)}(x)\}^2\,dx = \sum_{i=1}^N \int_{x_{i-1}}^{x_i} \{f^{(n)}(x) - S_\Delta^{(n)}(x)\}^2\,dx. \quad (5.10.3)$$

Next we integrate each of the integrals in the right-hand member of (5.10.3) by parts n times and obtain

$$\begin{aligned}\int_{x_{i-1}}^{x_i} &\{f^{(n)}(x) - S_\Delta^{(n)}(x)\}^2\,dx\\ &= \sum_{\alpha=1}^n (-1)^{\alpha+1}\{f^{(n-\alpha)}(x) - S_\Delta^{(n-\alpha)}(x)\}\{f^{(n+\alpha-1)}(x) - S_\Delta^{(n+\alpha-1)}(x)\}\Big|_{x_{i-1}}^{x_i}\\ &\quad + (-1)^n \int_{x_{i-1}}^{x_i} \{f(x) - S_\Delta(x)\}\{f^{(2n)}(x) - S_\Delta^{(2n)}(x)\}\,dx;\end{aligned} \quad (5.10.4)$$

$$\begin{aligned}\|f - S_\Delta\|^2 &= \sum_{i=1}^N \sum_{\alpha=1}^n \Big\{(-1)^{\alpha+1} \cdot D^{n-\alpha}(f - S_\Delta) \cdot D^{n+\alpha-1}(f - S_\Delta)\Big|_{x_{i-1}}^{x_i}\Big\}\\ &\quad + (-1)^n \int_a^b (f - S_\Delta) \cdot D^{2n} f\,dx.\end{aligned} \quad (5.10.5)$$

The identity (5.10.5) is the analog of the identity (3.9.4). Under a variety of conditions on $f(x) - S_\Delta(x)$, the identity (5.10.5) reduces to the relation

$$\|f - S_{\Delta,f}\|^2 - (-1)^n \int_a^b (f - S_{\Delta,f}) \cdot D^{2n} f\,dx, \quad (5.10.6)$$

which we call the *second integral relation*. We observe that, for a spline of interpolation $S_\Delta(f; x)$ to $f(x)$ on Δ of type k, the second integral relation normally is not true. We have, however, the following two theorems.

Theorem 5.10.1. *Let* Δ: $a = x_0 < x_1 < \cdots < x_N = b$ *and* $f(x)$ *in* $\mathscr{K}^{2n}(a, b)$ *be given. If* $S_\Delta(f; x)$ *is a polynomial spline of degree* $2n - 1$ *which interpolates to* $f(x)$ *on* Δ *and* $S_\Delta(f; x)$ *satisfies one of the conditions,* (a) $f(x) - S_\Delta(f; x)$ *is of type I′,* (b) $f(x) - S_\Delta(f; x)$ *is of type II′,* (c) $f(x)$ *and* $S_\Delta(f; x)$ *are periodic, then*

$$\|f - S_{\Delta,f}\|^2 = (-1)^n \int_a^b (f - S_{\Delta,f}) \cdot D^{2n} f\,dx.$$

Theorem 5.10.2. *Let Δ: $a = x_0 < x_1 < \cdots < x_N = b$ and $f(x)$ in $\mathscr{K}^{2n}(a, b)$ be given. If $S_\Delta(f; x)$ is a polynomial spline of degree $2n - 1$ and deficiency k which interpolates to $f(x)$ on Δ, satisfies the interpolation conditions*

$$S^{(\alpha)}(f; x_i) = f^{(\alpha)}(x_i) \qquad (\alpha = 1, 2, \ldots, k - 1; \quad i = 1, 2, \ldots, N - 1), \quad (5.10.7)$$

and one of the conditions, (a) $f(x) - S_\Delta(f; x)$ *is of type I',* (b) $f(x) - S_\Delta(f; x)$ *is of type II',* (c) $f(x)$ *and $S_\Delta(f; x)$ are periodic, then*

$$\| f - S_{\Delta,f} \|^2 = (-1)^n \int_a^b (f - S_{\Delta,f}) \cdot D^{2n} f \, dx.$$

As we have already pointed out, the second integral relation generally is not valid for splines of type k. If we consider splines satisfying the slightly modified end conditions

$$S_\Delta^{(\alpha)}(f; x_i) = f^{(\alpha)}(x_i)$$
$$(\alpha = 0, 1, \ldots, k - 1; \quad \alpha = n, n + 1, \ldots, 2n - k - 1; \quad i = 0, N), \qquad (5.10.8)$$

the second integral relation is again valid. In this case, however, the minimum norm property fails, but the best approximation property holds. We refer to splines of interpolation of this form as splines of *modified type k*. A type II spline is a spline of modified type I.

5.11. Raising the Order of Convergence

In this section, we proceed very much as in Section 3.10. From (5.9.3), it follows that

$$| f^{(\alpha)}(x) - S_\Delta^{(\alpha)}(f; x) | \leqslant K_\alpha \cdot \left\{ \int_a^b \{ f^{(n)}(x) - S_\Delta^{(n)}(f; x) \}^2 \, dx \right\}^{1/2} \cdot \| \Delta \|^{(2n-2\alpha-1)/2} \qquad (5.11.1)$$

for a suitable choice of the constant K_α. If the second integral relation is valid, (5.11.1) is equivalent to

$$| f^{(\alpha)}(x) - S_\Delta^{(\alpha)}(f; x) |$$
$$\leqslant K_\alpha \cdot \left\{ (-1)^n \int_a^b \{ f(x) - S_\Delta(f; x) \} \cdot f^{(2n)}(x) \, dx \right\}^{1/2} \cdot \| \Delta \|^{(2n-2\alpha-1)/2};$$

hence, we have

$$\sup_x | f^{(\alpha)}(x) - S_\Delta^{(\alpha)}(f; x) |$$
$$\leqslant K_\alpha \cdot \{ V_a{}^b [f^{(2n-1)}] \}^{1/2} \cdot \{ \sup_x | f(x) - S_\Delta(f; x) | \}^{1/2} \cdot \| \Delta \|^{(2n-2\alpha-1)/2}. \qquad (5.11.2)$$

As in Section 3.10, we set $\alpha = 0$ and solve (5.11.2) for $\sup_x |f(x) - S_\Delta(f; x)|$, which is possible except in the trivial case when $f(x) \equiv S_\Delta(f; x)$. Thus,

$$\sup_x |f(x) - S_\Delta(f; x)| \leqslant K_0^2 \cdot V_a^b[f^{(2n-1)}] \cdot \|\Delta\|^{2n-1}, \tag{5.11.3}$$

which, together with (5.11.2), implies

$$|f^{(\alpha)}(x) - S_\Delta^{(\alpha)}(f; x)| \leqslant K_\alpha \cdot K_0 \cdot V_a^b[f^{(2n-1)}] \cdot \|\Delta\|^{2n-\alpha-1}. \tag{5.11.4}$$

We are now able to reformulate Theorems 5.9.1 and 5.9.2.

Theorem 5.11.1. *Let $f(x)$ be in $\mathscr{K}^{2n}(a, b)$, and let*

$$\{\Delta_N : a = x_0^N < \cdots < x_{m_N}^N = b\}$$

be a sequence of meshes with $\|\Delta_N\| \to 0$ as $N \to \infty$. Let $\{S_{\Delta_N}(f; x)\}$ be a sequence of splines of interpolation to $f(x)$ satisfying one of the conditions (a) *$f(x) - S_{\Delta_N}(f; x)$ is of type I′ ($N = 0, 1,\ldots$),* (b) *$f(x)$ and $S_{\Delta_N}(f; x)$ are periodic ($N = 0, 1,\ldots$),* (c) *$f(x) - S_{\Delta_N}(f; x)$ is of type II′ ($N = 0, 1,\ldots$). Then*

$$f^{(\alpha)}(x) = S_\Delta^{(\alpha)}(f; x) + \eta_\alpha(x) \qquad (\alpha = 0, 1,\ldots, n-1), \tag{5.11.5.1}$$

where

$$|\eta_\alpha(x)| \leqslant n(n-1) \cdots (\alpha+1)[(n-1)!] \cdot 2^{-(2n-\alpha-1)} \cdot V_a^b[f^{(2n-1)}] \cdot \|\Delta_N\|^{2n-\alpha-1}. \tag{5.11.5.2}$$

When condition (c) *is satisfied, the factor $2^{-(2n-\alpha-1)}$ must be omitted for $x = a$ and $x = b$.*

In reformulating Theorem 5.9.2, we employ splines of modified type k rather than splines of type k.

Theorem 5.11.2. *Let $f(x)$ be in $\mathscr{K}^{2n}(a, b)$, and let*

$$\{\Delta_N : a = x_0^N < \cdots < x_{m_N}^N = b\}$$

be a sequence of meshes with $\|\Delta_N\| \to 0$ as $N \to \infty$. Let $\{S_{\Delta_N}(f; x)\}$ be a sequence of splines of interpolation to $f(x)$ satisfying one of the conditions (a) *$S_{\Delta_N}(f; x)$ is of modified type k ($N = 0, 1,\ldots$),* (b) *$f(x)$ is in $\mathscr{K}_p^{2n}(a, b)$, and $S_{\Delta_N}(f; x)$ is a periodic spline of type k ($N = 0, 1,\ldots$). Then*

$$f^{(\alpha)}(x) = S_{\Delta_N}^{(\alpha)}(f; x) + \eta_\alpha(x) \qquad (\alpha = 0, 1,\ldots, n-1), \tag{5.11.6.1}$$

where

$$|\eta_\alpha(x)| \leqslant \frac{(n-2k+2)\{(n-2k+1)!\}^2}{(\alpha-2k+2)!} \cdot 2^{-(2n-\alpha-1)} \cdot V_a{}^b[f^{(2n-1)}] \cdot \|\Delta_N\|^{2n-\alpha-1}. \tag{5.11.6.2}$$

When condition (a) *is satisfied, the factor* $2^{-(2n-\alpha-1)}$ *must be omitted when* $x = a$ *or* $x = b$ *and* $\alpha \geqslant k$. *If* $n - 2k + 2 < 1$ *in (5.11.6.2), it is replaced by* 1.

5.12. Convergence of Higher-Order Derivatives

Let Δ: $a = x_0 < \cdots < x_N = b$ be given, and let $f(x)$ be in $\mathscr{K}^{2n}(a, b)$. In addition, let $S_\Delta(f; x)$ be a polynomial spline of degree $2n - 1$ interpolating to $f(x)$ on Δ such that

$$|f(x) - S_\Delta(f; x)| \leqslant K_0{}^2 \cdot V_a{}^b[f^{(2n-1)}] \cdot \|\Delta\|^{2n-1} \tag{5.12.1}$$

is valid. For the equally spaced difference quotients

$$\delta^\alpha_{S_{\Delta,f}}[x_{i-1}, x_i] \qquad (i = 1, 2, \ldots, N; \alpha = 0, 1, \ldots, 2n-1),$$

where $\delta^0_{S_{\Delta,f}}[x_{i-1}, x_i] = S_\Delta(f; x_{i-1}) = f(x_{i-1})$, we can find quantities $x_{\alpha,i}$ with $x_{i-1} \leqslant x_{\alpha,i} \leqslant x_i$ such that

$$\delta^\alpha_{S_{\Delta,f}}[x_{i-1}, x_i] = S_\Delta^{(\alpha)}(f; x_{\alpha,i}) \qquad (i = 1, 2, \ldots, N;\ \alpha = 0, 1, \ldots, 2n-1). \tag{5.12.2}$$

As a consequence, the equations

$$\delta^\alpha_{S_{\Delta,f}}[x_{i-1}, x_i] = \sum_{j=1}^{2n} c_{ij} u_j^{(\alpha)}(x_{\alpha,i} - x_{i-1}) \qquad (i = 1, 2, \ldots, N;\ \alpha = 0, 1, \ldots, 2n-1) \tag{5.12.3}$$

can be used to determine the coefficients c_{ij} for small values of $\|\Delta\|$, since

$$\sum_{j=1}^{2n} c_{ij} u_j^{(\alpha)}(x_{\alpha,i} - x_{i-1}) \to c_{i,\alpha+1}$$

as $\|\Delta\| \to 0$ uniformly with respect to both the number and location of the mesh intervals $[x_{i-1}, x_i]$. Moreover, since $\delta^\alpha_f[a, b]$ is a linear operation with respect to f,

$$|\delta^\alpha_{S_{\Delta,f}}[x_{i-1}, x_i] - \delta^\alpha_f[x_{i-1}, x_i]| = |\delta^\alpha_{S_{\Delta,f}-f}[x_{i-1}, x_i]|. \tag{5.12.4}$$

It follows that

$$| \delta^{\alpha}_{S_{\Delta,f}}[x_{i-1}, x_i] - \delta^{\alpha}_{f}[x_{i-1}, x] | \leqslant (2\alpha R_{\Delta})^{\alpha} \cdot K_0{}^2 \cdot V_a{}^b[f^{(2n-1)}] \cdot \| \Delta \|^{2n-\alpha-1}$$
$$(i = 1, 2,..., N; \quad \alpha = 0, 1,..., 2n - 1), \qquad (5.12.5.1)$$

where

$$R_{\Delta} = \max_i \frac{\| \Delta \|}{| x_i - x_{i-1} |}. \qquad (5.12.5.2)$$

Theorem 5.12.1. *Let $f(x)$ be in $\mathscr{K}^{2n}(a, b)$ and*

$$\{\Delta_N : a = x_0{}^N < \cdots < x^N_{m_N} = b\}$$

be a sequence of meshes such that $\| \Delta_N \| \to 0$ as $N \to \infty$. Let R_{Δ_N}, defined by (5.12.5.2), be bounded with respect to N, and let $\{S_{\Delta_N}(f; x)\}$ be a sequence of polynomial splines of degree $2n - 1$ which interpolate to $f(x)$ on corresponding meshes Δ_N and which satisfy one of the conditions (a) *$f(x) - S_{\Delta_N}(f; x)$ is of type I' ($N = 1, 2,...$),* (b) *$f(x) - S_{\Delta_N}(f; x)$ is of type II' ($N = 1, 2,...$),* (c) *$f(x)$ and $S_{\Delta_N}(f; x)$ are periodic ($N = 1, 2,...$). Then*

$$f^{(\alpha)}(x) = S^{(\alpha)}_{\Delta_N} f; x) + O(\| \Delta_N \|^{2n-\alpha-1}) \qquad (\alpha = 0, 1,..., 2n - 1) \quad (5.12.6)$$

uniformly for x in $[a, b]$.

The proof is essentially the same as that of Theorem 3.11.1.

By a completely parallel argument, we have Theorem 5.12.2, which should be compared with Theorem 5.11.2. Where Theorem 5.11.2 applies it is sharper, particularly when $k > 1$. Details of the proof of the final assertion of Theorem 5.12.2 can be found in Section 6.12.

Theorem 5.12.2. *Let $f(x)$ be in $\mathscr{K}^{2n}(a, b)$ and*

$$\{\Delta_N : a = x_0{}^N < \cdots < x^N_{m_N} = b\}$$

be a sequence of meshes such that $\| \Delta_N \| \to 0$ as $N \to \infty$. Let R_{Δ_N}, defined by (5.12.5.2), be bounded with respect to N, and let $\{S_{\Delta_N}(f; x)\}$ be a sequence of polynomial splines of degree $2n - 1$ which interpolate to $f(x)$ on corresponding meshes Δ_N and which satisfy one of the conditions (a) *$S_{\Delta_N}(f; x)$ is of modified type k ($N = 1, 2,...$),* (b) *$f(x)$ is in $\mathscr{K}^{2n}_P(a, b)$ and $S_{\Delta_N}(f; x)$ is a periodic spline of type k ($N = 1, 2,...$). Then we have, uniformly for x in $[a, b]$,*

$$f^{(\alpha)}(x) = S^{(\alpha)}_{\Delta_N}(f; x) + O(\| \Delta_N \|^{2n-\alpha-k}) \qquad (\alpha = 0, 1,..., 2n - k). \quad (5.12.7)$$

Moreover, $\lim_{N\to\infty} S^{(\alpha)}_{\Delta_N}(f; x) = f^{(\alpha)}(x)$ uniformly in x for $\alpha = 0, 1,..., 2n - 2$.

5.13. Limits on the Order of Convergence

The discussion of limitations on the convergence of cubic splines contained in Section 3.12 carries over essentially unchanged to polynomial splines of odd degree. In general, we have

$$f^{(\alpha)}(x) = S_{\Delta_N}^{(\alpha)}(f; x) + O(\| \Delta_N \|^{2n-\alpha-1}) \qquad (\alpha = 0, 1,..., 2n - 1). \quad (5.13.1)$$

For $\alpha = 0, 1,..., n - 1$, no restrictions are imposed on the meshes, but for $\alpha = n, n + 1,..., 2n - 1$, the mesh parameters R_{Δ_N} must be bounded as a function of N. For uniform spacing we obtained in the periodic case (cf. Section 4.6, Theorem 4.6.3) the stronger result that

$$f^{(\alpha)}(x) = S_{\Delta_N}^{(\alpha)}(f; x) + O(\| \Delta_N \|^{2n-\alpha}) \qquad (\alpha = 0, 1,..., 2n - 1). \quad (5.13.2)$$

In the case of (5.13.1), the rate of convergence is proportional to $V_a^b[f^{(2n-1)}]$, whereas for (5.13.2) the rate of convergence is proportional to $\| f^{(2n)} \|_\infty$ for $f(x)$ in $C^{2n}(a, b)$.

The rate of convergence in (5.13.2), insofar as it depends on $\| \Delta_N \|$, cannot be improved. We have, in fact, the following theorem, the proof of which is the same as that of Theorem 3.12.1.

Theorem 5.13.1. *Let $\{\Delta_N\}$ be a sequence of meshes with $\| \Delta_N \| \to 0$ as $N \to \infty$, and let R_{Δ_N} be bounded with respect to N. Let $f(x)$ be in $C^{2n}(a, b)$ and $\mu > 0$. If, uniformly for x in $[a, b]$,*

$$f(x) = S_{\Delta_N}(f; x) + O(\| \Delta_N \|^{2n+\mu}), \quad (5.13.3)$$

then

$$D^{2n}f = 0.$$

REMARK 5.13.1. The splines involved in Theorem 5.13.1 need not be of deficiency one; the key hypothesis is (5.13.3).

5.14. Hilbert Space Interpretation

We continue here the discussion begun in Section 3.13. The class $\mathscr{K}^n(a, b)$, under the pseudo-inner product

$$(f, g) = \int_a^b f^{(n)}(x) \cdot g^{(n)}(x)\, dx \quad (5.14.1)$$

is a Hilbert space if we identify functions that differ by a polynomial of degree $n - 1$; without these identifications and the inner product (f, g),

$\mathscr{K}^n(a, b)$ is simply a linear space. Let Δ: $a = x_0 < x_1 < \cdots < x_N = b$ be given, and let $F_\Delta(n, k)$ denote the family of polynomial splines on Δ of degree $2n - 1$ and deficiency k ($k \leqslant n$). As a linear subspace of $\mathscr{K}^n(a, b)$, $F_\Delta(n, k)$ has dimension $k(N - 1) + 2n$, and as a Hilbert space, where splines differing by a polynomial of degree $n - 1$ are identified, it has dimension $k(N - 1) + n$. If $P_\Delta(n, k)$ denotes the family of periodic polynomial splines on Δ of degree $2n - 1$ and deficiency k, then $P_\Delta(n, k)$ is a subspace of $F_\Delta(n, k)$. As a linear space (without any identifications), $P_\Delta(n, k)$ has dimension $N \cdot k$; as a Hilbert space (with splines differing by a constant identified), $P_\Delta(n, k)$ has dimension $Nk - 1$. If Δ_2 refines Δ_1, $F_{\Delta_1}(n, k)$ is a subspace of $F_{\Delta_2}(n, k)$, and $P_{\Delta_1}(n, k)$ is a subspace of $P_{\Delta_2}(n, k)$. Since they are finite dimensional, $F_\Delta(n, k)$ and $P_\Delta(n, k)$ are always closed subspaces. If $\Delta_1 \subset \Delta_2$, then $[F_{\Delta_2}(n, k) - F_{\Delta_1}(n, k)]$ and $[P_{\Delta_2}(n, k) - P_{\Delta_1}(n, k)]$ denote the splines in $F_{\Delta_2}(n, k)$ or $P_{\Delta_2}(n, k)$, respectively, whose defining values (including any derivatives*) on Δ_1 are zero. We employ similar notation for other spaces when required. The orthogonality of the component spaces in the decompositions in the remainder of this section is demonstrated in Section 5.15. Observe that the linear spaces $[F_{\Delta_l}(n, k) - F_{\Delta_{l-1}}(n, k)]$, etc., unlike the spaces $F_\Delta(n, k)$, are unaffected when systems differing by a polynomial of degree $n - 1$ are identified. Thus, we can regard elements in these spaces as functions rather than equivalence classes even after identifications are made.

Consider now a sequence of meshes $\{\Delta_N\}$ on $[a, b]$ with $\Delta_N \subset \Delta_{N+1}$ ($N = 1, 2, \ldots$). It is true that

$$F_{\Delta_N}(n, k) = F_{\Delta_1}(n, k) \oplus [F_{\Delta_2}(n, k) - F_{\Delta_1}(n, k)] \oplus \cdots \oplus [F_{\Delta_N}(n, k) - F_{\Delta_{N-1}}(n, k)], \tag{5.14.2.1}$$

$$P_{\Delta_N}(n, k) = P_{\Delta_1}(n, k) \oplus [P_{\Delta_2}(n, k) - P_{\Delta_1}(n, k)] \oplus \cdots \oplus [P_{\Delta_N}(n, k) - P_{\Delta_{N-1}}(n, k)]. \tag{5.14.2.2}$$

Define $F_{\Delta_\infty}(n, k)$ and $P_{\Delta_\infty}(n, k)$ as the infinite direct sums

$$F_{\Delta_\infty}(n, k) = F_{\Delta_1}(n, k) \oplus \sum_{N=2}^{\infty} \oplus [F_{\Delta_N}(n, k) - F_{\Delta_{N-1}}(n, k)] \tag{5.14.3.1}$$

and

$$P_{\Delta_\infty}(n, k) = P_{\Delta_1}(n, k) \oplus \sum_{N=2}^{\infty} \oplus [P_{\Delta_N}(n, k) - P_{\Delta_{N-1}}(n, k)], \tag{5.14.3.2}$$

* Here and in the remainder of this chapter we take these defining values to be the entries in (5.7.3.10), (5.7.3.11), or (5.7.3.12) associated with Δ_1.

respectively. Clearly, we have the inclusion relations

$$P_{\Delta_\infty}(n, k) \subset F_{\Delta_\infty}(n, k), \tag{5.14.4.1}$$

$$F_{\Delta_\infty}(n, k) \subseteq \mathscr{K}^n(a, b). \tag{5.14.4.2}$$

In Section 5.15, we establish for $k \neq 0$ that $F_{\Delta_\infty}(n, k) = \mathscr{K}^n(a, b)$ and that $P_{\Delta_\infty}(n, k) = \mathscr{K}^n(a, b)$ provided $\| \Delta_N \| \to 0$ as $N \to \infty$. Since, by definition, $F_{\Delta_\infty}(n, k)$ and $P_{\Delta_\infty}(n, k)$ are closed with respect to the norm

$$\| f \| = (f, f)^{1/2}, \tag{5.14.5}$$

this is equivalent to showing that $F_{\Delta_\infty}(n, k)$ is dense in $\mathscr{K}^n(a, b)$ and $P_{\Delta_\infty}(n, k)$ is dense in $\mathscr{K}^n(a, b)$. First, however, we single out two additional subspaces of $F_\Delta(n, k)$ which are of considerable importance. The first of these subspaces is the family of type II′ polynomial splines on Δ of degree $2n - 1$ and deficiency k; the second is the family of type k polynomial splines on Δ of degree $2n - 1$.* We denote these subspaces by $F'_\Delta(n, k)$ and $T_\Delta(n, k)$, respectively. Observe that $F'_\Delta(n, k) \subset T_\Delta(n, k) \subset F_\Delta(n, k)$. Given a sequence of meshes $\{\Delta_N\}$ on $[a, b]$ with $\Delta_N \subset \Delta_{N+1}$ $(N = 1, 2, \ldots)$, the subspaces $F'_\Delta(n, k)$ and $T_\Delta(n, k)$ allow us to define the infinite direct sums $F'_{\Delta_\infty}(n, k)$ and $T_{\Delta_\infty}(n, k)$. We define $F'_{\Delta_\infty}(n, k)$ as

$$F'_{\Delta_\infty}(n, k) = F'_{\Delta_1}(n, k) \oplus \sum_{N=2}^{\infty} \oplus [F'_{\Delta_N}(n, k) - F'_{\Delta_{N-1}}(n, k)] \tag{5.14.6.1}$$

and $T_{\Delta_\infty}(n, k)$ as

$$T_{\Delta_\infty}(n, k) = T_{\Delta_1}(n, k) \oplus \sum_{N=2}^{\infty} \oplus [T_{\Delta_N}(n, k) - T_{\Delta_{N-1}}(n, k)]. \tag{5.14.6.2}$$

We establish in Section 5.15 that, for $k \neq 0$,

$$T_{\Delta_\infty}(n, k) = F'_{\Delta_\infty}(n, k) = \mathscr{K}^n(a, b), \tag{5.14.7}$$

if $\| \Delta_N \| \to 0$ as $N \to \infty$.

5.15. Convergence in Norm

Theorem 5.15.1. *Let* $\{\Delta_N : a = x_0^N < \cdots < x_{n_N}^N = b\}$ *be a sequence of meshes with* $\Delta_N \subset \Delta_{N+1}$ $(N = 1, 2, \ldots)$, $\| \Delta_N \| \to 0$ *as* $N \to \infty$, *let*

* A spline is of type k if for some function $f(x)$ it is a spline of interpolation to $f(x)$ of type k.

$f(x)$ be in $\mathcal{K}^n(a, b)$, and let $\{S_{\Delta_N}(f; x)\}$ be a sequence of polynomial splines of degree $2n - 1$ and deficiency k $(k \leqslant n)$ with $S^{(\alpha)}_{\Delta_N}(f; x_i^N) = f^{(\alpha)}(x_i^N)$ $(i = 1, 2,..., m_N - 1; \alpha = 0, 1,..., k - 1)$ for each N. If, in addition, one of the conditions, (a) *$f(x) - S_{\Delta_N}(f; x)$ is of type I' $(N = 1, 2,...)$,* (b) *$S_{\Delta_N}(f; x)$ is of type II' $(N = 1, 2,...)$,* (c) *$S_{\Delta_N}(f; x)$ is of type k $(N = 1, 2,...)$,* (d) *$f(x)$ and $S_{\Delta_N}(f; x)$ are in $\mathcal{K}_P{}^n(a, b)$, $(N = 1, 2,...)$, is satisfied, then $\| f - S_{\Delta_{N,f}} \| \to 0$ as $N \to \infty$.*

Proof. Since the minimum norm property and the first integral relation are valid, the proof is a replica of the proof of Theorem 3.14.1. Here the nth derivative plays the role of the second derivative in the proof of Theorem 3.14.1 and the $(n - 1)$th derivative the role of the first derivative.

REMARK 5.15.1. The norm of functions in Theorem 5.15.1 is the Hilbert space norm; i.e.,

$$\| f \| = (f, f)^{1/2}. \tag{5.15.1}$$

In any Hilbert space, the concept of an infinite direct sum is meaningful. As indicated earlier, if V_i is orthogonal to V_j $(i \neq j)$ and

$$V = \sum_{N=1}^{\infty} \oplus V_N , \tag{5.15.2}$$

then V is the smallest closed subspace containing all the component spaces V_N. Moreover, we can choose a basis for V which is simultaneously the extension to V of a basis for each V_N. Consequently, Theorem 5.15.2 follows from Theorem 5.15.1, since a dense subspace that is closed must be the whole space.*

Theorem 5.15.2. *Let $\{\Delta_N\}$ be a sequence of meshes on $[a, b]$ with $\Delta_N \subset \Delta_{N+1}$ $(N = 1, 2,...)$ and $\| \Delta_N \| \to 0$ as $N \to \infty$. Then*

$$F_{\Delta_\infty}(n, k) = F'_{\Delta_\infty}(n, k) = T_{\Delta_\infty}(n, k) = \mathcal{K}^n(a, b), \tag{5.15.3.1}$$

$$P_{\Delta_\infty}(n, k) = \mathcal{K}^n(a, b). \tag{5.15.3.2}$$

In Section 3.14, we pursued essentially the same approach, and we established for the analogs of our direct sums $F_{\Delta_\infty}(n, k)$, $F'_{\Delta_\infty}(n, k)$, $T_{\Delta_\infty}(n, k)$, and $P_{\Delta_\infty}(n, k)$ that the component spaces are mutually orthogonal so that the indicated decompositions are decompositions in the Hilbert space sense. This is still true; we have, in fact, the following lemma, which is an extension of Lemma 3.14.1.

* A proof that $P_{\Delta_\infty}(n, k)$ is dense in $\mathcal{K}^n(a, b)$ is given in Section 6.14.

Lemma 5.15.1. *Let Δ_1 and Δ_2 be two meshes on $[a, b]$ with $\Delta_1 \subset \Delta_2$, and let $S_{\Delta_1}(x)$ and $S_{\Delta_2}(x)$ be two polynomial splines on Δ_1 and Δ_2, respectively, each of degree $2n - 1$ and deficiency k $(k \leqslant n)$. If $S_{\Delta_2}^{(\alpha)}(x)$ $(\alpha = 0, 1,..., k - 1)$ vanishes at the interior mesh points of Δ_1 and, in addition, one of the conditions,* (a) *$S_{\Delta_1}(x)$ is of type II′,* (b) *$S_{\Delta_2}(x)$ is of type I′,* (c) *$S_{\Delta_1}(x)$ and $S_{\Delta_2}(x)$ are of type k with $S_{\Delta_2}^{(\alpha)}(a) = S_{\Delta_2}^{(\alpha)}(b) = 0$ $(\alpha = 0, 1,..., k - 1)$,* (d) *$S_{\Delta_1}(x)$ and $S_{\Delta_2}(x)$ are in $\mathscr{K}_p{}^n(a, b)$ with $S_{\Delta_2}^{(\alpha)}(a) = 0$ $(\alpha = 0, 1,..., k - 1)$, is satisfied, then $(S_{\Delta_1}, S_{\Delta_2}) = 0$.*

Proof. Let Δ_1 be defined by $a = x_0 < x_1 < \cdots < x_N = b$. Then,

$$(S_{\Delta_1}, S_{\Delta_2}) = \int_a^b S_{\Delta_1}^{(n)}(x) \cdot S_{\Delta_2}^{(n)}(x)\, dx = \sum_{i=1}^{N} \int_{x_{i-1}}^{x_i} S_{\Delta_1}^{(n)}(x) \cdot S_{\Delta_2}^{(n)}(x)\, dx.$$

If we integrate by parts n times, we obtain

$$(S_{\Delta_1}, S_{\Delta_2}) = \sum_{i=1}^{N} \left\{ \sum_{\alpha=1}^{n} (-1)^{\alpha+1} S_{\Delta_2}^{(n-\alpha)}(x) \cdot S_{\Delta_1}^{(n+\alpha-1)}(x) \Big|_{x_{i-1}}^{x_i} \right\} = 0,$$

and the lemma follows.

Consider now any one of the infinite direct sums $F_{\Delta_\infty}(n, k)$, $F'_{\Delta_\infty}(n, k)$, $T_{\Delta_\infty}(n, k)$, or $P_{\Delta_\infty}(n, k)$; for instance,

$$F_{\Delta_\infty}(n, k) = F_{\Delta_1}(n, k) \oplus \sum_{N=2}^{\infty} \oplus [F_{\Delta_N}(n, k) - F_{\Delta_{N-1}}(n, k)]. \qquad (5.15.4)$$

If $S_{\Delta_N}(x)$ is in $[F_{\Delta_N}(n, k) - F_{\Delta_{N-1}}(n, k)]$, then $S_{\Delta_N}^{(\alpha)}(x)$ $(\alpha = 0, 1,..., k - 1)$ vanishes at the interior mesh points of Δ_{N-1} and is of type I′. Thus Lemma 5.15.1 applies, and we can conclude that (5.15.4) is an orthogonal decomposition.

Theorem 5.15.3. *Let $\{\Delta_N\}$ be a sequence of meshes on $[a, b]$ with $\Delta_N \subset \Delta_{N+1}$ $(N = 1, 2,...)$ and such that $\|\Delta_N\| \to 0$ as $N \to \infty$. Then the indicated infinite direct sums*

$$F_{\Delta_\infty}(n, k) = F_{\Delta_1}(n, k) \oplus \sum_{N=2}^{\infty} \oplus [F_{\Delta_N}(n, k) - F_{\Delta_{N-1}}(n, k)], \qquad (5.15.5.1)$$

$$F'_{\Delta_\infty}(n, k) = F'_{\Delta_1}(n, k) \oplus \sum_{N=2}^{\infty} \oplus [F'_{\Delta_N}(n, k) - F'_{\Delta_{N-1}}(n, k)], \qquad (5.15.5.2)$$

$$T_{\Delta_\infty}(n, k) = T_{\Delta_1}(n, k) \oplus \sum_{N=2}^{\infty} \oplus [T_{\Delta_N}(n, k) - T_{\Delta_{N-1}}(n, k)], \qquad (5.15.5.3)$$

$$P_{\Delta_\infty}(n, k) = P_{\Delta_1}(n, k) \oplus \sum_{N=2}^{\infty} \oplus [P_{\Delta_N}(n, k) - P_{\Delta_{N-1}}(n, k)] \qquad (5.15.5.4)$$

are orthogonal decompositions with respect to the inner product (5.14.1), and all are identical with $\mathscr{K}^n(a, b)$.

5.16. Canonical Mesh Bases and Their Properties

Canonical mesh bases were introduced in Section 3.15 for $\mathscr{K}^2(a, b)$ and $\mathscr{K}_P^2(a, b)$. Similar bases can be obtained for $\mathscr{K}^n(a, b)$ and $\mathscr{K}_P^n(a, b)$; in fact, we now obtain such bases for $F_{\Delta_\infty}(n, k)$, $F'_{\Delta_\infty}(n, k)$, $T_{\Delta_\infty}(n, k)$, and $P_{\Delta_\infty}(n, k)$. Consequently, in view of Theorem 5.15, we also obtain a variety of orthonormal bases for both $\mathscr{K}^n(a, b)$ and $\mathscr{K}_P^n(a, b)$. Since the constructions are essentially the same, we consider, explicitly, only the construction of a mesh basis for $F_{\Delta_\infty}(n, k)$. Even here, we simplify the procedure over that of Section 3.15 by limiting ourselves to a single straightforward enumeration of mesh points and thereby omit mesh bases that are not canonical.

Let $\{\Delta_N\}$ be a sequence of meshes on $[a, b]$ such that $\Delta_N \subset \Delta_{N+1}$ $(N = 1, 2,\ldots)$. Let M be the set of all distinct mesh points contained in the meshes Δ_N, excluding the mesh points of Δ_1. Give M the enumeration $\{M: P_1, P_2, \ldots\}$, where mesh points are enumerated starting with the mesh points of Δ_2 and counting from left to right, then proceeding to the mesh points of Δ_3, etc., in each case passing over mesh points previously enumerated. Now define a new sequence of meshes $\{\pi_m\}$ $(m = 0, 1,\ldots)$ where $\pi_0 = \Delta_1$, $\pi_1 = \Delta_1 \cup \{P_1\}$, and, in general, $\pi_m = \pi_{m-1} \cup \{P_m\}$. We assume that we are given an orthonormal basis for $F_{\Delta_1}(n, k)$, and we construct an orthonormal basis for $[F_{\Delta_\infty}(n, k) - F_{\Delta_1}(n, k)]$, thus extending the original basis to an orthonormal base for $F_{\Delta_\infty}(n, k)$.

For each m $(m = 1, 2,\ldots)$, we let $h_{mj}(x)$ $(j = 1, 2,\ldots, k)$ be type I′ polynomial splines on π_m of degree $2n - 1$ and deficiency k such that each $h_{mj}^{(\alpha)}(x)$ $(\alpha = 0, 1,\ldots, k - 1)$ vanishes on π_{m-1} and the $h_{mj}(x)$ are orthonormal. We can take $g_{mj}(x)$ $(j = 1, 2,\ldots, k)$ to be the type I′ splines on Δ_m such that $g_{mj}^{(\alpha)}(x)$ $(\alpha = 0, 1,\ldots, k - 1)$ vanishes on Δ_{m-1} and $g_{mj}^{(\alpha)}(P_m) = \delta_j^{\alpha+1}$; the Gram-Schmidt process now yields the desired $h_{mj}(x)$. If for $i = k(m - 1) + j$, where $k(m - 1) < i \leqslant km$, we set

$$S_i(n, k; x) = h_{mj}(x) \qquad (m = 1, 2,\ldots;\ j = 1, 2,\ldots, k), \tag{5.16.1}$$

we obtain the desired orthonormal basis for $[F_{\Delta_\infty}(n, k) - F_{\Delta_1}(n, k)]$. Indeed, the subset $\{S_i(n, k; x) \mid i = 1, 2,\ldots, km\}$ is an orthonormal basis for $[F_{\pi_m}(n, k) - F_{\pi_0}(n, k)]$ $(m = 1, 2,\ldots)$, and for each N $(N = 1, 2,\ldots)$ the $S_i(n, k; x)$ which, together with their first $k - 1$ derivatives, do not vanish at every mesh point of Δ_N, constitute an orthonormal basis for

$[F_{\Delta_N}(n, k) - F_{\Delta_1}(n, k)]$. When there is no ambiguity, we denote $S_i(n, k; x)$ by $S_i(x)$ and $F_\Delta(n, k)$ by F_Δ.

We call the set of $S_i(x)$ $(i = 1, 2,...)$, together with the preassigned orthonormal basis for F_{Δ_1}, *a canonical mesh basis* for F_{Δ_∞}; their analogs for F'_{Δ_∞}, T_{Δ_∞}, and P_{Δ_∞} are called *canonical mesh bases* for these spaces. We have the following theorem, which is now immediate from Theorem 5.15.

Theorem 5.16.1. *Let $\{\Delta_N\}$ be a sequence of meshes on $[a, b]$ with $\Delta_N \subset \Delta_{N+1}$ $(N = 1, 2,...)$ and $\| \Delta_N \| \to 0$ as $N \to \infty$. Then $F_{\Delta_\infty}(n, k)$, $F'_{\Delta_\infty}(n, k)$, and $T_{\Delta_\infty}(n, k)$ have canonical mesh bases that are orthonormal bases for $\mathscr{K}^n(a, b)$; $P_{\Delta_\infty}(n, k)$ has a canonical mesh basis that is an orthonormal basis for $\mathscr{K}_P{}^n(a, b)$ and $\mathscr{K}^n(a, b)$.*

REMARK 5.16.1. In the preceding theorem, both $\mathscr{K}^n(a, b)$ and $\mathscr{K}_P{}^n(a, b)$ are meant to be interpreted as Hilbert spaces under the inner product (f, g) defined by (5.14.1). However, to be precise, $\mathscr{K}_P{}^n(a, b)$ is a pre-Hilbert space.

We formulate next the analog of Lemma 3.15.1 which furnishes extremely useful information regarding the magnitude of $S_i^{(\alpha)}(x)$ $(\alpha = 0, 1,..., n - 1)$.

Lemma 5.16.1. *Let $\{S_i(n, k; x)\}$ be a canonical mesh basis for $[F_{\Delta_\infty}(n, k) - F_{\Delta_1}(n, k)]$, $[F'_{\Delta_\infty}(n, k) - F'_{\Delta_1}(n, k)]$, $[T_{\Delta_\infty}(n, k) - T_{\Delta_1}(n, k)]$, or $[P_{\Delta_\infty}(n, k) - P_{\Delta_1}(n, k)]$ determined by a sequence of meshes $\{\Delta_N\}$ with $\Delta_N \subset \Delta_{N+1}$ $(N = 1, 2,...)$. Let $\{\pi_m\}$ $(m = 0, 1,...)$ be the related sequence of meshes used in the construction of $\{S_i(n, k; x)\}$. Then, for $i = k(m-1) + j$, $0 < j \leqslant k$, we have*

$$| S_i^{(\alpha)}(n, k; x) | \leqslant K_\alpha \cdot \| \pi_{m-1} \|^{(2n-2\alpha-1)/2} \qquad (\alpha = 0, 1,..., n - 1), \quad (5.16.2.1)$$

where

$$K_\alpha = \frac{(n - 2k + 2)^{1/2}(n - 2k + 1)!}{(\alpha - 2k + 2)!} \cdot 2^{-(2n-2\alpha-1)/2} \qquad (\alpha = 0, 1,..., n - 1). \quad (5.16.2.2)$$

The factor $2^{-(2n-2\alpha-1)/2}$ is omitted at $x = a$ and $x = b$ for

$$[F'_{\Delta_\infty}(n, k) - F'_{\Delta_1}(n, k)] \quad \text{and} \quad [T_{\Delta_\infty}(n, k) - T_{\Delta_1}(n, k)].$$

If $n - 2k + 2 < 1$ in (5.16.2.2), it is replaced by 1.

Proof. Except possibly at $x = a$ and $x = b$, we can find points $\bar{x}_i$ such that $S_i^{(n-1)}(\bar{x}_i) = 0$ and $| x - \bar{x}_i | \leqslant \frac{1}{2}(n - 2k + 2)^{1/2} \cdot \| \pi_{m-1} \|$

by repeated application of Rolle's theorem and the fact that $S_i^{(k-1)}(x)$ vanishes at every mesh point of π_{m-1}. In view of this, it follows that

$$| S_i^{(n-1)}(x) | \leqslant \int_{\bar{x}_i}^{x} | S_i^{(n)}(x) | \, | dx | \leqslant [\tfrac{1}{2}(n - 2k + 2) \cdot \| \pi_{m-1} \|]^{1/2} \quad (5.16.3)$$

by Schwarz's inequality. By applying the same argument to $S_i^{(n-2)}(x)$ and using inequality (5.16.3) rather than Schwarz's inequality, we obtain

$$| S_i^{(n-2)}(x) | \leqslant (n - 2k + 2)^{1/2} \cdot (n - 2k + 1) \cdot (\tfrac{1}{2})^{3/2} \cdot \| \pi_{m-1} \|^{3/2},$$

which may be written as

$$| S_i^{(n-2)}(x) | \leqslant \frac{(n - 2k + 2)^{1/2}(n - 2k + 1)!}{(n - 2k)!} \cdot (\tfrac{1}{2})^{3/2} \cdot \| \pi_{m-1} \|^{3/2}. \quad (5.16.4)$$

We obtain (5.16.2) by further repetition of this argument. Since the modifications required at $x = a$ and $x = b$ for $[F'_{\Delta_\infty} - F'_{\Delta_1}]$ and $[T_{\Delta_\infty} - T_{\Delta_1}]$ are trivial, the lemma is established.

We conclude Section 5.16 with Theorem 5.16.2, which is fundamental to Sections 5.17 and 5.18.

Theorem 5.16.2. *Let $\{S_i(x)\}$ be a canonical mesh basis such that $\| \pi_m \| = O(1/m)$. Then there exist real numbers $\beta_\alpha > 0$ such that*

$$S^{(\alpha)}(x) \equiv \sum_{i=1}^{\infty} \{S_i^{(\alpha)}(x)\}^2 < \beta_\alpha \qquad (\alpha = 0, 1,..., n - 2). \quad (5.16.5)$$

Proof. We have

$$S^{(\alpha)}(x) \leqslant K \sum_{m=1}^{\infty} K_\alpha^2 \left(\frac{1}{m - 1}\right)^{2n-2\alpha-1} < \beta_\alpha < \infty \qquad (\alpha = 0, 1,..., n - 2) \quad (5.16.6)$$

for some positive constants K and β_α. The theorem follows.

REMARK 5.16.2. It would be desirable to have (5.16.5) hold for $\alpha = n - 1$, but inequalities (5.16.2) are not sharp enough. This is reflected later, when we obtain exact replicas of (5.16.2) for generalized splines, indicating that the generality of our methods limits, to a small degree, their sharpness.

REMARK 5.16.3. In this discussion, it has been tacitly assumed that $\Delta_1 = \pi_0$ is sufficiently large so that the splines $S_i(n, k; x) = S_i(x)$

exist. We also have employed the relation $i = k(m-1)+j$, where $k(m-1) < i \leqslant km$, which was introduced earlier. We henceforth assume that the statement "$\lim_{N\to\infty} \| \Delta_N \| = 0$" or the assertion that a basis is a canonical mesh basis for $\mathscr{K}^n(a, b)$ or $\mathscr{K}_P{}^n(a, b)$ includes $\| \pi_i \| = O(1/i)$.

5.17. Kernels and Integral Representations

In Section 3.16, we determined kernels giving integral representations for the remainders

$$R(x) = f(x) - S_\Delta(f; x); \tag{5.17.1}$$

now, we determine kernels $H_\alpha(n, k; x, t)$ such that

$$f^{(\alpha)}(x) = \int_a^b H_\alpha(n, k; x, t) f^{(n)}(t)\, dt + P_{n-1}^{(\alpha)}(x) \tag{5.17.2}$$

for functions $f(x)$ in $\mathscr{K}^n(a, b)$. If $f(x)$ is in $\mathscr{K}^n(a, b)$, it follows that $f(x) - S_\Delta(f; x)$ is in $\mathscr{K}^n(a, b)$; consequently, (5.17.2) applies to (5.17.1). The remainder $P_{n-1}(x)$ is a polynomial of degree $n-1$ to be discussed further at the end of this section.

Theorem 5.17.1. *Let $f(x)$ be in $\mathscr{K}^n(a, b)$ or $\mathscr{K}_P{}^n(a, b)$, and $\{S_i(n, k; x)\}$ $(i = 1, 2, \ldots)$, together with a basis $u_i(n, k; x)$ $(i = 1, 2, \ldots, m)$ for $F_\Delta(n, k)$ be a canonical mesh basis that is an orthonormal basis for $\mathscr{K}^n(a, b)$ or $\mathscr{K}_P{}^n(a, b)$. Then for every x in $[a, b]$*

$$f^{(\alpha)}(x) = \lim_{N\to\infty} \int_a^b H_{\alpha,N}(n, k; x, t) \cdot f^{(n)}(t)\, dt + P_{n-1}^{(\alpha)}(x) \qquad (\alpha = 0, 1, \ldots, n-1), \tag{5.17.3.1}$$

where $P_{n-1}(x)$ is a polynomial of degree $n-1$,

$$H_{\alpha,N}(n, k; x, t) \equiv \sum_{i=1}^{m} u_i^{(\alpha)}(x) \cdot u_i^{(n)}(t) + \sum_{i=1}^{N} S_i^{(\alpha)}(x) \cdot S_i^{(n)}(t), \tag{5.17.3.2}$$

and the limit exists uniformly with respect to x in $[a, b]$.

Proof. Let $\{\pi_i\}$ $(i = 0, 1, \ldots)$ be the mesh sequence occurring in the construction of $\{S_i(x)\}$. By assumption, $\| \pi_i \| \to 0$ as $i \to \infty$; consequently,

$$\begin{aligned} f^{(\alpha)}(x) &= \lim_{N\to\infty} S_{\pi_N}^{(\alpha)}(f; x) \\ &= \lim_{N\to\infty} \left\{ \sum_{i=1}^{m} (u_i, f)\, u_i^{(\alpha)}(x) + \sum_{i=1}^{N} (S_i, f)\, S_i^{(\alpha)}(x) \right\} + P_{n-1}^{(\alpha)}(x), \end{aligned} \tag{5.17.4}$$

which implies

$$f^{(\alpha)}(x) = \lim_{N\to\infty} \int_a^b \Big\{ \sum_{i=1}^{m} u_i^{(\alpha)}(x) \cdot u_i^{(n)}(t)$$

$$+ \sum_{i=1}^{N} S_i^{(\alpha)}(x) \cdot S_i^{(n)}(x) \Big\} f^{(n)}(t)\, dt + P_{n-1}^{(\alpha)}(x), \qquad (5.17.5)$$

where the limits exist uniformly with respect to x by Theorem 5.9.2. The theorem is now immediate, since (5.17.5) holds for $\alpha = 0, 1,..., n - 1$.

The method of proof for Theorem 5.17.1 depends on the pointwise convergence of $S_\Delta^{(\alpha)}(f; x)$ to $f^{(\alpha)}(x)$. As a consequence, if we restrict ourselves to suitable canonical mesh bases for F_{Δ_∞} or P_{Δ_∞}, we have the following corollary.*

Corollary 5.17.1. *Let $f(x)$ be in $\mathscr{K}^{2n}(a, b)$ or $\mathscr{K}_P^{2n}(a, b)$, and let $\{S_i(n, k; x)\}$ $(i = 1, 2,...)$, together with $u_i(n, k; x)$ $(i = 1, 2,..., m)$, be a canonical mesh basis for $F_{\Delta_\infty}(n, k)$ or $P_{\Delta_\infty}(n, k)$, which is an orthonormal basis for $\mathscr{K}^{2n}(a, b)$ or $\mathscr{K}_P^{2n}(a, b)$, respectively. Then for every x in $[a, b]$ and $\alpha = 0, 1,..., 2n - k - 1$, (5.17.3) is valid.*

REMARK 5.17.1. Observe that $H_{\alpha,N}(n, k; x, t)$ is obtained from $H_{\alpha-1,N}(n, k; x, t)$ by formal term-by-term differentiation with respect to x.

In itself, Theorem 5.17.1 does not establish the existence in $L(a, b)$ of the desired kernels $H_\alpha(n, k; x, t)$ for each x. We show, however, that, for $\alpha = 0, 1,..., n - 2$, the kernel $H_\alpha(n, k; x, t)$ exists and is in $L^2(a, b)$; it is the limit, in the mean square sense, of the partial sums $H_{\alpha,N}(n, k; x, t)$.

Theorem 5.17.2. *Let $\{\pi_i\}$ $(i = 0, 1,...)$ be a sequence of meshes on $[a, b]$ determining a canonical mesh basis that is an orthonormal basis for $\mathscr{K}^n(a, b)$ or $\mathscr{K}_P^n(a, b)$. If $H_{\alpha,N}(n, k; x, t)$ is defined by (5.17.3.2), then, as a function of t, $\{H_{\alpha,N}\}$ $(\alpha = 0, 1,..., n - 2;\ N = 1, 2,...)$ is a Cauchy sequence in $L^2(a, b)$ and, consequently, a Cauchy sequence in $L(a, b)$. If $H_\alpha(n, k; x, t)$ $(\alpha = 0, 1,..., n - 2)$ denotes the common limit, then*

$$f^{(\alpha)}(x) = \int_a^b H_\alpha(n, k; x, t) f^{(n)}(t)\, dt + P_{n-1}^{(\alpha)}(x) \quad (\alpha = 0, 1,..., n - 2), \quad (5.17.6)$$

where $P_{n-1}(x)$ is a polynomial of degree $n - 1$. The convergence is uniform with respect to x in $[a, b]$, and $H_\alpha(n, k; x, t)$ is obtained from $H_{\alpha-1}(n, k; x, t)$ by formal term-by-term differentiation with respect to x.

* For the auxiliary mesh sequence $\{\pi_i\}$ $(i = 0, 1,...)$, we assume R_{π_i} to be bounded as a function of i.

Proof. Because of the orthonormality of the mesh basis and Lemma 5.10.1, we have

$$\int_a^b | H_{\alpha,N+P} - H_{\alpha,N} |^2 \, dt = \int_a^b \left| \sum_{i=N+1}^{N+P} S_i^{(\alpha)}(x) \cdot S_i^{(n)}(t) \right|^2 dt$$

$$= \sum_{i=N+1}^{N+P} | S_i^{(\alpha)}(x) |^2$$

$$= O\left(\sum_{i=N+1}^{N+P} \left(\frac{1}{m}\right)^{2n-2\alpha-1} \right)$$

$$[i = k(m-1) + j, \quad 0 < j \leqslant k]. \tag{5.17.7}$$

Consequently, for $\alpha \leqslant n-2$, we have a Cauchy sequence, and (5.17.6) follows from (5.17.3); this completes the proof, since the limits exist uniformly with respect to x in $[a, b]$.

We conclude this section with some further comments on mesh bases. In choosing bases for F_{Δ_1}, F'_{Δ_1}, T_{Δ_1}, and P_{Δ_1}, we can consider them as linear spaces (without identifications) rather than Hilbert spaces. For instance, we can select a basis for F_{Δ_1} including n independent polynomials of degree less than n. These basis elements are identified with the null spline when F_{Δ_1} is interpreted as a Hilbert space. This is consistent, since these polynomials are orthogonal to every element in F_{Δ_1}, including themselves. Their inclusion in the basis allows us to express $S_{\Delta_N}^{(\alpha)}(f; x)$ as

$$S_{\pi_N}^{(\alpha)}(f; x) = \sum_{i=1}^{m} (u_i, f)\, u_i^{(\alpha)}(x) + \sum_{i=1}^{N} (S_i, f)\, S_i^{(\alpha)}(x) + P_{n-1}^{(\alpha)}(x) \tag{5.17.8}$$

and, consequently, to obtain Theorem 5.17.1 and Corollary 5.17.1. Here the polynomials of degree less than n in the basis contribute the term $P_{n-1}^{(\alpha)}(x)$, and the remainder of the basis

$$[u_1(n, k; x), u_2(n, k; x), \ldots, u_m(n, k; x)]$$

contributes the summation

$$\sum_{i=1}^{m} (f, u_i)\, u_i^{(\alpha)}(x).$$

Alternatively, we can consider F_{Δ_1} as a Hilbert space with an orthonormal basis $u_1(n, k; x)$, $u_2(n, k; x), \ldots, u_m(n, k; x)$. We then define $P_{n-1}(x)$ as

$$P_{n-1}(x) = S_{\Delta_1}(f; x) - \sum_{i=1}^{m} (f, u_i) \cdot u_i(x), \tag{5.17.9}$$

and (5.17.8) will still be valid.* Both alternatives are in agreement with the formulation of our theorems.

5.18. Representation and Approximation of Linear Functionals

In this section, we examine the representation of linear functionals by means of integrals involving kernels. We consider also the approximation of functionals by other functionals and obtain integral representations for the remainders incurred. We do not limit ourselves, as in Section 3.17, to the point functionals $\mathscr{L}_x : f \to f(x)$. The representation theorems we establish are of the type established by Peano [1913] and Sard [1963]; their close connection with spline theory was first realized by Schoenberg [1964b]. The approach we take is novel but has considerable generality and utilizes heavily the material we have developed here and in Chapter III. As a consequence of our approach, the theorems we obtain are, in some senses, stronger, and, in other senses, weaker than those obtained by Peano, Sard, and Schoenberg.

Let $f(x)$ be in $\mathscr{K}^n(a, b)$ or $\mathscr{K}_p{}^n(a, b)$, and let $\mathscr{L}$ be a linear functional on $\mathscr{K}^n(a, b)$ or $\mathscr{K}_p{}^n(a, b)$ of the form

$$\mathscr{L} o f = \sum_{j=0}^{\eta} \int_a^b f^{(j)}(t)\, d\mu_j(t) \qquad (\eta \leqslant n-1), \tag{5.18.1}$$

where each $\mu_j(t)$ is a function of bounded variation on $[a, b]$. A detailed treatment of functionals of this type can be found in Sard [1963, Chapter I]. Let us consider the possibility of representing $\mathscr{L} o f$ in the form

$$\mathscr{L} o f = \int_a^b H(t) f^{(n)}(t)\, dt + \mathscr{L} o\, P_{n-1}\,, \tag{5.18.2}$$

where $H(t)$ is a function in $L^2(a, b)$ which is independent of $f(x)$ and $P_{n-1}(x)$ is a polynomial of degree $n - 1$. As in the preceding section, we establish first the more general result that there exist sequences $\{H_N(n, k; t)\}$ $(N = 1, 2, \ldots)$ of functions in $\mathscr{K}^{n-k}(a, b)$ such that

$$\mathscr{L} o f = \lim_{N\to\infty} \int_a^b H_N(n, k; t) f^{(n)}(t)\, dt + \mathscr{L} o\, P_{n-1}\,. \tag{5.18.3}$$

More precisely, we prove the following theorem.

* In (5.17.9), we are thinking of each $u_i(x)$ as a particular member of an equivalence class rather than as an equivalence class.

Theorem 5.18.1. *Let $f(x)$ be in $\mathcal{K}^n(a, b)$ or $\mathcal{K}_P{}^n(a, b)$, and let $\{S_i(n, k; x)\}$ $(i = 1, 2,\ldots)$, together with $\{u_i(n, k; x)\}$ $(i = 1, 2,\ldots, m)$, be a canonical mesh basis that is an orthonormal basis for $\mathcal{K}^n(a, b)$ or $\mathcal{K}_P{}^n(a, b)$. If $\mathcal{L}$ is a linear functional of the form (5.18.1), then*

$$\mathcal{L}o\, f = \lim_{N\to\infty} \int_a^b H_N(n, k; t) \cdot f^{(n)}(t)\, dt + \mathcal{L}o\, P_{n-1}, \qquad (5.18.4.1)$$

where

$$H_N(n, k; x) = \sum_{i=1}^{m} \alpha_i \cdot u_i^{(n)}(x) + \sum_{i=1}^{N} \beta_i \cdot S_i^{(n)}(x), \qquad (5.18.4.2)$$

$$\alpha_i = \sum_{j=0}^{\eta} \int_a^b u_i^{(j)}(s)\, d\mu_j(s) \qquad (i = 1, 2,\ldots, m), \qquad (5.18.4.3)$$

$$\beta_i = \sum_{j=0}^{\eta} \int_a^b S_i^{(j)}(s)\, d\mu_j(s) \qquad (i = 1, 2,\ldots, N), \qquad (5.18.4.4)$$

and $P_{n-1}(x)$ is a polynomial of degree $n - 1$.

Proof. We can represent $f^{(\alpha)}(x)$ $(\alpha = 0, 1,\ldots, n - 1)$ as

$$f^{(\alpha)}(x) = \lim_{N\to\infty} \left\{ \sum_{i=1}^{m} (f, u_i)\, u_i^{(\alpha)}(x) + \sum_{i=1}^{N} (f, S_i)\, S_i^{(\alpha)}(x) \right\} + P_{n-1}^{(\alpha)}(x),$$

where the limit exists uniformly with respect to x; hence,

$$\mathcal{L}o\, f = \sum_{j=0}^{\eta} \int_a^b \lim_{N\to\infty} \left\{ \sum_{i=1}^{m} (f, u_i)\, u_i^{(j)}(s) + \sum_{i=1}^{N} (f, S_i)\, S_i^{(j)}(s) \right\} d\mu_j(s) + \mathcal{L}o\, P_{n-1}.$$

Since the convergence is uniform with respect to x,

$$\mathcal{L}o\, f = \lim_{N\to\infty} \sum_{j=0}^{\eta} \int_a^b \left\{ \sum_{i=1}^{m} (f, u_i)\, u_i^{(j)}(s) + \sum_{i=1}^{N} (f, S_i)\, S_i^{(j)}(s) \right\} d\mu_j(s) + \mathcal{L}o\, P_{n-1}.$$

However, by definition we have

$$(f, g) = \int_a^b f^{(n)}(t)\, g^{(n)}(t)\, dt; \qquad (5.18.5)$$

consequently, after substituting for (f, u_i) and (f, S_i) and changing the order of summation, we obtain

$$\mathcal{L}o\, f = \lim_{N\to\infty} \int_a^b \left\{ \sum_{i=1}^{m} \left\{ \sum_{j=0}^{\eta} \int_a^b u_i^{(j)}(s)\, d\mu_j(s) \right\} u_i^{(n)}(t) \right.$$

$$\left. + \sum_{i=1}^{N} \left\{ \sum_{j=0}^{\eta} \int_a^b S_i^{(j)}(s)\, d\mu_j(s) \right\} S_i^{(n)}(t) \right\} f^{(n)}(t)\, dt + \mathcal{L}o\, P_{n-1},$$

from which the theorem follows.

Corollary 5.18.1. *Let $f(x)$ be in $\mathscr{K}^{2n}(a, b)$ or $\mathscr{K}_P^{2n}(a, b)$, and let $\{S_i(n, k; x)\}$ $(i = 1, 2, \ldots)$, together with $\{u_i(n, k; x)\}$ $(i = 1, 2, \ldots, m)$, be a canonical mesh basis that is an orthornomal basis for $\mathscr{K}^n(a, b)$ or $\mathscr{K}_P{}^n(a, b)$. If $\mathscr{L}$ is a linear functional of the form*

$$\mathscr{L} o f = \sum_{j=0}^{\eta} \int_a^b f^{(j)}(t)\, d\mu_j(t) \qquad (\eta \leqslant 2n - 2), \tag{5.18.6}$$

where each $\mu_j(t)$ is a function of bounded variation on $[a, b]$, then (5.18.4) holds except that $\eta \leqslant 2n - 2$.

For functionals of the form

$$\mathscr{L} o f = \sum_{j=0}^{\eta} \int_a^b f^{(j)}(t)\, d\mu_j(t) \qquad (\eta \leqslant n - 2), \tag{5.18.7}$$

where each $\mu_j(t)$ is a function of bounded variation on $[a, b]$, we obtain representations of the special form (5.18.2).

Theorem 5.18.2. *Let $\{\pi_i\}$ $(i = 0, 1, \ldots)$ be a sequence of meshes on $[a, b]$ determining a canonical mesh basis that is an orthonormal basis for $\mathscr{K}^n(a, b)$ or $\mathscr{K}_P{}^n(a, b)$. If $H_N(n, k; x)$ is defined by (5.18.4) except that $\eta \leqslant n - 2$, then $\{H_N(n, k; x)\}$ $(N = 1, 2, \ldots)$ is a Cauchy sequence in $L^2(a, b)$ and, consequently, a Cauchy sequence in $L(a, b)$. If $H(n, k; x)$ denotes the common limit, then*

$$\mathscr{L} o f = \int_a^b H(n, k; t) f^{(n)}(t)\, dt + \mathscr{L} o P_{n-1}, \tag{5.18.8}$$

where $P_{n-1}(x)$ is a polynomial of degree $n - 1$

Proof. The proof of Theorem 5.17.2 applies, essentially unchanged.

We are now in position to consider the approximation of a linear functional $\mathscr{L} o f$ the form (5.18.1) by linear functionals of the special form

$$B o f = \sum_{i=0}^{r} \sum_{j=0}^{k-1} a_{ij} f^{(j)}(x_i) \qquad (k < n), \tag{5.18.9}$$

determined by a set of constants a_{ij} $(i = 0, 1, \ldots, r;\ j = 0, 1, \ldots, k - 1)$ and a mesh Δ: $a = x_0 < \cdots < x_r = b$. If we let $\mu_j(t)$ be a step function with jumps a_{ij} at x_i $(i = 0, 1, \ldots, r)$, then (5.18.9) takes the form

$$B o f = \sum_{j=0}^{k-1} \int_a^b f^{(j)}(t)\, d\mu_j(t), \tag{5.18.10}$$

where each $\mu_j(t)$ is a function of bounded variation on $[a, b]$; thus, our representation theorems apply. Let $\mu_1(n, k; x)$, $u_2(n, k; x), \ldots, u_m(n, k; x)$ be an orthonormal basis for $F_\Delta(n, k)$, and let $\{S_i(n, k; x)\}$ $(i = 1, 2, \ldots)$ extend this basis to an orthonormal basis for $\mathscr{K}^n(a, b)$. We could equally well consider $T_\Delta(n, k)$ or, in the case of $\mathscr{K}_p{}^n(a, b)$, $P_\Delta(n, k)$; but $F'_\Delta(n, k)$ encounters difficulties at $x = a$ and $x = b$.

We now make two important observations. The first observation is that, since $S_i^{(\alpha)}(x_j) = 0$ $(\alpha = 0, 1, \ldots, k-1; j = 0, 1, \ldots, r; i = 1, 2, \ldots)$, the coefficients $\beta_i (i = 1, 2, \ldots, N)$, defined by (5.18.4.4), all vanish for B. This occurs since all the mass of the measures $\mu_j(t)$ is concentrated at the mesh points of Δ; moreover, this is true for every N. Consequently, if we apply either Theorem 5.18.1 or Theorem 5.18.2 to $\mathscr{L} - B$, the coefficients β_i for $\mathscr{L} - B$ are determined by $\mathscr{L}$ alone and are unaffected by B.Our second observation is that

$$\mathscr{L} o\, S_{\Delta,f} = \int_a^b \left\{ \sum_{i=1}^{m} \alpha_i u_i^{(n)}(n, k; t) \cdot f^{(n)}(t)\, dt \right\} + \mathscr{L} o\, P_{n-1} \qquad (5.18.11)$$

so that

$$\mathscr{L} o f = \mathscr{L} o\, S_{\Delta,f} + \lim_{N\to\infty} \int_a^b \left\{ \sum_{i=1}^{N} \beta_i \cdot S_i^{(n)}(t) \cdot f^{(n)}(t)\, dt \right\}, \qquad (5.18.12)$$

as a re-examination of the proof of Theorem 5.18.1 reveals. Since we can determine the coefficients a_{ij} in (5.18.9) such that

$$B\, o f = \mathscr{L} o\, S_{\Delta,f}\,, \qquad (5.18.13)$$

we have the following two theorems.

Theorem 5.18.3. *If $\mathscr{L}$ is a linear functional defined by (5.18.1) and if B is the linear functional defined by (5.18.13), then*

$$\mathscr{L} o f - B\, o f = \lim_{N\to\infty} \int_a^b \left\{ \sum_{i=1}^{N} \beta_i \cdot S_i^{(n)}(n, k; t) \cdot f^{(n)}(t)\, dt \right\}, \qquad (5.18.14.1)$$

where

$$\beta_i = \sum_{j=0}^{\eta} \int_a^b S_i^{(j)}(n, k; s)\, d\mu_j(s) \qquad (\eta < n) \qquad (5.18.14.2)$$

and the $\mu_j(s)$ $(j = 0, 1, \ldots, \eta)$ are functions of bounded variation on $[a, b]$ determined by $\mathscr{L}$ alone.

Theorem 5.18.4. *If $\mathscr{L}$ is a linear functional of the form (5.18.7) and B is a linear functional of the form (5.18.13), then*

$$\mathscr{L} o f - B o f = \int_a^b H(n, k; t) f^{(n)}(t)\, dt, \tag{5.18.15.1}$$

where $H(n, k; t)$ is in $L^2(a, b)$ and is the limit, in the mean square sense, of

$$H_N(n, k; t) = \sum_{i=1}^{m} \alpha_i u_i^{(n)}(n, k; t) + \sum_{i=1}^{N} \beta_i S_i^{(n)}(n, k; t), \tag{5.18.15.2}$$

$$\alpha_i = \sum_{j=k}^{\eta} \int_a^b u_i^{(j)}(n, k; s)\, d\mu_j(s), \tag{5.18.15.3}$$

$$\beta_i = \sum_{j=0}^{\eta} \int_a^b S_i^{(j)}(n, k; s)\, d\mu_j(s). \tag{5.18.15.4}$$

The $\mu_j(s)$ are functions of bounded variation on $[a, b]$ and depend on $\mathscr{L}$ alone, being given by the representation (5.18.7) for $\mathscr{L}$. If B is any linear functional of the form (5.18.9) and $\mathscr{L} - B$ annihilates polynomials of degree less than n, then

$$\mathscr{L} o f - B o f = \int_a^b H(n, k; t) f^{(n)}(t)\, dt, \tag{5.18.16}$$

where $H(n, k; t)$ is in $L^2(a, b)$ and is defined as in Theorem 5.18.2. Moreover,

$$\int_a^b \{H(n, k; t)\}^2\, dt \tag{5.18.17}$$

is minimized when B is of the form (5.18.13).

The application of the methods of this section to the point functionals $\mathscr{L}_x : f \to f(x)$ is illuminating, but we defer further discussion of these functionals until Chapter VI. There we also examine other functionals of considerable interest. For instance, if we do not wish the approximating functional B to involve the value of $f(x)$ at x_i, we cannot merely set $a_{i0} = 0$ in (5.18.9) and, in general, satisfy (5.18.13). Approximating functionals exist, however, which meet these requirements. This is a desirable property in obtaining predictor or corrector formulas for numerical integration, since stability requirements often require the suppression of certain values of the function and its derivatives in these formulas.

This page intentionally left blank

Chapter VI

Generalized Splines

6.1. Introduction

The theory of polynomial splines of odd degree can be approached from two points of view: (1) the algebraic, which depends primarily on the examination in detail of the linear system of equations defining the spline; or (2) the intrinsic, which exploits the consequences of basic integral relations existing between functions in $\mathscr{K}^n(a, b)$, or $\mathscr{K}^{2n}(a, b)$, and approximating spline functions. The first approach reaches its high point for the cubic and doubly cubic spline but ebbs noticeably even for polynomial splines of higher odd degree. For generalized splines, there is at present no algebraic theory, although special theories for particular generalized splines could well evolve. The intrinsic approach, however, carries over undiminished and reaches its fullest maturity in the generalized setting. In Chapter VI, we develop this theory as a continuation of the intrinsic theory of polynomial splines.

In general, we assume that we have a linear differential operator L defined by

$$L \equiv a_n(x) \cdot D^n + a_{n-1}(x) \cdot D^{n-1} + \cdots + a_0(x), \tag{6.1.1}$$

where each $a_j(x)$ $(j = 0, 1,..., n)$ is in $C^n[a, b]$, and $a_n(x)$ does not vanish on $[a, b]$. Let L^* be the formal adjoint of L; thus,

$$L^* = (-1)^n \cdot D^n\{a_n(x) \cdot\} + (-1)^{n-1} \cdot D^{n-1}\{a_{n-1}(x) \cdot\} + \cdots - D\{a_1(x) \cdot\} + a_0(x). \tag{6.1.2}$$

If $\Delta: a = x_0 < x_1 < \cdots < x_N = b$ is a mesh on $[a, b]$, then a generalized spline of deficiency k $(0 \leqslant k \leqslant n)$ with respect to Δ is a function $S_\Delta(x)$ which is in $\mathscr{K}^{2n-k}(a, b)$ and satisfies the differential equation

$$L^*LS_\Delta = 0 \tag{6.1.3}$$

on each open mesh interval of Δ. We also say that $S_\Delta(x)$ has order $2n$ when we want to indicate the order of the operator L^*L defining $S_\Delta(x)$.

If $k = 0$ and L has analytic coefficients, then $S_\Delta(x)$ has continuous derivatives of all orders and satisfies (6.1.3) throughout $[a, b]$; in this case, continuity of the $(2n - 1)$th derivative implies continuity of the $2n$th and all higher derivatives. Thus, for this important class of differential operators, $k = 0$ is equivalent to continuity of all derivatives. The ordinary spline (deficiency one) allows discontinuities in the $(2n - 1)$th derivative, but only at mesh points. In general, the deficiency of a spline is a measure of the failure of the spline to satisfy (6.1.3) on $[a, b]$.

6.2. The Fundamental Identity

If L is a differential operator of order n and L^* is its formal adjoint, then we have the identity

$$Lu(x) \cdot v(x) = (d/dx)\, P[u(x), v(x)] + u(x) \cdot L^*v(x); \tag{6.2.1.1}$$

here $P[u(x), v(x)]$ is the bilinear concomitant and is defined by

$$P[u(x), v(x)] = \sum_{j=0}^{n-1} \sum_{k=0}^{n-j-1} (-1)^k \cdot u^{(n-j-k-1)}(x) \cdot \{a_{n-j}(x) \cdot v(x)\}^{(k)}. \tag{6.2.1.2}$$

The right-hand side of (6.2.1.2) can be regrouped so that

$$P[u(x), v(x)] = \sum_{j=0}^{n-1} u^{(n-j-1)}(x) \cdot \sum_{k=0}^{j} (-1)^k \cdot \{a_{n-j-k}(x) \cdot v(x)\}^{(k)}. \tag{6.2.2}$$

Now let Δ: $a = x_0 < x_1 < \cdots < x_N = b$ be given, and let $S_\Delta(x)$ be a generalized spline on Δ of order $2n$. If in Eqs. (6.2.1) we set $u(x) = f(x) - S_\Delta(x)$ and $v(x) = LS_\Delta(x)$, then we obtain, after integration over the interval $[x_{i-1}, x_i]$, the relation

$$\int_{x_{i-1}}^{x_i} L\{f(x) - S_\Delta(x)\} \cdot LS_\Delta(x)\, dx$$
$$= \left\{ \sum_{j=0}^{n-1} \{f(x) - S_\Delta(x)\}^{(n-j-1)} \cdot \sum_{k=0}^{j} (-1)^k \cdot \{a_{n-j-k}(x) \cdot LS_\Delta(x)\}^{(k)} \right\} \Bigg|_{x_{i-1}}^{x_i}$$
$$(i = 1, 2, \ldots, N), \tag{6.2.3}$$

since $L^*LS_\Delta(x) = 0$ on the open mesh interval (x_{i-1}, x_i). Consequently, in view of the general identity

$$\int_a^b \{L[f(x) - S_\Delta(x)]\}^2\, dx$$
$$= \int_a^b \{Lf(x)\}^2\, dx - 2\int_a^b L\{f(x) - S_\Delta(x)\} \cdot LS_\Delta(x)\, dx - \int_a^b \{LS_\Delta(x)\}^2\, dx, \tag{6.2.4}$$

it follows from (6.2.3) that

$$\int_a^b \{L[f(x) - S_\Delta(x)]\}^2\,dx$$
$$= \int_a^b \{Lf(x)\}^2\,dx - 2\sum_{i=1}^{N}\left\{\sum_{j=0}^{n-1}\{f(x) - S_\Delta(x)\}^{(n-j-1)}\right.$$
$$\left.\cdot\sum_{k=0}^{j}(-1)^k\cdot\{a_{n-j-k}(x)\cdot LS_\Delta(x)\}^{(k)}\right\}\Bigg|_{x_{i-1}}^{x_i} - \int_a^b \{LS_\Delta(x)\}^2\,dx. \quad (6.2.5)$$

The identity (6.2.5) is the *fundamental identity* for generalized splines; the only restrictions are (1) $S_\Delta(x)$ is a spline with respect to Δ, and (2) $f(x)$ is in $\mathscr{K}^n(a, b)$.

6.3. The First Integral Relation

Under certain restrictions on $S_\Delta(x)$, the fundamental identity reduces to

$$\int_a^b |Lf(x)|^2\,dx = \int_a^b |LS_\Delta(f;x)|^2\,dx + \int_a^b |Lf(x) - LS_\Delta(f;x)|^2\,dx, \quad (6.3.1)$$

which we call the *first integral relation* for generalized splines. If $S_\Delta(x)$ is of deficiency k, then $\{LS_\Delta(x)\}^{(n-j)}$ ($j = 0, 1,..., k$) normally will have discontinuities at the mesh points of Δ. Let

$$\beta_r(v; x) = \sum_{i=0}^{r}(-1)^i\{a_{n-r-i}(x)\,Lv(x)\}^{(i)} \qquad (r = 0, 1,..., n-1); \quad (6.3.2)$$

then $\beta_r(S_\Delta\,; x)$ is the coefficient of $\{f(x) - S_\Delta(x)\}^{(n-r-1)}$ in (6.2.3). Since we do not require $\beta_r(S_\Delta\,; x)$ to be continuous at mesh points for $r \geqslant n-k$, we compensate for any lack of continuity by requiring that $f^{(\alpha)}(x) - S_\Delta^{(\alpha)}(x)$ ($\alpha = 0, 1,..., k-1$) vanish at the interior mesh points of Δ; if, in addition, we impose suitable end conditions at $x = a$ and $x = b$, then (6.3.1) is valid.

One acceptable set of end conditions is that $f(x) - S_\Delta(x)$ vanish at $x = a$ and $x = b$ and $f(x) - S_\Delta(x)$ be of type I′; another is that $f(x) - S_\Delta(x)$ vanish at $x = a$ and $x = b$ and that $S_\Delta(x)$ be of type II′. We emphasize here that the concepts "type I′" and "type II′" depend on the underlying operator L. We say that a function $f(x)$ is of *type I′* provided $f^{(\alpha)}(x)$ vanishes at $x = a$ and $x = b$ for $\alpha = 1, 2,..., n-1$, where n is the order of the operator L. On the other hand, we now say that a function $f(x)$ is of *type II'* provided $\{Lf(x)\}^{(\alpha)}$ vanishes at $x = a$ and $x = b$ for $\alpha = 0, 1, \ldots, n-2$. For $L \equiv D^n$, this agrees with the earlier definition.* Equivalence classes, etc., can be introduced as in Chapters III and V. As before, a spline is *simple* if it is in $C^{2n-2}[a, b]$.

For generalized splines of interpolation of type k, this condition is also sufficient; a generalized spline $S_\Delta(f; x)$ of deficiency k on Δ is *a spline of interpolation of type k if* $S_\Delta^{(\alpha)}(f; x)$ $(\alpha = 0, 1, \ldots, k-1)$ interpolates to the values of $f^{(\alpha)}(x)$ at the mesh points of Δ and $\{LS_\Delta(x)\}^{(\alpha)} = 0$ $(\alpha = 0, 1, \ldots, n-k-1)$ at $x = a$ and $x = b$. In the periodic case we require that $f^{(\alpha)}(x) - S_\Delta^{(\alpha)}(f; x)$ $(\alpha = 0, 1, \ldots, k-1)$ vanish on all of Δ and $S_\Delta(f; x)$ be in $C^{2n-k-1}[a, b]$. Theorem 6.3.1 summarizes these conditions under which we have indicated the validity of the first integral relation (6.3.1).

Theorem 6.3.1. *Let Δ: $a = x_0 < x_1 < \cdots < x_N = b$ and $f(x)$ in $\mathscr{K}^n(a, b)$ be given. If $S_\Delta(f; x)$ is a generalized spline of deficiency k on Δ such that $f^{(\alpha)}(x) - S_\Delta^{(\alpha)}(f; x)$ $(\alpha = 0, 1, \ldots, k-1)$ vanishes at the interior mesh points of Δ and, in addition, one of the conditions,* (a) *$f(x) - S_\Delta(f; x)$ is of type I', and $f(x_i) - S_\Delta(f; x_i) = 0$ $(i = 0, N)$,* (b) *$f(x_i) - S_\Delta(f; x_i) = 0$ $(i = 0, N)$ and $S_\Delta(f; x)$ is of type II',* (c) *$S_\Delta(f; x)$ is of type k,* (d) *$f^{(\alpha)}(x_i) - S_\Delta^{(\alpha)}(f; x_i) = 0$ $(\alpha = 0, 1, \ldots, k-1;\ i = 0, 1, \ldots, N)$ $f(x)$ is in $\mathscr{K}_P^n(a, b)$, and $S_\Delta(f; x)$ is periodic, is satisfied, then the first integral relation (6.3.1) is valid.*

The first integral relation is valid for another broad class of generalized splines, besides the classes covered by Theorem 6.3.1. These splines have the property that some of their first $n-1$ derivatives are prescribed at mesh points. At a given mesh point, the specified derivatives need not be consecutive, as in the case of splines of deficiency k, and at different mesh points different derivatives may be prescribed. For example, the even derivatives may be specified at alternate mesh points and odd derivatives at the remaining mesh points; we include $f(x)$ among the even derivatives. In addition, we require $S_\Delta^{(\alpha)}(x)$ $(\alpha = 0, 1, \ldots, n-1)$ to be continuous. However, when $S_\Delta^{(j)}(x_i) = f^{(j)}(x_i)$, $\beta_{n-j-1}(S_\Delta; x)$ need not be continuous at x_i, but when $S_\Delta^{(j)}(x_i) \neq f^{(j)}(x_i)$, we require

$$\lim_{x \to x_i+} \beta_{n-j-1}(S_\Delta; x) = \lim_{x \to x_i-} \beta_{n-j-1}(S_\Delta; x). \tag{6.3.3}$$

Finally, if $S_\Delta^{(j)}(x) \neq f^{(j)}(x_i)$ at $x = a$ or $x = b$, then $\beta_{n-j-1}(S_\Delta; x)$ must vanish there. We refer to splines determined by such conditions as *heterogeneous splines*. For heterogeneous splines, the following theorem is a direct consequence of the fundamental identity.

* This is equivalent to $\beta_\alpha(f; a) = \beta_\alpha(f; b) = 0$ $(\alpha = 0, 1, \ldots, n-2)$.

Theorem 6.3.2. *Let $\Delta: a = x_0 < x_1 < \cdots < x_N = b$ and $f(x)$ in $\mathcal{K}^n(a, b)$ be given. If $S_\Delta(f; x)$ is a heterogeneous spline on Δ such that, when $S^{(\alpha)}(f; x_i)$ $(\alpha = 0, 1,..., n-1;\ i = 0, 1,..., N)$ is prescribed, we have $S_\Delta^{(\alpha)}(f; x_i) = f^{(\alpha)}(x_i)$, then*

$$\int_a^b |Lf(x)|^2\,dx = \int_a^b |LS_\Delta(f; x)|^2\,dx + \int_a^b |Lf(x) - LS_\Delta(f; x)|^2\,dx.$$

6.4. The Minimum Norm Property

Under the hypotheses of either Theorem 6.3.1 or Theorem 6.3.2, we know from the first integral relation that

$$\int_a^b \{Lf(x)\}^2\,dx \geqslant \int_a^b \{LS_\Delta(f; x)\}^2\,dx. \tag{6.4.1}$$

We carry over to the setting of generalized splines the terminology of polynomial splines and refer to this extremal property as the *minimum norm property*; for $L \equiv D^n$, inequality (6.4.1) expresses the minimum norm property for polynomial splines, as it should.

Theorem 6.4.1. *Let $\Delta: a = x_0 < x_1 < \cdots < x_N = b$ and $Y \equiv \{y_{i\alpha} \mid i = 0, 1,..., N;\ \alpha = 0, 1,..., k-1\}$ be given. Then of all functions $f(x)$ in $\mathcal{K}^n(a, b)$ such that $f^{(\alpha)}(x_i) = y_{i\alpha}$ $(i = 0, 1,..., N;$ $\alpha = 0, 1,..., k-1)$, the generalized spline $S_\Delta(Y; x)$ of type k, when it exists, minimizes*

$$\int_a^b \{Lf(x)\}^2\,dx. \tag{6.4.2}$$

If $g(x)$ also minimizes (6.4.2), then $g(x)$ and $S_\Delta(Y; x)$ differ by a solution of $Lf = 0$. Moreover, if $y_{0\alpha} = y_{N\alpha}$ $(\alpha = 0, 1,..., k-1)$, then of all functions in $\mathcal{K}_P^n(a, b)$, the periodic generalized spline of type k, if it exists, minimizes (6.4.2) and is unique in this sense to within a periodic solution of $Lf = 0$.

For $k = 1$ and $L \equiv D^n$, Theorem 6.4.1 reduces to the main assertions of Theorem 5.4.1. Although we could formulate the theorem in terms of the other conditions under which Theorem 6.3.1 asserts the validity of the first integral relation, we formulate it only for heterogeneous splines and consider these alternative theorems as special cases of the latter.

Theorem 6.4.2. *Let $\Delta: a = x_0 < x_1 < \cdots < x_N = b$ and $Y = \{y_{i\alpha_i}\}$ be given, where i ranges over a subset of $0, 1,..., N$ and α_i ranges* *over a subset of* 0, 1,..., $n - 1$ *which varies with* i. *Then of all functions* $f(x)$ *in* $\mathcal{K}^n(a, b)$ *such that* $f^{(\alpha_i)}(x_i) = y_{i\alpha_i}$ *when* $y_{i\alpha_i}$ *is in* Y, *the heterogeneous generalized spline* $S_\Delta(Y; x)$ *for which* Y *is sufficient to define* $S_\Delta(Y; x)$, *if it exists, minimizes*

$$\int_a^b \{Lf(x)\}^2 \, dx. \tag{6.4.2}$$

If $g(x)$ *satisfies the required conditions and also minimizes (6.4.2), then* $g(x)$ *and* $S_\Delta(Y; x)$ *differ by a solution of* $Lf = 0$.

Generalized splines do not exist for all operators L on every mesh; ordinarily, when there are sufficiently many mesh points they do exist. We cannot, however, be as explicit with respect to the number of mesh points required for existence as we can for polynomial splines. For this reason, we have explicitly required the existence of the splines $S_\Delta(f; x)$ in the statement of Theorems 6.4.1 and 6.4.2. For polynomial splines, the mesh was required to have sufficient points so that the splines involved exist. This question is discussed further in Section 6.7.

6.5. Uniqueness

The methods of Chapters III and V carry over directly and yield the expected uniqueness theorems. We need only observe that, if $S_\Delta(Y; x)$ and $\bar{S}_\Delta(Y; x)$ are two generalized splines interpolating to a common interpolation vector Y on Δ, then their difference $S_\Delta(Y; x) - \bar{S}_\Delta(Y; x)$ is a generalized spline on Δ of the same type, but its interpolation vector is the zero vector. In addition, $S_\Delta(Y; x) - \bar{S}_\Delta(Y; x)$ has the same continuity properties at mesh points which $S(Y; x)$ and $\bar{S}_\Delta(Y; x)$ have. We can now argue, using the minimum norm property, that $S_\Delta(Y; x) - \bar{S}_\Delta(Y; x)$ is the zero function $Z(x)$. This argument establishes both Theorem 6.5.1 and Theorem 6.5.2, which follow.

Theorem 6.5.1. *Let* Δ: $a = x_0 < x_1 < \cdots < x_N = b$ *and* $Y = \{y_{i\alpha} \mid i = 0, 1,..., N;\ \alpha = 0, 1,..., k - 1\}$ *be given. In addition, let* L *and* Δ *be such that, if* $Lg = 0$ *and* $g^{(\alpha)}(x_i) = 0$ $(i = 0, 1,..., N;$ $\alpha = 0, 1,..., k - 1)$, *then* $g(x) = 0$. *Under these conditions, there is at most one generalized spline* $S_\Delta(Y; x)$ *of type* k *on* Δ *such that* $S_\Delta^{(\alpha)}(Y; x_i) = y_{i\alpha}$ $(i = 0, 1,..., N;\ \alpha = 0, 1,..., k - 1)$; *the periodic generalized spline of deficiency* k *is also unique under these hypotheses.*

Theorem 6.5.2. *Let* Δ: $a = x_0 < x_1 < \cdots < x_N = b$ *and* $Y = \{y_{i\alpha_i}\}$ *be given, where* i *ranges over a subset of* 0, 1,..., N *and* α_i *ranges* *over a subset of* 0, 1,..., $n - 1$ *which varies with* i. *In addition, let* L *and* Δ *be such that, if* $Lg \equiv 0$ *and* $g^{(\alpha_i)}(x_i) = 0$ *for all allowable values of* i *and* α_i, *then* $g(x) \equiv 0$. *Under these conditions, there is at most one heterogeneous spline* $S_\Delta(Y; x)$ *such that* $S_\Delta^{(\alpha_i)}(Y; x_i) = y_{i\alpha_i}$ *for all allowable values of* i *and* α_i *and for which* Y *is sufficient to define* $S_\Delta(Y; x)$.

6.6. Defining Equations

Let $u_1(x), u_2(x),..., u_{2n}(x)$ be a fundamental set of solutions of the differential equation $L^*Lf = 0$ on $[a, b]$ such that $u_j^{(\alpha)}(a) = \delta_{j,\alpha+1}$ ($j = 1, 2,..., 2n$; $\alpha = 0, 1,..., 2n - 1$). If a mesh Δ:

$$a = x_0 < x_1 < \cdots < x_N = b$$

is given, then in each mesh interval $x_{i-1} \leqslant x \leqslant x_i$ ($i = 1, 2,..., N$) a generalized spline $S_\Delta(x)$ has a unique representation

$$S_\Delta(x) = \sum_{j=1}^{2n} c_{ij} u_j(x). \tag{6.6.1}$$

Interpolation requirements, continuity requirements, and end conditions determine a system of $2nN$ linear equations for obtaining the $2nN$ coefficients c_{ij}. We defer until the next section the question of the existence of a solution to these equations and content ourselves in this section with the task of formulating the appropriate equations for a number of important cases.

The appropriate equations for periodic and type I generalized splines of deficiency k can be obtained from Eqs. (5.7.4) and (5.7.3) by the following modifications:

(1) Equation (5.7.4.1) must be evaluated at x_i rather than at h_i.
(2) Equation (5.7.3.7) must be evaluated at x_N rather than at h_N.
(3) Equation (5.7.4.2) must be replaced by

$$B_n = \begin{bmatrix} u_1(x_i) & u_2(x_i) & \cdots & u_{2n}(x_i) \\ u_1'(x_i) & u_2'(x_i) & \cdots & u_{2n}'(x_i) \\ \cdots & & & \cdots \\ u_1^{(k-1)}(x_i) & u_2^{(k-1)}(x_i) & \cdots & u_{2n}^{(k-1)}(x_i) \\ u_1(x_i) & u_2(x_i) & \cdots & u_{2n}(x_i) \\ \cdots & & & \cdots \\ u_1^{(2n-k-1)}(x_i) & u_2^{(2n-k-1)}(x_i) & \cdots & u_{2n}^{(2n-k-1)}(x_i) \end{bmatrix}. \tag{6.6.2.1}$$

In the case of generalized splines of type II, in addition to modifications (1) and (3), we must also have

$$C_{0n}^{\mathrm{II}} = \begin{bmatrix} 1 & 0 & \cdots & 0 \\ \{Lu_1\}_a & \{Lu_2\}_a & \cdots & \{Lu_{2n}\}_a \\ \{Lu_1\}_a' & \{Lu_2\}_a' & \cdots & \{Lu_{2n}\}_a' \\ \cdots & & & \cdots \\ \cdots & & & \cdots \\ \{Lu_1\}_a^{(n-2)} & \{Lu_2\}_a^{(n-2)} & \cdots & \{Lu_{2n}\}_a^{(n-2)} \end{bmatrix} \tag{6.6.2.2}$$

and

$$C_{1n}^{\mathrm{II}} = \begin{bmatrix} u_1(b) & u_2(b) & \cdots & u_{2n}(b) \\ \{Lu_1\}_b & \{Lu_2\}_b & \cdots & \{Lu_{2n}\}_b \\ \{Lu_1\}_b' & \{Lu_2\}_b' & \cdots & \{Lu_{2n}\}_b' \\ \cdots & & & \cdots \\ \cdots & & & \cdots \\ \{Lu_1\}_b^{(n-2)} & \{Lu_2\}_b^{(n-2)} & \cdots & \{Lu_{2n}\}_b^{(n-2)} \end{bmatrix} \tag{6.6.2.3}$$

instead of (5.7.3.6) and (5.7.3.8). For generalized splines of type k, the situation is the same as for type II splines except that (5.6.2.2) and (5.6.2.3) are replaced by

$$C_{0n}^{k} = \begin{bmatrix} \overbrace{1 \quad 0 \quad 0 \quad \cdots}^{k} & & & & 0 \\ 0 & 1 & 0 & \cdots & 0 \\ & \cdots & & & \\ 0 & \cdots & & 1 & 0 \\ \{Lu_1\}_a & \{Lu_2\}_a & & \cdots & \{Lu_{2n}\}_a \\ \{Lu_1\}_a' & \{Lu_2\}_a' & & \cdots & \{Lu_{2n}\}_a' \\ \cdots & & & & \cdots \\ \{Lu_1\}_a^{(n-k-1)} & \{Lu_2\}_a^{(n-k-1)} & & \cdots & \{Lu_{2n}\}_a^{(n-k-1)} \end{bmatrix} \tag{6.6.2.4}$$

and

$$C_{1n}^{k} = \begin{bmatrix} u_1(b) & u_2(b) & \cdots & u_{2n}(b) \\ u_1'(b) & u_2'(b) & \cdots & u_{2n}'(b) \\ \cdots & & & \cdots \\ u_1^{(k-1)}(b) & u_2^{(k-1)}(b) & \cdots & u_{2n}^{(k-1)}(b) \\ \{Lu_1\}_b & \{Lu_2\}_b & \cdots & \{Lu_{2n}\}_b \\ \{Lu_1\}_b' & \{Lu_2\}_b' & \cdots & \{Lu_{2n}\}_b' \\ \cdots & & & \cdots \\ \{Lu_1\}_b^{(n-k-1)} & \{Lu_2\}_b^{(n-k-1)} & \cdots & \{Lu_{2n}\}_b^{(n-k-1)} \end{bmatrix}. \tag{6.6.2.5}$$

In the preceding equations, the notation $\{Lv\}_c^{(\alpha)}$ signifies the αth derivative of Lv evaluated at $x = c$. The fact that the linear differential operator L does not, in general, have constant coefficients forces us to evaluate the $u_j(x)$ at x_i rather than at h_i, since in the general case $u_j(x - a)$ is not a solution of $Lf = 0$ even though $u_j(x)$ is a solution.

Heterogeneous splines have no systematic pattern and have to be handled individually. One should observe, however, that at each interior mesh point $S_\Delta^{(\alpha)}(x)$ is continuous for $\alpha = 0, 1,..., n - 1$. In addition, either $S_\Delta^{(\alpha)}(x)$ is specified or $\beta_\gamma(S_\Delta ; x)$ is required to be continuous for $\alpha = 0, 1,..., n - 1$ and $\alpha + \gamma = n - 1$. Thus we have $2n(N - 1)$ linear equations from these conditions. At $x = a$ and $x = b$, either $S_\Delta^{(\alpha)}(x)$ is prescribed or $\beta_\gamma(S_\Delta ; x)$ is required to vanish for $\alpha = 0, 1,..., n - 1$ and $\alpha + \gamma = n - 1$. This gives us $2n$ additional equations or a total of $2nN$ equations; there are exactly the same number of coefficients c_{ij} to be determined. In formulating the system of equations appropriate to a heterogeneous spline, one should note that $\beta_\gamma(S_\Delta ; x)$ operates on S_Δ in a linear fashion. Thus,

$$\beta_\gamma(S_\Delta ; x) = \sum_{j=1}^{2n} c_{ij}\beta_\gamma(u_j ; x) \qquad (x_{i-1} \leqslant x \leqslant x_i). \tag{6.6.3}$$

6.7. Existence

We are now in position to apply the analysis of the preceding three sections to establishing the existence of generalized splines. The proof proceeds along the same lines as the existence proofs of Chapters III and V.

Theorem 6.7.1. *Let* Δ: $a = x_0 < x_1 < \cdots < x_N = b$ *and* $Y \equiv \{y_{i\alpha} \mid i = 0, 1,..., N; \alpha = 0, 1,..., k - 1\}$ *be given. In addition, let* L *and* Δ *be such that, if* $Lg \equiv 0$ *and* $g^{(\alpha)}(x_i) = 0$ $(i = 0, 1,..., N;$ $\alpha = 0, 1,..., k - 1)$, *then* $g(x) \equiv 0$. *Under these conditions, the generalized spline* $S_\Delta(Y; x)$ *of type* k *on* Δ *such that* $S_\Delta^{(\alpha)}(Y; x_i) = y_i$ $(i = 0, 1,..., N;$ $\alpha = 0, 1,..., k - 1)$ *exists; the periodic generalized spline of type* k $S_\Delta(Y; x)$ *also exists.*

Proof. We know that, if $S_\Delta(Y; x)$ exists, it is unique by Theorem 6.4.1. Moreover, from Section 6.6 we know that we can obtain a system of linear equations for determining $S_\Delta(x)$ of the form

$$AC = Y, \tag{6.7.1}$$

where the components of the vector C are the coefficients c_{ij}, A is a matrix, and Y is a vector. Since two distinct sets of c_{ij} define two distinct splines, $AC = 0$ has a unique solution; therefore, A^{-1} exists. The theorem follows.

Similarly, we can establish the following existence theorem for heterogeneous splines.

Theorem 6.7.2. *Let Δ: $a = x_0 < x_1 < \cdots < x_N = b$ and $Y = \{y_{i\alpha_i}\}$ be given, where i ranges over a subset of 0, 1,..., N and α_i ranges over a subset of 0, 1,..., $n - 1$ which varies with i. In addition, let L and Δ be such that, if $Lg \equiv 0$ and $g^{(\alpha_i)}(x_i) = 0$ for all allowable values of i and α_i, then $g(x) \equiv 0$. Under these conditions, the heterogeneous spline $S_\Delta(Y; x)$, such that $S_\Delta^{(\alpha_i)}(Y; x_i) = y_{i\alpha_i}$ for all allowable values of i and α_i and Y is sufficient to define $S_\Delta(Y; x)$, exists.*

The existence arguments we have used depend on first establishing uniqueness. The question of uniqueness, in turn, centers on the question of how often a solution f of $L^*Ly = 0$ and its derivatives can vanish on $[a, b]$ without vanishing identically. For a specific differential operator L such as $L = D^n$, this question usually has a very precise answer. For the general case, the situation is somewhat less precise. We have, however, two basic results whose easy proofs we omit. First, for the operators L under consideration, there is a maximum number of times a solution of $L^*Ly = 0$ and certain of its derivatives can vanish without vanishing identically. The maximum number, unfortunately, is not explicitly given. The second result is that, in any sufficiently small interval, $2n$ independent zero interpolation requirements on y and certain of its derivatives force $y(x)$ to vanish identically; the maximum length of such an interval is again elusive.

6.8. Best Approximation

Both generalized splines of type k and heterogeneous splines depend linearly on their defining values. Thus we have in both cases

$$S_\Delta(f - g; x) = S_\Delta(f; x) - S_\Delta(g; x).$$

Let Δ: $a = x_0 < x_1 < \cdots < x_N = b$ and $f(x)$ in $\mathscr{K}^n(a, b)$ be given. If $S_\Delta(x)$ is any spline on Δ, we have

$$\begin{aligned} S_\Delta(f - S_\Delta ; x) &= S_\Delta(f; x) - S_\Delta(S_\Delta ; x) \\ &= S_\Delta(f; x) - S_\Delta(x), \end{aligned}$$

provided $S_\Delta(f - S_\Delta ; x)$, $S_\Delta(f; x)$, $S_\Delta(S_\Delta ; x)$ have their defining values determined by $f(x) - S_\Delta(x)$, $f(x)$, and $S_\Delta(x)$, respectively; continuity requirements must also be compatible, however. It now follows from the Minimum Norm Property that

$$\| f - S_\Delta \|^2 - \| S_{\Delta, f-S_\Delta} \|^2 = \| f - S_\Delta - S_{\Delta, f-S_\Delta} \|^2$$

or,

$$\| f - S_\Delta \|^2 - \| S_{\Delta, f} - S_\Delta \|^2 = \| f - S_\Delta - S_{\Delta, f} + S_\Delta \|^2.$$

Consequently,

$$\| f - S_\Delta \| \geqslant \| f - S_{\Delta, f} \|.$$

This establishes the following theorem.

Theorem 6.8.1. *Let Δ: $a = x_0 < x_1 < \cdots < x_N = b$ and $f(x)$ in $\mathcal{K}^n(a, b)$ be given. Then of all generalized splines $S_\Delta(x)$ of type k on Δ, the spline of interpolation $S_\Delta(f; x)$ with $S^{(\alpha)}(f; x_i) = f^{(\alpha)}(x_i)$ $(i = 0, 1, \ldots, N;\ \alpha = 0, 1, \ldots, k - 1)$, if it exists, minimizes*

$$\int_a^b \{Lf(x) - LS_\Delta(x)\}^2 \, dx. \tag{6.8.1}$$

If $S_\Delta(x)$ also minimizes (6.8.1), then $S_\Delta(x)$ and $S_\Delta(f; x)$ differ by a solution of $Ly = 0$. Furthermore, if $f(x)$ and $S_\Delta(x)$ are required to be periodic, the spline of interpolation of type k again minimizes (6.8.1) and is unique in this sense up to a periodic solution of $Ly = 0$.

We have, in addition, the following theorem.

Theorem 6.8.2. *Let Δ: $a = x_0 < x_1 < \cdots < x_N = b$ and $f(x)$ in $\mathcal{K}^n(a, b)$ be given. Then of all generalized heterogeneous splines $S_\Delta(x)$ on Δ, determined by a specified set of continuity conditions and defining values $S_\Delta^{(\alpha_i)}(x_i)$, where i ranges over a subset of $0, 1, \ldots, N$ and α_i ranges over a subset of $0, 1, \ldots, n - 1$ which varies with i, the spline of interpolation $S_\Delta(f; x)$ with $S_\Delta^{(\alpha_i)}(f; x_i) = f^{(\alpha_i)}(x_i)$ for allowable values of i and α_i and for which the interpolation requirements are sufficient to define $S_\Delta(f; x)$, if it exists, minimizes (6.8.1). If $S_\Delta(x)$ also minimizes (6.8.1), then $S_\Delta(x)$ and $S_\Delta(f; x)$ differ by a solution of $Ly = 0$.*

6.9. Convergence of Lower-Order Derivatives

In discussing convergence, we confine ourselves to generalized splines of type k; we point out, however, that the periodic generalized spline of type k, the type I generalized spline of deficiency k, and the type II generalized spline of deficiency k also have regularly occurring interpolation points to an approximated function $f(x)$ and its derivatives, so that Rolle's theorem can be applied to them in the same manner as it is to polynomial splines in Section 5.9. Thus, analogous convergence properties are obtainable. We formulate our theorems to include all these splines, but for the most part the proofs and discussions apply explicitly only to the case of type k splines. The heterogeneous splines that we consider have the irregularities in their interpolation and continuity properties confined to the initial mesh of a given mesh sequence $\{\Delta_N\}$ $(N = 1, 2, \ldots)$, and we assume that $\Delta_1 \subseteq \Delta_N (N = 1, 2, \ldots)$. Simplicity is gained by requiring that $S_{\Delta_N}(f; x) = f(x)$ at the mesh points of Δ_N not in Δ_1 and that $S_{\Delta_N}(f; x)$ be of deficiency 1 (Section 1.2) at these points. The pattern of the convergence argument in this section is that of Section 5.9, with one important change involving an application of Minkowski's inequality.

Let $f(x)$ be in $\mathscr{K}^n(a, b)$, and let $\{S_{\Delta_N}(f; x)\}$ $(N = 1, 2, \ldots)$ be a sequence of generalized splines of type k. If $\{\Delta_N : a = x_0^N < x_1^N < \cdots < x_{m_N}^N = b\}$ is the associated sequence of meshes, then $S_{\Delta_N}^{(\alpha)}(f; x_i^N) = f^{(\alpha)}(x_i^N)$ $(i = 0, 1, \ldots, m_N;\ \alpha = 0, 1, \ldots, k - 1)$. By repeated application of Rolle's theorem, we know that $S_{\Delta_N}^{(\alpha)}(f; x)$ interpolates to $f^{(\alpha)}(x)$ at least once in every $\alpha - 2k + 2$ consecutive mesh intervals for $\alpha \geqslant 2k$ and at least once in every mesh interval for $0 \leqslant \alpha \leqslant 2k - 1$. Consequently, for each x in $[a, b]$ we can find an $x_{\alpha N}$ such that $S_{\Delta_N}^{(\alpha)}(f; x_{\alpha N}) = f^{(\alpha)}(x_{\alpha N})$ $(0 \leqslant \alpha \leqslant n)$ and $|x - x_{\alpha N}| \leqslant K_\alpha \|\Delta_N\|$, where $K_\alpha = \alpha - 2k + 2$ if $2k \leqslant \alpha \leqslant n - 1$ and $K_\alpha = 1$ if $0 \leqslant \alpha \leqslant \min(2k, n - 1)$. Furthermore, if $x \neq a$ or $x \neq b$ and N is sufficiently large so that there are points of interpolation both to the left and right of x, then $K_\alpha = (\alpha - 2k + 3)/2$ if $2k \leqslant \alpha \leqslant n - 1$. It follows that

$$|f^{(n-1)}(x) - S_{\Delta_N}^{(n-1)}(f; x)| \leqslant \left| \int_{x_{n-1,N}}^{x} \{f^{(n)}(x) - S_{\Delta_N}^{(n)}(f; x)\}\, dx \right| \leqslant J \cdot K_{n-1}^{1/2} \cdot \|\Delta_N\|^{1/2}, \tag{6.9.1.1}$$

$$J^2 = \int_a^b \{f^{(n)}(x) - S_{\Delta_N}^{(n)}(f; x)\}^2\, dx. \tag{6.9.1.2}$$

Here, as in earlier chapters, we have made use of Schwarz's inequality. We repeat this process for $\alpha = n - 2$ but employ Eqs. (6.9.1) rather than Schwarz's inequality; thus,

$$|f^{(n-2)}(x) - S_{\Delta_N}^{(n-2)}(f; x)| \leqslant J \cdot \{K_{n-1}\}^{1/2} \cdot K_{n-2} \cdot \|\Delta_N\|^{3/2}. \tag{6.9.2}$$

The general case is described by

$$|f^{(\alpha)}(x) - S^{(\alpha)}_{\Delta_N}(f; x)| \leqslant J \cdot \{K_{n-1}\}^{1/2} \cdot K_{n-2} \cdots \cdot K_\alpha \cdot \| \Delta_N \|^{(2n-2\alpha-1)/2}$$
$$(\alpha = 0, 1, \ldots, n-1). \quad (6.9.3)$$

We can now use (6.9.3) to establish a bound for J, which in turn can replace J in (6.9.3); this will establish the uniform convergence of $S^{(\alpha)}_{\Delta_N}(f; x)$ to $f^{(\alpha)}(x)$ ($\alpha = 0, 1, \ldots, n-1$) for x in $[a, b]$.

We have by definition

$$L\{f(x) - S_{\Delta_N}(f; x)\} \equiv a_n(x) D^n\{f(x) - S_{\Delta_N}(f; x)\}$$
$$+ a_{n-1}(x) D^{n-1}\{f(x) - S_{\Delta_N}(f; x)\} + \cdots + a_0(x)\{f(x) - S_{\Delta_N}(f; x)\}, \quad (6.9.4)$$

which implies

$$\left\{\int_a^b [a_n(x) D^n\{f(x) - S_{\Delta_N}(f; x)\}]^2 \, dx\right\}^{1/2} \leqslant \left\{\int_a^b [L\{f(x) - S_{\Delta_N}(f; x)\}]^2 \, dx\right\}^{1/2}$$
$$+ \cdots + \left\{\int_a^b [a_0(x)\{f(x) - S_{\Delta_N}(f; x)\}]^2 \, dx\right\}^{1/2} \quad (6.9.5)$$

by Minkowski's inequality. If we transpose terms and make use of (6.9.3), we obtain

$$K^{-1} \cdot J \leqslant \left\{\int_a^b \{Lf(x) - LS_{\Delta_N}(f; x)\}^2 \, dx\right\}^{1/2}, \quad (6.9.6.1)$$

where

$$K^{-1} = \inf_{x \in [a,b]} | a_n(x)| - \sum_{j=0}^{n-1} [(b-a)^{1/2} \sup_{x \in [a,b]} | a_j(x)|$$
$$\cdot \{K_{n-1}\}^{1/2} \cdot K_{n-2} \cdot \cdots \cdot K_j \cdot \| \Delta_N \|^{(2n-2j-1)/2}]. \quad (6.9.6.2)$$

Since $a_n(x)$ does not vanish and $a_j(x)$ ($j = 0, 1, \ldots, n$) is continuous on $[a, b]$, for $\| \Delta_N \|$ sufficiently small K is positive and bounded. Thus, if either the minimum norm property holds or the best approximation property holds with $\Delta_1 \subset \Delta_N$ ($N \geqslant 1$), then J is bounded. This implies Theorems 6.9.1 and 6.9.2, which follow.

Theorem 6.9.1. *Let $f(x)$ in $\mathscr{K}^n(a, b)$ and*

$$\{\Delta_N : a = x_0^N < x_1^N < \cdots < x_{m_N}^N = b\} \quad (N = 1, 2, \ldots)$$

with $\| \Delta_N \| \to 0$ as $N \to \infty$ be given. Let $\{S_{\Delta_N}(f; x)\}$ ($N = 1, 2, \ldots$) be a sequence of generalized splines of deficiency k where $S_{\Delta_N}(f; x)$ is a spline on Δ_N with

$$S^{(\alpha)}_{\Delta_N}(f; x_i^N) = f^{(\alpha)}(x_i^N) \quad (\alpha = 0, 1, \ldots, k-1; \ i = 1, 2, \ldots, m_N - 1)$$

such that one of the conditions, (a) *each* $S_{\Delta_N}(f; x)$ *is of type* k, (b) $f(x)$ *is in* $\mathscr{K}_P{}^n(a, b)$, $S_{\Delta_N}^{(\alpha)}(f; x_i{}^N) = f^{(\alpha)}(x_i{}^N)$ $(\alpha = 0, 1,..., k - 1; i = 0)$, *and each* $S_{\Delta_N}(f; x)$ *is periodic,* (c) $f(x) - S_{\Delta_N}(f; x)$ *vanishes at* $x = a$ *and* $x = b$ *and is of type* I' $(N = 1, 2,...)$, (d) $f(x) - S_{\Delta_N}(f; x)$ *vanishes at* $x = a$ *and* $x = b$, $\Delta_1 \subset \Delta_N$ $(N \geqslant 1)$, *and* $S_{\Delta_1}(f; x) - S_{\Delta_N}(f; x)$ *is of type* II' $(N = 1, 2,...)$, *is satisfied, then* $S_{\Delta_N}^{(\alpha)}(f; x)$ *converges uniformly to* $f^{(\alpha)}(x)$ *on* $[a, b]$ *for* $\alpha = 0, 1,..., n - 1$ *and*

$$|f^{(\alpha)}(x) - S_{\Delta_N}^{(\alpha)}(f; x)| = O(\| \Delta_N \|^{(2n-2\alpha-1)/2}). \tag{6.9.7}$$

Theorem 6.9.2. *Let* $f(x)$ *in* $\mathscr{K}^n(a, b)$ *and*

$$\{\Delta_N : a = x_0{}^N < x_1{}^N < \cdots < x_{m_N}^N = b\} \quad (N = 1, 2,...)$$

with $\| \Delta_N \| \to 0$ *as* $N \to \infty$ *and* $\Delta_1 \subseteq \Delta_N$ $(N \geqslant 1)$ *be given. Let* $\{S_{\Delta_N}(f; x)\}$ $(N = 1, 2,...)$ *be a sequence of generalized heterogeneous splines where* $S_{\Delta_N}(f; x)$ *is a spline on* Δ_N *which has deficiency one at each mesh point not in* Δ_1 *and interpolates to* $f(x)$ *at these points. In addition, for* i *ranging over a subset of* $0, 1,..., m_1$ *and* α_i *ranging over a subset of* $0, 1,..., n - 1$ *which varies with* i *but is independent of* N, *let* $S_{\Delta_N}^{(\alpha_i)}(f; x_i{}^1) = f^{(\alpha_i)}(x_i{}^1)$, *and let these interpolation requirements be sufficient to define each* $S_{\Delta_N}(f; x)$. *Then* $S_{\Delta_N}^{(\alpha_i)}(f; x)$ *converges uniformly to* $f^{(\alpha)}(x)$ *on* $[a, b]$ *for* $\alpha = 0, 1,..., n - 1$, *and (6.9.7) applies.*

6.10. The Second Integral Relation

As when we deduced the first integral relation, our point of departure is the basic identity

$$\{Lu(x)\} \cdot v(x) = (d/dx)\, P[u(x), v(x)] + u(x) \cdot \{L^*v(x)\} \tag{6.10.1}$$

existing between a linear differential operator L and its formal adjoint L^*. Let Δ: $a = x_0 < x_1 < \cdots < x_N = b$ and $f(x)$ in $\mathscr{K}^{2n}(a, b)$ be given. If we set $u(x) = f(x) - S_\Delta(x)$ and $v(x) = Lf(x) - LS_\Delta(x)$, where $S_\Delta(x)$ is a generalized spline on Δ associated with the operator L, then

$$\int_{x_{i-1}}^{x_i} \{Lf(x) - LS_\Delta(x)\}^2\, dx = P[f(x) - S_\Delta(x), Lf(x) - LS_\Delta(x)] \Big|_{x_{i-1}}^{x_i} + \int_{x_{i-1}}^{x_i} \{f(x) - S_\Delta(x)\}\, L^*Lf(x)\, dx \quad (i = 1, 2,..., N). \tag{6.10.2}$$

If we let

$$\beta_r(f - S_\Delta ; x) = \sum_{j=0}^{r} (-1)^j [a_{n-r-j}(x) \cdot \{Lf(x) - LS_\Delta(x)\}]^{(j)}$$

$$(r = 0, 1, \ldots, n-1), \quad (6.10.3)$$

then we can express $P[f(x) - S_\Delta(x), Lf(x) - LS_\Delta(x)]$ as

$$P[f(x) - S_\Delta(x), Lf(x) - LS_\Delta(x)] = \sum_{j=0}^{n-1} \{f(x) - S_\Delta(x)\}^{(n-j-1)} \cdot \beta_j(f - S_\Delta ; x). \quad (6.10.4)$$

The relation (6.10.4) follows from (6.2.2), and the notation (6.10.4) is consistent with the notation in Section 6.3. As a consequence of (6.10.2) and (6.10.4), we obtain the identity

$$\int_a^b \{Lf(x) - LS_\Delta(x)\}^2 \, dx = \sum_{i=1}^{N} \left[\sum_{j=0}^{n-1} \{f(x) - S_\Delta(x)\}^{(n-j-1)} \cdot \beta_j(f - S_\Delta ; x) \right] \Bigg|_{x_{i-1}}^{x_i} + \int_a^b \{f(x) - S_\Delta(x)\} \, L^*Lf(x) \, dx. \quad (6.10.5)$$

When the summation

$$\sum_{i=1}^{N} \left[\sum_{j=0}^{n-1} \{f(x) - S_\Delta(x)\}^{(n-j-1)} \cdot \beta_j(f - S_\Delta ; x) \right] \Bigg|_{x_{i-1}}^{x_i} \quad (6.10.6)$$

vanishes, we obtain

$$\int_a^b \{Lf(x) - LS_\Delta(x)\}^2 \, dx = \int_a^b \{f(x) - S_\Delta(x)\} \, L^*Lf(x) \, dx; \quad (6.10.7)$$

this is the *second integral relation* for generalized splines. If in the summation (6.10.6) we have $f^{(\alpha)}(x_i) = S_\Delta^{(\alpha)}(x_i)$ for α $(0 \leqslant \alpha < n)$ at an interior mesh point x_i, then there is no contribution from

$$\{f(x) - S_\Delta(x)\}^{(\alpha)} \cdot \beta_{n-\alpha-1}(f - S_\Delta ; x)$$

at x_i to the summation (6.10.6). On the other hand, if $f^{(\alpha)}(x_i) \neq S_\Delta^{(\alpha)}(x_i)$, we require

$$\lim_{x \to x_i +} \beta_{n-\alpha-1}(f - S_\Delta ; x) = \lim_{x \to x_i -} \beta_{n-\alpha-1}(f - S_\Delta ; x) \quad (6.10.8)$$

in order that there be no contribution to the summation. At either $x = a$ or $x = b$ if $f^{(\alpha)}(x) - S_\Delta^{(\alpha)}(x)$ does not vanish, we require $\beta_{n-\alpha-1}(f - S_\Delta ; x)$ to vanish at the point in question to avoid a contribution. Theorems 6.10.1 and 6.10.2 now follow.

Theorem 6.10.1. *Let $f(x)$ in $\mathcal{K}^{2n}(a, b)$ and Δ:*

$$a = x_0 < x_1 < \cdots < x_N = b$$

be given. Let $S_\Delta(f; x)$ be a generalized spline on Δ of deficiency k with $S_\Delta^{(\alpha)}(f; x_i) = f^{(\alpha)}(x_i)$ ($\alpha = 0, 1,..., k - 1$; $i = 1, 2,..., N - 1$) such that one of the conditions, (a) $S_\Delta^{(\alpha)}(f; x_i) = f^{(\alpha)}(x_i)$ ($\alpha = 0, 1,..., k - 1; i = 0, N$) *and* $\{Lf(x_i) - LS_\Delta(f; x_i)\}^{(\alpha)} = 0$ ($\alpha = 0, 1,..., n - k - 1$; $i = 0, N$), (b) *$f(x)$ is in $\mathcal{K}_P^{2n}(a, b)$, $S_\Delta(f; x)$ is periodic, and $S_\Delta^{(\alpha)}(f; x_i) = f^{(\alpha)}(x_i)$* ($\alpha = 0, 1,..., k - 1$; $i = 0$), (c) *$f(x) - S_\Delta(f; x)$ vanishes at $x = a$ and $x = b$ and is of type I',* (d) *$f(x) - S_\Delta(f; x)$ vanishes at $x = a$ and $x = b$ and is of type II', is satisfied; then*

$$\int_a^b \{Lf(x) - LS_\Delta(f; x)\}^2 \, dx = \int_a^b \{f(x) - S_\Delta(f; x)\} L^*Lf(x) \, dx.$$

Theorem 6.10.2. *Let $f(x)$ in $\mathcal{K}^{2n}(a, b)$ and Δ:*

$$a = x_0 < x_1 < \cdots < x_N = b$$

be given. Let $S_\Delta(f; x)$ be a generalized heterogeneous spline on Δ such that $S_\Delta^{(\alpha_i)}(f; x_i) = f^{(\alpha_i)}(x_i)$ as i ranges over a subset of 0, 1,..., N *and α_i ranges over a subset of* 0, 1,..., $n - 1$ *which varies with i, and let these interpolation requirements be sufficient to define $S_\Delta(f; x)$. If for any i ($i = 0, 1,..., N$) and any α ($\alpha = 0, 1,..., n - 1$) we have $S_\Delta^{(\alpha)}(f; x_i) \neq f^{(\alpha)}(x_i)$, let*

$$\lim_{x \to x_i +} \beta_{n-\alpha-1}(f - S_\Delta\, ; x) = \lim_{x \to x_i -} \beta_{n-\alpha-1}(f - S_\Delta\, ; x)$$

if $i \neq 0$ and $i \neq N$, and

$$\beta_{n-\alpha-1}(f - S_\Delta\, ; x_i) = 0$$

if $i = 0$ or $i = N$. Under these conditions,

$$\int_a^b \{Lf(x) - LS_\Delta(f; x)\}^2 \, dx = \int_a^b \{f(x) - S_\Delta(f; x)\} L^*Lf(x) \, dx.$$

6.11. Raising the Order of Convergence

For most of the generalized splines in which we are interested, it follows from (6.9.1.2), (6.9.3), and (6.9.6) that

$$|f^{(\alpha)}(x) - S_{\Delta_N}^{(\alpha)}(f; x)| \leqslant K \cdot \{K_{n-1}\}^{1/2} \cdot K_{n-2} \cdot \cdots \cdot K_\alpha \cdot \left[\int_a^b \{Lf(x) - LS_\Delta(f; x)\}^2 \, dx\right]^{1/2} \cdot \| \Delta_N \|^{(2n-2\alpha-1)/2}$$

$$(\alpha = 0, 1,..., n - 1). \quad (6.11.1)$$

The conditions under which (6.11.1) is valid are considered in Section 6.9, and the constants K and K_α ($\alpha = 0, 1, \ldots, n-1$) are defined there. Even if the splines are heterogeneous, (6.11.1) applies with $\| \Delta_N \|$ multiplied by an appropriate constant, provided the irregularities in interpolation and continuity properties are confined to a limited number of meshes in a mesh sequence. If we assume both the validity of (6.11.1) and the second integral relation, it follows by the same argument as that given in Section 5.11 that

$$\| f^{(\alpha)} - S^{(\alpha)}_{\Delta_N, f} \|_\infty \leqslant K \cdot \{K_{n-1}\}^{1/2} \cdot K_{n-2} \cdot \cdots \cdot K_0$$

$$\cdot V_a{}^b[f]_L \cdot \| \Delta_N \|^{2n-1-\alpha} \qquad (\alpha = 0, 1, \ldots, n-1). \qquad (6.11.2)$$

In (6.11.2), we have employed the standard notation

$$\| f \|_\infty = \sup_{x \in [a,b]} | f(x) | \qquad (6.11.3)$$

and the special notation

$$V_a{}^b[f]_L = \int_a^b | L^* L f(x) | \, dx \qquad (6.11.4)$$

to illustrate the analogy with Chapter V. From (6.11.2), we obtain Theorems 6.11.1 and 6.11.2, which follow.

Theorem 6.11.1. *Let $f(x)$ in $\mathscr{K}^{2n}(a, b)$ and*

$$\{\Delta_N : a = x_0{}^N < x_1{}^N < x^N_{m_N} = b\} \quad (N = 1, 2, \ldots)$$

with $\| \Delta_N \| \to 0$ as $N \to \infty$ be given. If $\{S_{\Delta_N}(f; x)\}$ ($N = 1, 2, \ldots$) is a sequence of generalized splines of deficiency k such that $S_{\Delta_N}(f; x)$ is a spline on Δ_N with $S^{(\alpha)}_{\Delta_N}(f; x_i{}^N) = f^{(\alpha)}(x_i{}^N)$ ($\alpha = 0, 1, \ldots, k-1$; $i = 1, 2, \ldots, m_{N-1}$) and, in addition, one of the conditions (a) *for $N = 1, 2, \ldots$, $f(x) - S_{\Delta_N}(f; x)$ vanishes at $x = a$ and $x = b$ and is of type I',* (b) *$f(x)$ is in $\mathscr{K}_P^{2n}(a, b)$, each $S_{\Delta_N}(f; x)$ is periodic, and $f^{(\alpha)}(x_i{}^N) = S^{(\alpha)}_{\Delta_N}(f; x_i{}^N)$ ($\alpha = 0, 1, \ldots, k-1$; $i = 0$; $N = 1, 2, \ldots$),* (c) *for $N = 1, 2, \ldots$, $f(x) - S_{\Delta_N}(f; x)$ vanishes at $x = a$ and $x = b$, $f(x) - S_{\Delta_N}(f; x)$ is of type II', and $\Delta_1 \subseteq \Delta_N$,* (d) *for $N = 1, 2, \ldots$, $\{f^{(\alpha)}(x) - S_{\Delta_N}(f; x)\}^{(\alpha)}$ ($\alpha = 0, 1, \ldots, k-1$) and $\{Lf(x) - LS_{\Delta_N}(f; x)\}^{(\alpha)}$ ($\alpha = 0, 1, \ldots, n-k-1$) vanish at $x = a$ and $x = b$, is satisfied, then*

$$f^{(\alpha)}(x) = S^{(\alpha)}_{\Delta_N}(f; x) + O(\| \Delta_N \|^{2n-1-\alpha}) \qquad (\alpha = 0, 1, \ldots, n-1)$$

uniformly for x in $[a, b]$.

Theorem 6.11.2. *Let $f(x)$ in $\mathscr{K}^{2n}(a, b)$ and*

$$\{\Delta_N : a = x_0^N < x_1^N < \cdots < x_{m_N}^N = b\} \quad (N = 1, 2, \ldots)$$

with $\| \Delta_N \| \to 0$ as $N \to \infty$ and $\Delta_1 \subset \Delta_N$ $(N \geqslant 1)$ be given. Let $\{S_{\Delta_N}(f; x)\}$ $(N = 1, 2, \ldots)$ be a sequence of generalized heterogeneous splines where $S_{\Delta_N}(f; x)$ is a heterogeneous spline on Δ_N which has deficiency one at each mesh point not in Δ_1 and interpolates to $f(x)$ at these points. In addition, for i ranging over a subset of $0, 1, \ldots, m_1$ and α_i ranging over a subset of $0, 1, \ldots, n-1$ which varies with i but is independent of N, let $S_{\Delta_N}^{(\alpha_i)}(f; x_i^1) = f^{(\alpha_i)}(x_i^1)$. If, in the requirements on a heterogeneous spline involving $\beta_r(S_{\Delta,f}\,; x)$, the latter is replaced by $\beta_r(f - S_{\Delta,f}\,; x)$, then

$$f^{(\alpha)}(x) = S_{\Delta_N}^{(\alpha)}(f; x) + O(\| \Delta_N \|^{2n-1-\alpha}) \qquad (\alpha = 0, 1, 2, \ldots, n-1)$$

uniformly for x in $[a, b]$ provided the interpolation requirements are sufficient to define each $S_{\Delta_N}(f; x)$.

6.12. Convergence of Higher-Order Derivatives

Let Δ: $a = x_0 < x_1 < \cdots < x_N = b$ and $f(x)$ in $\mathscr{K}^{2n}(a, b)$ be given. If $S_\Delta(f; x)$ is a generalized spline of deficiency k interpolating on Δ, together with its first $k-1$ derivatives, to $f(x)$ and its first $k-1$ derivatives, then $S_\Delta^{(\alpha)}(f; x)$ interpolates to $f^{(\alpha)}(x)$ at least once in every $\alpha - 2k + 2$ mesh intervals if $2k \leqslant \alpha \leqslant 2n - k - 1$ and once in every mesh interval for $0 \leqslant \alpha \leqslant 2k$. Thus,

$$|f^{(\alpha)}(x) - S_\Delta^{(\alpha)}(f; x)| \leqslant \left| \int_{x_{\alpha_i}}^{x} \{f^{(\alpha+1)}(x) - S_\Delta^{(\alpha+1)}(f; x)\}\, dx \right|$$

$$\leqslant K_\alpha \cdot \| f^{(\alpha+1)} - S_{\Delta,f}^{(\alpha+1)} \|_\infty \cdot \| \Delta \| \quad (\alpha = 0, 1, \ldots, 2n-k-1), \tag{6.12.1}$$

where K_α is defined as in Section 6.9 but for values of α up to $2n - k - 1$ and x_{α_i} is a suitably chosen point of interpolation of $S_\Delta^{(\alpha)}(f; x)$ to $f^{(\alpha)}(x)$. Consequently, if we can establish a bound on $\| f^{(\alpha+1)} - S_{\Delta,f}^{(\alpha+1)} \|_\infty$ which is independent of the magnitude of $\| \Delta \|$, the convergence of $S_\Delta^{(\alpha)}(f; x)$ to $f^{(\alpha)}(x)$ $(\alpha = 0, 1, \ldots, 2n - k - 1)$ as $\| \Delta \| \to 0$ will follow.

We know that, for $x_{i-1} \leqslant x \leqslant x_i$, we have the representation

$$S_\Delta(f; x) = \sum_{j=1}^{2n} c_{ij} \cdot u_j(x), \tag{6.12.2}$$

where the $u_j(x)$ and the c_{ij} are defined in Section 6.6. Hence, if we can show that the c_{ij} are bounded as $\| \Delta \| \to 0$, then $\| S_{\Delta,f}^{(\alpha)} \|_\infty$ $(\alpha = 0, 1, \ldots, 2n - k - 1)$ is bounded. Since $\| f^{(\alpha)} \|_\infty$ $(\alpha = 0, 1, \ldots, 2n - k - 1)$ is also bounded, the desired convergence will result. To show the c_{ij} are bounded, we revert to the methods of Section 5.12. As in Section 5.12, for some $x_{\alpha i}$ in $[x_{i-1}, x_i]$,

$$\delta_{S_{\Delta,f}}^{\alpha}[x_{i-1}, x_i] = S_\Delta^{(\alpha)}(f; x_{\alpha i}). \tag{6.12.3}$$

Moreover, from Section 6.11, we have

$$\| f - S_{\Delta,f} \|_\infty \leqslant B_0 \cdot V_a{}^b[f]_L \cdot \| \Delta_N \|^{2n-1}, \tag{6.12.4}$$

where $B_0 = K \cdot \{K_{n-1}\}^{1/2} \cdot K_{n-2}' \cdot \cdots \cdot K_0$. As a result of (6.12.2) and (6.12.3), we obtain

$$\delta_{S_{\Delta,f}}^{\alpha}[x_{i-1}, x_i] = \sum_{j=1}^{2n} c_{ij} \cdot u_j^{(\alpha)}(x_{\alpha i}) \qquad (\alpha = 0, 1, \ldots, 2n - 1;\ i = 1, 2, \ldots, N). \tag{6.12.5}$$

For the left-hand member of (6.12.5), we have the bound

$$| \delta_{S_{\Delta,f}}^{\alpha}[x_{i-1}, x_i]| \leqslant \{2\alpha R_\Delta\}^\alpha \cdot B_0 \cdot V_a{}^b[f]_L \cdot \| \Delta \|^{2n-\alpha-1} + | \delta_f{}^\alpha[x_{i-1}, x_i]|$$
$$(i = 1, 2, \ldots, N;\ \alpha = 0, 1, \ldots, 2n - 1), \tag{6.12.6.1}$$

where

$$R_\Delta = \max_i \frac{\| \Delta \|}{| x_i - x_{i-1} |}. \tag{6.12.6.2}$$

Since

$$\max_{j,i} | u_j^{(\alpha)}(x_i) - u^{(\alpha)}(x_{\alpha i}) | \qquad (\alpha = 0, 1, \ldots, 2n - 1)$$

approaches 0 as $\| \Delta \| \to 0$ uniformly with respect to both the number and location of the mesh intervals $[x_{i-1}, x_i]$ and since the $u_j(x)$ are a fundamental set of solutions to $L^*Lf = 0$, it follows that the c_{ij} are bounded provided R_Δ is bounded.

Theorem 6.12.1. *Let $f(x)$ in $\mathscr{K}^{2n}(a, b)$ and*

$$\{\Delta_N : a = x_0{}^N < x_1{}^N < \cdots < x_{m_N}^N = b\} \quad (N = 1, 2, \ldots)$$

with $\| \Delta \| \to 0$ as $N \to \infty$ be given. Let $\{S_{\Delta_N}(f; x)\}$ $(N = 1, 2, \ldots)$ be a sequence of generalized splines of deficiency k where $S_{\Delta_N}(f; x)$ is a spline on Δ_N with $S_{\Delta_N}^{(\alpha)}(f; x_i{}^N) = f^{(\alpha)}(x_i{}^N)$ $(\alpha = 0, 1, \ldots, k - 1;\ i = 1, 2, \ldots, m_N - 1)$ such that one of the conditions, (a) $S_{\Delta_N}^{(\alpha)}(f; x_i{}^N) = f^{(\alpha)}(x_i{}^N)$ $(\alpha = 0, 1, \ldots, k - 1;$

$i = 0,\ m_N)$, $\{LS_{\Delta_N}(f; x_i^N) - Lf(x_i^N)\}^{(\alpha)} = 0$ $(\alpha = 0, 1,..., n - k - 1;$ $i = 0, m_N)$ *and* $\Delta_1 \subseteq \Delta_N$ *all hold for* $N = 1, 2,...,$ (b) $f(x)$ *is in* $\mathscr{K}_P^{2n}(a, b)$, $S_{\Delta_N}^{(\alpha)}(f; x_i^N) = f^{(\alpha)}(x_i^N)$ $(\alpha = 0, 1,..., k - 1;\ i = 0;\ N = 1, 2,...)$ *and each* $S_{\Delta_N}(f; x)$ *is periodic,* (c) $f(x) - S_{\Delta_N}(f; x)$ *vanishes at* $x = a$ *and* $x = b$ *and is of type I'* $(N = 1, 2,...)$, (d) $f(x) - S_{\Delta_N}(f; x)$ *vanishes at* $x = a$ *and* $x = b$ *and is of type II'* $(N = 1, 2,...)$ *and* $\Delta_1 \subseteq \Delta_N$ $(N \geqslant 1)$, *is satisfied; then* $S_{\Delta_N}^{(\alpha)}(f; x)$ *converges uniformly to* $f^{(\alpha)}(x)$ *on* $[a, b]$ *for* $\alpha = 0, 1,..., 2n - k - 1$ *and*

$$f^{(\alpha)}(x) = S_{\Delta_N}^{(\alpha)}(f; x) + O(\| \Delta_N \|^{2n-\alpha-k})$$

provided the R_{Δ_N} *defined by (6.12.6.2) are bounded.*

Theorem 6.12.2. *Let* $f(x)$ *in* $\mathscr{K}^{2n}(a, b)$ *and*

$$\{\Delta_N : a = x_0^N < x_1^N < \cdots < x_{m_N}^N = b\} \quad (N = 1, 2,...)$$

with $\| \Delta_N \| \to 0$ *as* $N \to \infty$ *and* $\Delta_1 \subseteq \Delta_N$ $(N \geqslant 1)$ *be given. Let* $\{S_{\Delta_N}(f; x)\}$ $(N = 1, 2,...)$ *be a sequence of generalized heterogeneous splines where* $S_{\Delta_N}(f; x)$ *is a spline on* Δ_N *which has deficiency one at each mesh point not in* Δ_1 *and interpolates to* $f(x)$ *at these points. In addition, for* α_i *ranging over a subset of* $0, 1,..., n - 1$ *which varies with i but is independent of N, let* $S_{\Delta_N}^{(\alpha_i)}(f; x_i^1) = f^{(\alpha_i)}(x_i^1)$. *If in the requirements on a heterogeneous spline involving* $\beta_r(S_{\Delta,f}\,; x)$ *the latter is replaced by* $\beta_r(f - S_{\Delta,f}\,; x)$, *then we have*

$$f^{(\alpha)}(x) = S_{\Delta_N}^{(\alpha)}(f; x) + O(\| \Delta_N \|^{2n-\alpha-1}) \qquad (\alpha = 0, 1,..., 2n - 2) \quad (6.12.7)$$

uniformly for x in $[a, b]$ *provided the* R_{Δ_N} *defined by (6.12.6.2) are bounded and provided the interpolation requirements imposed on each* $S_{\Delta_N}(f; x)$ *are sufficient as defining conditions.*

REMARK 6.12.1. If at the mesh points not in Δ_1 we have $S_{\Delta_N}^{(\alpha)}(f; x_i^N) = f^{(\alpha)}(x_i^N)$ $(\alpha = 0, 1,..., k - 1)$ and each $S_\Delta(f; x)$ has deficiency k at these points, then (6.12.7) is valid for $\alpha = 0, 1,..., 2n - k - 1$ but with $2n - \alpha - 1$ replaced by $2n - \alpha - k$.

We can, however, modify the argument used in the proof of the preceding two theorems and obtain the following theorem.

Theorem 6.12.3. *Under the hypotheses of either Theorem 6.12.1 or Theorem 6.12.2,*

$$\lim_{N\to\infty} S_{\Delta_N}^{(\alpha)}(f; x) = f^{(\alpha)}(x) \qquad (\alpha = 0, 1,..., 2n - 2) \qquad (6.12.8)$$

uniformly on $[a, b]$.

Proof. We know that

$$\delta^{\alpha}_{S_{\Delta_N},f}[x^N_{i-1}, x_i^N] = \delta_f{}^{\alpha}(x^N_{i-1}, x_i^N) + O(\| \Delta_N \|^{2n-\alpha-1}) \qquad (\alpha = 0, 1, \ldots, 2n-1). \tag{6.12.9}$$

In addition, the boundedness of the c_{ij} with respect to N implies that the $S^{(\alpha)}_{\Delta_N}(f; x)$ $(\alpha = 0, 1, \ldots, 2n-2)$ are uniformly bounded and equicontinuous on mesh intervals if we take one-sided limits at mesh points where discontinuities occur. Moreover, we can find points $x^N_{i\alpha}$ and $\bar{x}^N_{i\alpha}$ in any mesh interval $[x_{i-1}, x_i]$ such that

$$\delta^{\alpha}_{f-S_{\Delta_N},f}[x^N_{i-1}, x_i^N] = f^{(\alpha)}(x^N_{i\alpha}) - S^{(\alpha)}_{\Delta_N}(f; \bar{x}^N_{i\alpha}). \tag{6.12.10}$$

An application of the triangle inequality now establishes (6.12.8), since

$$\delta^{\alpha}_{g+h} = \delta_g{}^{\alpha} + \delta_h{}^{\alpha}.$$

6.13. Limits on the Order of Convergence

It may be possible to increase the order of convergence of a sequence of generalized splines $\{S_{\Delta_N}(f; x)\}$ $(N = 1, 2, \ldots)$ to a function $f(x)$ in $C^{2n}[a, b]$ over that indicated in Theorem 6.12.1, but there is a definite limit. For cubic splines this limit was investigated in Section 3.12 and for polynomial splines of odd degree in Section 5.13. The investigation for generalized splines proceeds along similar lines.

Theorem 6.13.1. *Let $\{\Delta_N\}$ $(N = 1, 2, \ldots)$ be a sequence of meshes with $\| \Delta_N \| \to 0$ as $N \to \infty$ and $R \equiv \sup_N R_{\Delta_N} < \infty$. Let $f(x)$ be in $C^{2n}[a, b]$ and $\mu > 0$. If for each N $(N = 1, 2, \ldots)$ $S_{\Delta_N}(f; x)$ is a generalized spline on Δ_N of deficiency k and*

$$f(x) = S_{\Delta N}(f; x) + O(\| \Delta_N \|^{2n+\mu}) \tag{6.13.1}$$

uniformly for x in $[a, b]$, then

$$L^*Lf(x) \equiv 0.$$

Proof. By the methods of Section 6.12, we can establish under the hypotheses of the theorem that

$$\lim_{N\to\infty} S^{(\alpha)}_{\Delta_N}(f; x) = f^{(\alpha)}(x) \qquad (\alpha = 0, 1, \ldots, 2n); \tag{6.13.2}$$

at each step, $2n - \alpha - 1$ can now be replaced by $2n - \alpha + \mu$. As a consequence,

$$L^*Lf(x) = \lim_{N\to\infty} \{L^*Lf(x) - L^*LS_{\Delta N}(f; x)\} = 0$$

for almost every x. The theorem now follows.

The limitations imposed by Theorem 6.13.1 on an approximated function $f(x)$ by an approximating sequence of splines of interpolation are not the only restrictions. In Chapter IV, we encountered other restrictions of a somewhat similar nature. For generalized splines, they take the following form.

Theorem 6.13.2. *Let $f(x)$ be in $C[a, b]$, and let $\{S_{\Delta_N}(f; x)\}$ $(N = 1, 2,...)$ be a sequence of splines of deficiency k which interpolate to $f(x)$ on a sequence of meshes $\{\Delta_N\}(N = 1, 2,...)$ with $\| \Delta_N \| \to 0$ as $N \to \infty$. If*

$$S_{\Delta_N}(f; x) = \sum_{j=1}^{2n} c_{ij}^N u_j(x) \qquad (x_{i-1}^N \leqslant x \leqslant x_i^N)$$

and the c_{ij}^N are bounded with respect to N, then $f(x)$ is in $C^{2n-k-1}[a, b]$.

Proof. It follows from the boundedness of the c_{ij}^N that for $\alpha = 0, 1,..., 2n - k - 1$ the sequence $\{S_{\Delta_N}^{(\alpha)}(f; x)\}$ is uniformly bounded and equicontinuous. Consequently, we can find functions $F_\alpha(x)$ such that for a suitable subsequence $\{\Delta_m\}$ $(m = 1, 2,...)$ of meshes

$$\lim_{m\to\infty} S_{\Delta_{N_m}}^{(\alpha)}(f; x) = F_\alpha(x) \qquad (\alpha = 0, 1,..., 2n - k - 1)$$

uniformly for x in $[a, b]$. Thus each $F_\alpha(x)$ is continuous. Moreover, since the convergence is uniform,

$$F_\alpha(x) = \lim_{m\to\infty} S_{\Delta_{N_m}}^{(\alpha)}(f; x) = \lim_{m\to\infty} S_{\Delta_{N_m}}^{(\alpha)}(f; a) + \lim_{m\to\infty} \int_a^x S_{\Delta_{N_m}}^{(\alpha+1)}(f; x)\, dx$$

$$= F_\alpha(a) + \int_a^x F_{\alpha+1}(x)\, dx \qquad (\alpha = 0, 1,..., 2n - k - 2).$$

We conclude that $F_0(x)$ is in $C^{2n-k-1}[a, b]$ and that $F_0(x)$ is identical with $f(x)$, since both $F_0(x)$ and $f(x)$ are continuous and they agree on a dense subset of $[a, b]$ because of the interpolation properties of the sequence $\{S_{\Delta_N}(f; x)\}$. This completes the proof.

Remark 6.13.1. The requirement that the splines be splines of interpolation to $f(x)$ can be replaced by the requirement that they converge to $f(x)$.

6.14. Hilbert Space Interpretation

As we have indicated in Section 5.1, the class $\mathscr{K}^n(a, b)$, under the inner product

$$(f, g)_L = \int_a^b Lf(x) \cdot Lg(x)\, dx, \tag{6.14.1}$$

is a Hilbert space provided functions differing by a solution of $Lf = 0$ are identified. Given a sequence of meshes $\{\Delta_N\}$ $(N = 1, 2,\ldots)$ on $[a, b]$ with $\Delta_N \subset \Delta_{N+1}$, we can, as in Chapter V, form the finite dimensional subspaces $F_{\Delta_N}(k, L)$ consisting of all generalized splines of deficiency k on Δ_N and the subspaces $[F_{\Delta_{N+1}}(k, L) - F_{\Delta_N}(k, L)]$ consisting of those elements in $F_{\Delta_{N+1}}(k, L)$ whose defining values* on Δ_N are zero. Also of interest are the analogous subspaces $P_{\Delta_N}(k, L)$ and $[P_{\Delta_{N+1}}(k, L) - P_{\Delta_N}(k, L)]$ of periodic generalized splines as well as the subspaces $F'_{\Delta_N}(k, L)$ and $[F'_{\Delta_{N+1}}(k, L) - F'_{\Delta_N}(k, L)]$ of type II′ splines and the subspaces $T_{\Delta_N}(k, L)$ and $[T_{\Delta_{N+1}}(k, L) - T_{\Delta_N}(k, L)]$ of type k splines.

We can also consider linear subspaces of heterogeneous splines having the same continuity requirements at mesh points but varying defining values. It will be convenient in this case to restrict ourselves to heterogeneous splines that at mesh points not in Δ_1 are of deficiency k. We denote the subspaces analogous to $F_{\Delta_N}(k, L)$ and $[F_{\Delta_{N+1}}(k, L) - F_{\Delta_N}(k, L)]$ by $H_{\Delta_N}(k, L)$ and $[H_{\Delta_{N+1}}(k, L) - H_{\Delta_N}(k, L)]$, respectively. In general, we suppress indication of the dependence on k and L when there is no ambiguity; thus, $F_{\Delta_N}(k, L)$ will be at times denoted by F_{Δ_N}. We emphasize the fact that we obtain different subspaces H_{Δ_N} depending on the continuity requirements imposed on the heterogeneous splines at the mesh points of Δ_1

We now can form the infinite direct sums

$$F_{\Delta_\infty}(k, L) = F_{\Delta_1}(k, L) \oplus \sum_{N=1}^{\infty} \oplus [F_{\Delta_{N+1}}(k, L) - F_{\Delta_N}(k, L)], \tag{6.14.2.1}$$

$$P_{\Delta_\infty}(k, L) = P_{\Delta_1}(k, L) \oplus \sum_{N=1}^{\infty} \oplus [P_{\Delta_{N+1}}(k, L) - P_{\Delta_N}(k, L)], \tag{6.14.2.2}$$

$$F'_{\Delta_\infty}(k, L) = F'_{\Delta_1}(k, L) \oplus \sum_{N=1}^{\infty} \oplus [F'_{\Delta_{N+1}}(k, L) - F'_{\Delta_N}(k, L)], \tag{6.14.2.3}$$

* We understand by "defining values," here and in the remainder of Chapter VI, the prescribable values of the spline and its derivatives.

$$T_{\Delta_\infty}(k, L) = T_{\Delta_1}(k, L) \oplus \sum_{N=1}^{\infty} \oplus [T_{\Delta_{N+1}}(k, L) - T_{\Delta_N}(k, L)], \qquad (6.14.2.4)$$

$$H_{\Delta_\infty}(k, L) = H_{\Delta_1}(k, L) \oplus \sum_{N=1}^{\infty} \oplus [H_{\Delta_{N+1}}(k, L) - H_{\Delta_N}(k, L)]. \qquad (6.14.2.5)$$

The orthogonality of the component spaces is established in Section 6.15. Also in Section 6.15 we establish that, if $\| \Delta_N \| \to 0$ as $N \to \infty$, all these infinite direct sums, with the possible exception of $P_{\Delta_\infty}(k, L)$, are the same and are identical with $\mathscr{K}^n(a, b)$.

In Chapter V, we inferred that, for each integer $n > 0$, $\mathscr{K}_P{}^n(a, b)$ is dense in $\mathscr{K}^n(a, b)$ under the norm

$$\| f \|_{D^n} = \left\{ \int_a^b \{D^n f(x)\}^2 \, dx \right\}^{1/2}. \qquad (6.14.3)$$

Theorem 6.14.1, which follows, establishes that $\mathscr{K}_P{}^n(a, b) + P_{n-1}(a, b)$ is dense in $\mathscr{K}^n(a, b)$ under the norm

$$\| f \|_L = \left\{ \int_a^b \{Lf(x)\}^2 \, dx \right\}^{1/2} \qquad (6.14.4)$$

defined by the inner product (6.14.1). Here $P_{n-1}(a, b)$ is the linear space of polynomials on $[a, b]$ of degree $n - 1$, and $\mathscr{K}_P{}^n(a, b) + P_{n-1}(a, b)$ is the linear space spanned by $\mathscr{K}_P{}^n(a, b)$ and $P_{n-1}(a, b)$.

Theorem 6.14.1. *The linear subspace* $\mathscr{K}_P{}^n(a, b) + P_{n-1}(a, b)$ *is dense in* $\mathscr{K}^n(a, b)$ *under the norm*

$$\| f \|_L = \left\{ \int_a^b \{Lf(x)\}^2 \, dx \right\}^{1/2}.$$

If $L \equiv D^n$, $\mathscr{K}_P{}^n(a, b)$ *is dense in* $\mathscr{K}^n(a, b)$.

Proof. Consider the special case where $L \equiv D^n$, and let $f(x)$ be an arbitrary function in $\mathscr{K}^n(a, b)$. Since $D^n f(x)$ is in $L^2(a, b)$, $D^n f(x)$ has a Fourier expansion whose partial sums $S_N(x)$ are periodic on $[a, b]$. We can integrate each of these partial sums n times and choose the constants of integration (set them equal to zero) such that the resultant functions $F_N(x)$ are periodic. Since $\| f - F_N \|_{D^n} \to 0$ as $N \to \infty$, the theorem is established for the special case $L \equiv D^n$. We establish the general case by showing that, if n is the order of the differential operator L, then convergence in the norm $\| \cdot \|_{D^n}$ implies convergence in the norm $\| \cdot \|_L$.

Since $\mathscr{K}_P{}^n(a, b)$ is dense in $\mathscr{K}^n(a, b)$ under the norm $\| \cdot \|_{D^n}$, we can find a sequence of functions $\{\tilde{F}_N(x)\}$ $(N = 1, 2,\ldots)$ in $\mathscr{K}_P{}^n(a, b)$ such that $\| f - \tilde{F}_N \|_{D^n} \to 0$ as $N \to \infty$. We replace the sequence of functions $\tilde{F}_N(x)$ by a new sequence $\{F_N(x)\}$ $(N = 1, 2,\ldots)$, where $F_N(x) = \tilde{F}_N(x) + P_N(x)$. Here $P_N(x)$ is a polynomial of degree $n - 1$ so chosen that $F^{(\alpha)}(a) = f^{(\alpha)}(a)$ $(\alpha = 0, 1,\ldots, n - 1)$. With the help of Schwarz's inequality, we are led to the following system of inequalities:

$$|f^{(n-1)}(x) - F_N^{(n-1)}(x)| \leqslant K_{n-1} \left\{ \int_a^b \{f^{(n)}(x) - F_N^{(n)}(x)\}^2 \, dx \right\}^{1/2}, \quad (6.14.5.1)$$

$$|f^{(n-2)}(x) - F_N^{(n-2)}(x)| \leqslant K_{n-2} \left\{ \int_a^b \{f^{(n)}(x) - F_N^{(n)}(x)\}^2 \, dx \right\}^{1/2}, \quad (6.14.5.2)$$

$$\vdots \qquad\qquad\qquad \vdots$$

$$|f(x) - F_N(x)| \leqslant K_0 \cdot \left\{ \int_a^b \{f^{(n)}(x) - F_N^{(n)}(x)\}^2 \, dx \right\}^{1/2}, \quad (6.14.5.n)$$

where the constants K_j $(j = 0,\ldots, n - 1)$ are independent of N. From the definition of $L[f(x) - F_N(x)]$ and Minkowski's inequality, together with inequalities (6.14.5), we know that

$$\left\{ \int_a^b \{L[f(x) - F_N(x)]\}^2 \, dx \right\}^{1/2} \leqslant \left\{ \int_a^b \{a_n(x) \cdot D^n[f(x) - F_N(x)]\}^2 \right\}^{1/2}$$

$$+ \cdots + \left\{ \int_a^b \{a_0(x) \cdot [f(x) - F_N(x)]\}^2 \, dx \right\}^{1/2}$$

$$\leqslant K \left\{ \int_a^b \{D^n[f(x) - F_N(x)]\}^2 \, dx \right\}^{1/2}.$$

This implies that $\| f - F_N \|_L \to 0$ as $N \to \infty$ and establishes the theorem.

It has been asserted in Chapter III that $\mathscr{K}^2(a, b)$ is a Hilbert space under the norm $\| \cdot \|_{D^2}$, in Chapter V that $\mathscr{K}^n(a, b)$ is a Hilbert space under the norm $\| \cdot \|_{D^n}$, and in the present section that $\mathscr{K}^n(a, b)$ is a Hilbert space under the norm $\| \cdot \|_L$. Once allowances are made for the pseudo character of the norm, all properties but the completeness of the spaces under the respective norms are immediate. This latter property is also easy to establish.

Theorem 6.14.2. *The space $\mathscr{K}^n(a, b)$ is complete under the norm $\| \cdot \|_L$.*

Proof. Let $\{f_N\}$ $(N = 1, 2,\ldots)$ be a Cauchy sequence in $\mathscr{K}^n(a, b)$ with respect to the norm $\| \cdot \|_L$. Then $\{Lf_N\}$ $(N = 1, 2,\ldots)$ is a Cauchy sequence in $L^2(a, b)$. Since L^2 is complete, this sequence has a limit $g(x)$ in $L^2(a, b)$. If $f(x)$ is any solution of $Lf(x) = g(x)$,* then $f(x)$ is in $\mathscr{K}^n(a, b)$ and $\| f_N - f \|_L \to 0$ as $N \to \infty$; thus, $\mathscr{K}^n(a, b)$ is complete under the norm $\| \cdot \|_L$.

6.15. Convergence in Norm

Theorem 6.15.1. *Let $f(x)$ in $\mathscr{K}^n(a, b)$ and*

$$\{\Delta_N : a = x_0^N < x^N < \cdots < x_{m_N}^N = b\} \quad (N = 1, 2, \ldots)$$

with $\Delta_N \subset \Delta_{N+1}$ and $\| \Delta_N \| \to 0$ as $N \to \infty$. Let $\{S_{\Delta_N}(f; x)\}$ $(N = 1, 2, \ldots)$ be a sequence of generalized splines of deficiency k which interpolate to $f(x)$ on Δ and, in addition, $f^{(\alpha)}(x_i^N) = S_{\Delta_N}^{(\alpha)}(f; x_i^N)$ $(\alpha = 1, 2, \ldots, k-1;$ $i = 1, 2, \ldots, m_N - 1;$ $N = 1, 2, \ldots)$. If one of the conditions, (a) $f(x) - S_{\Delta_N}(f; x)$ is of type I′ $(N = 1, 2, \ldots)$, (b) $f(x) - S_{\Delta_N}(f; x)$ is of type II′ $(N = 1, 2, \ldots)$, (c) $f^{(\alpha)}(x_i^N) = S_{\Delta}^{(\alpha)}(f; x_i^N)$ $(\alpha = 1, 2, \ldots, k-1;$ $i = 0, m_N;$ $N = 1, 2, \ldots)$ and each $S_{\Delta_N}(f; x)$ is of type k, (d) $f^{(\alpha)}(x_i^N) = S_{\Delta_N}^{(\alpha)}(f; x_i^N)$ $(\alpha = 1, 2, \ldots, k-1;$ $i = 0;$ $N = 1, 2, \ldots)$, $f(x)$ is in $\mathscr{K}_P^n(a, b)$, and each $S_{\Delta_N}(f; x)$ is periodic, is satisfied, then

$$\lim_{N \to \infty} \| f - S_{\Delta_N, f} \| = 0.$$

Proof. Since $S_{\Delta_N}(f; x)$ can be regarded as a spline of interpolation to $S_{\Delta_{N+M}}(f; x)$ $(M \geqslant 1)$, the sequence $\{\| S_{\Delta_N}(f; x) \|_L\}$ $(N = 1, 2, \ldots)$ is monotonic increasing and is bounded above by $\| f \|_L$. This is a consequence of the first integral relation, which also implies that

$$\| S_{\Delta_{N+M}, f} - S_{\Delta_N, f} \|_L^2 = \| S_{\Delta_{N+M}, f} \|_L^2 - \| S_{\Delta_N, f} \|_L^2.$$

It follows that the sequence $\{S_{\Delta_N}(f; x)\}$ is a Cauchy sequence with respect to the norm $\| \cdot \|_L$, since the sequence $\{\| S_{\Delta_N, f} \|_L\}$ converges. Moreover, by the same argument as used to establish (6.9.6), we have

$$\| S_{\Delta_{N+M}, f} - S_{\Delta_N, f} \|_{D^n} \leqslant K \| S_{\Delta_{N+M}, f} - S_{\Delta_N, f} \|_L$$

for $\| \Delta_N \|$ sufficiently small and some positive constant K that is independent of N. Consequently, $\{S_{\Delta_N}^{(n)}(f; x)\}$ is a Cauchy sequence in $L^2(a, b)$. If $g(x)$ is the limit in $L^2(a, b)$ of this sequence and

$$G(x) = f^{(n-1)}(a) + \int_a^x g(x)\, dx,$$

* The solution can be taken in the sense of Carathéodory (cf. Sansone and Conti [1964, p. 11]).

then

$$|S_{\Delta_N}^{(n-1)}(f;x) - G(x)| \leqslant (b-a)^{1/2}\left\{\int_a^b \{S_{\Delta_N}^{(n)}(f;x) - g(x)\}^2\,dx\right\}^{1/2}$$
$$+ |S_{\Delta_N}^{(n-1)}(f;a) - f^{(n-1)}(a)|, \tag{6.15.1}$$

and, as $N \to \infty$, the right-hand member of (6.15.1) approaches zero. It follows that $f^{(n-1)}(x)$ is identical with $G(x)$ on $[a, b]$; hence,

$$\lim_{N\to\infty} \| S_{\Delta_N,f} - f \|_{D^n} = 0. \tag{6.15.2}$$

In addition, we have the inequalities

$$|S_{\Delta_N}^{(n-1)}(f;x) - f^{(n-1)}(x)| \leqslant (b-a)^{1/2}\| S_{\Delta_N,f} - f \|_{D^n}$$
$$+ |S_{\Delta_N}^{(n-1)}(f;a) - f^{(n-1)}(a)|, \tag{6.15.3.1}$$

$$|S_{\Delta_N}^{(n-2)}(f;x) - f^{(n-2)}(x)| \leqslant (b-a)^{3/2}\cdot\| S_{\Delta_N,f} - f \|_{D^n}$$
$$+ (b-a)\,|S_{\Delta_N}^{(n-1)}(f;a) - f^{(n-1)}(a)|$$
$$+ |S_{\Delta_N}^{(n-2)}(f;a) - f^{(n-2)}(a)|, \tag{6.15.3.2}$$

$$\vdots \qquad\qquad \vdots$$

$$|S_{\Delta_N}(f;x) - f(x)| \leqslant (b-a)^{(2n-1)/2}\cdot\| S_{\Delta_N,f} - f \|_{D^n}$$
$$+ \sum_{j=1}^{n}(b-a)^{n+1-j}\cdot|S_{\Delta_N}^{(n-j)}(f;a) - f^{(n-j)}(a)|, \tag{6.15.3.n}$$

which, in turn, imply the inequality (for N sufficiently large)

$$\| f - S_{\Delta_N,f} \|_L \leqslant K \| f - S_{\Delta_N,f} \|_{D^n}, \tag{6.15.4}$$

where K is a positive constant independent of N. The theorem now follows.

The same argument can be applied to a sequence of heterogeneous splines; Theorem 6.15.2 is the result.

Theorem 6.15.2. *Suppose $f(x)$ is in $\mathscr{K}^n(a, b)$ and*

$$\{\Delta_N : a = x_0^N < x_1^N < \cdots < x_{m_N}^N = b\} \quad (N = 1, 2, \ldots)$$

with $\Delta_N \subset \Delta_{N+1}$ *and* $\|\Delta_N\| \to 0$ *as* $N \to \infty$. *Let* $\{S_{\Delta_N}(f; x)\}$ $(N = 1, 2, \ldots)$ *be a sequence of generalized heterogeneous splines satisfying the hypotheses of Theorem 6.9.2. Then*

$$\lim_{N\to\infty} \|f - S_{\Delta_N, f}\|_L = 0.$$

Lemma 5.15.1 and Theorem 5.15.3 have direct analogs for generalized splines; in particular, we have the following lemma.

Lemma 6.15.1. *Let* Δ_1 *and* Δ_2 *be two meshes on* $[a, b]$ *with* $\Delta_1 \subset \Delta_2$, *and let* $S_{\Delta_1}(x)$ *and* $S_{\Delta_2}(x)$ *be two generalized splines on* Δ_1 *and* Δ_2, *respectively, each having the same quantities prescribed on* Δ_1 *and the same continuity requirements on* Δ_1. *If the prescribed values (defining values) of* $S_{\Delta_2}(x)$ *at the mesh points of* Δ_1 *are zero, then*

$$(S_{\Delta_1}, S_{\Delta_2})_L = 0.$$

Proof. Let Δ_1 be defined by $a = x_0 < x_1 < \cdots < x_N = b$. Then

$$\begin{aligned}
(S_{\Delta_1}, S_{\Delta_2})_L &= \int_a^b LS_{\Delta_2}(x) \cdot LS_{\Delta_1}(x)\, dx \\
&= \sum_{i=1}^{N} \int_{x_{i-1}}^{x_i} LS_{\Delta_2}(x) \cdot LS_{\Delta_1}(x)\, dx \\
&= \sum_{i=1}^{N} P[S_{\Delta_2}(x), LS_{\Delta_1}(x)] \Big|_{x_{i-1}}^{x_i} + \int_{x_{i-1}}^{x_i} S_{\Delta_2}(x) \cdot L^*LS_{\Delta_1}(x)\, dx \\
&= \sum_{i=1}^{N} P[S_{\Delta_2}(x), LS_{\Delta_1}(x)] \Big|_{x_{i-1}}^{x_i} = 0,
\end{aligned}$$

the final equality holding because, whenever a term in

$$\sum_{i=1}^{N} P[S_{\Delta_2}(x), LS_{\Delta_1}(x)] \Big|_{x_{i-1}}^{x_i}$$

is not cancelled directly by another term, because of continuity, it is multiplied by a defining value of $S_{\Delta_2}(x)$ on Δ_1 and is thus zero. This proves the lemma, which in turn establishes Theorem 6.15.3.

Theorem 6.15.3. *Let* $\{\Delta_N\}$ $(N = 1, 2, \ldots)$ *be a sequence of meshes on* $[a, b]$ *with* $\Delta_N \subset \Delta_{N+1}$ *and such that* $\|\Delta_N\| \to 0$ *as* $N \to \infty$. *Then the* *infinite direct sums (6.14.2) are orthogonal decompositions with respect to* $(f, g)_L$ *and, with the possible exception of* $P_{\Delta_\infty}(k, L)$, *are identical with* $\mathscr{K}^n(a, b)$. *In the case of* $P_{\Delta_\infty}(k, L)$,

$$\mathscr{K}_P{}^n(a, b) \subseteq P_{\Delta_\infty}(k, L) \subseteq \mathscr{K}^n(a, b).$$

6.16. Canonical Mesh Bases

The definition and construction of canonical mesh bases for $F_{\Delta_\infty}(k, L)$, $F'_{\Delta_\infty}(k, L)$, $T_{\Delta_\infty}(k, L)$, $H_{\Delta_\infty}(k, L)$, and $P_{\Delta_\infty}(k, L)$ is identical with the construction already given in Chapter V and will be omitted here. Both the statement and proof of the analog of Lemma 5.16.1, however, require some modification. The proof is more complicated to the extent that we need to show that, if $S_i(L; x)$ is an element of a canonical mesh basis associated with the linear differential operator L of order n, then

$$\| S_i(L; x)\|_{D^n} \leq K \cdot \| S_i(L; x)\|_L \tag{6.16.1}$$

for some positive constant K that is independent of i; the analog of the inequalities (5.16.2) will involve this constant.

We proceed as in Section 6.9. Because of the vanishing of the defining values of $S_i(L; x)$ at the mesh points of preceding meshes in the mesh sequence $\{\pi_i\}$ $(i = 0, 1, \ldots)$ arising in the construction of the canonical mesh basis, we can take $f(x)$ as the zero function; thus, we modify (6.9.1) by setting

$$J^2 = \int_a^b \{S_i^{(n)}(L; x)\}^2 \, dx. \tag{6.16.2}$$

By essentially the same method of argument as in Section 6.9, however, the existence of a positive constant K such that (6.16.1) holds is clear. Consequently, there exist positive constants K_α independent of i such that the analog of Lemma 5.16.1 is valid. Since these constants admit no simple representation, we do not state them explicitly.

Lemma 6.16.1. *Let* $\{S_i(L; x)\}$ $(i = 1, 2, \ldots)$ *be a canonical mesh basis for* $[F_{\Delta_\infty}(k, L) - F_{\Delta_1}(k, L)]$, $[F'_{\Delta_\infty}(k, L) - F'_{\Delta_1}(k, L)]$, $[T_{\Delta_\infty}(k, L) - T_{\Delta_1}(k, L)]$, $[H_{\Delta_\infty}(k, L) - H_{\Delta_1}(k, L)]$, *or* $[P_{\Delta_\infty}(k, L) - P_{\Delta_1}(k, L)]$ *determined by a sequence of meshes* $\{\Delta_N\}$ $(N = 1, 2, \ldots)$ *with* $\Delta_N \subset \Delta_{N+1}$. *Let* $\{\pi_i\}$ $(i = 0, 1, \ldots)$ *be the related sequence of meshes used in the construction of* $\{S_i(L; x)\}$. *Then there exist positive constants* K_α, *independent of i, such that*

$$| S_i^{(\alpha)}(L; x)| \leq K_\alpha \cdot \| \pi_{i-1} \|^{(2n-2\alpha-1)/2} \qquad (\alpha = 0, 1, \ldots, n-1). \tag{6.16.3}$$

From the preceding lemma, we obtain the following analog of Theorem 5.16.2.

Theorem 6.16.1. *Let* $\{S_i(L; x)\}$ $(i = 1, 2, \ldots)$ *be a canonical mesh basis such that* $\| \pi_i \| = O(1/i)$. *Then there exist real numbers* $\beta_\alpha > 0$ *such that*

$$S_\alpha(x) = \sum_{i=1}^{\infty} \{S_i^{(\alpha)}(L; x)\}^2 < \beta_\alpha \qquad (\alpha = 0, 1, \ldots, n-2). \tag{6.16.4}$$

The elements $S_i(L; x)$ of a canonical mesh basis not only have the property of orthogonality, but if $\Delta_N \subset \Delta_{N+1}$ the basis for $F_{\Delta_{N+1}}$ is simply an extension of the basis for F_{Δ_N}. If Δ_N is defined by $a = x_0 < x_1 < \cdots < x_N = b$ and if, to obtain a basis for F_{Δ_N}, we employ cardinal splines $S_i(\Delta_N; x)$ whose defining values at all but the mesh point x_i vanish and there only one defining value is nonzero, we not only lose orthogonality, but in passing from F_{Δ_N} to $F_{\Delta_{N+1}}$ a completely new set of basis elements is needed. There is a definite analogy here between this situation and the use of Newtonian interpolation formulas rather than Lagrangian interpolation formulas. When additional interpolation points are added, a whole new set of Lagrangian unit functions is needed (Davis [1963, p. 41]); on the other hand, the set of Newtonian functions can be supplemented to accomodate the new interpolation points.

6.17. Kernels and Integral Representations

In this section, we state the analogs for the case of generalized splines of the theorems contained in Section 5.17. The statement of the theorems, however, is such that heterogeneous splines are included. The proofs differ in no essential way from the earlier proofs and are consequently omitted.

Theorem 6.17.1. *Let* $f(x)$ *be in* $\mathscr{K}^n(a, b)$ *or* $\mathscr{K}_P{}^n(a, b)$, *and let* $\{S_i(L, k; x)\}$ $(i = 1, 2, \ldots)$, *together with* $\{u_i(L, k; x)\}$ $(i = 1, 2, \ldots, m)$, *be a canonical mesh basis for* $F_{\Delta_\infty}(k, L), F'_{\Delta_\infty}(k, L)$, $T_{\Delta_\infty}(k, L)$, $H_{\Delta_\infty}(k, L)$, *or* $P_{\Delta_\infty}(k, L)$, *which is an orthonormal basis for* $\mathscr{K}^n(a, b)$ *or* $\mathscr{K}_P{}^n(a, b)$. *Then for every* x *in* $[a, b]$

$$f^{(\alpha)}(x) = \lim_{N\to\infty} \int_a^b H_{\alpha,N}(L, k; x, t) \cdot Lf(t)\, dt + G^{(\alpha)}(x) \qquad (\alpha = 0, 1, \ldots, n-1) \tag{6.17.1}$$

where $LG(x) \equiv 0$ *for* x *in* $[a, b]$,

$$H_{\alpha,N}(L, k; x, t) = \sum_{i=1}^{m} u_i^{(\alpha)}(L, k; x) \cdot Lu_i(L, k; t)$$

$$+ \sum_{i=1}^{N} S_i^{(\alpha)}(L, k; x) \cdot LS_i(L, k; t), \qquad (6.17.2)$$

and the limit exists uniformly with respect to x *in* $[a, b]$.

Corollary 6.17.1. *Let* $f(x)$ *be in* $\mathscr{K}^{2n}(a, b)$ *or* $\mathscr{K}_P^{2n}(a, b)$, *and let* $\{S_i(L, k; x)\}$ $(i = 1, 2,...)$, *together with* $\{u_i(L, k; x)\}$ $(i = 1, 2,..., m)$, *be a canonical mesh basis (cf. footnote Section 5.17) for* $F_{\Delta_\infty}(k, L)$, $F'_{\Delta_\infty}(k, L)$, $T_{\Delta_\infty}(k, L)$, $H_{\Delta_\infty}(k, L)$, *or* $P_{\Delta_\infty}(k, L)$, *which is an orthonormal basis for* $\mathscr{K}^n(a, b)$ *or* $\mathscr{K}_P{}^n(a, b)$. *Then for every* x *in* $[a, b]$ *and* $\alpha = 0, 1,..., 2n - 2$, *Eq. (6.17.1) is valid. In the case of heterogeneous splines, the maximum deficiency is assumed not to exceed* k.

Theorem 6.17.2. *Let* $\{\pi_i\}$ $(i = 0, 1,...)$ *be a sequence of meshes on* $[a, b]$ *determining a canonical mesh basis for* $F_{\Delta_\infty}(k, L)$, $F'_{\Delta_\infty}(k, L)$, $T_{\Delta_\infty}(k, L)$, $H_{\Delta_\infty}(k, L)$, *or* $P_{\Delta_\infty}(k, L)$, *which is an orthonormal basis for* $\mathscr{K}^n(a, b)$ *or* $\mathscr{K}_P{}^n(a, b)$. *If* $H_{\alpha,N}(L, k; x, t)$ *is defined by (6.17.1.2), then for each* x $\{H_{\alpha,N}\}$ $(\alpha = 0, 1,..., n - 2;\ N = 1, 2,...)$ *is a Cauchy sequence in* $L^2(a, b)$ *and, consequently, a Cauchy sequence in* $L(a, b)$. *If* $H_\alpha(L, k; x, t)$ $(\alpha = 0, 1,..., n - 2)$ *denotes the common limit, then for* $f(x)$ *in* $\mathscr{K}^n(a, b)$ *or* $\mathscr{K}_P{}^n(a, b)$

$$f^{(\alpha)}(x) = \int_a^b H_\alpha(L, k; x, t) \cdot Lf(t)\, dt + G^{(\alpha)}(x), \qquad (6.17.3)$$

where $LG(x) = 0$ *for* x *in* $[a, b]$. *Moreover, the convergence is uniform with respect to* x *in* $[a, b]$, *and* $H_\alpha(L, k; x, t)$ *is obtained from* $H_{\alpha-1}(L, k; x, t)$ *by formal term-by-term differentiation with respect to* x.

REMARK 6.17.1. We are tacitly assuming, when we have a canonical mesh basis for $\mathscr{K}^n(a, b)$ or $\mathscr{K}_P{}^n(a, b)$, that $\| \pi_i \| = O(1/i)$.

6.18. Representation and Approximation of Linear Functionals

Analogs of the four theorems contained in Section 5.18 remain valid for generalized splines, and again the arguments needed to prove the theorems for generalized splines are essentially unchanged. Consequently, we again content ourselves with just the statement of the theorems and omit the proofs. We do, however, consider some examples of approximating linear functionals in which we approximate an integral using these equally spaced values of the integrand. These same examples are considered by Sard [1963, Chapter II], and they illustrate the manner in which spline theory provides many of the "best approximations" obtained by Sard. We also connect generalized spline theory to the calculation of the eigenvalues of a linear differential operator. We conclude this section with an application of heterogeneous splines to the approximation of point functionals $\mathscr{L}_x : f \to f(x)$.

Theorem 6.18.1. *Let $f(x)$ be in $\mathscr{K}^n(a, b)$ or $\mathscr{K}_P{}^n(a, b)$, and let $\{S_i(k, L; x)\}$ $(i = 1, 2, \ldots)$, together with $\{u_i(k, L; x)\}$ $(i = 1, 2, \ldots, m)$, be a canonical mesh basis for $F_{\Delta_\infty}(k, L)$, $F'_{\Delta_\infty}(k, L)$, $T_{\Delta_\infty}(k, L)$, $H_{\Delta_\infty}(k, L)$, or $P_{\Delta_\infty}(k, L)$, which is an orthonormal basis for $\mathscr{K}^n(a, b)$ or $\mathscr{K}_P{}^n(a, b)$. If $\mathscr{L}$ is a linear functional of the form (5.18.1), then*

$$\mathscr{L} o f = \lim_{N \to \infty} \int_a^b H_N(k, L; t) \cdot Lf(t)\, dt + \mathscr{S} o G, \tag{6.18.1.1}$$

where

$$H_N(k, L; x) = \sum_{i=1}^{m} \alpha_i L\mu_i(k, L; t) + \sum_{i=1}^{N} \beta_i LS_i(k, L; x), \tag{6.18.1.2}$$

$$\alpha_i = \sum_{j=0}^{\eta} \int_a^b u_i^{(j)}(k, L; s)\, d\mu_j(s) \qquad (i = 0, 1, \ldots, m), \tag{6.18.1.3}$$

$$\beta_i = \sum_{j=0}^{\eta} \int_a^b S_i^{(j)}(k, L; s)\, d\mu_j(s) \qquad (i = 1, 2, \ldots, N), \tag{6.18.1.4}$$

and $LG(x) = 0$ for every x in $[a, b]$.

Corollary 6.18.1. *Let $f(x)$ be in $\mathscr{K}^{2n}(a, b)$ or $\mathscr{K}_P^{2n}(a, b)$, and let $\{S_i(k, L; x)\}$ $(i = 1, 2, \ldots)$, together with $\{u_i(k, L; x)\}$ $(i = 1, 2, \ldots, m)$, be a canonical mesh basis for $F_{\Delta_\infty}(k, L)$, $F'_{\Delta_\infty}(k, L)$, $T_{\Delta_\infty}(k, L)$, $H_{\Delta_\infty}(k, L)$, or $P_{\Delta_\infty}(k, L)$, which is an orthonormal basis for $\mathscr{K}^n(a, b)$ or $\mathscr{K}_P{}^n(a, b)$. If $\mathscr{L}$ is a linear functional of the form*

$$\mathscr{L} o f = \sum_{j=0}^{\eta} \int_a^b f^{(j)}(t)\, d\mu_j(t), \tag{6.18.2}$$

where each $\mu_j(t)$ is a function of bounded variation on $[a, b]$, then (5.18.1) *holds except that in this case $\eta < 2n - k - 1$.*

REMARK 6.18.1. In both the theorem and the corollary, the function $G(x)$ is dependent on the function $f(x)$, but the kernels $H_N(k, L; x)$ are not. The method of proof essentially depends on the uniform convergence of the spline sequence and its derivatives to $f(x)$ and its derivatives, and not on the rate of convergence. Thus, in view of Theorem 6.12.3, we need only require $\eta < 2n - 2$ rather than $2n - k - 1$ in Corollary 6.18.1.

Theorem 6.18.2. *Let $f(x)$ be in $\mathscr{K}^n(a, b)$ or $\mathscr{K}_P{}^n(a, b)$, and let $\{S_i(k, L; x)\}$ $(i = 1, 2,...)$, together with $\{u_i(k, L; x)\}$ $(i = 1, 2,..., m)$, be a canonical mesh basis for $F_{\Delta_\infty}(k, L)$, $F'_{\Delta_\infty}(k, L)$, $T_{\Delta_\infty}(k, L)$, $H_{\Delta_\infty}(k, L)$, or $P_{\Delta_\infty}(k, L)$, which is an orthonormal basis for $\mathscr{K}^n(a, b)$ or $\mathscr{K}_P{}^n(a, b)$. If $\mathscr{L}$ is a linear functional of the form (5.18.1) except that $\eta \leqslant n - 2$, then $\{H_N(k, L; x)\}$ is a Cauchy sequence in $L^2(a, b)$ and, consequently, a Cauchy sequence in $L(a, b)$. If $H(k, L; x)$ denotes the common limit, then*

$$\mathscr{L} o f = \int_a^b H(k, L; t) \cdot Lf(t)\, dt + \mathscr{L} o\, G, \tag{6.18.3}$$

where $LG(x) = 0$ for every x in $[a, b]$.

Turning from the representation of linear functionals to the approximation of linear functionals, we have the analogs of Theorems 5.18.3 and 5.18.4.

Theorem 6.18.3. *If $\mathscr{L}$ is a linear functional of the form (5.18.1) and if B is the linear functional such that*

$$B\, o f = \mathscr{L} o\, S_{\Delta, f}\,, \tag{6.18.4}$$

$S_\Delta(f; x)$ being the spline of interpolation to $f(x)$ which is a linear combination of $\{u_i(k, L; x)\}$ $(i = 1, 2,..., m)$ and $G(x)$, then

$$\mathscr{L} o f - B\, o f = \lim_{N\to\infty} \int_a^b \left\{ \sum_{i=1}^{N} \beta_i \cdot LS_i(k, L; t) \right\} \cdot Lf(t)\, dt, \tag{6.18.5.1}$$

where

$$\beta_i = \sum_{j=0}^{\eta} \int_a^b S_i^{(j)}(k, L; s)\, d\mu_j(s) \qquad (i = 1, 2,..., N) \tag{6.18.5.2}$$

[$f(x)$ is in $\mathscr{K}^n(a, b)$ or $\mathscr{K}_P{}^n(a, b)$], and the $\mu_j(s)$ $(j = 0, 1,..., \eta)$ are functions of bounded variation on $[a, b]$ determined by $\mathscr{L}$ alone through the representation (6.18.1).

Theorem 6.18.4. *If $\mathscr{L}$ is a linear functional of the form (5.18.1) and B is a linear functional of the form (6.18.4) with $\eta < n - 1$, then*

$$\mathscr{L} o f - B o f = \int_a^b H(k, L; t) \cdot Lf(t)\, dt.$$

$H(k, L; t)$ is in $L^2(a, b)$ and is the limit, in the mean square sense, of

$$H_N(k, L; x) = \sum_{i=1}^{N} \beta_i \cdot LS_i(k, L; x), \qquad (6.18.6.1)$$

where

$$\beta_i = \sum_{j=1}^{\eta} \int_a^b S_i^{(j)}(k, L; s)\, d\mu_j(s) \qquad (\eta < n); \qquad (6.18.6.2)$$

the $\mu_j(s)$ are functions of bounded variation on $[a, b]$ and depend on $\mathscr{L}$ alone [(Again $f(x)$ is in $\mathscr{K}^n(a, b)$ or $\mathscr{K}_P{}^n(a, b)$.)] If B is any linear functional of the form (5.18.9) and $\mathscr{L} - B$ annihilates solutions of $Lf(x) = 0$, then for $k < n$

$$\mathscr{L} o f - B o f = \int_a^b H(k, L; t) \cdot Lf(t)\, dt, \qquad (6.18.7)$$

where $H(k, L; t)$ is in $L^2(a, b)$ and is defined as in Theorem 6.18.2 with $\mathscr{L}$ replaced by $\mathscr{L} - B$. Moreover, the integral

$$\int_a^b \{H(k, L; t)\}^2\, dt \qquad (6.18.8)$$

is minimized if B is of the form (6.18.4).

REMARK 6.18.2. If the coefficients a_{ij} defining B in (5.18.9) are subject to additional constraints, it may not be possible to satisfy (6.18.4). Generally, however, this can be done if heterogeneous splines are used. This is particularly true if certain of the a_{ij} are required to be zero. Furthermore, if $f(x)$ is in $\mathscr{K}^{2n}(a, b)$ or $\mathscr{K}_P^{2n}(a, b)$, the restriction $\eta < n$ imposed by (5.18.1) can be replaced by the condition $\eta < 2n - 2$ in Theorem 6.18.3. We remind the reader that the deficiency k of a spline is never allowed to exceed n, the order of the operator L.

We now consider the approximation of an integral of the form

$$\mathscr{L} o f = \int_{-1}^{1} f(x)\, dx \qquad (6.18.9)$$

by functionals of the form

$$B o f = a_1 f(-1) + a_2 f(0) + a_3 f(1). \qquad (6.18.10)$$

We could equally well consider an arbitrary interval $[a, b]$ and take

$$B\,o\,f = a_1 f(a) + a_2 f\left(\frac{a+b}{2}\right) + a_3 f(b), \tag{6.18.11}$$

but the calculations would become more cumbersome. Moreover, there is no loss of generality in the simplification (6.18.9), since

$$\int_a^b f(x)\,dx = \frac{b-a}{2}\int_{-1}^1 g(t)\,dt, \qquad g(t) = f\left(\frac{b-a}{2}t + \frac{b+a}{2}\right),$$

so that

$$\begin{aligned}\frac{b-a}{2} B\,o\,g &= \frac{b-a}{2}\{a_1 g(-1) + a_2 g(0) + a_3 g(1)\}\\ &= \frac{b-a}{2}\left\{a_1 f(a) + a_2 f\left(\frac{a+b}{2}\right) + a_3 f(b)\right\},\end{aligned}$$

which is of the form (6.18.11).

Let us impose the additional requirement that the approximation is exact for linear functions. Then by either Theorem 5.18.4 or Theorem 6.18.4.

$$\mathscr{L} o\,f - B\,o\,f = \int_{-1}^1 H_B(t)\cdot D^2 f(x)\,dt, \tag{6.18.12}$$

and

$$\int_{-1}^1 \{H_B(t)\}^2\,dt \tag{6.18.13}$$

is minimized when $B\,o\,f = \mathscr{L} o\, S_{\Delta,f}$, where $S_\Delta(f; x)$ is the type II′ cubic spline of interpolation to $f(x)$ on Δ: $-1 < 0 < 1$. Let

$$u_1(x) = 1, \qquad u_2(x) = x, \qquad u_3(x) = x^2/2, \qquad u_4(x) = x^3/6; \tag{6.18.14}$$

then

$$S_\Delta(f; x) = c_{11}u_1(x) + c_{12}u_2(x) + c_{13}u_3(x) + c_{14}u_4(x) \quad (-1 \leqslant x \leqslant 0), \tag{6.18.15.1}$$

$$S_\Delta(f; x) = c_{21}u_1(x) + c_{22}u_2(x) + c_{23}u_3(x) + c_{24}u_4(x) \quad (0 \leqslant x \leqslant 1), \tag{6.18.15.2}$$

and

$$\begin{aligned}\mathscr{L} o\, S_{\Delta,f} = c_{11}\int_{-1}^0 u_1(x)\,dx + c_{12}\int_{-1}^0 u_2(x)\,dx + c_{13}\int_{-1}^0 u_3(x)\,dx\\ + c_{14}\int_{-1}^0 u_4(x)\,dx + c_{21}\int_0^1 u_1(x)\,dx + c_{22}\int_0^1 u_2(x)\,dx\\ + c_{23}\int_0^1 u_3(x)\,dx + c_{24}\int_0^1 u_4(x)\,dx.\end{aligned}$$

But we have

$$\int_0^1 u_1(x)\,dx = 1, \qquad \int_{-1}^0 u_1(x)\,dx = 1,$$
$$\int_0^1 u_2(x)\,dx = \tfrac{1}{2}, \qquad \int_{-1}^0 u_2(x)\,dx = -\tfrac{1}{2},$$
$$\int_0^1 u_3(x)\,dx = \tfrac{1}{6}, \qquad \int_{-1}^0 u_3(x)\,dx = \tfrac{1}{6},$$
$$\int_0^1 u_4(x)\,dx = \tfrac{1}{24}, \qquad \int_{-1}^0 u_4(x)\,dx = -\tfrac{1}{24},$$

so that

$$\mathscr{L} o\, S_{\Delta,f} = c_{11} - \tfrac{1}{2}c_{12} + \tfrac{1}{6}c_{13} - \tfrac{1}{24}c_{14} + c_{21} + \tfrac{1}{2}c_{22} + \tfrac{1}{6}c_{23} + \tfrac{1}{24}c_{24}\,.$$

The interpolation properties of $S_\Delta(f;x)$ imply that

$$f(0) = c_{11} = c_{21}\,,$$
$$f(-1) = c_{11} - c_{12} + \tfrac{1}{2}c_{13} - \tfrac{1}{6}c_{14}\,,$$
$$f(1) = c_{21} + c_{22} + \tfrac{1}{2}c_{23} + \tfrac{1}{6}c_{24}\,,$$

whereas from the continuity of $S_\Delta'(f;x)$ and $S_\Delta''(f;x)$ at $x = 0$ we have $c_{12} = c_{22}$ and $c_{13} = c_{23}$.

Finally, since the spline is of type II′, we must have

$$0 = c_{13} - c_{14}\,, \qquad 0 = c_{23} + c_{24}\,.$$

As a result,

$$c_{13} = c_{23} = c_{14} = -c_{24}\,,$$

and

$$\mathscr{L} o\, S_{\Delta,f} = 2c_{11} + \tfrac{1}{4}c_{13}\,.$$

However, $c_{11} = f(0)$, so that

$$f(-1) - f(0) = -c_{12} + \tfrac{1}{3}c_{13}\,,$$

$$f(1) - f(0) = c_{12} + \tfrac{1}{3}c_{13}\,,$$

from which it follows that

$$c_{13} = \frac{3f(-1) - 6f(0) + 3f(1)}{2}\,,$$

and which in turn implies

$$\mathscr{L} o\, S_{\Delta,f} = \frac{3f(-1) + 10f(0) + 3f(1)}{8}. \tag{6.18.16}$$

This is the rule of 3 — 10 — 3 obtained by Sard [1963, p. 42] through direct minimization of (6.18.13).

If we require B to be exact for quadratic functions of x, we obtain a better known approximation with less effort. In this instance,

$$\mathscr{L} o f - B\, o f = \int_{-1}^{1} H_B(t) \cdot D^3 f(t)\, dt, \tag{6.18.17}$$

and (6.18.13) is minimized when $B\, o f = \mathscr{L} o\, S_{\Delta,f}$, $S_\Delta(f; x)$ being the type II′ quintic spline of interpolation to $f(x)$ on Δ. Since

$$y(x) = \frac{f(-1) - 2f(0) + f(1)}{2} \cdot x^2 + \frac{f(1) - f(-1)}{2} \cdot x + f(0) \tag{6.18.18}$$

interpolates to $f(x)$ on Δ and is a type II′ quintic spline on Δ, the uniqueness of $S_\Delta(f; x)$ asserts that

$$S_\Delta(f; x) \equiv y(x).$$

Consequently,

$$\mathscr{L} o\, S_{\Delta,f} = \frac{f(-1) - 2f(0) + f(1)}{3} + 2f(0)$$
$$= \frac{f(-1) + 4f(0) + f(1)}{3},$$

which is simply Simpson's rule. Again the result was obtained by Sard through direct minimization of (6.18.13). In addition, Sard showed that, if B is exact for cubics, the remainder has a representation

$$\mathscr{L} o f - B\, o f = \int_{-1}^{1} H_B(t)\, D^4 f(t)\, dt \tag{6.18.19}$$

for which (6.18.13) is still minimized when B is given by Simpson's rule.

From the standpoint of spline theory, this gives rise to a serious difficulty, since the type II′ polynomial spline of degree seven is not uniquely defined on Δ. The quadratic $y(x)$ defined by (6.18.18) is one possibility, and $\mathscr{L} o\, y$ does yield Simpson's rule. If, however, we add an arbitrary fourth point p to Δ to form a new mesh $\bar{\Delta}$, then the type II′ polynomial spline of degree seven $S_{\bar{\Delta}}(f; x)$ is uniquely defined and is the cubic polynomial of interpolation to $f(x)$ on Δ. In addition, if $B \circ f = \mathscr{L} \circ S_{\Delta,f}$, B is exact for cubics, (6.18.19) is valid, and this choice of B minimizes (6.18.13).

Let

$$u(x) = \frac{x^3 - x}{p^3 - p};$$

then $u(x)$ is a cubic polynomial that vanishes on Δ and has the value 1 at p. Moreover,

$$S_\Delta(f; x) = y(x) + \{f(p) - y(p)\}\, u(x),$$

and $\mathscr{L} \circ S_{\Delta,f} = \mathscr{L} \circ y + \{f(p) - y(p)\}\, \mathscr{L} \circ u = \mathscr{L} \circ y$. Consequently, we have verified the well-known result that Simpson's rule is exact for cubics, and we are still in agreement with Sard that, given an approximating functional of the form (6.18.10) which is exact for cubics, the remainder can be represented in the form (6.18.19), and (6.18.13) is minimized when B is identical with Simpson's rule. In addition, we have shown that, if we add an arbitrary fourth point p to Δ, distinct from the mesh points of Δ, and consider approximating functionals B of the form

$$B \circ f = af(-1) + bf(0) + cf(1) + df(p),$$

we cannot improve the approximation with respect to the measure (6.18.13).

The previous application required only polynomial splines; the next application involves generalized splines. Consider the problem of determining the eigenvalues of a linear differential operator L of the form (6.1.1), subject to a set of n linearly independent auxiliary conditions, each specifying that $f(x)$ or one of its first $n - 1$ derivatives vanish at some point in $[a, b]$. We restrict ourselves to a simple case in which the auxiliary conditions involve only the endpoints of the interval. Thus, we require

$$\begin{aligned} f^{(\alpha_i)}(a) &= 0 \qquad (i = 1, 2,..., I; \quad \alpha_i \neq \alpha_j, \quad i \neq j), \\ f^{(\gamma_j)}(b) &= 0 \qquad (j = 1, 2,..., J; \quad \gamma_i \neq \gamma_j, \quad i \neq j), \end{aligned} \tag{6.18.20}$$

and $I + J = n$. In addition, the α_i and γ_j are less than n. Let Δ: $a = x_0 < x_1 < \cdots < x_N = b$ be given, and let $\mathscr{F}_\Delta$ denote the family of simple generalized splines $S_\Delta(L; x)$ associated with the operator L, which satisfy the boundary conditions (6.18.20) together with the additional conditions

$$\begin{aligned} \beta_{n-\alpha_i-1}(S_\Delta; a) &= 0 \qquad (i = 1, 2,..., I), \\ \beta_{n-\gamma_j-1}(S_\Delta; b) &= 0 \qquad (j = 1, 2,..., J), \end{aligned} \tag{6.18.21}$$

$\beta_j(v; x)$ being defined by (6.3.2). Moreover, we assume that if $Ly \equiv 0$ and y satisfies (6.18.20), then $y \equiv 0$.

Before considering the eigenvalue problem determined by L and the constraints (6.18.20), let us consider the problem of finding a solution to the nonhomogeneous equation

$$Lf(x) = g(x), \qquad a \leqslant x \leqslant b, \tag{6.18.22}$$

which satisfies the constraints

$$\begin{aligned} f^{(\alpha_i)}(a) &= A_i \qquad (i = 1, 2,..., I; \;\; \alpha_i \neq \alpha_j\,, \;\; i \neq j), \\ f^{(\gamma_j)}(b) &\quad B_j \qquad (j = 1, 2,..., J; \;\; \gamma_i \neq \gamma_j\,, \;\; i \neq j), \end{aligned} \tag{6.18.23}$$

where we have $I + J = n$ and the α_i and γ_j are less than n. If the homogeneous equation has a solution satisfying (6.18.23), the non-homogeneous problem is solved if we can find a particular solution of (6.18.22) that satisfies the homogeneous boundary conditions (6.18.20).

We observe that $\mathscr{F}_\Delta$ is an inner product space under the inner product

$$(f, g)_L = \int_a^b Lf(x) \cdot Lg(x)\, dx.$$

Let the dimension of $\mathscr{F}_\Delta$ be m, and let $\{u_i(L; x)\}$ $(i = 1, 2,..., m)$ be an orthonormal basis. Let $\{P_i\}$ $(i = 1, 2,...)$ be a sequence of distinct points in $[a, b]$ which are distinct from the mesh points of Δ. We require that the sequence $\{P_i\}$ be such that, if we form a sequence of meshes $\{\pi_i\}$ $(i = 0, 1,...)$ by adding the points P_i one at a time in their enumerated order starting with $\pi_0 = \Delta$, then $\| \pi_i \| = O(1/i)$. We can consequently introduce additional orthonormal splines $S_i(L; x)$ which satisfy the boundary conditions (6.18.20) and (6.18.21), with the result that $\{S_i(L; x)\}$ $(i = 1, 2,...)$, together with $\{u_i(L; x)\}$ $(i = 1, 2,..., m)$, comprise a canonical mesh basis for $\mathscr{K}^n(a, b)$. Let $f(x)$ satisfy (6.18.22) and (6.18.20). Then, by Theorem 6.17.2, if the boundary conditions (6.18.20) uniquely determine a solution of the differential equation (6.18.22), we have

$$f(x) = \int_a^b H(L; x, t)\, Lf(t)\, dt; \tag{6.18.24}$$

here $H(L; x, t)$ is the mean square limit of $\{H_N(L; x, t)\}$ $(N = 1, 2,...)$, where

$$H_N(L; x, t) = \sum_{i=1}^{m} u_i(L; x) \cdot Lu_i(L; t) + \sum_{i=1}^{N} S_i(L; x) \cdot LS_i(L; t). \tag{6.18.25}$$

Moreover, from Lemma 6.16.1 we know

$$|S_i(L; x)| \leqslant K(1/i)^{n-1/2} \qquad (i = 1, 2, \ldots). \tag{6.18.26}$$

The solution $f(x)$ of (6.18.22) and (6.18.23) is now given by

$$f(x) = G(x) + \int_a^b H(L; x, t)\, g(t)\, dt, \tag{6.18.27}$$

where $G(x)$ is a solution of the homogeneous problem. We can interpret the kernel $H(L; x, t)$ as a Green's function.

The eigenvalue problem

$$Lv(x) = \lambda v(x), \tag{6.18.28}$$

where $v(x)$ satisfies the conditions (6.18.20), similarly is equivalent to the eigenvalue problem

$$v(x) = \lambda \int_a^b H(L; x, t)\, v(t)\, dt. \tag{6.18.29}$$

Here we have the important advantage that $H(L; x, t)$ is the mean square limit of the degenerate kernels $H_N(L; x, t)$ provided $n \geqslant 2$. In this case, an approximate solution can be obtained by solving a problem where the kernel is degenerate. The inequality (6.18.26) is useful in justifying the approximation and estimating the rate of convergence.

The preceding application of generalized splines is not limited to the rather special boundary conditions defined by (6.18.20). The main requirement on the boundary conditions is that they be such that the first integral relation is valid. Given a mesh Δ: $a = x_0 < x_1 < \cdots < x_N = b$ and a linear differential operator L, we require for the validity of the first integral relation that

$$\sum_{i=1}^{N} P[f - S_{\Delta,f}, LS_{\Delta,f}] \Big|_{x_{i-1}}^{x_i} = 0, \tag{6.18.30}$$

where $P[u, v]$ is the bilinear concomitant of L. Observe now that the continuity and interpolation requirements imposed on $S_\Delta(f; x)$ at the interior mesh points of Δ reduce (6.18.30) to

$$P[f - S_{\Delta,f}, LS_{\Delta,f}]\big|_a^b = 0. \tag{6.18.31}$$

Consequently, if $f(x) - S_\Delta(f; x)$ satisfies a linear homogeneous set of n boundary conditions sufficient to imply that (6.18.22) has a unique solution on $[a, b]$, and if $LS_\Delta(f; x)$ satisfies an adjoint set of boundary conditions, then (6.18.31) holds, and the theory goes through as before.

Another important observation is that, if we are given a self-adjoint differential operator $R = L^*L$, where L contains no singularities on $[a, b]$, then we can apply the same methods to solution of the equation

$$Rf(x) = g(x), \qquad (6.18.32)$$

subject to a set of self-adjoint linear homogeneous boundary conditions, provided the boundary conditions imply the validity of (6.18.31). This will be the case, for instance, if we require

$$f^{(\alpha)}(a) = f^{(\alpha)}(b) = 0 \qquad (\alpha = 0, 1, \ldots, n-1). \qquad (6.18.33)$$

We then have

$$f(x) = \int_a^b H(R; x, t)\, Rf(t)\, dt; \qquad (6.18.34)$$

in this case, $H(R; x, t)$ is the uniform limit of $\{H_N(R; x, t)\}$ $(N = 1, 2, \ldots)$, where

$$H_N(R; x, t) = \sum_{i=1}^{m} U_i(L; x)\, U_i(L; t) + \sum_{i=1}^{N} S_i(L; x)\, S_i(L; t). \qquad (6.18.35)$$

The proof of (6.18.34) is analogous to that of (6.18.24). We need only observe that in this case

$$\int_a^b LS_i(L; x)\, Lf(x)\, dx = \int_a^b S_i(L; x)\, L^*Lf(x)\, dx.$$

Similar remarks apply to the associated eigenvalue problem

$$Rf(x) = \lambda f(x).$$

When R is of the second order, L is of the first order; consequently, the inequality (6.18.26) is too weak to establish the uniform convergence of $H_N(R; x, t)$ to $H(R; x, t)$. However, if in obtaining our canonical mesh basis we add new mesh points in sweeps moving from left to right, at each step of the sweep the new point bisecting a mesh interval, uniform convergence can still be established. The important fact here is that the basis elements $S_i(L; x)$ vanish identically except in the two adjacent mesh intervals separated by the mesh point in the associated mesh π_i at which $S_i(L; x)$ does not interpolate to zero. This follows from the uniqueness of the spline $S_i(L; x)$ and the fact that, since L is of first order, only $S_i(L; x)$ but not its derivatives is required to be continuous on $[a, b]$. Thus, if $S_i(L; x)$ does not vanish identically on any mesh interval at both ends of which it vanishes, then uniqueness is contradicted, since a second spline with the same interpolation and continuity properties as $S_i(L; x)$ results when the definition of $S_i(L; x)$ is altered so that it vanishes on the mesh interval in question. Thus, given x in $[a, b]$, there are only two basis elements in each sweep which do not vanish at x. Since in each sweep all mesh intervals are halved, uniform convergence follows from Lemma 6.16.1.

We conclude this chapter with an example in which the approximation of a linear functional $\mathscr{L}$ requires heterogeneous splines. The example comes from numerical analysis, more specifically from the numerical integration of ordinary differential equations. Assume that our integration steps are of equal length. Since the dependence on step size can be shown to be linear, we assume unit length. Consider two consecutive intervals defined by three points x_{n-1}, x_n, x_{n+1} which we can take as 0, 1, 2, respectively. Thus, given the mesh $0 < 1 < 2$, we desire a corrector formula for estimating the value of a function $f(x)$ at $x = 2$ from its values at $x = 0$, $x = 1$ and the values of its first derivative at $x = 0$, $x = 1$, $x = 2$. Moreover, we desire the approximation to be exact for cubics. [Here we are assuming that we have obtained satisfactory values of $f(x)$ and $f'(x)$ at $x = 0$ and $x = 1$, and, with the aid of a predictor formula and the differential equation, we have obtained an acceptable value of $f'(x)$ at $x = 2$ for use in the corrector formula.] Finally, we desire that the corrector formula be a linear function of the five quantities $f(0)$, $f(1)$, $f'(0)$, $f'(1)$, $f'(2)$ and that these quantities reflect the total dependence of the formula on the function $f(x)$.

Our general theory now tells us that we can approximate the linear functional $\mathscr{L} \circ f = f(2)$, subject to the preceding conditions, if we employ a heterogeneous polynomial spline $S_\Delta(f; x)$ of degree seven. We then have

$$f(2) = S_\Delta(f; 2) + \mathscr{R}(2),$$

where the remainder $\mathscr{R}(2)$ can be represented as

$$\mathscr{R}(2) = \int_0^2 H(2, t)\, D^4 f(t)\, dt. \tag{6.18.36}$$

Moreover, the integral

$$\int_0^2 \{H(2, t)\}^2\, dt \tag{6.18.37}$$

is minimized by taking $S_\Delta(f; 2)$ as the approximating functional. The following set of conditions completely defines $S_\Delta(f; x)$:

$$\left.\begin{aligned} &S_\Delta(f; 0) = f(0), \qquad S_\Delta(f; 1) = f(1); \\ &S'_\Delta(f; 0) = f'(0), \qquad S'_\Delta(f; 1) = f'(1), \qquad S'_\Delta(f; 2) = f'(2); \\ &S_\Delta^{(\alpha)}(f; 1+) = S_\Delta^{(\alpha)}(f; 1-) \qquad (\alpha = 0, 1, 2, 3, 4, 5); \\ &S_\Delta^{(\alpha)}(f; 0) = 0 \qquad (\alpha = 4, 5); \\ &S_\Delta^{(\alpha)}(f; 2) = 0 \qquad (\alpha = 4, 5, 7). \end{aligned}\right\} \tag{6.18.38}$$

If $u_i(x)$ $(i = 1, 2,..., 8)$ are the polynomials x^i, and we let

$$\begin{aligned} S_\Delta(f; x) &= c_{11}u_1(x) + c_{12}u_2(x) + \cdots + c_{18}u_8(x) \qquad 0 \leqslant x \leqslant 1, \\ S_\Delta(f; x) &= c_{21}u_1(x) + c_{22}u_2(x) + \cdots + c_{28}u_8(x) \qquad 1 \leqslant x \leqslant 2, \end{aligned}$$

then the conditions (6.18.38) yield a set of 16 independent linear equations for obtaining the 16 quantities c_{ij} in terms of $f(0)$, $f(1)$, $f'(0)$, $f'(1)$, and $f'(2)$. Their exact solution results in the predictor formula

$$f(2) = \tfrac{8}{43}f(1) + \tfrac{35}{43}f(0) + \tfrac{15}{43}f'(2) + \tfrac{52}{43}f'(1) + \tfrac{11}{43}f'(0) \tag{6.18.39}$$

obtained by Sard [1963, p. 83], and, as he points out, it is stable and convergent in the sense of Dahlquist [1956]. Numerical solution of the system of equations arising from the conditions (6.18.38) gives the approximate coefficients

$$\left.\begin{aligned} \tfrac{8}{43} &\sim 0.1860464 \\ \tfrac{35}{43} &\sim 0.8139536 \\ \tfrac{15}{43} &\sim 0.3488372 \\ \tfrac{52}{43} &\sim 1.209302 \\ \tfrac{11}{43} &\sim 0.2558140. \end{aligned}\right\} \tag{6.18.40}$$

This page intentionally left blank

CHAPTER VII

The Doubly Cubic Spline

7.1. Introduction

Our development of spline theory has been one-dimensional up to this point; the theory, however, generalizes readily to higher dimensions. Just as the simple cubic spline is of fundamental importance in one-dimensional spline theory, the simple doubly cubic spline (Section 1.2) is basic in two-dimensional spline theory. We limit ourselves to the consideration of simple two-dimensional splines in this chapter; a very general theory is developed in Chapter VIII.

Suppose that we are given a rectangular region $\mathscr{R}$: $a \leqslant t \leqslant b$; $c \leqslant s \leqslant d$ of the plane. Then, if we are given two one-dimensional meshes Δ_t: $a = t_0 < t_1 < \cdots < t_N = b$ and $\Delta_s : c = s_0 < s_1 < \cdots < s_M = d$, the resulting two-dimensional mesh $\pi = \{P_{ij}\}$ $(i = 0, 1,..., N; j = 0, 1,..., M)$, where $P_{ij} = (t_i, s_j)$, partitions $\mathscr{R}$ into a family of subrectangles

$$\{\mathscr{R}_{ij} : t_{i-1} \leqslant t \leqslant t_i \,;\, s_{j-1} \leqslant s \leqslant s_j\} \qquad (i = 1, 2,..., N; \; j = 1, 2,..., M).$$

A *simple doubly cubic spline* $S_\pi(t, s)$ on $\mathscr{R}$ with respect to π is (1) a double cubic in each rectangle $\mathscr{R}_{ij}$, and (2) an element of $C_2^{4}(\mathscr{R})$, where $C_r^{n}(R)$ is the family of functions $f(t, s)$ on $\mathscr{R}$ whose nth order partial derivatives, involving no more than rth order differentiation with respect to a single variable, exist and are continuous.

As in the one-dimensional case, we can distinguish between a spline and its representations. It is possible to express a two-dimensional spline as a linear function of a finite set of linearly independent parameters; the choice of these parameters, or defining values as we often refer to them, is far from unique. In this chapter, we confine ourselves to a limited but important group of these representations. A *type I* representation of a spline includes among the defining values of the spline the following values of its partial derivatives:

$$\left.\begin{array}{lll}
\text{(a)} & \dfrac{\partial S_\pi}{\partial t} \text{ at the mesh points } \{P_{ij}\} & (i = 0, N;\ j = 0, 1,..., M), \\[2ex]
\text{(b)} & \dfrac{\partial S_\pi}{\partial s} \text{ at the mesh points } \{P_{ij}\} & (i = 0, 1,..., N;\ j = 0, M), \\[2ex]
\text{(c)} & \dfrac{\partial^2 S_\pi}{\partial t\, \partial s} \text{ at the mesh points } \{P_{ij}\} & (i = 0, N;\ j = 0, M).
\end{array}\right\} \qquad (7.1.1)$$

The remaining parameters needed to represent $S_\pi(t, s)$ uniquely at times may not be specified, but, for splines of interpolation on π, they are the values of $S_\pi(t, s)$ at the mesh points of π. In a similar fashion, we define a *type II* representation as one including among the defining values of a spline the values of

$$\left.\begin{array}{lll}
\text{(a)} & \dfrac{\partial^2 S_\pi}{\partial t^2} \text{ at the mesh points } \{P_{ij}\} & (i = 0, N;\ j = 0, 1,..., M), \\[2ex]
\text{(b)} & \dfrac{\partial^2 S_\pi}{\partial s^2} \text{ at the mesh points } \{P_{ij}\} & (i = 0, 1,..., N;\ j = 0, M), \\[2ex]
\text{(c)} & \dfrac{\partial^4 S_\pi}{\partial t^2\, \partial s^2} \text{ at the mesh points } \{P_{ij}\} & (i = 0, N;\ j = 0, M).
\end{array}\right\} \qquad (7.1.2)$$

A two-dimensional spline is *periodic in t* if $S_\pi(t, s)$, $\partial S_\pi(t, s)/\partial t$, and $\partial^2 S_\pi(t, s)/\partial t^2$ are periodic functions of t with period $b - a$. The definition of a spline *periodic in s* is analogous. A *doubly periodic* spline is periodic in both t and s with period $b - a$ in t and $d - c$ in s. The most convenient set of defining values for a doubly periodic spline consists of its values at the mesh points $\{P_{ij}\}$ $(i = 1, 2,..., N; j = 1, 2,..., M)$, and this is what is implied by the terminology *a doubly periodic spline of interpolation on* π. At times, the words *doubly* or *on* π may be suppressed.

If the values of partial derivatives specified by (7.1.1) are zero, we speak of the spline as a *type I′* spline, and if the values of partial derivatives specified by (7.1.2) are zero, we speak of the spline as a *type II′* spline. As in the one-dimensional case, it is desirable to go a step further and separate functions $f(t, s)$ defined on $\mathscr{R}$ into *type I and type II equivalence classes*. Thus two functions are in the same *type I* equivalence class if the partial derivatives specified by (7.1.1) are defined and equal. A function for which the quantities in (7.1.1) are defined and zero is a *type I′ function*. The equivalent definitions for *type II* and *type II′ functions* are immediate. We point out, however, that, unlike the one-dimensional analogues, these definitions are mesh-dependent, since they depend on both the number and spacing of the mesh points on the boundary of $\mathscr{R}$.

Historically, two-dimensional spline theory lagged its one-dimensional counterpart by more than 15 years. Birkhoff and Garabedian [1960] attempted a generalization, but it represented only a beginning. A year later, DeBoor [1962] inaugurated two-dimensional spline theory by establishing the existence of the simple type I spline of interpolation to a function $f(t, s)$ on a rectangular mesh. The minimum norm property, best approximation property, convergence properties, and orthogonality properties were obtained by Ahlberg, Nilson, and Walsh [abs. 1964a; 1965b] in 1964.

Before developing the theory of doubly cubic splines further, we consider a useful generalization.

7.2. Partial Splines

Let a rectangle $\mathscr{R}$: $a \leqslant t \leqslant b$; $c \leqslant s \leqslant d$, together with a mesh Δ_t : $a = t_0 < t_1 < \cdots < t_N = b$, be given. In addition, we assume that we are given $N + 1$ functions $f_i(s)$ $(i = 0, 1,..., N)$ defined on the interval $c \leqslant s \leqslant d$. For each s, we can form the one-dimensional type II′ cubic spline $S_{\Delta_t}(Y(s); t)$, where

$$Y(s) = [f_0(s), f_1(s),..., f_N(s)]^{\mathrm{T}}. \tag{7.2.1}$$

In the same manner if $f_0(s) = f_N(s)$, we can form the periodic spline $S_{\Delta_t}(Y(s); t)$, or, if we are given two additional functions $g_0(s)$ and $g_N(s)$, we can form type I and type II splines, where the additional derivatives with respect to t at $t = a$ and $t = b$, for a given value of s, are specified by the functions $g_0(s)$ and $g_N(s)$, respectively. For each s, we have the minimum norm property and the best approximation property holding in a one-dimensional sense. If we require the functions $f_i(s)$ $(i = 0, 1,..., N)$, $g_0(s)$, and $g_N(s)$ to be in $L(c, d)$, then, since $S_{\Delta_t}(Y(s); t)$ depends linearly on these functions and since they reflect its total dependence on s, it follows that $S_{\Delta_t}(Y(s); t)$, $\partial S_{\Delta_t}(Y(s); t)/\partial t$ and $\partial^2 S_{\Delta_t}(Y(s); t)/\partial t^2$ are all in $L(c, d)$. Under these conditions, Theorem 7.2.1, which follows, is typical of the type of theorem valid for partial splines; its proof is immediate from one-dimensional spline theory. Aside from a few remarks regarding convergence and the effect of linear operators on partial splines, we leave the translation of one-dimensional spline theory into a theory for partial splines to the reader.

Theorem 7.2.1. *Let $N + 1$ functions $f_i(s)$ $(i = 0, 1,..., N)$, each in $L(c, d)$, be given, together with a mesh $\Delta_t : a = t_0 < t_1 < \cdots < t_N = b$. Then of all functions $f(t, s)$ defined on the rectangle $\mathscr{R}$: $a \leqslant t \leqslant b$;*

$c \leqslant s \leqslant d$, which coincide with $f_i(s)$ at $t = t_i$ $(i = 0, 1,..., N)$ and which are in $\mathscr{K}^2(a, b)$ for each s in $[c, d]$, the type II′ partial spline $S_{\Delta_t}(Y(s); t)$, where $Y(s)$ is given by (7.2.1), minimizes

$$\int_c^d \int_a^b \left\{\frac{\partial^2 f(t, s)}{\partial t^2}\right\}^2 dt\, ds$$

and is the unique admissible function that minimizes this integral.

As we refine the mesh Δ_t, for each s the functions $S_{\Delta_t}(Y(s); t)$ and $\partial S_{\Delta_t}(Y(s); t)/\partial t$ converge to $f(t, s)$ and $\partial f(t, s)/\partial t$, respectively, uniformly with respect to t. Furthermore, if

$$\int_a^b \left\{\frac{\partial^2 f(t, s)}{\partial t^2}\right\}^2 dt$$

is uniformly bounded as a function of s, the convergence will be uniform with respect to s as well. It is of importance to note that, because of the linear dependence of $S_{\Delta_t}(Y(s); t)$ on the functions $f_i(s)$ $(i = 0, 1,..., N)$, $g_0(s)$, and $g_N(s)$, we have

$$\partial^\alpha S_{\Delta_t}(Y(s); t)/\partial s^\alpha = S_{\Delta_t}(\partial^\alpha Y(s)/\partial s^\alpha; t)$$

for all α for which $\partial^\alpha Y(s)/\partial s^\alpha$ is defined. Indeed, this applies in general to linear operators, provided they are well defined. As a further example, we have

$$\int_c^d S_{\Delta_t}(Y(s); t)\, ds = S_{\Delta_t}\left(\left(\int_c^d Y(s)\, ds; t\right)\right).$$

In what follows, we speak of simple partial splines. We understand by this terminology that the induced one-dimensional splines obtained by fixing the variable s are simple splines.

7.3. Relation of Partial Splines to Doubly Cubic Splines

The concept of a partial spline allows a very direct approach to the construction of doubly cubic splines which reduces the construction to the construction of one-dimensional splines. We proceed as follows. Let $\mathscr{R}$: $a \leqslant t \leqslant b$; $c \leqslant s \leqslant d$ be given, and let $f(t, s)$ be defined on $\mathscr{R}$. If a mesh π on $\mathscr{R}$ is defined by $\Delta_t : a = t_0 < t_1 < \cdots < t_N = b$ and $\Delta_s : c = s_0 < s_1 < \cdots < s_M = d$ and if the partial derivatives occurring in (7.1.1) exist for $f(t, s)$, then we can set

$$\begin{aligned} f_i(s) &= f(t_i, s) \qquad (i = 0, 1,..., N), \\ g_i(s) &= \frac{\partial f(t_i, s)}{\partial t} \qquad (i = 0, N), \end{aligned} \tag{7.3.1}$$

and, for $i = 0, 1, \ldots, N$, construct the type I spline $S_{\Delta_s}(f_i ; s)$ of interpolation to $f_i(s)$ on Δ_s such that $f_i(s) - S_{\Delta_s}(f_i ; s)$ is of type I′. In addition, let $S_{\Delta_s}(g_i ; s)$ $(i = 0, N)$ be similarly defined for $g_0(s)$ and $g_N(s)$, respectively. Now $S_{\Delta_s}(f_i ; s)$ $(i = 0, 1, \ldots, N)$, together with $S_{\Delta_s}(g_i ; s)$ $(i = 0, N)$, defines a type I partial spline, denoted $S_\pi(f; t, s)$, which is easily verified to be a simple doubly cubic spline of interpolation to $f(t, s)$ on π. One need only observe that, for $t_{i-1} \leqslant t \leqslant t_i$,

$$S_\pi(f; t, s) = \sum_{k=0}^{N} A_{ik}(t) \cdot S_{\Delta_s}(f_k ; s) + B_{i0}(t) \cdot S_{\Delta_s}(g_0 ; s) + B_{iN}(t) \cdot S_{\Delta_s}(g_N ; s), \tag{7.3.2}$$

where $A_{ij}(t)$ $(j = 0, 1, \ldots, N)$ and $B_{ij}(t)$ $(j = 0, N)$ are cubic functions of t. But for $s_{j-1} \leqslant s \leqslant s_j$ $(j = 0, 1, \ldots, M)$, we know that $S_{\Delta_s}(f_i ; s)$ $(i = 0, 1, \ldots, N)$, $S_{\Delta_s}(g_i ; s)$ $(i = 0, N)$ are cubic functions of s; consequently, in each rectangle $\mathscr{R}_{ij}$: $t_{i-1} \leqslant t \leqslant t_i$; $s_{j-1} \leqslant s \leqslant s_j$ $(i = 1, 2, \ldots, N;\ j = 1, 2, \ldots, M)$, $S_\pi(f; t, s)$ is a double cubic. It is in $C_2^4(\mathscr{R})$ by the nature of its construction.

The preceding construction has established the existence of at least one simple type I doubly cubic spline of interpolation to $f(t, s)$ on π such that $f(t, s) - S_\pi(f; t, s)$ is of type I′. This, however, immediately raises the question of uniqueness, since a second such spline can be obtained by interchanging the roles of s and t. In order to establish uniqueness, we first extend the minimum norm property to doubly cubic splines; once this is done, a simple uniqueness argument can be given. Uniqueness can also be established through a more careful examination of Eqs. (7.3.2).

The construction of periodic and type II splines of interpolation to $f(t, s)$ on $\mathscr{R}$ proceeds in the same manner. We observe that the cubics in s or t, to which $S_\pi(f; t, s)$ reduces on the boundary of each rectangle $\mathscr{R}_{ij}$,* furnish sufficient information to determine $S_\pi(f; t, s)$ on $\mathscr{R}_{ij}$; these cubics can be obtained from the one-dimensional splines used in the construction of $S_\pi(f; t, s)$. Since the values of $f(t, s)$ and certain of its partial derivatives are required only at a finite number of points, $f(t, s)$ is essentially an arbitrary function on $\mathscr{R}$.

* This statement needs to be qualified to the extent that quantities such as $\partial^2 S_\pi / \partial s\, \partial t$ at the vertices of $\mathscr{R}_{ij}$ are obtained by constructing the one-dimensional splines of interpolation to $\partial S/\partial s$ along the grid lines $s = s_{j-1}$ and $s = s_j$ and then differentiating with respect to t.

7.4. The Fundamental Identity

We assume that $f(t, s)$ is in $C_2^4(\mathscr{R})$ and that the rectangle $\mathscr{R}$: $a \leqslant t \leqslant b$; $c \leqslant s \leqslant d$ is partitioned into subrectangles $\mathscr{R}_{ij} : t_{i-1} \leqslant t \leqslant t_i$; $s_{j-1} \leqslant s \leqslant s_j$ ($i = 1, 2, \ldots, N$; $j = 1, 2, \ldots, M$; $t_0 = a$, $t_N = b$, $s_0 = c$, $s_M = d$) by a mesh π. We have the obvious identity

$$\begin{aligned}\int_c^d \int_a^b \left\{\frac{\partial^4 f(t, s)}{\partial s^2\, \partial t^2}\right\}^2 dt\, ds &= \int_c^d \int_a^b \left\{\frac{\partial^4 S_\pi(t, s)}{\partial s^2\, \partial t^2}\right\}^2 dt\, ds \\ &+ \int_c^d \int_a^b \left\{\frac{\partial^4 f(t, s)}{\partial s^2\, \partial t^2} - \frac{\partial^4 S_\pi(t, s)}{\partial s^2\, \partial t^2}\right\}^2 dt\, ds \\ &+ 2 \int_c^d \int_a^b \left\{\frac{\partial^4 f(t, s)}{\partial s^2\, \partial t^2} - \frac{\partial^4 S_\pi(t, s)}{\partial s^2\, \partial t^2}\right\} \frac{\partial^4 S_\pi(t, s)}{\partial s^2\, \partial t^2}\, dt\, ds.\end{aligned} \tag{7.4.1}$$

We modify the last term in the right-hand member of (7.4.1) by integrating it twice by parts with respect to t. We then have

$$\begin{aligned}&\int_c^d \int_a^b \left\{\frac{\partial^4 f(t, s)}{\partial s^2\, \partial t^2} - \frac{\partial^4 S_\pi(t, s)}{\partial s^2\, \partial t^2}\right\} \frac{\partial^4 S_\pi(t, s)}{\partial s^2\, \partial t^2}\, dt\, ds \\ &= \int_c^d \left\{\sum_{i=1}^N \int_{t_{i-1}}^{t_i} \left\{\frac{\partial^4 f(t, s)}{\partial s^2\, \partial t^2} - \frac{\partial^4 S_\pi(t, s)}{\partial s^2\, \partial t^2}\right\} \frac{\partial^4 S_\pi(t, s)}{\partial s^2\, \partial t^2}\, dt\right\} ds \\ &= \int_c^d \sum_{i=1}^N \left\{- \left\{\frac{\partial^2 f(t, s)}{\partial s^2} - \frac{\partial^2 S_\pi(t, s)}{\partial s^2}\right\} \frac{\partial^5 S_\pi(t, s)}{\partial s^2\, \partial t^3}\right. \\ &\quad \left. + \left\{\frac{\partial^3 f(t, s)}{\partial s^2\, \partial t} - \frac{\partial^3 S_\pi(t, s)}{\partial s^2\, \partial t}\right\} \frac{\partial^4 S_\pi(t, s)}{\partial s^2\, \partial t^2}\right\} \Bigg|_{t_{i-1}}^{t_i} ds,\end{aligned}$$

and, after two more integrations by parts this time with respect to s,

$$\begin{aligned}&\int_c^d \int_a^b \left\{\frac{\partial^4 f(t, s)}{\partial s^2\, \partial t^2} - \frac{\partial^4 S_\pi(t, s)}{\partial s^2\, \partial t^2}\right\} \frac{\partial^4 S_\pi(t, s)}{\partial s^2\, \partial t^2}\, dt\, ds \\ &= \sum_{j=1}^M \left\{ \sum_{i=1}^N \left\{ \{f(t, s) - S_\pi(t, s)\} \frac{\partial^6 S_\pi(t, s)}{\partial s^3\, \partial t^3} \right.\right. \\ &\quad - \left\{\frac{\partial f(t, s)}{\partial s} - \frac{\partial S_\pi(t, s)}{\partial s}\right\} \frac{\partial^5 S_\pi(t, s)}{\partial s^2\, \partial t^3} \\ &\quad - \left\{\frac{\partial f(t, s)}{\partial t} - \frac{\partial S_\pi(t, s)}{\partial t}\right\} \frac{\partial^5 S_\pi(t, s)}{\partial s^3\, \partial t^2} \\ &\quad \left.\left. + \left\{\frac{\partial^2 f(t, s)}{\partial s\, \partial t} - \frac{\partial^2 S_\pi(t, s)}{\partial s\, \partial t}\right\} \frac{\partial^4 S_\pi(t, s)}{\partial s^2\, \partial t^2}\right\} \Bigg|_{t_{i-1}}^{t_i} \right\} \Bigg|_{s_{j-1}}^{s_j}.\end{aligned}$$

If we substitute this result into (7.4.1), we are led to the identity

$$\int_c^d \int_a^b \left\{ \frac{\partial^4 f(t, s)}{\partial s^2\, \partial t^2} \right\}^2 dt\, ds$$

$$= \int_c^d \int_a^b \left\{ \frac{\partial^4 S_\pi(t, s)}{\partial s^2\, \partial t^2} \right\}^2 dt\, ds + \int_c^d \int_a^b \left\{ \frac{\partial^4 f(t, s)}{\partial s^2\, \partial t^2} - \frac{\partial^4 S_\pi(t, s)}{\partial s^2\, \partial t^2} \right\}^2 dt\, ds$$

$$+ 2 \sum_{j=1}^{M} \left\{ \sum_{i=1}^{N} \left[\{f(t, s) - S_\pi(t, s)\} \frac{\partial^6 S_\pi(t, s)}{\partial s^3\, \partial t^3} \right.\right.$$

$$- \left\{ \frac{\partial f(t, s)}{\partial s} - \frac{\partial S_\pi(t, s)}{\partial s} \right\} \frac{\partial^5 S_\pi(t, s)}{\partial s^2\, \partial t^3}$$

$$- \left\{ \frac{\partial f(t, s)}{\partial t} - \frac{\partial S_\pi(t, s)}{\partial t} \right\} \frac{\partial^5 S_\pi(t, s)}{\partial s^3\, \partial t^2}$$

$$\left.\left. + \left\{ \frac{\partial^2 f(t, s)}{\partial s\, \partial t} - \frac{\partial^2 S_\pi(t, s)}{\partial s\, \partial t} \right\} \frac{\partial^4 S_\pi(t, s)}{\partial s^2\, \partial t^2} \right] \Bigg|_{t_{i-1}}^{t_i} \right\} \Bigg|_{s_{j-1}}^{s_j}. \tag{7.4.2}$$

In this identity, which we call the *fundamental identity*, $S_\pi(t, s)$ is a double cubic in each rectangle $\mathscr{R}_{ij}$ $(i = 1, 2,\ldots, N;\ j = 1, 2,\ldots, M)$, but we have not assumed that $S_\pi(t, s)$ is in $C_2^4(\mathscr{R})$. If the latter assumption is made, $S_\pi(t, s)$ is then a simple doubly cubic spline on $\mathscr{R}$, and (7.4.2) reduces to

$$\int_c^d \int_a^b \left\{ \frac{\partial^4 f(t, s)}{\partial s^2\, \partial t^2} \right\}^2 dt\, ds$$

$$= \int_c^d \int_a^b \left\{ \frac{\partial^4 S(t, s)}{\partial s^2\, \partial t^2} \right\}^2 dt\, ds + \int_c^d \int_a^b \left\{ \frac{\partial^4 f(t, s)}{\partial s^2\, \partial t^2} - \frac{\partial^4 S_\pi(t, s)}{\partial s^2\, \partial t^2} \right\}^2 dt\, ds$$

$$+ 2 \sum_{j=1}^{M} \left\{ \sum_{i=1}^{N} \{f(t, s) - S_\pi(t, s)\} \frac{\partial^0 S_\pi(t, s)}{\partial s^3\, \partial t^3} \Bigg|_{t_{i-1}}^{t_i} \right\} \Bigg|_{s_{j-1}}^{s_j}$$

$$- 2 \left\{ \sum_{i=1}^{N} \left\{ \frac{\partial f(t, s)}{\partial s} - \frac{\partial S_\pi(t, s)}{\partial s} \right\} \frac{\partial^5 S_\pi(t, s)}{\partial s^2\, \partial t^3} \Bigg|_{t_{i-1}}^{t_i} \right\} \Bigg|_c^d$$

$$- 2 \left\{ \sum_{j=1}^{M} \left\{ \frac{\partial f(t, s)}{\partial t} - \frac{\partial S_\pi(t, s)}{\partial t} \right\} \frac{\partial^5 S_\pi(t, s)}{\partial t^3\, \partial s^2} \Bigg|_{s_{j-1}}^{s_j} \right\} \Bigg|_a^b$$

$$+ 2 \left\{ \frac{\partial^2 f(t, s)}{\partial s\, \partial t} - \frac{\partial^2 S_\pi(t, s)}{\partial s\, \partial t} \right\} \frac{\partial^4 S_\pi(t, s)}{\partial s^2\, \partial t^2} \Bigg|_a^b \Bigg|_c^d. \tag{7.4.3}$$

It is important to note that, although we cannot expect $\partial^5 S_\pi(t, s)/\partial s^2\, \partial t^3$ to be continuous at a grid line $t = t_j$, both its left-hand and right-hand limits as $t \to t_j$ are continuous functions of s. A similar observation applies to $\partial^5 S_\pi(t, s)/\partial s^3\,\partial t^2$ with the roles of s and t interchanged. This fact has been used in the reduction of the fundamental identity to the form (7.4.3), which it assumes for simple doubly cubic splines.

7.5. The First Integral Relation

Under a variety of auxiliary conditions, the fundamental identity reduces to the integral relation

$$\int_c^d \int_a^b \left\{\frac{\partial^4 f(s, t)}{\partial s^2\,\partial t^2}\right\}^2 dt\,ds = \int_c^d \int_a^b \left\{\frac{\partial^4 S_\pi(t, s)}{\partial s^2\,\partial t^2}\right\}^2 dt\,ds + \int_c^d \int_a^b \left\{\frac{\partial^4 f(t, s)}{\partial s^2\,\partial t^2} - \frac{\partial^4 S_\pi(t, s)}{\partial s^2\,\partial t^2}\right\}^2 dt\,ds \tag{7.5.1}$$

which we call the *first integral relation*. Again, this is a direct generalization of the one-dimentional situation. For simple doubly cubic splines of interpolation, we have the following theorem.

Theorem 7.5.1. *Let $\mathscr{R}$: $a \leqslant t \leqslant b$; $c \leqslant s \leqslant d$ be given along with a mesh π defined by Δ_t: $a = t_0 < t_1 < \cdots < t_N = b$ and Δ_s: $c = s_0 < s_1 < \cdots < s_M = d$. Let $f(t, s)$ be in $C_2^4(\mathscr{R})$. If $S_\pi(f; t, s)$ is a simple doubly cubic spline of interpolation to $f(t, s)$ on π such that one of the conditions,* (a) *$f(t, s) - S_\pi(f; t, s)$ is of type I',* (b) *$S_\pi(f; t, s)$ is of type II',* (c) *$f(t, s)$ and $S_\pi(f; t, s)$ are doubly periodic, is satisfied, then*

$$\int_c^d \int_a^b \left\{\frac{\partial^4 f(t, s)}{\partial s^2\,\partial t^2}\right\}^2 dt\,ds = \int_c^d \int_a^b \left\{\frac{\partial^4 S_\pi(f; t, s)}{\partial s^2\,\partial t^2}\right\}^2 dt\,ds + \int_c^d \int_a^b \left\{\frac{\partial^4 f(t, s)}{\partial s^2\,\partial t^2} - \frac{\partial S^4(f; t, s)}{\partial s^2\,\partial t^2}\right\}^2 dt\,ds.$$

Of course, the first integral relation is valid under other end conditions.

7.6. The Minimum Norm Property

As a direct corollary of Theorem 7.5.1, we obtain a generalization to doubly cubic splines of the minimum norm property of one-dimensional splines. We formalize this in Theorem 7.6.1, which follows.

Theorem 7.6.1. *Let $\mathscr{R}$: $a \leqslant t \leqslant b$; $c \leqslant s \leqslant d$ be given along with a mesh π defined by Δ_t: $a = t_0 < t_1 < \cdots < t_N = b$ and Δ_s:*

$c = s_0 < s_1 \cdots < s_M = d$. *In addition, let* $\{f_{ij}\}$ $(i = 0, 1, 2, \ldots, N;$ $j = 0, 1, \ldots, M)$ *be a prescribed set of real numbers, where* f_{ij} *is associated with the mesh point* (t_i, s_j). *Then of all functions* $f(t, s)$ *in* $C_2^4(\mathscr{R})$ *the type II′ spline of interpolation to the values* f_{ij} *on* π *minimizes*

$$\int_c^d \int_a^b \left\{\frac{\partial^4 f(t, s)}{\partial s^2\, \partial t^2}\right\}^2 dt\, ds \tag{7.6.1}$$

and is the unique admissible function that minimizes this integral. If, in addition, $\partial f(t, s)/\partial t$ *is prescribed at* (t_i, s_j) $(i = 0, N;\ j = 0, 1, \ldots, M)$, $\partial f(t, s)/\partial s$ *is prescribed at* (t_i, s_j) $(i = 0, 1, \ldots, N;\ j = 0, M)$, *and* $\partial^2 f(t, s)/\partial t\, \partial s$ *is prescribed at* (t_i, s_j) $(i = 0, N;\ s = 0, M)$, *then (7.6.1) is minimized by the corresponding type I spline of interpolation. If* $f_{0j} = f_{Nj}$ $(j = 0, 1, \ldots, M)$ *and* $f_{i0} = f_{iM}$ $(i = 0, 1, \ldots, N)$, *then (7.6.1) is minimized by the doubly periodic spline of interpolation. In both these cases we also have uniqueness.*

As indicated, the fact that (7.6.1) is minimized follows from the first integral relation. The latter also implies that any other function $g(t, s)$ minimizing (7.6.1) differs from the spline of interpolation by a linear function of s and t; it follows from the interpolation requirements that the linear function vanishes identically.

7.7. Uniqueness and Existence

With the establishment of Theorem 7.6.1, we have provided an easy means of demonstrating the uniqueness of type I, type II, and doubly periodic, doubly cubic splines of interpolation, for the argument can now proceed along the same lines as in the one-dimensional case.* The doubly periodic spline of interpolation is typical. Thus, let $S_\pi(f; t, s)$ and $\hat{S}_\pi(f; t, s)$ be two doubly periodic splines interpolating on a mesh π to a function $f(t, s)$ defined on a rectangle $\mathscr{R}$. Then their difference $S_\pi(f; t, s) - \hat{S}_\pi(f; t, s)$ is a doubly cubic spline that interpolates to the zero function $Z(t, s)$ on π, and consequently it follows from the minimum norm property that $S_\pi(f; t, s) - \hat{S}_\pi(f; t, s)$ must differ from $Z(x)$ by a solution of

$$\partial^4 f/\partial s^2\, \partial t^2 = 0,$$

that is, by a linear function of s and t. Interpolation requirements then ensure that

$$S_\pi(f; t, s) \equiv \hat{S}_\pi(f; t, s).$$

* For splines possessing the minimum norm property, uniqueness is an immediate corollary of Theorem 7.6.1.

Theorem 7.7.1. *Let* $\mathscr{R}$: $a \leqslant t \leqslant b$; $c \leqslant s \leqslant d$ *be given along with a mesh* π *defined by* Δ_t : $a = t_0 < t_1 < \cdots < t_N = b$ *and* Δ_s : $c = s_0 < s_1 < \cdots < s_M = d$. *If* $f(t, s)$ *is defined on* $\mathscr{R}$ *and if* $S_\pi(f; t, s)$ *is a simple doubly cubic spline of interpolation to* $f(t, s)$ *on* π *such that one of the conditions,* (a) $f(t, s) - S_\pi(f; t, s)$ *is of type I'*, (b) $f(t, s) - S_\pi(f; t, s)$ *is of type II'*, (c) $f(t, s)$ *and* $S_\pi(f; t, s)$ *are doubly periodic, is satisfied, then* $S_\pi(f; t, s)$ *is unique.*

REMARK 7.7.1. Since $f(t, s)$ is only specified at mesh points, Theorem 7.7.1 asserts that in any type I or type II equivalence class there is at most one spline of interpolation to $f(t, s)$ on π.

The existence proof in Chapter III for one-dimensional cubic splines consists of exhibiting a linear system of equations which ensures that the interpolation and continuity requirements imposed on $S_\pi(f; t, s)$ are satisfied, and of then using uniqueness to show that the system of linear equations is solvable. In two-dimensions, it is not trivial to write down in a straightforward manner a finite system of linear equations which will ensure the desired continuity of $S_\pi(f; t, s)$ and its derivatives along grid lines. Existence, however, follows from the construction of $S_\pi(f; t, s)$ contained in Section 7.3, since the latter requires only the existence of one-dimensional splines. Once existence has been established, the doubly cubic nature of $S_\pi(f; t, s)$ in each mesh rectangle $\mathscr{R}_{ij}$ allows an appropriate system of independent linear equations (cf. Ahlberg *et al.* [1965b]) to be formulated.

7.8. Best Approximation

Because of the linear dependence of a spline on its defining values, we have, under appropriately chosen end conditions, the decomposition

$$S_\pi(f + g; t, s) = S_\pi(f; t, s) + S_\pi(g; t, s) \tag{7.8.1}$$

for splines of interpolation on a mesh π. In particular, (7.8.1) is valid if any one of the conditions,

(a) $S_\pi(f + g; t, s) - S_\pi(f; t, s) - S_\pi(g; t, s)$ is of type I',

(b) $S_\pi(f + g; t, s) - S_\pi(f; t, s) - S_\pi(g; t, s)$ is of type II',

(c) $f(t, s), g(t, s), S_\pi(f + g; t, s), S_\pi(f; t, s)$, and $S_\pi(g; t, s)$ are doubly periodic,

is satisfied. If we apply the decomposition (7.8.1) to $f(t, s) - S_\pi(t, s)$, where $S_\pi(t, s)$ is an arbitrary simple spline with respect to π, then in virtue of the minimum norm property we have

$$\int_c^d \int_a^b \{f''(t, s) - S''_\pi(t, s)\}^2\, dt\, ds$$

$$= \int_c^d \int_a^b \{f''(t, s) - S''_\pi(t, s) - S''_\pi(f - S_\pi\,; t, s)\}^2\, dt\, ds$$

$$+ \int_c^d \int_a^b \{S''_\pi(f - S_\pi\,; t, s)\}^2\, dt\, ds$$

$$= \int_c^d \int_a^b \{f''(t, s) - S''_\pi(f; t, s)\}^2\, dt\, ds + \int_c^d \int_a^b \{S''_\pi(f - S_\pi\,; t, s)\}^2\, dt\, ds,$$

provided end conditions are such that $S_\pi(S_\pi\,; t, s) = S_\pi(t, s)$. This argument establishes the *best approximation property* of simple doubly cubic splines.

Theorem 7.8.1. *Let a rectangle* $\mathscr{R}$: $a \leqslant t \leqslant b$; $c \leqslant s \leqslant d$ *be given along with a mesh* π *defined by* $\Delta_t : a = t_0 < t_1 < \cdots < t_N = b$ *and* Δ_s : $c = s_0 < s_1 < \cdots < s_M = d$. *Then if* $f(t, s)$ *is in* $C_2^4(\mathscr{R})$, $S_\pi(t, s)$ *is any simple spline with respect to* π, *and* $S_\pi(f; t, s)$ *is the simple spline of interpolation to* $f(t, s)$ *on* π *such that* $f(t, s) - S_\pi(f; t, s)$ *is of type* I', *we have*

$$\int_c^d \int_a^b \{f''(t, s) - S''_\pi(t, s)\}^2\, dt\, ds \geqslant \int_c^d \int_a^b \{f''(t, s) - S''_\pi(f; t, s)\}^2\, dt\, ds, \quad (7.8.2)$$

and $S_\pi(f; t, s)$ *is unique in this sense up to a solution of* $\partial^4 f(t, s)/\partial s^2\, \partial t^2 = 0$. *If all functions are required to be doubly periodic or to be in a prescribed type II equivalence class, then (7.8.2) is valid if* $S_\pi(f; t, s)$ *is interpreted as the corresponding spline of interpolation. In the doubly periodic case,* $S_\pi(f; t, s)$ *is unique up to a constant; otherwise, uniqueness is up to a solution of* $\partial^4 f(t, s)/\partial s^2\, \partial t^2 = 0$.

7.9. Cardinal Splines

Cardinal splines have occurred elsewhere in this book (cf. Section 2.7); in interpreting the representation (7.3.2) for a doubly cubic spline, they again serve a useful purpose. In a very broad sense, we can define a cardinal spline to be a spline for which exactly one defining value is one and all others are zero. The functions

$$\left.\begin{array}{lll} A_j(t) = A_{ij}(t), & t_{i-1} \leqslant t \leqslant t_i & (i = 1, 2,..., N; j = 0, 1,..., N), \\ B_0(t) = B_{i0}(t), & t_{i-1} \leqslant t \leqslant t_i & (i = 1, 2,..., N), \\ B_N(t) = B_{iN}(t), & t_{i-1} \leqslant t \leqslant t_i & (i = 1, 2,..., N), \end{array}\right\} \quad (7.9.1)$$

which enter into (7.3.2), are one-dimensional cardinal splines. We have, however, the one-dimensional representations

$$\left.\begin{aligned}
S_{\Delta_s}(f_i\,;s) &= \sum_{j=0}^{M} \bar{A}_j(s) f(t_i\,, s_j) + \bar{B}_0(s)\frac{\partial f(t_i\,, s_0)}{\partial s} + \bar{B}_M(s)\frac{\partial f(t_i\,, s_M)}{\partial s} \\
&\qquad\qquad\qquad\qquad (i = 0, 1,\ldots, N), \\
S_{\Delta_s}(g_0\,;s) &= \sum_{j=0}^{M} \bar{A}_j(s)\frac{\partial f(t_0\,, s_j)}{\partial t} + \bar{B}_0(s)\frac{\partial^2 f(t_0\,, s_0)}{\partial s\,\partial t} + \bar{B}_M(s)\frac{\partial^2 f(t_0\,, s_M)}{\partial s\,\partial t}, \\
S_{\Delta_s}(g_N\,;s) &= \sum_{\partial=0}^{M} \bar{A}_j(s)\frac{\partial f(t_N\,, s_j)}{\partial t} + \bar{B}_0(s)\frac{\partial^2 f(t_N\,, s_0)}{\partial s\,\partial t} \\
&\quad + \bar{B}_M(s)\frac{\partial^2 f(t_N\,, s_M)}{\partial s\,\partial t},
\end{aligned}\right\} \tag{7.9.2}$$

where the functions $\bar{A}_j(s)$, $\bar{B}_0(s)$, and $\bar{B}_M(s)$ are the corresponding one-dimensional cardinal splines defined by the mesh Δ_s :

$$c = s_0 < s_1 < \cdots < s_M = d.$$

If the representations (7.9.2) are used in (7.3.2), we obtain

$$\begin{aligned}
S_\pi(f; t, s) &= \sum_{i=0}^{N}\sum_{j=0}^{M} C_{ij}(t, s) f(t_i\,, s_j) \\
&\quad + \sum_{j=0}^{M} D_{0j}(t, s)\frac{\partial f(t_0\,, s_j)}{\partial t} + \sum_{j=0}^{M} D_{Nj}(t, s)\frac{\partial f(t_N\,, s_j)}{\partial t} \\
&\quad + \sum_{i=0}^{N} E_{i0}(t, s)\frac{\partial f(t_i\,, s_0)}{\partial s} + \sum_{i=0}^{N} E_{iM}(t, s)\frac{\partial f(t_i\,, s_M)}{\partial s} \\
&\quad + F_{00}(t, s)\frac{\partial^2 f(t_0\,, s_0)}{\partial s\,\partial t} + F_{N0}(t, s)\frac{\partial^2 f(t_N\,, s_0)}{\partial s\,\partial t} \\
&\quad + F_{0M}(t, s)\frac{\partial^2 f(t_0\,, s_M)}{\partial s\,\partial t} + F_{NM}(t, s)\frac{\partial^2 f(t_N\,, s_M)}{\partial s\,\partial t},
\end{aligned} \tag{7.9.3.1}$$

where

$$\left.\begin{aligned}
C_{ij}(t, s) &= A_i(t)\,\bar{A}_j(s) && (i = 0, 1,\ldots, N;\ \ j = 0, 1,\ldots, M), \\
D_{ij}(t, s) &= B_i(t)\,\bar{A}_j(s) && (i = 0, N;\ \ j = 0, 1,\ldots, M), \\
E_{ij}(t, s) &= A_i(t)\,\bar{B}_j(s) && (i = 0, 1,\ldots, N;\ \ j = 0, M), \\
F_{ij}(t, s) &= B_i(t)\,\bar{B}_j(s) && (i = 0, N;\ \ j = 0, M).
\end{aligned}\right\} \tag{7.9.3.2}$$

The functions $C_{ij}(t, s)$, $D_{ij}(t, s)$, $E_{ij}(t, s)$, $F_{ij}(t, s)$ are clearly the two-dimensional cardinal splines needed to represent $S_\pi(f; t, s)$, and as (7.9.3.2) demonstrates, they are obtainable by forming pairwise products of one-dimensional cardinal splines. Thus, although $S_\pi(f; t, s)$ is not normally representable as the product of a function of t and a function of s, it is always representable as a finite sum of such products.

7.10. Convergence Properties

The convergence properties of doubly cubic splines are virtually immediate consequences of the representation (7.3.2) which may be written as

$$S_\pi(f; t, s) = \sum_{i=0}^{N} A_i(t) S_{\Delta_s}(f_i\,; s) + B_0(t) S_{\Delta_s}(g_0\,; s) + B_N(t) S_{\Delta_s}(g_N\,; s) \qquad (7.10.1)$$

with the aid of the notation of (7.9.1). Consequently,

$$\lim_{\|\Delta_s\| \to 0} S_\pi(f; t, s) = \sum_{i=0}^{N} A_i(t) f(t_i\,, s) + B_0(t) \frac{\partial f(t_0\,, s)}{\partial t} + B_N(t) \frac{\partial f(t_N\,, s)}{\partial t},$$

and

$$\lim_{\|\Delta_t\| \to 0} \lim_{\|\Delta_s\| \to 0} S_\pi(f; t, s) = f(t, s).$$

If $f(t, s)$ is in $C_2^4(\mathscr{R})$, convergence is uniform with respect to both t and s, and the iterated limit can be taken as the double limit. By differentiating $S_\pi(f; t, s)$ and using similar arguments, we obtain the following theorem.

Theorem 7.10.1. *Let* $\mathscr{R}$: $a \leqslant t \leqslant b$; $c \leqslant s \leqslant d$ *be given, together with a mesh* π *defined by* $\Delta_t : a = t_0 < t_1 < \cdots < t_N = b$ *and* $\Delta_s : c = s_0 < s_1 < \cdots < s_M = d$. *If* $f(t, s)$ *is in* $C_2^4(\mathscr{R})$, *and* $\|\pi\| \to 0$, *then* $\partial^\gamma S_\pi(f; t, s)/\partial s^\alpha\, \partial t^\beta$ *converges to* $\partial^\gamma f(t, s)/\partial s^\alpha\, \partial t^\beta$ *uniformly with respect to* t *and* s *for* $\gamma = \alpha + \beta \leqslant 2$, $\alpha \leqslant 1$, $\beta \leqslant 1$, *and*

$$\frac{\partial^\gamma f(t, s)}{\partial s^\alpha\, \partial t^\beta} = \frac{\partial^\gamma S_\pi(f; t, s)}{\partial s^\alpha\, \partial t^\beta} + O(\|\Delta_t\|^{2-\beta-1/2} + \|\Delta_s\|^{2-\alpha-1/2}). \qquad (7.10.2)$$

If $f(t, s)$ *is in* $C_4^8(\mathscr{R})$, *then*

$$\frac{\partial^\gamma f(t, s)}{\partial s^\alpha\, \partial t^\beta} = \frac{\partial^\gamma S_\pi(f; t, s)}{\partial s^\alpha\, \partial t^\beta} + O(\|\Delta_t\|^{3-\beta} + \|\Delta_s\|^{3-\alpha}); \qquad (7.10.3)$$

moreover, (7.10.3) is valid for $\gamma = \alpha + \beta \leqslant 6$, $\alpha \leqslant 3$, $\beta \leqslant 3$, *provided the ratios of the mesh norms to the minimum distance between adjacent mesh points are uniformly bounded as* $\| \Delta_s \|$ *and* $\| \Delta_t \|$ *approach zero; indeed, under these conditions the exponents* $3 - \beta$ *and* $3 - \alpha$ *may be replaced by* $4 - \beta$ *and* $4 - \alpha$, *respectively.*

REMARK 7.10.1. The end conditions required of $S_\pi(f; t, s)$ are essentially dictated by one-dimensional spline theory. In particular, Theorem 7.10.1 is valid if $S_\pi(f; t, s)$ is a spline of interpolation to $f(t, s)$ on π such that $f(t, s) - S_\pi(f; t, s)$ is of either type I′ or type II′. If both $f(t, s)$ and $S_\pi(f; t, s)$ are doubly periodic, the theorem is valid. For (7.10.2) to apply, the splines $S_\pi(f; t, s)$ need only be restricted to a fixed type II equivalence class.

7.11. The Second Integral Relation

There is an analog of the second integral relation for one-dimensional splines which applies to doubly cubic splines. It asserts that under suitable end conditions

$$\int_c^d \int_a^b \left\{ \frac{\partial^4 f(t, s)}{\partial s^2\, \partial t^2} - \frac{\partial^4 S_\pi(f; t, s)}{\partial s^2\, \partial t^2} \right\}^2 dt\, ds$$
$$= \int_c^d \int_a^b \{ f(t, s) - S_\pi(f; t, s) \} \frac{\partial^8 f(t, s)}{\partial s^4\, \partial t^4}\, dt\, ds; \qquad (7.11.1)$$

however, since convergence properties can be established directly from the analogous convergence properties of one-dimensional splines via the representation (7.10.1), its importance is diminished. Theorem 7.11.1 gives several conditions under which (7.11.1) is valid; its proof proceeds along the same general lines as the proof used to establish the first integral relation for doubly cubic splines.

Theorem 7.11.1. *Let a rectangle* $\mathscr{R}$: $a \leqslant t \leqslant b$; $c \leqslant s \leqslant d$ *be given along with a mesh* π *defined by* $\Delta_t : a = t_0 < t_1 < \cdots < t_N = b$ *and* $\Delta_s : c = s_0 < s_1 < \cdots < s_M = d$. *Let* $f(t, s)$ *be in* $C_4^{\,8}(\mathscr{R})$ *and* $S_\pi(f; t, s)$ *be a spline of interpolation to* $f(t, s)$ *on* π. *If one of the conditions,* (a) $f(t, s) - S_\pi(f; t, s)$ *is of type I′,* (b) $f(t, s) - S_\pi(f; t, s)$ *is of type II′,* (c) $f(t, s)$ *and* $S_\pi(f; t, s)$ *are doubly periodic, is satisfied, then*

$$\int_c^d \int_a^b \left\{ \frac{\partial^4 f(t, s)}{\partial s^2\, \partial t^2} - \frac{\partial^4 S_\pi(f; t, s)}{\partial s^2\, \partial t^2} \right\}^2 dt\, ds$$
$$= \int_c^d \int_a^b \{ f(t, s) - S_\pi(f; t, s) \} \frac{\partial^8 f(t, s)}{\partial s^4\, \partial t^4}\, dt\, ds.$$

7.12. The Direct Product of Hilbert Spaces

Let H_1 and H_2 be separable Hilbert spaces with bases $\{e_i\}$ $(i = 1, 2, ...)$ and $\{f_j\}$ $(j = 1, 2, ...)$, respectively, and let $\bar{H}$ denote the linear space generated by the quantities $\{h_{ij}\} = \{e_i f_j\}$ $(i = 1, 2, ...;\ j = 1, 2, ...)$. If we define

$$(h_{ij}, h_{kl})_{\bar{H}} = (e_i, e_k)_{\bar{H}_1} \cdot (f_j, f_l)_{\bar{H}_2}, \tag{7.12.1}$$

where $(\cdot, \cdot)_{H_1}$ and $(\cdot, \cdot)_{H_2}$ are the inner products associated with H_1 and H_2, then $(\cdot, \cdot)_{\bar{H}}$ can be extended by linearity to an inner product for $\bar{H}$. Let

$$\| u \|_{\bar{H}} = (u, u)_{\bar{H}}^{1/2}; \tag{7.12.2}$$

then we can complete $\bar{H}$ with respect to $\| \cdot \|_{\bar{H}}$ and extend the inner product $(\cdot, \cdot)_{\bar{H}}$ to the completion of $\bar{H}$. We denote the latter by H and the extended inner product by $(\cdot, \cdot)_H$. It is readily verified that H is a separable Hilbert space with respect to $(\cdot, \cdot)_H$. A more detailed discussion of this construction is given by Sard [1963, p. 354].

Our motivation for discussing the direct product of Hilbert spaces is to form the direct product of $\mathscr{K}^2(a, b)$ and $\mathscr{K}^2(c, d)$. In Chapter III, we considered $\mathscr{K}^2(a, b)$ as a pseudo-Hilbert space under the pseudo-inner product

$$(f, g) = \int_a^b f''(t) g''(t)\, dt,$$

and we determined several orthonormal bases for $\mathscr{K}^2(a, b)$. The most important of these bases for our purposes are the canonical mesh bases. Let $\{u_i(t)\}$ $(i = 1, 2, ...)$ be a canonical mesh basis for $\mathscr{K}^2(a, b)$ and $\{v_j(s)\}$ $(j = 1, 2, ...)$ be a canonical mesh basis for $\mathscr{K}^2(c, d)$. If $\mathscr{R}$: $a \leqslant t \leqslant b$; $c \leqslant s \leqslant d$ denotes the rectangle determined by (a, b) and (c, d), we let $\mathscr{K}^2(\mathscr{R})$ denote the direct product of $\mathscr{K}^2(a, b)$ and $\mathscr{K}^2(c, d)$. It follows that

$$(f, g) = \int_c^d \int_a^b \left\{ \frac{\partial^4 f(t, s)}{\partial s^2\, \partial t^2} \cdot \frac{\partial^4 g(t, s)}{\partial s^2\, \partial t^2} \right\} dt\, ds \tag{7.12.3}$$

is the proper inner product for $\mathscr{K}^2(\mathscr{R})$, since

$$\int_c^d \int_a^b \left\{ \frac{\partial^4 u_i(t)\, v_j(s)}{\partial s^2\, \partial t^2} \cdot \frac{\partial^4 u_l(t)\, v_k(s)}{\partial s^2\, \partial t^2} \right\} dt\, ds$$
$$= \int_a^b u_i''(t) \cdot u_l''(t)\, dt \int_c^d v_j''(s)\, v_k''(s)\, ds.*$$

We now show that $C_2^4(\mathscr{R}) \subseteq \mathscr{K}^2(\mathscr{R})$.

* This relation justifies interpreting $\mathscr{K}^2(\mathscr{R})$ as a space of classes of functions on $\mathscr{R}$ and the symbolic product $u_i v_j$ as the pointwise product of the functions $u_i(t)$ and $v_j(s)$. We must, however, identify functions differing by a linear function of t and s.

Let $\{\pi_N\}$ $(N = 1, 2, \ldots)$ be a sequence of meshes on $\mathscr{R}$ defined by Δ_t^N: $a = t_0^N < t_1^N < \cdots < t_{n_N}^N = b$ and Δ_s^N: $c = s_0^N < s_1^N < \cdots < s_{m_N}^N = d$, where π_M refines π_N if $M > N$, and let $\{S_N(f; t, s)\}$ $(N = 1, 2, \ldots)$ be an associated sequence of splines of interpolation on these meshes to a function $f(t, s)$ in $C_2^4(\mathscr{R})$. Since, for $M > N$, $S_N(f; t, s)$ is a spline of interpolation to $S_M(f; t, s)$ on π_N, it follows, if the first integral relation applies, that

$$\int_c^d \int_a^b \left\{ \frac{\partial^4 S_M(f; t, s)}{\partial s^2\, \partial t^2} - \frac{\partial^4 S_N(f; t, s)}{\partial s^2\, \partial t^2} \right\}^2 dt\, ds$$
$$= \int_c^d \int_a^b \left\{ \frac{\partial^4 S_M(f; t, s)}{\partial s^2\, \partial t^2} \right\}^2 dt\, ds - \int_c^d \int_a^b \left\{ \frac{\partial^4 S_N(f; t, s)}{\partial s^2\, \partial t^2} \right\}^2 dt\, ds.$$

Therefore, the sequence of real numbers

$$\int_c^d \int_a^b \left\{ \frac{\partial^4 S_N(f; t, s)}{\partial s^2\, \partial t^2} \right\}^2 dt\, ds \qquad (N = 1, 2, \ldots)$$

is monotonically increasing and is bounded above by

$$\int_c^d \int_a^b \left\{ \frac{\partial^4 f(t, s)}{\partial s^2\, \partial t^2} \right\}^2 dt\, ds;$$

consequently, the sequence

$$\left\{ \frac{\partial^4 S_N(f; t, s)}{\partial s^2\, \partial t^2} \right\} \qquad (N = 1, 2, \ldots)$$

is a Cauchy sequence in $L^2(\mathscr{R})$ and has a limit $g(t, s)$ in $L^2(\mathscr{R})$. Proceeding as in Chapter III, we let

$$G(t, s) = \frac{\partial^2 f(a, c)}{\partial s\, \partial t} + \int_c^s \int_a^t g(x, y)\, dx\, dy.$$

We then have

$$G(t, s) - \frac{\partial^2 S_N(f; t, s)}{\partial s\, \partial t} = \left\{ \frac{\partial^2 f(a, c)}{\partial s\, \partial t} - \frac{\partial^2 S_N(f; a, c)}{\partial s\, \partial t} \right\}$$
$$+ \int_c^s \int_a^t \left\{ g(x, y) - \frac{\partial^4 S_N(f; x, y)}{\partial y^2\, \partial x^2} \right\} dx\, dy.$$

We can now conclude from Theorem 7.10.1, the definition of $g(t, s)$, and Schwarz's inequality

$$\lim_{N \to \infty} \frac{\partial^2 S_N(f; t, s)}{\partial s\, \partial t} = G(t, s),$$

from which it follows that

$$G(t, s) \equiv \frac{\partial^2 f(t, s)}{\partial s\, \partial t}.$$

Consequently, we have

$$g(t, s) = \frac{\partial^4 f(t, s)}{\partial s^2\, \partial t^2} \quad \text{a.e.,}$$

$$\lim_{N\to\infty} \| f - S_{N,f} \|_{\mathscr{K}^2(R)} = 0.$$

Theorem 7.12.1. *Let* $\mathscr{R}$: $a \leqslant t \leqslant b$; $c \leqslant s \leqslant d$ *be given, together with a sequence of meshes* $\{\pi_N\}$ $(N = 1, 2,...)$, *where* π_N *is defined by* Δ_t^N: $a = t_0^N < t_1^N < \cdots < t_{n_N}^N = b$ *and* Δ_s^N: $c = s_0^N < s_1^N < \cdots < s_{m_N}^N = d$ *for each N. Let* $\| \pi_N \| \to 0$ *as* $N \to \infty$ *and* π_N *refine* $\pi_{N'}$ *for* $N' < N$.* *If* $f(t, s)$ *is in* $C_2^4(\mathscr{R})$ *and if one of the conditions,* (a) $f(t, s) - S_N(f; t, s)$ *is of type I'* $(N = 1, 2,...)$, (b) *each* $S_N(f; t, s)$ *is of type II'* $(N = 1, 2,...)$, (c) $f(t, s)$ *and each* $S_N(f; t, s)$ *are doubly periodic, where* $S_N(f; t, s)$ *is a spline of interpolation to* $f(t, s)$ *on* π_N, *is satisfied, then*

$$\lim_{N\to\infty} \| f - S_{N,f} \|_{\mathscr{K}^2(R)} = 0.$$

Corollary 7.12.1. $C_2^4(\mathscr{R}) \subset \mathscr{K}^2(R)$.

7.13. The Method of Cardinal Splines

In Section 7.9, doubly cubic cardinal splines were constructed by multiplying together pairs of cubic cardinal splines; in this section, we exploit this and other properties of cardinal splines in order to approximate, under suitable conditions, solutions of second-order partial differential equations. Let $\mathscr{R}$: $a \leqslant t \leqslant b$; $c \leqslant s \leqslant d$ and $f(t, s)$ in $C_4^8(\mathscr{R})$ be given. If $\{u_i(t, s)\}$ $(i = 1, 2,...)$ is an orthonormal basis for $\mathscr{K}^2(\mathscr{R})$ which is obtained by forming the direct product of canonical mesh bases for $\mathscr{K}^2(a, b)$ and $\mathscr{K}^2(c, d)$, respectively, then

$$\left\| f - \sum_{i=1}^{\infty} a_i u_i \right\|_{\mathscr{K}^2(\mathscr{R})} = 0, \qquad (7.13.1.1)$$

$$a_i = \int_c^d \int_a^b \frac{\partial^4 f(t, s)}{\partial s^2\, \partial t^2} \cdot \frac{\partial^4 u_i(t, s)}{\partial s^2\, \partial t^2}\, dt\, ds \qquad (i = 1, 2,...). \qquad (7.13.1.2)$$

* We can define $\| \pi_N \|$ as $\max\{\| \Delta_t^N \|, \| \Delta_s^N \|\}$.

Moreover, if the constants b_1, b_2, b_3, b_4 are properly chosen, we have

$$f(t, s) = b_1 + b_2 t + b_3 s + b_4 ts + \sum_{i=1}^{\infty} a_i u_i(t, s). \tag{7.13.2}$$

If we let

$$S_N(f; t, s) = b_1 + b_2 t + b_3 s + b_4 ts + \sum_{i=1}^{N} a_i u_i(t, s) \qquad (N = 1, 2, \ldots) \tag{7.13.3}$$

and then restrict ourselves to a suitable subsequence, the $S_N(f; t, s)$ are splines of interpolation to $f(t, s)$ to which Theorem 7.10.1 applies. Thus, for $\gamma = \alpha + \beta$, where $0 \leqslant \alpha, \beta \leqslant 4$ and $f(t, s) = S_N(f; t, s) + E_N(f; t, s)$, we have

$$\begin{aligned} \frac{\partial^\gamma f(t, s)}{\partial s^\alpha\, \partial t^\beta} &= \frac{\partial^\gamma S_N(f; t, s)}{\partial s^\alpha\, \partial t^\beta} + \frac{(\partial^\gamma E_N(f; t, s)}{\partial s^\alpha\, \partial t^\beta} \\ &= \frac{\partial^\gamma S_N(f; t, s)}{\partial s^\alpha\, \partial t^\beta} + O(\| \Delta_t^N \|^{4-\beta} + \| \Delta_s^N \|^{4-\alpha}). \end{aligned} \tag{7.13.4}$$

In Eq. (7.13.4), Δ_t^N and Δ_s^N are intended to denote one-dimensional meshes arising in the construction of the canonical mesh bases from which $u_i(t, s)$ $(i = 1, 2, \ldots, N)$ were obtained. We observe that, if we assume $f(t, s)$ to be in $C_2^4(\mathscr{R})$ rather than in $C_4^8(\mathscr{R})$, then the proof of Theorem 7.10.1 holds in view of Theorem 2.3.4, and we have convergence for $0 \leqslant \alpha, \beta \leqslant 2$; but the rate of convergence is slower, and we cannot estimate the error in as precise a fashion. Thus, although we use (7.13.4) in demonstrating convergence, our results apply under much broader circumstances.

Assume that we are given a partial differential equation of the form

$$\begin{aligned} a_1(t, s)\, U_{tt} + a_2(t, s)\, U_{st} + a_3(t, s)\, U_{ss} + a_4(t, s)\, U_t \\ + a_5(t, s)\, U_s + a_6(t, s)\, U + g(t, s) = 0 \end{aligned} \tag{7.13.5}$$

defined on $\mathscr{R}$, together with a set of boundary conditions such that the problem is well set in the sense of Hadamard. Thus, we assume that (7.13.5) has a unique solution $U(t, s)$ which depends continuously on the prescribed boundary data. Since we are basically interested in demonstrating a method, we assume that the partial differential equation is elliptic and that $U(t, s)$ is prescribed on the boundary of $\mathscr{R}$ by a function $f(\tau)$, τ being the arc length along the boundary, such that $f''(\tau)$ is continuous along each side of $\mathscr{R}$. Hence $f(\tau)$ also defines $U_s(t, s)$ along vertical sides of $\mathscr{R}$ and $U_t(t, s)$ along horizontal sides of $\mathscr{R}$. Finally, we assume that the coefficients in (7.13.5) and boundary data are sufficiently smooth so that $U(t, s)$ is in $C_4^8(\mathscr{R})$. The assumption of "ellipticity" and "smoothness" does not obscure the generality of the method and allows a clearer exposition.

If for $N = 1, 2, 3,...$ we let $S_N(U; t, s)$ be the spline of interpolation to $U(t, s)$ such that $U(t, s) - S_N(U; t, s)$ is of type I′ for each N, then in the notation of Section 7.9 we can write $S_N(U; t, s)$ as

$$\begin{aligned} S_N(U; t, s) &= \sum_{i=0}^{n_N} \sum_{j=0}^{m_N} U(t_i, s_j)\, A_i(t)\, \bar{A}_j(s) \\ &+ \sum_{j=0}^{m_N} \{U_t(a, s_j)\, B_0(t) + U_t(b, s_j)\, B_{n_N}(t)\}\, \bar{A}_j(s) \\ &+ \sum_{i=0}^{n_N} \{U_s(t_i, c)\, \bar{B}_0(s) + U_s(t_i, d)\, \bar{B}_{m_N}(s)\}\, A_i(t) \\ &+ U_{st}(a, c)\, B_0(t)\, \bar{B}_0(s) + U_{st}(b, c)\, B_{n_N}(t)\, \bar{B}_0(s) \\ &+ U_{st}(a, d)\, B_{0N}(t)\, \bar{B}_{m_N}(s) + U_{st}(b, d)\, B_{n_N}(t)\, \bar{B}_{m_N}(s). \end{aligned} \tag{7.13.6}$$

We can rewrite (7.13.5) in the form

$$LU + g(t, s) = 0 \tag{7.13.7.1}$$

if we define

$$\begin{aligned} L \equiv\ & a_1(t, s) \frac{\partial^2}{\partial t^2} \cdot + a_2(t, s) \frac{\partial^2}{\partial s\, \partial t} \cdot + a_3(t, s) \frac{\partial^2}{\partial s^2} \cdot \\ & + a_4(t, s) \frac{\partial}{\partial t} \cdot + a_5(t, s) \frac{\partial}{\partial s} \cdot + a_6(t, s) \cdot. \end{aligned} \tag{7.13.7.2}$$

Consequently,

$$LS_N(U; t, s) = -g(t, s) - LE_N(U; t, s), \tag{7.13.8}$$

and the term $LE_N(U; t, s)$ can be made arbitrarily small in magnitude in view of (7.13.4) by choosing N sufficiently large. If we evaluate the members of (7.13.8) at the mesh points (t_i, s_j) $(i = 0, 1,..., n_N;$ $j = 0, 1,..., m_N)$, we obtain $(n_N + 1)(m_N + 1)$ linear equations for the unknowns

$$\left.\begin{array}{ll} U(t_i, s_j) & (i = 1, 2,..., n_N - 1;\ \ j = 1, 2,..., m_N - 1), \\ U_t(t_i, s_j) & (i = 0, n_N;\ \ j = 1, 2,..., m_N - 1), \\ U_s(t_i, s_j) & (i = 1, 2,..., n_N - 1;\ \ j = 0, m_N), \\ U_{st}(t_i, s_j) & (i = 0, n_N;\ \ j = 0, m_N). \end{array}\right\} \tag{7.13.9}$$

The remaining quantities $U(t_i, s_j)$, $U_t(t_i, s_j)$, $U_s(t_i, s_j)$ entering into (7.13.6) are determined by the boundary data. In matrix form, we have the equations

$$A_N U_N = G_N + E_N, \tag{7.13.10}$$

where A_N is the resulting matrix, U_N is the vector of unknowns, G_N is the vector arising from $-g(t, s)$ and the boundary data, and E_N is the vector arising from $-LE(U; t, s)$. Although the existence of A_N^{-1} is not guaranteed, it is likely, since $U(t, s)$ exists and is unique, and since $S_N(U; t, s)$ is uniquely determined by $U(t, s)$. If we assume A_N^{-1} to exist and $\| A_N^{-1}E_N \| \to 0$ as $N \to \infty$, then the solutions $\bar{U}_N$ of the approximate equations

$$A_N \bar{U}_N = G_N \tag{7.13.11}$$

determine doubly cubic splines $S_N(t, s)$ which converge to $U(t, s)$ as $N \to \infty$. The rate of convergence is determined by (7.13.4) and by the behavior of the matrix A_N^{-1}. Observe that the $S_N(U; t, s)$ do not satisfy the boundary conditions exactly, but only spline approximations of the boundary data; thus, it is important that the problem be "well set." For situations where $\mathscr{R}$ is partitioned into approximately 100 or less subrectangles, the matrices A_N can be inverted numerically by elimination methods; otherwise, iterative techniques are normally required. Since the $A_i(t)$, $\bar{A}_j(s)$, $B_i(t)$, and $\bar{B}_j(s)$ are cubic splines, their determination is greatly simplified. The resulting approximations are not completely numerical, since Eq. (7.13.6), or a more convenient rearrangement, provides intermediary values and can be used in analytic investigations. This latter feature makes the method attractive for ordinary differential equations as well. Since the error is given by $A_N^{-1}E_N$, error estimates can be calculated. When a considerable number of intermediate points are needed for a precision plot of the output, the method of cardinal splines is advantageous over methods of equal accuracy which yield only the values of $U(t, s)$ at mesh points.

7.14. Irregular Regions

Up to this point, we have confined ourselves to doubly cubic splines defined on rectangular regions. Our results extend readily, however, to other regions. One of the simplest extensions is to regions that are the union of a finite number of rectangles. In defining type I or type II representations for such regions, the same quantities are specified along the sides of the rectangles parallel to the t axis as are specified by (7.1.1) or (7.1.2), respectively. The same is true with respect to the sides of the rectangles parallel to the s axis. The quantities specified by (c) of (7.1.1) or by (c) of (7.1.2) must be prescribed at each corner of the rectangles. The first integral relation, the minimum norm property, the best approximation property, as well as all the other properties obtained for doubly cubic splines on a rectangular region, can be immediately generalized to regions of this type. We leave this development to the reader and turn to the consideration of regions, or perhaps more appropriately "surfaces," which under suitable mappings are mapped onto a rectangular region $\mathscr{R}$. The mappings are not $1 - 1$ (in fact they are not single-valued mappings), and so not all functions on $\mathscr{R}$ correspond to functions on the original surface.

Let S denote the surface depicted in Fig. 1. We assume that we are given a point P_0 in S together with a family $\{\Gamma_Q\}$ of smooth curves in S,

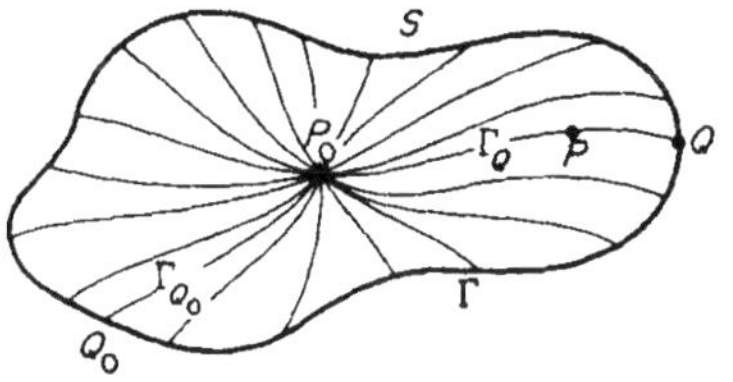

FIG. 1

each connecting P_0 to a point Q of Γ, the boundary of S. We assume that Γ is also a smooth curve in the sense that each of its describing coordinates has a continuous second derivative with respect to arc length, that the correspondence between the boundary points Q and the curves Γ_Q is $1 - 1$, and that any pair of these curves has only the point P_0 in common. The family of curves $\{\Gamma_Q\}$ is "surface-filling" in the sense that, except for P_0, there is precisely one curve of our family passing through any point P of S.

Let $d(P, P')$ denote the distance between P and P' measured along the curve Γ_Q passing through P. The distance function $d(P, P')$ is clearly not defined for an arbitrary pair of points P and P' of S, but, if P and P' can be joined by a curve Γ_Q, this can be done in only one way so that $d(P, P')$ is well defined in this event. Also, we let $t(P)$ denote the distance measured along Γ in a counterclockwise sense from a fixed point Q_0 of Γ to Q_P, where Q_P is the unique point of Γ such that P lies on Γ_{Q_P}. Now let $s(P)$ be defined by

$$s(P) = \frac{d(P, P_0)}{d(Q_P, P_0)}. \tag{7.14.1}$$

Thus, to each point of S not on Γ_{Q_0}, we can assign a unique pair of numbers $[t(P), s(P)]$. With each point $P \neq P_0$ of Γ_{Q_0} we have two distinct pairs: $[0, s(P)]$ and $[l, s(P)]$, where l denotes the length of Γ. For P_0, we have the infinity of pairs $(t, 0)$, where $0 \leqslant t \leqslant l$. Thus, the mapping F: $P \to [t(P), s(P)]$, although it is not single-valued, maps S onto the rectangle $\mathscr{R}$: $0 \leqslant t \leqslant l$; $0 \leqslant s \leqslant 1$. Under the mapping F, the curve $\Gamma_Q, Q \neq Q_0$, is mapped onto the line segment $t = t(Q)$ parallel to the s axis. The curve Γ_{Q_0} is mapped onto both the line segments $t = 0$ and $t = l$, the point P_0 is mapped onto the line segment $s = 0$, and the curve Γ is mapped onto the line segment $s = 1$. Observe that, although the mapping F is not single-valued, it has a single-valued inverse mapping F^{-1}, since each point (t, s) in $\mathscr{R}$ is the image of precisely one point of S. Consequently, with each function $f(P)$ defined on S we have the unique image function $f(t, s) = f[F^{-1}(t, s)]$. Because of the smoothness of the curve Γ and the curves Γ_Q, certain partial derivatives of $f(P)$ are expressible in terms of the partial derivatives of $f(t, s)$, and conversely. Thus, with a function $f(P)$ defined on S, we can associate splines of interpolation $S(f; P)$ which are in reality splines of interpolation to the corresponding functions $f(t, s) = f[F^{-1}(t, s)]$ defined on $\mathscr{R}$. Clearly, it is the functions $f(t, s)$ in $C_2^4(\mathscr{R})$ which are constant on $s = 0$ and periodic with respect to t that are important in this context.

A variation of the mapping just described is also very useful. Suppose that, in place of the family of curves Γ_Q joining P_0 to the boundary points Q, we have a surface-filling family of smooth curves $\{\Gamma_{Q,Q'}\}$, where both Q and Q' are on Γ. We consider two cases: (1) through each point P of S except for two points Q_0 and Q_1 on Γ there is a unique curve $\Gamma_{Q,Q'}$ of our family; and (2) there is one singular point P_0 through which every curve $\Gamma_{Q,Q'}$ passes. For the cases where there is no singular point, we associate with each point P of S the coordinate $t(P)$ equal to the distance from Q_0 measured along Γ in a counterclockwise direction to the end point Q_P (the first one encountered) of the curve $\Gamma_{Q_P,Q_P'}$ passing through P. Observe that we encounter the end point Q_P before we reach Q_1. We also are assuming that Γ is a rectifiable Jordan curve so that our surface S is simply connected. Figure 2 is representative of the surface under consideration. The assignment $t(P)$ to P is unique if 0 is assigned to Q_0 and the distance l' from Q_0 to Q_1 measured along Γ in a counterclockwise sense is assigned to Q_1.

For $P \neq Q_0$ and $P \neq Q_1$, we can uniquely assign a second coordinate $s(P)$ to P by defining

$$s(P) = \frac{d(Q_P, P)}{d(Q_P, Q_{P'})}; \tag{7.14.2}$$

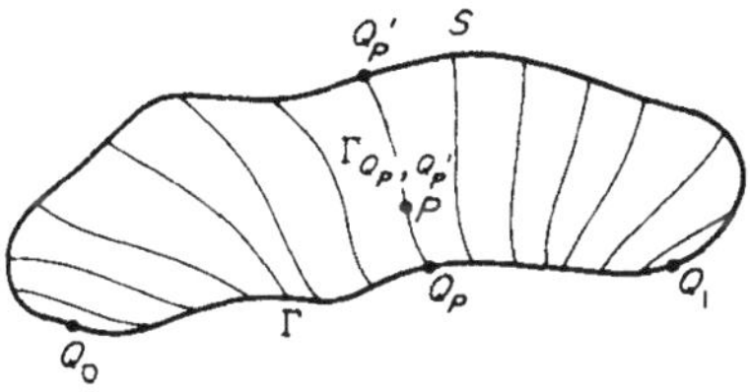

FIG. 2

for $P = Q_0$ or $P = Q_1$, this assignment is indeterminate, and we allow $s(Q_0)$ and $s(Q_1)$ to assume any value between 0 and 1. As before, the mapping

$$F: \quad P \to [t(P), s(P)]$$

maps S onto $\mathscr{R}$: $0 \leqslant t \leqslant l'$; $0 \leqslant s \leqslant 1$. The map F again is not single-valued but has a single-valued inverse F^{-1} so that we can associate with a function $f(P)$ defined on S a function $f(t, s) = f[F^{-1}(t, s)]$ defined on $\mathscr{R}$. We can now define splines of interpolation $S(f; P)$ as we did earlier. In this case, it is the functions in $C_2{}^4(\mathscr{R})$ that are constant on $t = 0$ and $t = l'$ which are relevant.

If we distinguish between the curves $\Gamma_{Q,Q'}$ and $\Gamma_{Q',Q}$, in the sense that they have opposite orientations, we can choose $\mathscr{R}$: $0 \leqslant t \leqslant l$; $0 \leqslant s \leqslant 1$, where l denotes the length of Γ as the image region. The curves $\Gamma_{Q,Q'}$ and $\Gamma_{Q',Q}$ are mapped by F into two line segments $t = \text{const}$ and $t' = \text{const}$. We refer to t and t' if they are related in this way as *conjugates* and the points (t, s) and $(t', 1 - s)$ as *conjugate points*. In this terminology, the functions in $C_2{}^4(\mathscr{R})$ which are of interest are constant on $t = 0$, $t = l'$, are periodic in t, and satisfy the relation $f(t, s) = f(t', 1 - s)$.

When a singular point P_0 is present, several modifications are required. We now take Q_0 as any point on Γ and define $t(P)$ as before. It is desirable to give P_0 the same s coordinate no matter on what curve $\Gamma_{Q_P,Q_P'}$ it is considered to lie; consequently, we let

$$s(P) = \frac{1}{2}\,\frac{d(Q_P\,, P)}{d(Q_P\,, P_0)} \tag{7.14.3.1}$$

for P between Q_P and P_0 on $\Gamma_{Q_P,Q_P'}$, and

$$s(P) = \frac{1}{2}\left(1 + \frac{d(P_0\,, P)}{d(P_0\,, Q_P')}\right) \tag{7.14.3.2}$$

for P between P_0 and Q_P' on $\Gamma_{Q_P,Q_P'}$. If we distinguish between $\Gamma_{Q,Q'}$ and $\Gamma_{Q',Q}$, then the image is again $\mathscr{R}$: $0 \leqslant t \leqslant l$; $0 \leqslant s \leqslant 1$. The pertinent functions in $C_2^4(\mathscr{R})$ are the functions periodic in t, constant along $s = \frac{1}{2}$, and satisfying $f(t, s) = f(t', 1 - s)$ for conjugate points (t, s) and $(t', 1 - s)$. Figure 3 gives a representative picture.

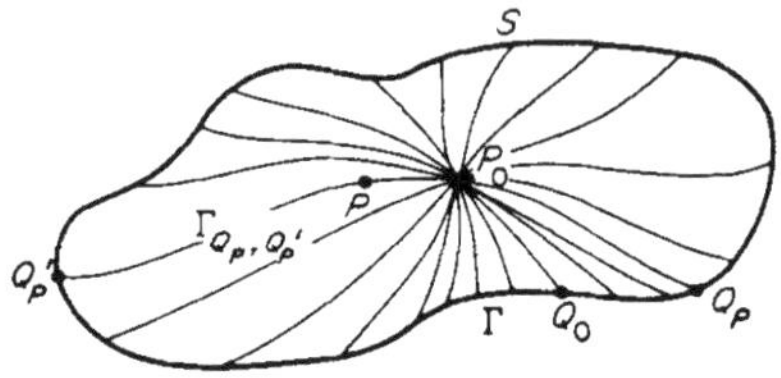

FIG. 3

The surfaces S that we have been considering need not be plane surfaces. Thus the curves Γ, Γ_Q, $\Gamma_{Q,Q'}$ need not be plane curves. The mapping F: $P \to [t(P), s(P)]$ introduces a set of intrinsic coordinates into S. It is important to note that the curves Γ, Γ_Q, $\Gamma_{Q,Q'}$ can be approximated by one-dimensional splines in the sense that their spacial coordinates can be approximated in this manner.* Thus surfaces, defined by a finite number of points, can be obtained and can be used to approximate other smooth surfaces. Convergence can be demonstrated not only in a pointwise sense, but with respect to tangent planes and curvature as well. In Section 7.15, we develop these ideas more fully.

7.15. Surface Representation

In this section, we extend the ideas of Section 7.14 to some other classes of smooth surfaces. Three classes of surfaces are considered: (1) smooth surfaces homeomorphic to the sphere; (2) smooth surfaces homeomorphic to the torus; and (3) smooth surfaces homeomorphic to a cylinder of finite length. We consider class 1 in some depth and then indicate the modifications that must be made for the other two classes. Two different points of view are possible: we can attempt to approximate a given surface by a second surface determined by a finite number of points, or we can endeavor simply to define a surface (in a reasonable rather than a unique manner) given a finite number of points.

Since the latter point of view is perhaps more basic, we adopt it. Assume that we are given $N + 1$ sets of points, each set consisting of

* Only a finite number of curves Γ_Q or $\Gamma_{Q,Q'}$ are approximated; these curves serve to determine grid lines parallel to the s axis.

coplanar points. We denote the planes by $\Omega_j (j = 0, 1,\ldots, N)$ and assume that in Ω_j there are $m_j + 1$ points $Q_{i,j}$ $(i = 0, 1,\ldots, m_j)$ with $Q_{0,j} = Q_{m_j,j}$ which roughly describe a simple closed curve Γ_j, except that Γ_0 and Γ_N degenerate to single points. We assume the points $Q_{0,j}$ $(j = 0, 1,\ldots, N)$ are coplanar. We think of the planes as ordered in the sense that they are parallel and that the directed distance from any plane Ω_j to Ω_{j+1} is positive, although this is not a necessary condition. In Fig. 4, we have a schematic representation.

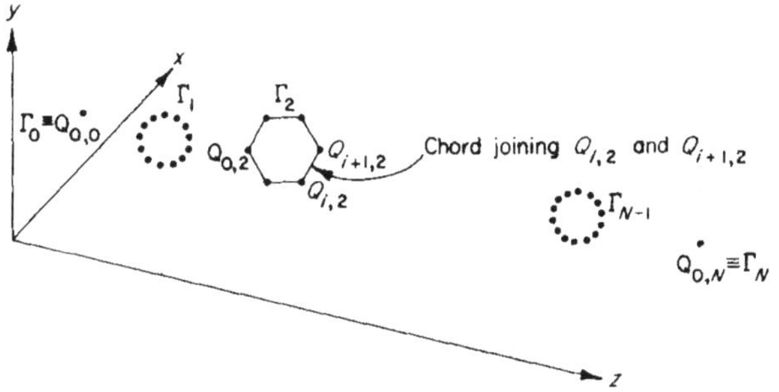

FIG. 4

Each point $Q_{i,j}$ is assumed to be defined by its cartesian coordinates $(x_{i,j}, y_{i,j}, z_{i,j})$. If $d(Q_{i,j}, Q_{k,j})$ denotes the cumulative chord length from $Q_{i,j}$ to $Q_{k,j}$ as i increases to k $(k > i)$ and l_j denotes the total cumulative chord length, i.e., $l_j = d(Q_{0,j}, Q_{m_j,j})$, we can define for each j $(j = 0, 1,\ldots, N)$ three periodic splines $\hat{S}_j(x_{i,j}; s)$, $\hat{S}_j(y_{i,j}; s)$, and $\hat{S}_j(z_{i,j}; s)$ which interpolate, respectively, to the $x_{i,j}$, $y_{i,j}$, and $z_{i,j}$ at $s = s_{i,j}$ $(i = 0, 1,\ldots, m_j)$, where

$$s_{i,j} = \frac{d(Q_{0,j}, Q_{i,j})}{l_j} \qquad (i = 0, 1,\ldots, m_j;\ \ j = 0, 1,\ldots, N). \qquad (7.15.1)$$

Next, partition the unit interval $0 \leqslant s \leqslant 1$ by a mesh Δ:

$$0 = s_0 < s_1 < \cdots < s_{k-1} < s_k = \tfrac{1}{2} < s_{k+1} < \cdots < s_{2k} = 1$$

and determine a new set of points $P_{i,j}$ in each Ω_j by evaluating $\hat{S}_j(x_{i,j}; s)$, $\hat{S}_j(y_{i,j}; s)$, and $\hat{S}_j(z_{i,j}; s)$ at $s_0, s_1,\ldots, s_{2k}$. In particular, $Q_{0,j} \equiv P_{0,j} \equiv P_{2k,j}$ $(j = 0, 1,\ldots, N)$, $P_{i,0} \equiv Q_{0,0}$ $(i = 0, 1,\ldots, 2k)$, and $P_{i,N} \equiv Q_{0,N}$ $(i = 0, 1,\ldots, 2k)$.

We can in each plane form new periodic splines of interpolation to the coordinates of the $P_{i,j}$ with respect to the mesh Δ. We denote these splines by $S_j(x; s)$, $S_j(y; s)$, and $S_j(z; s)$; they do not normally interpolate to the original coordinates, but the plane curves they define can generally be expected to resemble closely the original Γ_j. They have the useful property, however, that their coordinates are defined by periodic splines with respect to the common mesh Δ.

If for fixed i and $q = i + k \pmod{2k}$ we determine a set of x coordinates by

$$x_{00} = \bar{x}_{0,i} = S_0(x; s_i), \qquad \bar{x}_{1,i} = S_1(x; s_i),\ldots, \qquad \bar{x}_{N-1,i} = S_{N-1}(x; s_i),$$
$$x_{0,N} = \bar{x}_{N,i} = S_N(x; s_i), \qquad \bar{x}_{N+1,i} = S_{N-1}(x; s_q),\ldots,$$
$$\bar{x}_{2N+1,i} = S_0(x; s_q) = x_{00},$$

and similar sets of y coordinates and z coordinates, then we have $2k$ distinct ordered sets of coordinates. Note that the sets of points associated with $i = 0$ and $i = 2k$ are identical, and sets of points associated with i and q differ only in that the ordering is reversed. We can use these sets of coordinates to define $2k$ oriented closed-space curves by forming periodic splines $\mathscr{T}_i(x; t)$, $\mathscr{T}_i(y; t)$, and $\mathscr{T}_i(z; t)$ interpolating to these coordinate values. The independent variable t at the points of interpolation is defined by

$$\begin{aligned} t_{i,j} &= \frac{1}{2}\frac{d(P_{i,0}, P_{i,j})}{d(P_{i,0}, P_{i,N})} && (0 \leqslant j \leqslant N), \\ t_{i,j} &= \frac{1}{2}\left\{1 + \frac{d(P_{i,N}, P_{i,j})}{d(P_{i,N}, P_{i,2N})}\right\} && (N \leqslant j \leqslant 2N), \end{aligned} \tag{7.15.2}$$

where $d(P_{i,j}, P_{i,l})$ is the cumulative chord length between $P_{i,j}$ and $P_{i,l}$ as the second index increases from j to l. The point $Q_{0,N}$ is always associated with $t = \frac{1}{2}$ by the parametrization, and the point $Q_{0,0}$ is associated with both $t = 0$ and $t = 1$ because of the periodicity of the splines. There is generally no value of t for which there is interpolation to the original Q_{ij} aside from these values except for $i = 0$, $i = 2k$; and $i = K$, where all the interpolation points are the original points $Q_{0,j}$.

For each i, the splines $\mathscr{T}_i(x; t)$, $\mathscr{T}_i(y; t)$, and $\mathscr{T}_i(z; t)$ are associated with the mesh $\Delta_i : 0 = t_{i,0} < t_{i,1} < \cdots < t_{i,2N} = 1$ which varies with i. In order to remove this dependence, we partition the unit interval $0 \leqslant t \leqslant 1$ by a mesh π: $0 = t_0 < t_1 < \cdots < t_N = \frac{1}{2} < \cdots < t_{2N} = 1$ and evaluate the splines $\mathscr{T}_i(x; t)$, $\mathscr{T}_i(y; t)$, and $\mathscr{T}_i(z; t)$ for these values of t. In this way, we obtain $2k$ new sets of coordinates, and we form new periodic splines of interpolation to these quantities, but this time with respect to the common mesh π. We denote these splines by $\mathscr{T}_{\pi,i}(x; t)$,

$\mathscr{T}_{\pi,i}(y; t)$, $\mathscr{T}_{\pi,i}(z; t)$. Here i takes on the values 0, 1,..., $2k$, and we have $\mathscr{T}_{\pi,0}(x; t) \equiv \mathscr{T}_{\pi,2k}(t)$, $\mathscr{T}_{\pi,0}(y; t) = \mathscr{T}_{\pi,2k}(y; t)$, and $\mathscr{T}_{\pi,0}(z; t) \equiv \mathscr{T}_{\pi,2k}(z; t)$. Finally, we evaluate these splines for a fixed t_j and form periodic splines $S_{\Delta,j}(x; s)$, $S_{\Delta,j}(y; s)$, and $S_{\Delta,j}(z; s)$ with respect to the mesh Δ. For each j, these coordinate functions define simple closed curves that are analogous to the original curves Γ_j except that there are $2N + 1$ curves rather than $N + 1$, since we distinguish between orientations.

The periodic one-dimensional splines

$$\mathscr{T}_{\pi,i}(x; t), \qquad \mathscr{T}_{\pi,i}(y; t), \qquad \mathscr{T}_{\pi,i}(z; t) \qquad (i = 0, 1, \ldots, 2k), \tag{7.15.3.1}$$

$$S_{\Delta,j}(x; t), \qquad S_{\Delta,j}(y; t), \qquad S_{\Delta,j}(z; t) \qquad (j = 0, 1, \ldots, 2N) \tag{7.15.3.2}$$

define x, y, and z along the grid lines on the unit square $\mathscr{R}$: $0 \leqslant t \leqslant 1$, $0 \leqslant s \leqslant 1$ which are determined by the meshes π and Δ. A little reflection allows us to perceive that these one-dimensional splines provide sufficient and consistent information to define x, y, z as doubly periodic splines on $\mathscr{R}$ which for uniform meshes π and Δ are subject to the symmetry relations

$$\left.\begin{aligned} x(t, s) &= x(1 - t, 1 - s), \\ y(t, s) &= y(1 - t, 1 - s), \\ z(t, s) &= z(1 - t, 1 - s), \\ [x(0, s), y(0, s), z(0, s)] &= Q_{0,0}, \\ [x(\tfrac{1}{2}, s), y(\tfrac{1}{2}, s), z(\tfrac{1}{2}, s)] &= Q_{0,N}, \end{aligned}\right\} \tag{7.15.4}$$

It is only when the identifications made possible by (7.15.4) and the periodicity of the splines are made that the surface described by $x(t, s)$, $y(t, s)$, and $z(t, s)$ is homeomorphic with the sphere. Without the identification (7.15.4), it is more like two spheres with a common north pole.

For a surface that is homeomorphic to a torus, the two curves Γ_0 and Γ_N are not degenerate but are identical. Consequently, the splines with respect to the t variable are naturally periodic, and the desired surface does not effectively need to be doubled in order to make them periodic. This greatly simplifies the procedure. For a surface homeomorphic to a finite cylinder, the splines with respect to the t variable are type I or type II splines. This causes no difficulty except that additional information must be supplied to define the requisite derivatives at the ends of the cylinder.

The variables s and t used in these constructions can be used in situations where the surface even doubles back on itself. In more limited situations, other variables are often more convenient. In particular, the angle between the line joining a point on a curve Γ_j to a fixed point and a fixed line through that point can replace the s-variable in many instances. If the surface is toroidal, a similar variable can be used in place of the t variable. For a surface homeomorphic to a finite cylinder, the z coordinate itself often can be considered for the other independent variable. When it is possible to use independent variables like these, the number of times that the surface has to be redefined in order that a rectangular mesh result is significantly reduced or even eliminated.

7.16. The Surfaces of Coons

Coons [1964] has developed methods of surface representation where he divides a rectangular region $\mathscr{R}$: $a \leqslant t \leqslant b$; $c \leqslant s \leqslant d$ into subrectangles $\mathscr{R}_{ij}$: $t_{i-1} \leqslant t \leqslant t_j$; $s_{j-1} \leqslant s \leqslant s_j$ $(i = 1, 2,..., N; j = 1, 2,..., M)$, and then he defines a surface $S(t, s)$ over each $\mathscr{R}_{ij}$ which coincides along each of the four edges of $\mathscr{R}_{ij}$ with the restriction to that edge of one of a set of prescribed curves $f_i(s)$ $(i = 0, 1,..., N)$, $g_j(t)$ $(j = 0, 1,..., M)$ defined on the grid lines that partition R into subrectangles R_{ij}. This is accomplished in such a fashion that the first partial derivative of $S(t, s)$ in the direction normal to an edge of $\mathscr{R}_{ij}$ [we refer to this partial derivative as the normal derivative of $S(t, s)$] depends only on the values of the boundary data at the ends of the edge and the values of the first derivative of the boundary data (along the edge) at the ends of the edge. In particular, for each $\mathscr{R}_{ij}$ we have $S(t, s_{j-1}) = g_{j-1}(t)$, $t_{i-1} \leqslant t \leqslant t_i$, and $\partial S(t, s)/\partial s \,|_{s=s_{j-1}}$, $t_{i-1} \leqslant t \leqslant t_i$, depends only on the quantities $f_{j-1}(s_{i-1}), f_{j-1}(s_i), f'_{j-1}(s_{i-1}), f'_{j-1}(s_i)$ (and some quantities independent of the boundary data). Consequently, $g_{j-1}(t)$ can be redefined in the interval $t_{i-1} \leqslant t \leqslant t_i$ [as long as the values of $g_{j-1}(t)$ and $g'_{j-1}(t)$ at t_{i-1} and t_i are not altered] without affecting the normal derivative of $S(t, s)$. In addition, there is injected sufficient symmetry into the construction such that the normal derivative of $S(t, s)$ is continuous across the boundary between two adjacent subrectangles.

Although there is not a unique method for accomplishing these objectives, we outline one method that is very closely related to spline theory.

Let $g_{j-1}(t)$ and $g_j(t)$ define $S(t, s)$ along $s = s_{j-1}$ and $s = s_j$, respectively. Similarly, let $f_{i-1}(s)$ and $f_i(s)$ define $S(t, s)$ along $t = t_{i-1}$ and $t = t_i$, respectively. These four functions determine the values of $S(t, s)$, $\partial S(t, s)/\partial s$, and $\partial S(t, s)/\partial t$ at the vertices of $\mathscr{R}_{ij}$. Finally, specify $\partial^2 S(t, s)/\partial s\, \partial t$ in some fixed but arbitrary fashion at the vertices of $\mathscr{R}_{ij}$. (Adjacent rectangles should have consistent values.) There is in each $\mathscr{R}_{ij}$ a unique double cubic $\hat{S}(t, s)$ determined by these 16 quantities.

Let

$$
\left.\begin{aligned}
S_1(t, s) &= \{g_{j-1}(t) - \hat{S}(t, s_{j-1})\} \left\{-2 \left(\frac{s_j - s}{s_j - s_{j-1}}\right)^3 + 3 \left(\frac{s_j - s}{s_j - s_{j-1}}\right)^2\right\}, \\
S_2(t, s) &= \{g_j(t) - \hat{S}(t, s_j)\} \left\{-2 \left(\frac{s - s_{j-1}}{s_j - s_{j-1}}\right)^3 + 3 \left(\frac{s - s_{j-1}}{s_j - s_{j-1}}\right)^2\right\}, \\
S_3(t, s) &= \{f_{i-1}(s) - \hat{S}(t_{i-1}, s)\} \left\{-2 \left(\frac{t_i - t}{t_i - t_{i-1}}\right)^3 + 3 \left(\frac{t_i - t}{t_i - t_{i-1}}\right)^2\right\}, \\
S_4(t, s) &= \{f_i(s) - \hat{S}(t_i, s)\} \left\{-2 \left(\frac{t - t_{i-1}}{t_i - t_{i-1}}\right)^3 + 3 \left(\frac{t - t_{i-1}}{t_i - t_{i-1}}\right)^2\right\};
\end{aligned}\right\} \quad (7.16.1)
$$

then

$$
S(t, s) = \hat{S}(t, s) + \sum_{i=1}^{4} S_i(t, s) \quad (7.16.2)
$$

has the desired properties.

It is not difficult to determine $\hat{S}(t, s)$. In this regard, assume R_{ij} is a square with unit length edges, and let

$$
\begin{aligned}
\hat{S}(t, s) = {} & (s - s_{j-1})^3 \{a_{11}(t - t_{i-1})^3 + a_{12}(t - t_{i-1})^2 + a_{13}(t - t_{i-1}) + a_{14}\} \\
& + (s - s_{j-1})^2 \{a_{21}(t - t_{i-1})^3 + a_{22}(t - t_{i-1})^2 + a_{23}(t - t_{i-1}) + a_{24}\} \\
& + (s - s_{j-1}) \{a_{31}(t - t_{i-1})^3 + a_{32}(t - t_{i-1})^2 + a_{33}(t - t_{i-1}) + a_{34}\} \\
& + \{a_{41}(t - t_{i-1})^3 + a_{42}(t - t_{i-1})^2 + a_{43}(t - t_{i-1}) + a_{44}\}; \quad (7.16.3)
\end{aligned}
$$

then

$$
a_{44} = S(t_{i-1}, s_{j-1}), \qquad a_{34} = \partial S/\partial s\,|_{t_{i-1}, s_{j-1}}, \qquad a_{43} = \partial S/\partial t\,|_{t_{i-1}, s_{j-1}},
$$

$$
a_{33} = \partial^2 S/\partial s\,\partial t\,|_{t_{i-1}, s_{j-1}};
$$

$$
\begin{aligned}
a_{14} + a_{24} &= S(t_{i-1}, s_j) - a_{34} - a_{44}, \\
3a_{14} + 2a_{24} &= \partial S/\partial s\,|_{t_{i-1}, s_j} - a_{34}; \\
a_{13} + a_{23} &= \partial S/\partial t\,|_{t_{i-1}, s_j} - a_{33} - a_{43}, \\
3a_{13} + 2a_{23} &= \partial^2 S/\partial s\,\partial t\,|_{t_{i-1}, s_j} - a_{33}; \\
a_{41} + a_{42} &= S(t_i, s_{j-1}) - a_{43} - a_{44}, \\
3a_{41} + 2_{42} &= \partial S/\partial t\,|_{t_i, s_{j-1}} - a_{43}; \\
a_{31} + a_{32} &= \partial S/\partial s\,|_{t_i, s_{j-1}} - a_{33} - a_{34}, \\
3a_{31} + 2_{32} &= \partial^2 S/\partial s\,\partial t\,|_{t_i, s_{j-1}} - a_{33};
\end{aligned}
$$

$$
\begin{aligned}
a_{11} + a_{12} + a_{21} + a_{22} = {} & S(t_i, s_j) - a_{13} - a_{14} - a_{23} - a_{24} - a_{31} - a_{32} \\
& - a_{34} - a_{44} - a_{41} - a_{42} - a_{43} - a_{44},
\end{aligned}
$$

$$3a_{11} + 3a_{12} + 2a_{21} + 2a_{22} = \partial S/\partial s\,|_{t_i, s_j} - 3a_{13} - 3a_{14} - 2a_{23}$$
$$- 2a_{24} - a_{31} - a_{32} - a_{34} - a_{44}\,,$$
$$3a_{11} + 2a_{12} + 3a_{21} + 2a_{22} = \partial S/\partial t\,|_{t_i, s_j} - a_{13} - a_{23} - 3a_{31} - 2a_{32}$$
$$- a_{33} - 3a_{41} - 2a_{42} - a_{43}\,,$$
$$9a_{11} + 6a_{12} + 6a_{21} + 4a_{22} = \partial^2 S/\partial s\,\partial t\,|_{t_i, s_j} - 3a_{13} - 2a_{23} - 3a_{31}$$
$$- 2a_{21} - 2_{33}\,.$$

In addition, there are prescribed

$$S(t_{i-1}\,, s_{j-1}) = g_{j-1}(t_{i-1}) = f_{i-1}(s_{j-1}),$$
$$S(t_{i-1}\,, s_j) = g_j(t_{i-1}) = f_{i-1}(s_j),$$
$$S(t_i\,, s_{j-1}) = g_{j-1}(t_i) = f_i(s_{j-1}), \qquad S(t_i\,, s_j) = g_j(t_j) = f_j(s_j);$$
$$\partial S/\partial s\,|_{t_{i-1}, s_{j-1}} = f'_{i-1}(s_{j-1}), \qquad \partial S/\partial t\,|_{t_{i-1}, s_{j-1}} = g'_{j-1}(t_{i-1}),$$
$$\partial S/\partial s\,|_{t_{i-1}, s_j} = f'_{i-1}(s_j), \qquad \partial S/\partial t\,|_{t_{i-1}, s_j} = g_j{}'(t_{i-1}),$$
$$\partial S/\partial s\,|_{t_i, s_{j-1}} = f_i{}'(s_{j-1}), \qquad \partial S/\partial t\,|_{t_i, s_{j-1}} = g_{j-1}(t_i),$$
$$\partial S/\partial s\,|_{t_i, s_j} = f_i{}'(s_j), \qquad \partial S/\partial t\,|_{t_i, s_j} = g_j(t_i);$$
$$\partial^2 S/\partial s\,\partial t\,|_{t_{i-1}, s_{j-1}}\,, \quad \partial^2 S/\partial s\,\partial t\,|_{t_{i-1}, s_j}\,, \quad \partial^2 S/\partial s\,\partial t\,|_{t_i, s_{j-1}}\,, \quad \partial^2 S/\partial s\,\partial t\,|_{t_i, s_j}.$$

It is straightforward from these conditions to verify that $S(t, s)$ has the properties required of it. If it is desired to prescribe the normal derivative of $S(t, s)$ along the boundary of $\mathscr{R}_{ij}$, quintic weight functions are needed; for higher derivatives, higher-degree polynomials are needed.

The weight functions, however, are not restricted to polynomials. For instance, we might require $\hat{S}(t, s)$ and the analogues of the polynomial parts of (7.16.1) to satisfy the equation $L^*L\hat{S} = 0$ for fixed t and the equation $M^*M\hat{S} = 0$ for fixed s (L and M are linear differential operators and L^* and M^* their formal adjoints). If the functions $f_i(s)$ and $g_j(t)$ satisfy the same $2n$th order differential equation $L^*Lh = M^*Mu = 0$, so that only information at the vertices of the rectangles $\mathscr{R}_{ij}$ need be specified, then the surfaces of Coons are two-dimensional splines $S(t, s)$, where each of the one-dimensional splines obtained by restricting $S(t, s)$ to a grid line has deficiency n at each mesh point on the grid line. Since Coons essentially considers the individual rectangles separately rather than collectively, we must admit deficiency n as indicated.

CHAPTER VIII

Generalized Splines in Two Dimensions

8.1. Introduction

The material contained in this chapter is closely related to that of Chapter VII. In this instance, however, we focus our attention on splines $S_\pi(t, s)$ which in each subrectangle $\mathscr{R}_{ij}$ simultaneously satisfy two differential equations: one differential equation in the variable t, and the second differential equation (which may have no relation to the first) in the variable s. A second difference is that we do not require the one-dimensional splines obtained by holding one of the variables fixed to be simple splines. If we regard the fixed variable as a parameter, then all the splines in the one-parameter family of splines share a common mesh; in addition, we assume them to possess like continuity properties at interior mesh points and to satisfy end conditions of the same type.

We obtain a Hilbert space theory for the splines under consideration by forming the direct product of two Hilbert spaces of one-dimensional splines. On the other hand, we obtain a characterization of splines possessing best approximation properties or minimum norm properties by establishing conditions under which the first integral relation is valid. Questions of pointwise convergence in two dimensions are reduced to similar questions in one dimension where the answers are known.

The methods we employ generalize to higher dimensions with more or less difficulty: forming the direct product of more than two Hilbert spaces offers no difficulty; the establishment of conditions under which the first integral relation is valid, however, is beset with computational difficulties stemming primarily from the sheer length of the expressions involved. For this reason, we limit ourselves to two dimensions, where the basic method is not obscured. Although we do not consider the application of generalized two-dimensional splines to surface representation, that could be done.

8.2. Basic Definition

Let a rectangle $\mathscr{R}$: $a \leqslant t \leqslant b$; $c \leqslant s \leqslant d$ be given along with two differential operators:

$$\begin{aligned} L_t &= a_n(t)\, D_t^{\,n} \cdot + a_{n-1}(t)\, D_t^{n-1} \cdot + \cdots + a_0(t) \cdot, \\ L_s &= b_m(s)\, D_s^{\,m} \cdot + b_{m-1}(s)\, D_s^{m-1} \cdot + \cdots + b_0(s). \end{aligned} \tag{8.2.1}$$

In these differential operators, the coefficients $a_i(t)$ $(i = 0, 1,..., n)$ possess continuous nth derivatives, and $a_n(t)$ does not vanish on $[a, b]$; the coefficients $b_j(s)$ $(j = 0, 1,..., m)$ possess continuous mth derivatives, and $b_m(s)$ does not vanish on $[c, d]$; and $D_t \equiv d/dt$, $D_s \equiv d/ds$. We denote by L_t^* and L_s^* the formal adjoints of L_t and L_s, respectively. Finally, let $\Delta_t : a = t_0 < t_1 < \cdots < t_N = b$ and $\Delta_s : c = s_0 < s_1 < \cdots s_M = d$ determine a mesh π which partitions $\mathscr{R}$ into $N \cdot M$ subrectangles $\mathscr{R}_{ij}$ $(i = 1, 2,..., N;\ j = 1, 2,..., M)$.

Definition 8.2.1. $S_\pi(t, s)$ is a (two-dimensional generalized) spline on $\mathscr{R}$ with respect to π associated with the operators L_t and L_s provided (a) for each s in $[c, d]$ $S_\pi(t, s)$ is a heterogeneous spline on $[a, b]$ with respect to Δ_t associated with the operator L_t, and (b) for each t in $[a, b]$ $S_\pi(t, s)$ is a heterogeneous spline on $[c, d]$ with respect to Δ_s associated with the operator L_s.

It is of interest at this point to examine the significance of the requirement that $L_t^*L_tS_\pi = 0$ and $L_s^*L_sS_\pi = 0$ within each rectangle $\mathscr{R}_{ij}$. From the fact that $L_t^*L_tS_\pi = 0$, we have in $\mathscr{R}_{ij}$

$$S_\pi(t, s) = a_1(i, j; s)\, u_1(t) + a_2(i, j; s)\, u_2(t) + \cdots + a_{2n}(i, j; s)\, u_{2n}(t),$$

where the functions $u_i(t)$ $(i = 1, 2,..., 2n)$ are a fundamental set of solutions of $L_t^*L_tu = 0$. Consequently, $L_s^*L_sS_\pi = 0$ implies

$$0 = L_s^*L_sa_1(i, j; s)\, u_1(t) + L_s^*L_sa_2(i, j; s)\, u_2(t) + \cdots + L_s^*L_sa_{2n}(i, j; s)u_{2n}(t).$$

Hence, $L_s^*L_sa_k(i, j; s) = 0$ $(k = 1, 2,..., 2n)$. It follows that

$$a_k(i, j; s) = c_{k1}(i, j)\, v_1(s) + c_{k2}(i, j)\, v_2(s) + \cdots + c_{k,2m}(i, j)\, v_{2m}(s),$$

where the functions $v_l(s)$ $(l = 1, 2,..., 2m)$ are a fundamental set of solution of $L_s^*L_sv = 0$. This establishes the representation

$$S_\pi(t, s) = \sum_{k=1}^{2n} \sum_{l=1}^{2m} c_{kl}(i, j)\, u_k(t)\, v_l(s) \tag{8.2.2}$$

for (t, s) in $\mathscr{R}_{ij}$.

From the representation (8.2.2), it follows that, if $\partial^\alpha S_\pi(t, s)/\partial t^\alpha$ is continuous at $t = t_i$, then $\partial^{\beta+\alpha} S_\pi(t, s)/\partial s^\beta \partial t^\alpha$ $(\beta = 0, 1, \ldots, 2m)$ is continuous at $t = t_i$ with the possible exception of the points (t_i, s_j) $(j = 0, 1, \ldots, M)$. A similar result holds with the roles of t and s interchanged. We also observe that (8.2.2) permits us to interchange the order of differentiation in computing the partial derivatives of $S_\pi(t, s)$.

8.3. The Fundamental Identity

The bilinear concomitant $P(u, v)$ associated with the linear differential operator L_t can be expressed as

$$P[u, v] = \sum_{j=0}^{n-1} u^{(n-j-1)}(t)\, \beta_j(L_t, v; t), \tag{8.3.1.1}$$

where

$$\beta_j(L_t, v; t) = \sum_{i=0}^{j} (-1)^i \{a_{n-j-i}(t)\, v(t)\}^{(i)}. \tag{8.3.1.2}$$

[In Section 6.2, we denoted $\beta_j(L, LS_\pi; t)$ by $\beta_j(S_\pi; t)$.] Since the functions we are currently considering depend on two variables t and s and there are two operators L_t and L_s, we employ the modified notation

$$P_{L_t}[u, v] = \sum_{j=0}^{n-1} D_t^{n-j-1}\, u(t, s) \cdot \beta_j(L_t, v, s; t), \tag{8.3.2.1}$$

$$\beta_j(L_t, v, s; t) = \sum_{i=0}^{j} (-D_t)^i \{a_{n-j-1}(t)\, v(t, s)\}, \tag{8.3.2.2}$$

$$P_{L_s}[u, v] = \sum_{j=0}^{m-1} D_s^{m-j-1}\, u(t, s)\, \beta_j(L_s, v, t; s), \tag{8.3.2.3}$$

$$\beta_j(L_s, v, t; s) = \sum_{i=0}^{j} (-D_s)^i \{b_{m-j-1}(s)\, v(t, s)\}. \tag{8.3.2.4}$$

Let $f(t, s)$ defined on a rectangle $\mathscr{R}$: $a \leqslant t \leqslant b$; $c \leqslant s \leqslant d$ be a function whose partial derivatives not involving more than n differentiations with respect to t and not more than m differentiations with respect to s are continuous on $\mathscr{R}$. Let Δ_t: $a = t_0 < t_1 < \cdots < t_N = b$ and Δ_s: $c = s_0 < s_1 < \cdots < s_M = d$ define a mesh π on $\mathscr{R}$; let $S_\pi(t, s)$ be a spline on $\mathscr{R}$ with respect to π associated with the operators L_t and L_s; and consider the integral

$$I = \int_c^d \int_a^b L_t L_s\{f(t, s) - S_\pi(t, s)\} L_t L_s S_\pi(t, s)\, dt\, ds.$$

Since $L_t{}^* L_t S_\pi(t, s) = 0$ and $L_s{}^* L_s S_\pi(t, s) = 0$ within each subrectangle $\mathscr{R}_{ij}$, we have

$$\begin{aligned} I &= \int_c^d \sum_{i=1}^{N} \sum_{j=0}^{n-1} D_t^{n-j-1} L_s\{f(t, s) - S_\pi(t, s)\} \cdot \beta_j(L_t, L_s L_t S_\pi, s; t)\Big|_{t_{i-1}}^{t_i} ds \\ &= \sum_{i=1}^{N} \sum_{k=1}^{M} \sum_{j=0}^{n-1} \sum_{l=0}^{m-1} D_s^{m-l-1} D_t^{n-j-1}\{f(t, s) - S_\pi(t, s)\} \\ &\quad \cdot \beta_l[L_s, \beta_j(L_t, L_s L_t S_\pi, s; t), t; s]\Big|_{t_{i-1}}^{t_i}\Big|_{s_{k-1}}^{s_k}. \end{aligned} \tag{8.3.3}$$

If we insert I into the identity

$$\begin{aligned} \int_c^d \int_a^b &\{L_t L_s\{f(t, s) - S(t, s)\}\}^2\, dt\, ds \\ &= \int_c^d \int_a^b \{L_t L_s f(t, s)\}^2\, dt\, ds \\ &\quad -2 \int_c^d \int_a^b L_t L_s\{f(t, s) - S_\pi(t, s)\} L_t L_s S_\pi(t, s)\, dt\, ds \\ &\quad - \int_c^d \int_a^b \{L_t L_s S_\pi(t, s)\}^2\, dt\, ds, \end{aligned}$$

we obtain

$$\begin{aligned} \int_c^d \int_a^b \{L_t L_s f(t, s)\}^2\, dt\, ds &= \int_c^d \int_a^b \{L_t L_s S_\pi(t, s)\}^2\, dt\, ds \\ &\quad + \int_c^d \int_a^b \{L_t L_s f(t, s) - L_t L_s S_\pi(t, s)\}^2\, dt\, ds \\ &\quad - 2 \sum_{i=1}^{N} \sum_{k=1}^{M} \sum_{j=0}^{n-1} \sum_{l=0}^{m-1} D_t^{m-l-1} D_t^{n-j-1}\{f(t, s) - S_\pi(t, s)\} \\ &\quad \cdot \beta_l[L_s, \beta_j(L_t, L_s L_t S_\pi, s; t), t; s]\Big|_{t_{i-1}}^{t_i}\Big|_{s_{k-1}}^{s_k}, \end{aligned} \tag{8.3.4}$$

which is the *fundamental identity* for generalized splines in two dimensions. Although discontinuities may occur in β_l at mesh points or along grid lines, they are simple jump discontinuities; the evaluations indicated in I must be interpreted in terms of left-hand limits and right-hand limits.

8.4. Types of Splines

With respect to a mesh Δ: $a = t_0 < t_1 < \cdots < t_N = b$, there are many varieties of splines on $[a, b]$ associated with a linear differential operator L. Any particular spline $S_\Delta(t)$ depends on a finite number of independent parameters which we have termed defining values; $S_\Delta(t)$ is the result of a particular assignment of numerical values to these parameters. If there are k parameters and each is allowed to vary over the field of real numbers, a k-parameter family F_Δ of splines with respect to Δ results. The family F_Δ consists of splines differing only in the assignment of numerical values to these parameters and, consequently, consists of splines possessing similar continuity properties at mesh points. In this sense, F_Δ defines a type of spline.

Previously, for certain classes of splines, we have defined a cardinal spline as one for which all parameter values are zero except for one that is unity. In this manner, with F_Δ we can associate k linearly independent splines $e_i(t)$ $(i = 1, 2,..., k)$, and F_Δ is a linear space with the $e_i(t)$ as a basis. As a consequence, if $S_\Delta(t)$ is in F_Δ, then

$$S_\Delta(t) = \sum_{i=1}^{k} a_i e_i(t). \tag{8.4.1}$$

Cardinal splines arise if we impose, for example, the conditions of Definition 8.4.1 or Definition 8.4.2, which follow.*

Definition 8.4.1. Let $S_\Delta(t)$ be in F_Δ. Then F_Δ is a family of heterogeneous splines of *explicit type* if each a_i in (8.4.1) can be identified as the value of a derivative $S_\Delta^{(\alpha)}(t)$ for some α $(\alpha = 0, 1,..., n-1)$ at some mesh point of Δ (in a manner independent of the particular spline under consideration). Moreover, if any of the quantities $S_\Delta^{(\alpha)}(t_i)$ $(\alpha = 0, 1,..., n-1; i = 0, 1,..., N-1)$ does not appear in this way, then $\beta_\alpha(L, LS_\Delta; t)$ is continuous at $t = t_i$ $(i = 1, 2,..., N-1)$, or $\beta_\alpha(L, LS; t)$ vanishes at $t = t_i$ $(i = 0, N)$.

In the earlier part of the book, we considered a number of very specific types of splines; most of these are splines of explicit type (subject to a proper choice of basis elements). The present definition, however

* These definitions do not cover all classes of splines; for instance, periodic splines. Modified definitions are easily formulated.

(particularly its analog in two dimensions), greatly facilitates the statement of many basic results.

Definition 8.4.2. Let F_π be a family of two-dimensional splines on $\mathscr{R}$ with respect to π with a basis of k splines $h_i(t, s)$ $(i = 1, 2,..., k)$. The family F_π consists of heterogeneous splines of *explicit type* if

$$S_\pi(t, s) = \sum_{i=1}^{k} a_i h_i(t, s) \tag{8.4.2}$$

implies that each a_i can be identified [in a manner independent of the particular spline $S_\pi(t, s)$ under consideration] as the value of a partial derivative $\partial^{\alpha+\gamma} S_\pi(t, s)/\partial t^\alpha \, \partial s^\gamma$ at some mesh point of π for some $\alpha + \gamma$ $(\alpha = 0, 1,..., n - 1;\ \gamma = 0, 1,..., m - 1)$. Moreover, if any of the quantities $\partial^{\alpha+\gamma} S_\pi(t_i, s_j)/\partial t^\alpha \, \partial s^\gamma$ $(\alpha = 0, 1,..., n - 1;\ \gamma = 0, 1,..., m - 1;$ $i = 0, 1,..., N;\ j = 0, 1,..., M)$ does not appear in this manner, then $\beta_\gamma[L_s, \beta_\alpha(L_t, L_t L_s S\ \ , s; t), t; s]$ is continuous* in either t or s at (t_i, s_j) (at interior mesh points), or either $\beta_\gamma[L_s, \beta_\alpha(L_t, L_t L_s S_\pi, s; t), t; s]$ vanishes or is continuous along the boundary at (t_i, s_j) (at boundary mesh points that are not corner points) or $\beta_\gamma[L_s, \beta_\alpha(L_t, L_t L_s S_\pi, s; t), t; s]$ vanishes at (t_i, s_j) (at corner points).

When we say that $S_\pi(t, s)$ is a spline of interpolation to $f(t, s)$ on π, this asserts that $S_\pi(t, s) = f(t, s)$ at the mesh points of π. We now require a stronger concept.

Definition 8.4.3. Let F_π consist of splines of explicit type, and let $S_\pi(f; t, s)$ be in F_π. We say $S_\pi(f; t, s)$ is a spline of *strong interpolation* to $f(t, s)$ if the partial derivatives of $S_\pi(f; t, s)$ indicated in Definition 8.4.2, which actually appear, interpolate to corresponding partial derivatives of $f(t, s)$ at the indicated mesh points of π.

8.5. The First Integral Relation

Theorem 8.5.1. *Let $f(t, s)$ be a function defined on $\mathscr{R}$: $a \leqslant t \leqslant b$; $c \leqslant s \leqslant d$ whose partial derivatives involving not more than n differentiations with respect to t and not more than m differentiations with respect to s are continuous on $\mathscr{R}$. Let π be a mesh on $\mathscr{R}$ determined by Δ_t:*

$$a = t_0 < t_1 < \cdots < t_N = b$$

* By the statement $f(t, s)$ is continuous in t at (t_i, s_j) we imply both $f(t, s_j+)$ and $f(t, s_j-)$ are continuous if they differ.

and Δ_s :

$$c = s_0 < s_1 < \cdots < S_M = d,$$

and let $S_\pi(f; t, s)$ *be a spline on* $\mathscr{R}$ *with respect to* π *associated with the operators* L_t *and* L_s. *Then if* $S_\Delta(f; t, s)$ *is a spline of strong interpolation to* $f(t, s)$ *on* π, *the first integral relation*

$$\int_c^d \int_a^b \{L_s L_t f(t, s)\}^2 \, dt \, ds = \int_c^d \int_a^b \{L_s L_t S_\pi(f; t, s)\}^2 \, dt \, ds$$

$$+ \int_c^d \int_a^b \{L_s L_t f(t, s) - L_s L_t S_\pi(f; t, s)\}^2 \, dt \, ds$$

is valid.

Proof. From the fundamental identity and (8.3.4), we see that the theorem follows if I vanishes. Because of the special structure of $S_\pi(f; t, s)$ as exhibited by the representation (8.2.2), we are justified in making the following two observations: (1) at interior mesh points, there is no contribution to I at (t_i, s_j) from a summand if $\partial^{\alpha+\gamma} S_\pi(f; t, s)/\partial t^\alpha \, \partial s^\gamma$ interpolates to $\partial^{\alpha+\gamma} f(t, s)/\partial t^\alpha \, \partial s^\gamma$ or $\beta_\gamma[L_s, \beta_\alpha(L_t, L_s L_t S_\pi, s; t), t; s]$ is continuous in either t or s at (t_i, s_j); and (2) at boundary mesh points, there is no contribution if either $\beta_\gamma[L_s, \beta_\alpha(L_t, L_s L_t S_\pi, s; t), t; s]$ vanishes or is continuous there as a function on the boundary of $\mathscr{R}$. This, however, is precisely what is implied by strong interpolation of $S_\pi(f; t, s)$ to $f(t, s)$ on π. The theorem follows.

8.6. Uniqueness

Theorem 8.6.1, which follows, expresses the minimum norm property in the present setting. Again, it is a highly useful tool in investigating the uniqueness of splines of interpolation; again, it is a corollary of the first integral relation.

Theorem 8.6.1. *Let* $\mathscr{R}$: $a \leqslant t \leqslant b$; $c \leqslant s \leqslant d$ *be given, let* π *be a mesh on* $\mathscr{R}$ *determined by* Δ_t : $a = t_0 < t_1 < \cdots < t_N = b$ *and* Δ_s : $c = s_0 < s_1 < \cdots < s_M = d$, *and let* F_π *be a family of splines of definite type. If* $f(t, s)$ *is a function defined on* $\mathscr{R}$ *with the properties,* (a) *the partial derivatives of* $f(t, s)$ *involving not more than* $n - 1$ *differentiations with respect to* t *and not more than* $m - 1$ *differentiations with respect to* s *are continuous on* $\mathscr{R}$, (b) *the partial derivatives of the restrictions of* $f(t, s)$ *to each subrectangle* $\mathscr{R}_{ij}$ *involving* n *differentiations with respect to* t *and* m

differentiations with respect to s are continuous on $\mathscr{R}_{ij}$, *and if* $S_\pi(f; t, s)$ *is a spline of strong interpolation to* $f(t, s)$, *then*

$$\int_c^d \int_a^b \{L_s L_t f(t, s)\}^2 \, dt \, ds \geqslant \int_c^d \int_a^b \{L_s L_t S_\pi(t, s)\}^2 \, dt \, ds.$$

Given a family F_π of explicit type, any solution of $L_s L_t f = 0$ is a member of F_π.* In particular, the zero function $Z(t, s)$ (the null spline) is a member of F_π.

Definition 8.6.1. If the only spline in F_π satisfying $L_s L_t S_\pi = 0$ which is a spline of strong interpolation to $Z(t, s)$ is $Z(t, s)$ itself, we say F_π possesses the uniqueness property.

Observe that, if the restrictions of $S_\pi(t, s)$ to the grid lines (these are one-dimensional splines of strong interpolation to the zero function) are identically zero, then it follows from the representation (8.2.2) that $S_\pi(t, s)$ is identically zero.

Theorem 8.6.2. *If* F_π *has the uniqueness property and* $S_\pi(f; t, s)$ *is a spline of strong interpolation to a function* $f(t, s)$ *satisfying the conditions of Theorem 8.6.1, then* $S_\pi(f; t, s)$ *is unique.*

Proof. The difference of any two splines of strong interpolation to $f(t, s)$ is a spline of strong interpolation to $Z(t, s)$. From the first integral relation, it follows that the difference is a solution of $L_s L_t S_\pi = 0$. Consequently, the difference is identically zero, and the theorem follows.

8.7. Existence

Once the cardinal splines comprising a basis for a family F_π of splines of definite type have been determined, it is a simple matter to construct the spline $S_\pi(f; t, s)$ in F_π of strong interpolation to a function $f(t, s)$. Only certain partial derivatives of $f(t, s)$ need then be determined. This approach, though, assumes the existence and availability of the cardinal splines.

Two-dimensional splines, however, are defined in terms of one-dimensional splines. In particular, the representation (8.3.3) is a consequence of this fact. Let $\mathscr{R}$: $a \leqslant t \leqslant b$; $c \leqslant s \leqslant d$ be given, and let π be determined by Δ_t: $a = t_0 < t_1 < \cdots < t_N = b$ and Δ_s: $c = s_0 < s_1 < \cdots < s_M = d$. From the representation (8.3.3), it is evident that in each subrectangle $\mathscr{R}_{ij}$ there are $4nm$ coefficients c_{ij} that

* If $L_s L_t f = 0$, any spline of strong interpolation to $f(t, s)$ in π is $f(t, s)$ itself.

must be determined. If we can properly formulate a system of linear equations for determining the c_{ij} (there are a total of $4nmNM$ such coefficients), then we could use the uniqueness property to establish the solvability of the equations. As in earlier arguments, two solutions to the associated homogeneous system would yield two splines in F_π of strong interpolation to the zero function, which would be a contradiction.

In order to obtain a proper system of equations for the c_{ij}, however, we must ensure that the conditions imposed on $S_\pi(f; t, s)$ so that the first integral relation is valid are satisfied. At each interior mesh point (t_i, s_j) there are $4nm$ such conditions: (a) $\partial^{\alpha+\gamma}S_\pi(f; t, s)/\partial t^\alpha\, \partial s^\gamma$ ($\alpha = 0, 1,..., n-1$; $\gamma = 0, 1,..., m-1$) must be continuous at (t_i, s_j) with respect to both t and s (this amounts to $3nm$ conditions) and (b) either $\partial^{\alpha+\gamma}S_\pi(f; t, s)/\partial t^\alpha\, \partial s^\gamma$ interpolates to $\partial^{\alpha+\gamma}f(t, s)/\partial t^\alpha\, \partial s^\gamma$ or $\beta_\gamma[L_s, \beta_\alpha(L_t, L_tL_sS_\pi, s; t), t+; s]$ and $\beta_\gamma[L_s, \beta_\alpha(L_s, L_tL_sS_\pi, s; t), t-; s]$ are continuous in s at (t_i, s_j) for $\alpha = 0, 1,..., n-1$; $\gamma = 0, 1,..., m-1$ [the roles of t and s may be interchanged in (b)]. Thus, except when condition (a) and the first alternative in condition (b) apply, there are five conditions rather than four to be satisfied at (t_i, s_j). Since the conditions that must hold at boundary mesh points are unaffected, we find that in some cases there are apparently more conditions than available coefficients. Consequently, we can expect that (at least formally) there may be more than $4nmNM$ conditions to be imposed on the c_{ij}. In reality, however, these conditions are not necessarily overrestrictive.

For instance, suppose that F_{Δ_t} is a family of splines of explicit type on the interval $[a, b]$ and F_{Δ_s} is a second family of splines of explicit type, this time on the interval $[c, d]$. Let $\{h_i(t)\}$ ($i = 1, 2,..., k$) be the set of cardinal splines associated with F_{Δ_t}, and let $\{g_j(s)\}$ ($j = 1, 2,..., l$) be the set of cardinal splines associated with F_{Δ_s}. Consider the linear space F_π generated by the set $\{h_i(t)g_j(s)\}$ ($i = 1, 2,..., k; j = 1, 2,..., l$) of pairwise products. We leave it to the reader to verify that F_π consists of two-dimensional splines on $\mathscr{R}$ with respect to π; indeed, F_π is a family of splines of explicit type. Observe in this regard that

$$\beta_\gamma[L_s, \beta_\alpha(L_t, L_tL_sh_ig_j, s; t)\, t; s] = \beta(L_s, L_sg_j; s) \cdot \beta_\alpha(L_t, L_th_i; t).* \qquad (8.7.1)$$

The concept of partial splines can also be used (as in Chapter VII) to construct two-dimensional generalized splines. Again, however, the two families of splines involved in this construction should both be of

* For these splines there are, in view of (8.7.1), only four conditions to be imposed at each interior mesh point. It can be shown that under these circumstances there are $4(M-1)(N-1)nm$ conditions from the interior mesh points and $4(N+M+1)nm$ conditions from the boundary mesh points, a total of $4NMnm$ conditions.

explicit type. Under these conditions, the first integral relation prevails, and the uniqueness property will then permit the interchange of the roles of t and s as in Chapter VII.

8.8. Convergence

The convergence argument given in Section 7.10 applies here as well and reduces the question of convergence in two dimensions to questions of convergence in one dimension. It is required in this argument, however, that $f(t, s)$ and its partial derivatives have sufficient continuity to permit certain interchanges in the order of differentiation. Theorem 8.8.1, which follows, is representative of the type of convergence theorem obtainable by this means. Its proof patterns that used in Section 7.10 and is omitted. The rate of convergence could also be estimated, if desired, in terms of the rates of convergence of the one-dimensional splines involved.

Theorem 8.8.1. *Let* $\mathscr{R}$: $a \leqslant t \leqslant b$; $c \leqslant s \leqslant d$ *be given, together with a sequence of meshes* $\{\pi_k\}$ $(k = 1, 2,\ldots)$ *on* $\mathscr{R}$ *determined by two sequences* $\{\Delta_t^k: a = t_0^k < t_1^k < \cdots < t_{N_k}^k = b\}$ $(k = 1, 2,\ldots)$ *and* $\{\Delta_s^k: c = s_0^k < s_1^k < \cdots < s_{M_k}^k = d\}$ $(k = 1, 2,\ldots)$. *Let* $f(t, s)$ *have continuous partial derivatives involving no more than* n_1 *differentiations with respect to* t *and no more than* m_1 *differentiations with respect to* s. *Let* $\{S_{\pi_k}(f; t, s)\}$ $(k = 1, 2,\ldots)$ *be a sequence of two-dimensional splines determined by linear operators* L_t *and* L_s *as in (8.2.1) and require that* $n \leqslant n_1$ *and* $m \leqslant m_1$. *If for each* t_i^k *we have*

$$\lim_{k\to\infty} \frac{\partial^\gamma S_{\pi_k}(f; t_i^k, s)}{\partial s^\gamma} = \frac{\partial^\gamma f(t_i^k, s)}{\partial s^\gamma} \qquad (\gamma = 0, 1,\ldots, m_1)$$

uniformly in s *and* t_i^k, *and for each* s_j^k *we have*

$$\lim_{k\to\infty} \frac{\partial^\alpha S_{\pi_k}(f; t, s_j^k)}{\partial t^\alpha} = \frac{\partial^\alpha f(t, s_j^k)}{\partial t^\alpha} \qquad (\alpha = 0, 1,\ldots, n_1)$$

uniformly in t *and* s_j^k, *then*

$$\lim_{k\to\infty} \frac{\partial^{\alpha+\gamma} S_{\pi_k}(f; t, s)}{\partial t^\alpha\, \partial s^\gamma} = \frac{\partial^{\alpha+\gamma} f(t, s)}{\partial t^\alpha\, \partial s^\gamma} \qquad (\alpha = 0, 1,\ldots, n_1; \quad \gamma = 0, 1,\ldots, m_1)$$

uniformly in s *and* t.

8.9. Hilbert Space Theory

If we are given a rectangle $\mathscr{R}$: $a \leqslant t \leqslant b$; $c \leqslant s \leqslant d$ and canonical mesh bases $\{S_i(L_t\,; t)\}$ $(i = 1, 2,\ldots)$ and $\{S_j(L_s\,; s)\}$ $(j = 1, 2,\ldots)$ for $\mathscr{K}^n(a, b)$ and $\mathscr{K}^m(c, d)$, respectively, we can form the direct product of $\mathscr{K}^n(a, b)$ and $\mathscr{K}^m(c, d)$ in the Hilbert space sense (cf. Sard [1963, p. 354]). We denote this direct product by $\mathscr{K}_m{}^n(\mathscr{R})$. Moreover, $\mathscr{K}_m{}^n(\mathscr{R})$ can be interpreted as the closure with respect to the pseudo-norm defined by

$$\| f \|^2 = \int_a^b \int_c^d | L_t L_s f(t, s)|^2 \, ds \, dt \tag{8.9.1}$$

(here functions differing by a solution of $L_t L_s f = 0$ are identified) of the function space generated by the pairwise products of the elements of the canonical bases for $\mathscr{K}^n(a, b)$ and $\mathscr{K}^m(c, d)$. Consequently, the functions

$$S_{ij}(t, s) \equiv S_i(L_t\,; t)\, S_j(L_s\,; s) \qquad (i = 1, 2,\ldots; j = 1, 2,\ldots) \tag{8.9.2}$$

comprise a basis for $\mathscr{K}_m{}^n(\mathscr{R})$.

We denote the space of functions $f(t, s)$ whose αth partial derivatives involving no more than β differentiations with respect to t and no more than γ differentiations with respect to s are continuous on $\mathscr{R}$ by $C^{\alpha}_{\beta,\gamma}(\mathscr{R})$. In this terminology, the spaces $C^{n+n}_{n,m}(\mathscr{R})$ and $C^{2(n+m)}_{2n,2m}(\mathscr{R})$ are subspaces of $\mathscr{K}_m{}^n(\mathscr{R})$. Since the basis elements (8.9.2) are in $C^{n+m}_{n,m}(\mathscr{R})$, the latter is dense in $\mathscr{K}_m{}^n(\mathscr{R})$.

If $f(t, s)$ is in $C^{n+m}_{n,m}(\mathscr{R})$, then we can give $f(t, s)$ the representation

$$f(t, s) = g(t, s) + \sum_{i,j} a_{ij} S_{ij}(t, s), \tag{8.9.3}$$

$$a_{ij} = \int_a^b \int_c^d f(t, s)\, L_t L_s S_{ij}(t, s)\, ds\, dt \qquad (i = 1, 2,\ldots;\ \ j = 1, 2,\ldots),$$

$$L_t L_s g(t, s) = 0.$$

Moreover, we know from Theorem 8.8.1 that under mild restrictions the convergence is uniform in t and s. As a consequence, we can proceed just as in Section 5.17 and obtain the representation

$$f(t, s) = g(t, s) + \int_a^b \int_c^d \mathscr{K}(t, s; t', s') \cdot L_t L_s f(t', s')\, ds'\, dt', \tag{8.9.4.1}$$

where

$$\mathscr{K}(t, s; t', s') = \lim_{N\to\infty} \sum_{i,j<N} S_{i,j}(t, s) \cdot L_t L_s S_{i,j}(t', s'). \tag{8.9.4.2}$$

The application of Eqs. (8.9.4) to the solution of partial differential equations of the form

$$L_t L_s h(t, s) = f(t, s) \tag{8.9.5}$$

and the related eigenvalue problems proceeds along the same lines as in Section 6.18. The detracting feature is that the factorization of the partial differential operator required by (8.9.5) is not generally possible; moreover, we are restricted to the rectangle $\mathscr{R}$. A change of coordinates of the type described in Section 7.14 often can be used to remove the latter objection, but the coordinate change will generally destroy a factorization of the form (8.9.5) if it has been achieved.

With respect to the approximation and representation of linear functionals, the situation is much better. One reason for the amenability of linear functionals is that they are often defined intrinsically rather than in terms of a particular coordinate system. For example, let

$$Lf = \int_D f(p)\, dA, \tag{8.9.6}$$

where D is a simply connected closed region that is starlike with respect to a point p_0 and dA is an element of area. Introduce into D polar coordinates r and θ with the origin at p_0. In terms of these coordinates, let $\bar{r} = g(\theta)$ describe the boundary of D. In practice, $g(\theta)$ could be a simple cubic spline in the variable θ. If we now introduce new coordinates

$$\beta = r/\bar{r}, \qquad \alpha = \theta; \tag{8.9.7}$$

then

$$\begin{aligned} Lf &= \int_0^1 \int_0^{2\pi} f(\beta, \alpha) \begin{vmatrix} \dfrac{\partial r}{\partial \beta} & \dfrac{\partial r}{\partial \alpha} \\ \dfrac{\partial \theta}{\partial \beta} & \dfrac{\partial \theta}{\partial \alpha} \end{vmatrix} d\beta\, d\alpha \\ &= \beta \int_0^1 \int_0^{2\pi} f(\beta, \alpha)\, g(\alpha)^2\, d\beta\, d\alpha. \end{aligned} \tag{8.9.8}$$

The preceding example illustrates how a coordinate system may be introduced into a region D such that the range of the coordinates is rectangular. Once this is done, a large class of functionals can be represented and approximated just as in Chapters V and VI. The differences from the one-dimensional methods offer no difficulty.

Bibliography

Ahlberg, J. H., and Nilson, E. N.

abs. 1961 Convergence properties of the spline fit, *Notices Am. Math. Soc.* 61T-219.

1962 Convergence properties of the spline fit, *Intern. Congr. Math. Stockholm.*

1963 Convergence properties of the spline fit, *J. Soc. Ind. Appl. Math.* **11**, 95–104.

abs. 1964 Convergence properties of generalized splines, *Notices Am. Math. Soc.* 64T-485.

1965 Orthogonality properties of spline functions, *J. Math. Anal. Appl.* **11**, 321–327.

1966 The approximation of linear functionals, *J. Soc. Ind. Appl. Math., Numerical Anal. Ser. B*, **3**, 173–182.

Ahlberg, J. H., Nilson, E. N., and Walsh, J. L.

abs. 1963 Best approximation and convergence properties of higher order spline fits, *Notices Am. Math. Soc.* 63T-103.

abs. 1964 Orthogonality properties of the spline function, *Notices Am. Math. Soc.* 64T-338.

abs. 1964a Extremal, orthogonality, and convergence properties of multi-dimensional splines, *Notices Am. Math. Soc.* 64T-339.

abs. 1964b Fundamental properties of generalized splines, *Notices Am. Math. Soc.* 64T-451.

abs. 1964c Higher-order spline interpolation, *Notices Am. Math. Soc.* 64T-494.

1964 Fundamental properties of generalized splines, *Proc. Natl. Acad. Sci. U.S.* **52**, 1412–1419.

abs. 1965 Generalized splines and the best approximation of linear functionals, *Notices Am. Math. Soc.* 65T-125.

1965 Best approximation and convergence properties of higher order spline approximations, *J. Math. Mech.* **14**, 231–244.

1965a Convergence properties of generalized splines, *Proc. Natl. Acad. Sci. U.S.* **54**, 344–350.

1965b Extremal, orthogonality, and convergence properties of multidimensional splines, *J. Math. Anal. Appl.* **11**, 27–48.

abs. 1966 Convergence properties of cubic splines, *Notices Am. Math. Soc.* 66T-47.

Aitken, A. C.

1958 "Determinants and Matrices." Oliver & Boyd, Edinburgh and London.

Asker, B.

1962 The spline curve, a smooth interpolating function used in numerical design of ship-lines, *Nord. Tidskr. Inform. Behandling* **2**, 76–82.

Atteia, M.

1965 Généralisation de la définition et des propriétés des "spline function," *Compt. Rend.* **260**, 3550–3553.

Bellman, R. E., and Kalaba, R. E.

1965 "Modern Analytic and Computational Methods in Science and Mathematics." Elsevier, Amsterdam.

Birkhoff, G.

abs. 1964 Error bounds for spline fits, *Notices Am. Math. Soc.* 64T-296.

Birkhoff, G., and deBoor, C.
1964 Error bounds for spline interpolation, *J. Math. Mech.* **13**, 827–835.

Birkhoff, G., and Garabedian, H.
1960 Smooth surface interpolation, *J. Math. Phys.* **39**, 258–268.

Coons, S. A.
1964 Surfaces for computer-aided design of space figures (unpublished).

Dahlquist, G.
1956 Convergence and stability in the numerical integration of ordinary differential equations, *Math. Scand.* **4**, 33–53.

Davis, P. J.
1963 "Interpolation and Approximation." Random House (Blaisdell), New York.

deBoor, C.
abs. 1961 Bicubic "spline" interpolation, *Notices Am. Math. Soc.* 579-24.
1962 Bicubic spline interpolation, *J. Math. Phys.* **41**, 212–218.
1963 Best approximation properties of spline functions of odd degree, *J. Math. Mech.* **12**, 747–749.

deBoor, C., and Lynch, R. E.
abs. 1964 General spline functions and their minimum properties, *Notices Am. Math. Soc.* 64T-456.
1966 On splines and their minimum properties, *J. Math. Mech.* **15**, 953–969.

Fejér, L.
1916 Über Interpolation, *Nachr. Ges. Wiss. Göttingen, Math.-Physik. Kl.*
1930 Die Abschätzung eines Polynoms in einem Intervalle, wenn Schranken für seine Werte und ersten Ableitungswerte in einzelnen Punkten des Intervalles gegeben sind, und ihre Anwendung auf die Konvergenzfrage Hermiteschen Interpolations-reihen, *Math. Z.* **32**, 426–457.

Freeman, H.
1949 "Mathematics for Actuarial Students," Vol. II. Cambridge Univ. Press, London and New York.

Goursat, E., and Bergmann, S.
1964 "A Course in Mathematical Analysis," Vol. III, Part 2. Dover, New York.

Goursat, E., and Hedrick, E. R.
1904 "A Course in Mathematical Analysis," Vol. I. Ginn, Boston.

Greville, T. N. E.
1964 Numerical procedures for interpolation by spline functions, *Math. Res. Center Tech. Summary Rept.* 450, U.S. Army, Univ. of Wisconsin.
1964a Interpolation by generalized spline functions, *Math. Res. Center Tech. Summary Rept.* 476, U.S. Army, Univ. of Wisconsin.
1964b Numerical procedures for interpolation by spline functions, *J. Soc. Ind. Appl. Math., Numerical Anal. Ser. B* **1**, 53–68.

Hildebrand, F. B.

1956 "Introduction to Numerical Analysis." McGraw-Hill, New York.

Hille, E.

1962 "Analytic Function Theory," Vol. II. Ginn, Boston.

Holladay, J. C.

1957 Smoothest curve approximation, *Math. Tables Aids Computation* **11**, 233–243.

Johnson, R. S.

1960 On monosplines of least deviation, *Trans. Am. Math. Soc.* **96**, 458–477.

Landis, F., and Nilson, E. N.

1962 The determination of thermodynamic properties by direct differentiation techniques, *Progr. Intern. Res. Thermodyn. Transport Properties, Am. Soc. Mech. Engrs.*

Muir, T.

1960 "A Treatise on the Theory of Determinants." Dover, New York.

Peano, G.

1913 Resto nelle formule di quadratura expresso con un integrale definito, *Atti Accad. Nazl. Lincei, Rend. Classe Sci. Fis. Mat. Nat.* (5^a) $\mathbf{22}_1$, 562–569; Opere Scelte Roma **I**, 410–418 (1957).

Sansone, G., and Conti, R.

1964 "Non-linear Differential Equations." Pergamon Press, New York.

Sard, Arthur

1963 Linear approximation, "Mathematical Surveys," Number 9. Am. Math. Soc., Providence.

Schoenberg, I. J.

1946 Contributions to the problem of approximation of equidistant data by analytic functions, *Quart. Appl. Math.* **4**, 45–99, 112–141.

1951 On Pólya frequency functions and their Laplace transforms, *J. Anal. Math.* **1**, 331–374.

1958 Spline functions, convex curves, and mechanical quadrature, *Bull. Am. Math. Soc.* **64**, 352–357.

1964 Spline interpolation and the higher derivatives, *Proc. Natl. Acad. Sci. U.S.* **51**, 24–28.

1964a Spline interpolation and best quadrature formulae, *Bull. Am. Math. Soc.* **70**, 143–148.

1964b On the best approximation of linear operators, *Koninkl. Ned. Akad. Wetenschap. Proc. Ser. A* **67**, 155–163.

1964c On trigonometric spline interpolation, *J. Math. Mech.* **13**, 795–825.

1964d On interpolation by spline functions and its minimal properties. "International Series of Numerical Analysis," Vol. 5, pp. 109–129. Academic Press, New York.

1964e Spline functions and the problem of graduation, *Proc. Natl. Acad. Sci. U.S.* **52**, 947–950.

1965 On monosplines of least deviation and best quadrature formulae, *J. Soc. Ind. Appl. Math., Numerical Anal. Ser. B* **2**, 145–170.

Schoenberg, I. J., and Whitney, A.

1949 Sur la positivité des déterminants de translations de fonctions de fréquence de Pólya avec une application au problème d'interpolation par les fonctions "spline," *Compt. Rend.* **228**, 1996–1998.

1953 On Polya frequency functions. III, *Trans. Am. Math. Soc.* **74**, 246–259.

Schweikert, D. G.

1966 An interpolation curve using a spline in tension, *J. Math. Phys.* (to appear).

Secrest, D.

1965 Best integration formulas and best error bounds, *Math. Computation* **19**, 79–83.

1965a Error bounds for interpolation and differentiation by the use of spline functions, *J. Soc. Ind. Appl. Math., Numerical Anal. Ser. B* **2**, 440–447.

Seifert, H. S. (ed.)

1959 "Space Technology." Wiley, New York.

Sharma, A., and Meir, A.

abs. 1964 Convergence of spline functions, *Notices Am. Math. Soc.* 64T-496.

1966 Degree of approximation of spline interpolation, *J. Math. Mech.* **15**, 759–767.

Sokolnikoff, I. S.

1956 "Mathematical Theory of Elasticity." McGraw-Hill, New York.

Taylor, A. E.

1958 "Introduction to Functional Analysis." Wiley, New York.

Theilheimer, F., and Starkweather, W.

1961 The fairing of ship lines on a high-speed computer, *Numerical Tables Aids Computation* **15**, 338–355.

Todd, J. (ed.)

1962 "Survey of Numerical Analysis." McGraw-Hill, New York.

Walsh, J. L., Ahlberg, J. H., and Nilson, E. N.

1962 Best approximation properties of the spline fit, *J. Math. Mech.* **11**, 225–234.

Ziegler, Z.

abs. 1965 On the convergence of *n*th order spline functions, *Notices Am. Math. Soc.* 65T-354.

INDEX

Ahlberg, J. H., 2, 3, 4, 5, 6, 7, 70, 78, 136, 140, 142, 237
Atteia, M., 6
Auslender, S., 143

Beamfit
  see cubic spline
Beam theory, 1, 3, 77
Bellman, R. E., 56
Best approximation property, 4
  for cubic splines, 16–19, 77–78
  for doubly cubic splines, 244–245
  for generalized splines, 200–201
  for polynomial splines, 157–159
Bicubic splines, 5–6
  see also doubly cubic splines
Birkhoff, G., 4, 5, 29, 237

$C^{\alpha}_{\beta,\gamma}(\mathscr{R})$
  definition of, 275
Canonical mesh bases
  for cubic splines, 101–103
  for doubly cubic splines, 249
  for generalized splines, 219–220, 275
  for polynomial splines, 179–182
Cardinal splines, 52–58, 245–247, 251–254
Circulant matrix, 36, 133, 148–149
Convergence in norm
  for cubic splines, 98–101
  for doubly cubic splines, 247–248
  for generalized splines, 214–219
  for polynomial splines, 176–179
Convergence properties, 4–5
  for cubic splines, 19–34, 61–74, 87–96
  for doubly cubic splines, 247–248
  for generalized splines, 201–212, 274
  for polynomial splines, 135–143, 148–152, 166–174
  see also convergence in norm
Coons surfaces, 262–264
Cubic splines 1, 9–108
  best approximation property, 16–19, 77–78
  canonical mesh bases, 101–103
  cardinal splines, 52–58
  convergence, 19–34, 61–74, 87–96
  convergence in norm, 98–101
  curve fitting, 50–52
  deficiency of, 24
  defining values, 82, 97
  end conditions, 11, 13–14, 50
  equal intervals, 9, 34–42
  equations for, 10–16, 84–87
  existence, 16–19, 61–74, 84
  first integral relation, 77–82
  fundamental identity, 78–79
  Hilbert space theory of, 97–107
  integral equations, 57–59
  linear functionals, 103–107
  minimum norm property, 75–77
  orthogonality, 97–101
  parametric splines, 51
  periodic cubic splines, 10
  second integral relation, 89–91
  simple cubic splines, 78
  spline-on-a-spline, 44, 48–50
  type I, 75
  type I′, 75
  type II, 75
  type II′, 75
  uniqueness, 16–19, 82–83
Cumulative chord length, 51, 254–262
Curve fitting 1–2, 50–52, 143
  see also surfaces

Dahlquist, G., 233
Davis, P. J., 19, 220
de Boor, C., 4, 5, 6, 7, 29, 237
Deficiency of a spline, 7
  for cubic splines, 24
  for generalized splines, 191–192
  for polynomial splines, 123, 143–147, 157, 163–164
  for quintic splines, 123, 143–148
Defining values, 82, 97, 175, 235
Degree of a spline, 109
Differential equations, 52–57, 228–233
  see also partial differential equations
Differentiation, *see* numerical differentiation

Direct products (of Hilbert spaces) 249
Doubly cubic splines, 5, 235–264
best approximation property, 244–245
canonical mesh bases, 249
cardinal splines, 245–247, 251–254
convergence, 247–248
convergence in norm, 250
defining values, 235
doubly periodic splines, 236
existence, 239, 243–244
first integral relation, 242
fundamental identity, 240–242
Hilbert space theory, 249–251
irregular regions, 254–258
$\mathscr{K}_m^n(\mathscr{R})$, 275
minimum norm property, 242–243
partial differential equations, 251–254
partial splines, 237–239
second integral relation, 248
simple doubly cubic splines, 235
surfaces, 256–262
type I, 235–236
type I′, 236
type II, 236
type II′, 236
uniqueness, 239, 243–244
see also generalized splines (two-dimensional)
Doubly periodic splines, 236

Eigenvalue problem, 57–58, 228–230
Elastica, 1, 3
End conditions
cubic splines, 11, 13–14, 50
curve fitting, 50
modified type k, 170
polynomial splines, 122–123, 158
type I, 75, 113, 193–194, 235–236
type I′, 75, 113, 193–194, 236
type II, 75, 113, 193–194, 236
type II′, 75, 113, 193–194, 236
type *k*, 167–168, 194
see also periodic splines
Equal intervals
cubic splines, 9, 34–42
polynomial splines, 124–135, 148–152
see also uniform meshes
Existence of splines, 2
of cubic splines, 16–19, 61–74, 84
of doubly cubic splines, 239, 243–244
of generalized splines, 199–200, 272–274
of polynomial splines, 132–135, 165–166
Explicit type, 269–270

Fejér, L., 23–24, 147–148
First integral relation, 3
for cubic splines, 77–82
for doubly cubic splines, 242
for generalized splines, 193–195, 270, 271
for polynomial splines, 155–156
Fundamental identiy
for cubic splines, 78–79
for doubly cubic splines, 240–242
for generalized splines, 192–193, 267–269
for polynomial splines, 154–155

Garabedian, H., 5, 237
Generalized splines, 6, 191–233, 265–276
best approximation property, 200–201
canonical mesh bases, 219–220, 275
convergence, 201–212, 274
convergence in norm, 214–219
deficiency of, 191–192
differential equations, 228–233
equations for, 197–199
existence, 199–200, 272–274
explicit type, 269–270
first integral relation, 193–195, 270–271
fundamental identity, 192–193, 267–269
heterogeneous splines, 194
Hilbert space theory, 213–233, 275–276
integral equations, 230–232
linear functionals, 220–233, 275–276
minimum norm property, 195–196, 271–272
numerical integration, 224–228
order of, 191
orthogonality, 218
partial differential equations, 276
partial splines, 273
Peano kernels, 220–224
periodic splines, 194
second integral relation, 204–206
simple splines, 194
strong interpolation, 270
two-dimensional, 265–276
type I, 193–194
type I′, 193–194
type II, 193–194
type II′, 193–194

type *k*, 194
uniqueness, 196–197, 271–272
uniqueness property, 272
Gershgorin's theorem, 16
Golomb, M., 7–8
Greville, T. N. E., 4, 6, 105

Heterogeneous splines, 7, 194–196
Hilbert space theory, 3–4
for cubic splines, 97–107
for doubly cubic splines, 249–251
for generalized splines, 213–233, 275–276
for polynomial splines, 174–190
Hille, E., 134
Holladay, J. C., 3, 8, 46, 75, 77, 78, 80

Integral equations, 57–61, 230–232
Integration, *see* numerical integration
Irregular regions, 254–258

$\mathscr{K}^n(a, b)$
definition of, 75
$\mathscr{K}^n_m(\mathscr{R})$
definition of, 275
$\mathscr{K}^n_P(a, b)$
definition of, 75
Kalaba, R. E., 56

Limits on convergence, 95–96, 174, 211–212
Linear functionals, 6–7, 103–107, 185–189, 220–233, 275–276
Lynch, R. E., 4, 6, 7

Mathematical spline, 1, 9
Meir, A., 4, 27
Mesh bases, 101–103, 179–182
see also canonical mesh bases
Mesh restrictions, 22, 25, 94–95
Method of cardinal splines,
see cardinal splines
Minimum curvature property, 2, 3
see minimum norm property
Minimum norm property, 3
for cubic splines, 75–77
for doubly cubic splines, 242–243
for generalized splines, 195–196, 271–272
for polynomial splines, 156–157
Modified type *k*, 170
see also type *k*

Multidimensional splines, 5, 6
see also two-dimensional splines

Nilson, E. N., 2, 3, 4, 5, 6, 7, 70, 78, 136, 140, 142, 237
Nonlinear differential equations, 56
Numerical differentiation, 42–57
Numerical integration, 42–50, 145–146, 224–228

Order of a spline, 191
Orthogonality,
cubic splines, 97–101
generalized splines, 213–219
polynomial splines, 174–179
see also canonical mesh bases

Parametric splines, 51, 254–258
surfaces, 258–262
Partial differential equations
numerical solution of, 251–254, 276
Partial splines, 237–239, 273
Peano, G., 105, 185
Peano kernel, 6, 103–105, 182–189, 220–224
Periodic splines, 10, 148–152, 156, 167, 194, 236
Polynomial splines, 109–189
best approximation property, 157–159
canonical mesh bases, 179–182
convergence, 135–143, 148–152, 166–174
convergence in norm, 176–179
deficiency of, 123, 143–148, 157, 163–164
defining values, 175
degree of, 109
end conditions, 122–123, 158
equal intervals, 124–135, 148–152
equations for, 109–123, 160–165
even degree, 109–110, 153
existence of, 132–135, 165–166
first integral relation, 155–156
fundamental identity, 154–155
Hilbert space theory, 174–189
limits on convergence, 174
linear functionals, 185–189
minimum norm property, 156–157
modified type *k*, 170
numerical integration, 145–146
odd degree, 5, 153–189
orthogonality, 174–179
Peano kernels, 182–189

periodic splines, 148–152, 156, 167
quintic splines, 143–148
remainder formulas, 185–189
second integral relation, 168–170
simple splines, 113
type I, 113
type I′, 113
type II, 113
type II′, 113
type *k*, 167–168
uniform mesh, 148–152
uniqueness, 159–160

Quadrature, *see* numerical integration
Quintic splines, 143–148

Remainder formulas, 103–105, 185–189, 221–228

Sard, A., 6, 105, 185, 222, 227, 233, 275
Schoenberg, I. J., 2, 4, 5, 6, 7, 44, 75, 106, 185
Schweikert, D. G., 6
Second integral relation, 5
for cubic splines, 89–91
for double cubic splines, 248
for generalized splines, 204–206
for polynomial splines, 168–170
Secrest, D., 8
Sharma, A., 4, 27
Simple splines, 7, 78, 113, 194, 235
Sokolnikoff, I. S., 2, 3, 77
Space technology, 107–108
Spline equations
for cubic splines, 10–16, 84–87
for generalized splines, 197–199
for polynomial splines, 109–123, 160–165
Splines in tension, 6
Splines of even degree, 109–110, 153
Splines of odd degree, 153–189
see also polynomial splines, cubic splines
Spline-on-spline, 44, 48–50
Spline surfaces, 256–262
see also Coons surfaces
Strong interpolation, 270
Surfaces,
see spline surfaces, Coons surfaces

Two-dimensional splines
doubly cubic splines, 235–264
generalized splines, 265–276
Type I, 75, 113, 193–194, 235–236
Type I′, 75, 113, 193–194, 236
Type II, 75, 113, 193–194, 236
Type II′, 75, 113, 193–194, 236
Type *k*, 167–168, 170, 194

Uniform mesh, 148–152
see also equal intervals
Uniqueness
of cubic splines, 16–19, 82–83
of doubly cubic splines, 239, 243–244
of generalized splines, 196–197, 271–272
of polynomial splines, 159–160
Uniqueness property, 272

Walsh, J. L., 2, 3, 4, 5, 6, 7, 78, 136, 140, 142, 237
Weinberger, H. F., 7–8
Whitney, A., 2

Ziegler, Z., 5, 136

Made in United States
Orlando, FL
04 November 2026

90208972R00164